scars of war, wounds of peace

The Israeli–Arab Tragedy

SHLOMO BEN-AMI

Weidenfeld & Nicolson

LONDON

To Ruthy

First published in Great Britain in 2005
by Weidenfeld & Nicolson

1 3 5 7 9 10 8 6 4 2

© Shlomo Ben-Ami 2005

A CIP catalogue record for this book
is available from the British Library.

ISBN-13 9 780297 84883 7
ISBN-10 0 297 84883 6

Typeset, printed and bound in Great Britain by
Butler and Tanner Ltd, Frome and London

Weidenfeld & Nicolson

The Orion Publishing Group Ltd
Orion House
5 Upper Saint Martin's Lane
London, WC2H 9EA

www.orionbooks.co.uk

scars of war,
wounds of peace

Let war yield to peace, laurels to paeans.
(*Cedant arma togae, concedant laurea laudi*)

   Cicero, *De Officiis*, Book I, Chapter 77

Now this is not the end. It is not even the beginning of the end.
But it is, perhaps, the end of the beginning.

                    Sir Winston Churchill, speech at the Mansion House,
                                    London, 10 November 1942

Contents

Maps

Preface

'Do you think we can still make it?' I was asked by President Clinton when, on Saturday, 20 December 2000, I was leaving the Cabinet Room adjacent to the Oval Office in the White House where the President had just finished communicating to the Israeli and Palestinian delegations to the peace talks his final parameters for a settlement.

'I don't know, Mr President,' I replied, 'if we have enough political time left to wrap up an agreement, but what I am sure of is that if we fail, we'll all have plenty of time to write books about it.'

After the sad chapter of our failure, Israelis and Palestinians, to reach a final peace settlement during President Clinton's last year at the White House, I did write about it in a book published in France (*Quel avenir pour Israel?*) and, in a more comprehensive work written in Hebrew, my personal account and perspective of the evolution of the peace process in its last phases, *A Front Without a Home Front: A Voyage to the Boundaries of the Peace Process*.

When considering the preparation of an English version of those books, I decided that, however important a separate analysis of both the Oslo process and the latest chapter of the peace talks surely are for drawing the necessary lessons for any future attempt to solve the Israeli–Palestinian tragedy, it should not be seen in isolation from the wider history of the Arab–Israeli conflict and of earlier stages in the quest for peace in the Middle East. Our capacity to better understand the present and look with sobriety at the future needs to draw on, and be inspired by, a broader historical perspective. When we went to Camp David, Prime Minister Ehud Barak took with him Alistair Horne's book on the war of Algeria and the subsequent peace with France, *A Savage War of Peace*, while I looked for inspiration in Henry Kissinger's study on the Congress of Vienna and the aftermath of the Napoleonic wars, *A World Restored: the Politics of Conservatism in a Revolutionary Age*. Neither of these books is, of course, a bad adviser for anyone willing to draw lessons for a transition from war to peace. But I later thought that an insightful overview of the history of the Arab–Israeli conflict, and especially that of the Palestinian dilemma, might certainly have been no less helpful to us both.

It subsequently occurred to me that I might try some day to write such a book myself. After all, I have always kept abreast of the literature, old and new, about the subject. And for years the Arab–Israeli conflict and the frustrated attempts to solve it have been for me a profound personal and intellectual preoccupation. Throughout my public life, both in politics and outside it, I have participated in the heated debates on the subject of war and peace, I have written extensively on ways to solve the conflict, and I was privileged eventually to be allowed to make my own effort at peacemaking on the tortuous road of trial and error that is the Arab–Israeli peace process.

The 1967 war was was a watershed in the life of the Israelis of my generation. Zionism was being dangerously redefined, we thought, by the encounter of the Israelis with the biblical lands of Judaea and Samaria, and by an infatuation with the new territories. The occupation also turned Zionism into a highly loaded term, too frequently vilified outside Israel as a reproachable ideology. I am a Zionist, and an ardent one at that. But I have fought to define the boundaries of the idea by a respect for the right of Israel's Palestinian neighbours to a life of sovereignty and dignity. What drove me to look back at the source and at the history of the conflict, and later into the attempts to solve it, can be summed up in something that I said to an Israeli newspaper, *Yedioth Aharonoth*, before I departed for Taba to lead the Israeli team in a last-ditch attempt to save the Israeli–Palestinian peace process from collapse:

> A normal state is not supposed to settle beyond its legitimate borders. We have created a state, we have been admitted to the UN, we strive to have orderly relations with the international community, yet we still continue to behave as if we are a Yishuv. The entire peace enterprise of this government is aimed at leading the nation to choose, once and for all, between being a state or a Yishuv.

It is to the shaping of the Israeli mind by the legacy of the Yishuv, where the utter rejection by the Arabs of a Jewish entity in their midst died so hard, that one needs to go back in order to trace the origins and the evolution of Israel's penchant for formulating policies only on the basis of worst-case scenarios. Zionism was the territorial answer to the Jewish fear and this fear has never subsided since.

Raymond Aron was once asked why he, who had such a keen interest in politics, was never tempted to become a politician himself. 'The reason I am not a politician', he said, 'is that I want to understand.' This book is my own attempt to 'understand'. The need to look at the broader picture and to put the short, even if certainly significant, chapter where we played a role in its proper context accompanied me when I came for a two-year academic sabbatical to England. This gave me the opportunity to turn my intellectual preoccupation into an orderly effort of which this book is the result.

Though written by a historian who is aware and respectful of the requirements of the discipline, it should not be read as exhaustive academic research or as a meticulous narrative history, for it is neither. Rather, it is a general interpretative overview where my understanding of, and my insights about, the story of the pendulous move of Jews and Arabs between war and peace are intertwined in the very broad lines of the unfolding story. It might, therefore, be a relief to the general reader that the book is not loaded with a heavy apparatus of primary sources and archival material. I was fortunate, however, to have been allowed the time and the chance to consult a large body of literature on the subject, the essential part of which is referred to in the Bibliography.

The major works of the leading scholars in the field like Avi Shlaim and Benny Morris, both of whom have written excellent general histories as well as some enlightening monographs, have been an invaluable reference. I also greatly benefited from my talks with, and the generous advice of, Avi Shlaim. I am indebted to him, too, for reading my manuscript and making useful suggestions. A special mention needs to be made of Mr Avi Raz, a D.Phil. student at St Antony's College, Oxford, who is now completing his thesis on the Israeli–Palestinian problem in the immediate aftermath of the Six Day War. He was very generous in allowing me to read the second chapter of his still unfinished thesis where he analyses the so-called Israeli 'peace initiative' of 19 June 1967, as well as the confusion and disorientation of Israel's leaders with regard to the future of the West Bank. His findings are a major contribution to our knowledge of that period. The works of other scholars who are not defined as 'new historians' such as Yoram Porath, Anita Shapira, Itamar Rabinovitch or Yoav Gelber will always be an important reference for the understanding of key chapters and the central themes in the history of Arabs and Jews in the Middle East. The chapters of the book that cover the phases of the peace process in which I was personally involved, as well as the Sharon years that came later, are inevitably based mainly on my personal recollections. But the heated political debate and the war of conflicting versions on the reasons for the collapse of the peace process have already produced some literature that was obviously consulted.

I am also thankful to the Oxford Centre for Hebrew and Jewish Studies at Yarnton and particularly to its president, Mr Peter Oppenheimer, for giving me the opportunity to deliver a series of lectures at the Examination Schools on 'the Quest for Peace in the Arab–Israeli Conflict'.

The work on these lectures turned out to be an essential part of the preparation of this book. Lord (George) Weidenfeld's commitment to its publication – as well as his personal friendship – has been a major source of encouragement and inspiration throughout. Thanks are also due to Mr Benjamin Buchan of Weidenfeld and Nicolson and Peter Ginna of Oxford University Press (New York). Dena Matmon was not only exceptionally skilful in processing my manuscript, but also generous and thoughtful in her remarks. I am indebted, too, to Ms Claudia Medina, Ms Paula Navarro and Ms Olga Hornero of the Toledo Peace Centre for their intelligent assistance with the final corrections of the text. Needless to say, any shortcomings that this book suffers from are entirely my responsibility.

Shlomo Ben-Ami
Madrid, January 2005

I   Prelude: The Birth of an Intractable Conflict

... you ... [must] fight the enemies of religion, who wish to destroy your mosques, and who wish to expel you from your land.

A local Palestinian leader addressing villagers,
1 January 1936

On one side, the forces of destruction, the forces of the desert, have risen, and on the other hand stand firm the forces of civilisation, but we will not be stopped.

Chaim Weizmann's response to the Arab 'riots',
April 1936

... I want you to see things ... with Arab eyes ... they see emigration on a giant scale ... they see the lands passing into our hands. They see England identifying with Zionism.

Ben-Gurion addressing the Jewish Agency,
May 1936

An irrepressible conflict has arisen between two national communities within the narrow bounds of one small country ... there is no common ground between them ...

The Peel Commission Report,
July 1937

Judaism, being a religion, is not an independent nationality ... it is ... expansionist and colonial in its aims.

The Palestinian National Charter,
July 1968

The encounter between Zionism and the Palestinian Arabs started as an experiment in mutual ignorance, an obsessive determination by each to overlook the powerful, genuine national sentiments and the spirit of communal identity that motivated the other. It was not the existence of, or the threat posed by, the other that was denied, but the authenticity of that existence that was repressed. The Jews, however, gained a vantage ground in the struggle for Palestine by being the first to supersede the comfortable inertia of self-delusion and realise the nature of the conflict as a bitter national struggle.

Zionism (the word 'Zion' is one of the many Biblical names of Jerusalem) was born in Europe at the end of the nineteenth century as a national movement that gave political expression to the millenarian yearning of the Jews to return to Zion. It aimed at gathering the exiled Jews in their ancestral homeland, Eretz-Israel, and restoring Jewish sovereignty in what was now Palestine. Zionism was never a religious dogma. It was always a widely democratic and diversified movement that encompassed right and left, moderates and extremists, the champions of compromise with the Arabs in order to partition the land, and those who would settle for nothing less than the whole of Eretz-Israel. Nor were those who believed in a binational state where Jews and Arabs would live in perfect harmony rare birds. Differences and tendencies in the Zionist movement abounded then as they do today. But the fundamental definition of Zionism as the movement for the liberation of the Jewish people, and its justification as the inevitable response to the Jewish question, were shared by all.

That Jewish emancipation in Europe had failed was the premise that was accepted by all the founding fathers of the movement, chief among them Theodor Herzl, a Viennese Jewish journalist who was fired by the Dreifus Affair in France and its anti-Semitic implications to advocate a territorial solution to the Jewish problem. Herzl's book, *The Jewish State*, published in 1896, and the first Zionist congress he gathered in Basel a year later, established the foundations of the new Zionist enterprise. The Jews, he maintained, were not just a *religious minority* that needed either to assimilate among the nations or be emancipated as a distinct group. They were a *nation* that was entitled to its own independent political expression as a sovereign people. 'The aim of Zionism' was, as the Basel Congress defined it, 'to create for the Jewish people a home in Palestine secured by law.' 'At Basel I founded the Jewish State in Palestine', was how Herzl described the vision of Zionism.

'Zion', however, was not an empty land waiting only for the Jews to claim and possess it. When David Ben-Gurion, the future founder of the State of Israel and its first prime minister, arrived in Palestine in 1906, the country consisted of 700,000 inhabitants, 55,000 of which were Jews, and only 550 could be defined as Zionist pioneers. The bulk of the Jewish population was made up of religious communities that did not see themselves as political Zionists. They mostly lived in the 'four sacred cities' (Tiberias, Safed, Hebron and Jerusalem) whereas the Zionist pioneers went to establish agricultural colonies, for they believed in settling the land and working it as the only way to redeem the Jewish people through the principles of self-help and 'Jewish labour'.

Zionism was also a movement of conquest, colonisation and settlement in the service of a just and righteous but also self-indulgent national cause. An enterprise of national liberation and human emancipation that was forced to use the tools of colonial penetration, it was a schizophrenic movement, which suffered from an irreconcilable incongruity between its liberating message and the offensive practices it used to advance it. The cultivation of a righteous self-image and the ethos of the few against the many, the heroic David facing the brutal, bestial Arab Goliath, was one way Zionism pretended to reconcile its contradictions.

Zionism, however, cannot be seen as a typical colonialist movement, an extension of Europe's nineteenth-century grab for colonies and raw material throughout Asia and Africa. It certainly behaved as such, mainly after the Six Day War, when it could no longer claim with any credibility that its drive to occupy and settle the West Bank, exploit its human and natural resources and turn the Palestinian population into the hewers of wood and drawers of water of the Israeli economy was the affirmation of its natural right as a movement of national liberation. But in the years leading to the creation of the Jewish state the conditions were radically different.

One does not have to subscribe to Arieh Avneri's staunch negation of the Arab claim of dispossession in order to see that, though clearly an avant-garde that came to colonise and possess a new land, Zionism was a movement of national liberation. Decimated by the pogroms and persecutions, in short by the Jewish catastrophe in Eastern Europe, the Jews who came to build a national home in the midst of the vast Arab Middle East were the emissaries of no foreign power; they were idealistic pioneers. The Zionists were genuine in their aspiration not to exploit the local population. Their ideal was to create a new Jewish society based on self-help and manual labour. This is certainly a sad irony when viewed from the perspective of the post-1967 years, when the role of the Palestinians from the occupied territories as low-wage labourers became so central to Israeli life, and distorted key values of the Zionist enterprise. Before the clash with the Arabs drifted into open war, the Zionist settlers did not evict the Palestinian peasants, but bought poor land for their settlements from their legal owners and ameliorated them. The eventual eviction of Palestinian peasants was a sad by-product of the Zionists having bought the land from 'effendies' living in Turkey, and of their philosophy of Jewish manual labour as the way of redeeming the Jewish people from the bad habits of Diaspora life. Unlike the European settlers during the imperialist drive of the late nineteenth century, the Zionists were driven by an ideology of national revival based on human improvement and social Utopia and, rather than thinking of ways to dispossess by force the local population and exploit the new lands, they brought in their own capital in order to buy and settle the land.

Most revolts are an uprising against a system; Zionism was a revolt against Jewish destiny. Unlike the European colonialists who acted as the beachhead and promoters of the strategic interests of the mother country, the Zionists cut off their links with their countries of origin and inaugurated for themselves a new beginning as a community that represented a radical break with Jewish history. A new culture and an old-new language were to be two fundamental pillars of this fresh start. Zionism was a social and cultural revolution, a movement that, in its beginning, believed innocently that it would not even require the use of force in order to assert itself. When the early Zionists spoke of 'conquest' they referred to 'conquering' the wilderness and the desert. They wanted to redeem the Jewish people not by exploiting the Arab workforce, but by 'conquering' work and, as Martin Buber wrote to Mahatma Gandhi, by setting 'their shoulders to the plough' and spending 'their strength and their blood to make the land fruitful'.

But it is also true that in the early years the founding fathers of the Zionist movement tended to be blind to the native Arab population and scornful of its physical environment, the land the Jews had come to possess. To Israel Zangwill, Palestine was 'a land without a people for a people without a land', a 'virgin country', as Moshe Smilansky put it. David Ben-Gurion described Palestine on the eve of the Zionist colonisation as 'primitive, neglected and derelict'. A member of a later generation, Abba Eban, echoed the descriptions of the founding fathers when he wrote, in terms that were reminiscent of Mark Twain's contemptuous impressions of the Holy Land in 1867 (*The Innocents Abroad*), about a 'squalid, unpromising, almost repellent land'.

As a group with a collective or a national personality, the Arabs hardly existed in the perception of the early Zionists and were depicted, for example, by Yitzhak Ben-Zvi, later to be the President of the State of Israel, in his *The Jews in their Land*, as 'looters', 'robbers', 'cheaters' and 'plunderers'. This stereotype of the Arabs as primitive and tribal was not, of course, entirely original. The books written by European travellers in the nineteenth century were replete with such descriptions. Others, like Ber Borochov, who defended the assimilation of the Arabs within the stronger Jewish society, did it out of a conviction that there was no such thing as an Arab communal, let alone national, entity in Palestine. Moreover, the Zionist pioneering enterprise was initially clearly permeated with a sense of the White Man's Burden, a patronising conviction that the Palestinian Arabs as backward individuals, not necessarily as a national community, would reconcile themselves to the Zionist idea if they could only be allowed to share in the economic benefits that would be created by the Zionist revolution and by the industrious and resourceful Jewish pioneers. Conspicuously, this patronising attitude coincided with the view that prevailed among some of the supporters of Zionism in British political circles. To Winston Churchill, for example, Zionism was 'also good for the Arabs who dwell in Palestine. ... They shall share in the benefits and progress of Zionism.'

To be sure, an awareness of the plight of the Arabs – expressed in heated intellectual debates and in keen reflections on the 'Arab question', 'the hidden question', as Yitzhak Epstein defined it during the Second Aliyah – was by no means rare in Jewish political and intellectual circles. Some, like the Marxist Hashomer Hatzair, preached a class-orientated integration between Jews and Arabs; others, like the intellectuals of Brit-Shalom, went even further. They defended the rights of the Arabs on the land and even questioned the necessity of a Jewish state. They dismissed Zionism as a moral aberration. There was sometimes also an ambivalent, dual attitude among the Zionists to the Arabs of Palestine, a mixture of contempt and admiration, and even envy. Hebrew literature is not short of references to the Arab as a true native, a flesh of the land's flesh. The image of the Jew as an alien estranged foreigner in contrast to the Arab, an authentic son of the soil, was not a perception exclusive to the Arab detractors of Zionism; it can also be found in the writings of the Jews from Yosef Haim Brener to Yizhar Smilansky.

A clearly defined national consciousness did not exist among the Palestinian Arabs at the time of the arrival of the first Zionist settlers in Palestine. The local Arab population had of course an urban component, but it mostly consisted of fellahin, peasants who toiled on the land of absentee landlords. Tribal and local loyalties more than a defined national identity with a clear notion of its territorial horizons characterised the Palestinian population that the first Zionist pioneers encountered. Palestine was not even considered a distinct province of the Ottoman empire. It was part of the provinces of Syria; and indeed the Palestinians regarded themselves as part of Southern Syria. The secular concept of the nation, and its expression in a modern state, was essentially alien to the Arab peoples. The prevailing concept was more that of the 'Arab nation' than that of, say, the 'Palestinian' or the 'Iraqi' and 'Syrian' nation and state.

But Palestinian nationalism would emerge and crystallise in the first two decades of the century as a defensive response to the Zionist arrival. Just as Jewish modern nationalism was the response of the Jews to the threat posed by the Europeans to their distinct identity, so Palestinian nationalism can be largely seen as the collective reaction of the local Arabs to a Zionist enterprise that threatened their natural rights in Palestine. As the irresistible drive of the Zionist settlers to possess the land gained in strength, as their population increased in size and their political institutions became consolidated, the Palestinian Arabs were driven to respond more and more as a group, and articulate their national identity to counter the threatening advance of Zionism. In a way, Zionism and Palestinian nationalism developed as twin movements, each feeding and nurturing the other.

The Arabs were therefore not blind to the Zionist threat, especially as the Palestinian national consciousness started to evolve. But there was nevertheless an Arab tendency to overlook the *authentic* power of the Zionist drive. An unyielding rejection prevailed of any claim of a Jewish link to Palestine, even when defined in strictly religious terms, let alone when it came to national rights. As Yehoshafat Harkavi showed in his studies of the Arab perception of the Jews and of Zionism, Arab writers paid special attention to challenging the Jews' claim to a divine right over the land. The topical commonplace was that the Jews were a religious group, not a national entity, and as such they did not qualify for self-determination. They were regarded as alien trespassers who came to subvert and corrupt the indigenous culture. Their artificial presence in Arab lands was an aggression against Arab purity. Clearly, the threat posed by the Jews was also frequently described using anti-Semitic stigmas about their greed and immorality. The Jewish presence in Palestine, it was argued, could only lead to the subversion of the values of traditional family and communal life, and to the destruction of its Arab character. The clash between the Arabs' genuine sense of belonging and the artificial nationalism of the Jews in Palestine was represented as being in reality a clash between Islam's noble universalism and the parochial, tribal and selfish culture of the Jews.

The Zionist and the European presence in the Middle East was perceived in Arab circles as nothing but the reincarnation of the medieval Crusader state. The conquest of Palestine by General Allenby and the Balfour Declaration were seen as inherently complementary. They amounted to a joint Jewish-Western sinister conspiracy against the Muslim world. General Allenby, upon taking over Jerusalem, wittingly rushed to endorse the Crusaders' role by announcing in front of the Jaffa Gate of the Old City that he had come to redeem the legacy of Richard Lionheart (his French counterpart in Damascus, General Gouraud, went even further: he defiantly announced in front of Saladin's tomb that 'we have come back to the East, Monsieur le Sultan'), and the subsequent British support for the Zionist project in Palestine fuelled the worst fears of the

Arabs. A new Crusader entity as a beachhead of Western imperialism was about to be implanted in their midst.

That the Arab Revolt of 1936–9 was mainly directed against the British was perhaps the best reflection of the attitude of the Arabs to the Zionist presence in Palestine as an artificial extension of the colonial power. They really believed that the Yishuv (the Jewish community in Palestine and its institutions) would collapse once denied the political support of the mandatory power. The fallacy of the Arab perception did not lie in the fact that the Revolt was ultimately broken by the British, for the latter did eventually acquiesce to the Arabs' demands and imposed draconian limitations on the Yishuv's prospects of development and expansion. But the Arabs should have realised how wrong their notion was when, in spite of the wedge they succeeded in driving between the British and the Zionists, the Yishuv remained as solid and strong as ever. An artificial transplantation it certainly was not.

The Arab Revolt, however, which the Zionists, in a familiar pattern of self-denial, started by dismissing as 'incidents' or 'riots', was nevertheless a major watershed in the history of the conflict between Jews and Arabs in Palestine. It was during the Revolt that the intractable nature of the conflict as a profound clash between two national movements driven by diametrically opposed objectives and by irreconcilable beliefs became patently clear even to the moderates and the idealistic dreamers among the Zionist leaders. The Revolt was the prelude to what increasingly became an inevitable all-out war between Jews and Arabs for the exclusive ownership of Palestine.

The brutal repression of the Revolt by the British brought the Arab community in Palestine to the verge of collapse and dissolution in a way that anticipated, and created the conditions for, the Palestinian Naqbah ('Disaster') of 1948. At the same time the Zionists, always better organised and far more prepared for statehood than the leaderless Palestinian Arabs – and now also more acutely aware than ever before of the national character of the Revolt – assumed the imminence of the forthcoming all-out war for Palestine, readied themselves to face the challenge and eventually prevailed. The Arab Revolt and the consequent dismemberment of the Arab community laid the ground for the Zionist victory of 1948.

The Revolt was also a turning point in the relations between Zionism and the British mandatory power, for it ushered in a fundamental change in Britain's policy towards the Yishuv. The premise of a Jewish national home, established in the Balfour Declaration, was now redefined with draconian limitations on Jewish immigration and land acquisition, the two most vital elements of Zionism. For all practical purposes, the 1939 White Paper ended the possibility of the Jews ever reaching demographic supremacy in Palestine and condemned them, as a matter of policy, to a permanent minority status. The war in Europe made the support of the Arab world a strategic imperative Britain chose not to disregard; she now decided to depart from the philo-Zionist policies that had inspired the Balfour Declaration, and redefined her policies as a mandatory power in favour of cold, sober considerations of *realpolitik*. As the war approached, Britain's need to retain her bases in Palestine also became vital. This was not exactly the time to toy with the idea of independent Jewish and Arab states as stipulated by the 1937 Peel Report.

That the British who defeated the Revolt militarily compensated it nevertheless politically was not only due, however, to *realpolitik*. They finally assumed that the insurgence was not just a blind, irrational eruption of rage, but a determined, not unreasonable attempt to force them into reversing their policies on immigration and land acquisition. The Arab Revolt brought home to the British government in an especially dramatic way the message that the stark disregard of the national interests of the Arab community upon which the Mandate had been conceived would not be allowed to prevail. A major concession to the rebellious Palestinian Arabs was the shelving by the British government of the recommendations of the Peel Commission. These had vindicated the Zionist practice of faits accomplis by partitioning the country into a Jewish and an Arab state along the existing division of land ownership and population distribution.

The British colonial power might have had its biases and politico-cultural preferences, of which the Jews were the main beneficiaries, but it lacked nevertheless a clear course of action and undeviating policies; it tended to shift, sometimes abruptly, its strategy under pressure. This was not the first time that a violent Arab protest forced the British to appease the Arabs and qualify their pledges to the Jews. In the wake of the 1921 riots, High Commissioner Herbert Samuel did just that. He imposed limitations on Jewish immigration, proposed a degree of self-rule to the Arabs, established the post of Mufti to which he appointed the same young nationalist, Haj Amin el Husseini, who had instigated the Nebi-Moussa riots in 1920, and allowed the creation of the Supreme Muslim Council, which the Mufti would soon turn into the main political platform for the Arab national struggle for Palestine. The 1922 White Paper went a step further in meeting Arab demands by linking Jewish immigration to the 'economic capacity of the country' to absorb newcomers. The same pattern was repeated in the aftermath of the 1929 riots. Long months of incitement and riots that reached their peak in the massacre of Jewish families in Safed and Hebron resulted in Lord Passfield's White Paper, where severe limitations on land acquisition and Jewish immigration were imposed.

But the inconsistencies of British policy should not obscure the central legacy of the Mandate up to 1939 as the vital guarantor of the Zionist project in Palestine. Frequently driven by pro-Zionist sentiments, and notwithstanding the apprehension of many in the mandatory admin-istration at the ruthless drive of the Zionists, an apprehension sometimes fed by a strong anti-Semitic bias as much as it was driven by a genuine sympathy for the dispossessed Arab fellahin, or by a romantic, Lawrence of Arabia brand of admiration for the Arab 'wild man', the policy makers in London and the high commissioners on the ground were essentially the protectors of the Zionist enterprise. However erratic British policies might have been, the Jewish state was the product of the favourable conditions created by the Mandate.

The Zionists were of course enraged by the frequent limitations on immigration and land acquisition. But these were never insurmountable obstacles. To begin with, in most cases it was the Zionist leaders who proved incapable of meeting the generous immigration quotas allowed by the British. It was not until the wave of immigration unleashed by the rise of Hitler to power that the Zionists managed to mobilise the necessary resources for the absorption of immigrants. And when the immigration laws were an obstacle, illegal methods of immigration were resorted to. The Zionist leaders also proved to be able diplomats who knew how to move in the corridors of power at Whitehall and to derail, when necessary, anti-Zionist measures. Such was the case, for example, of the Passfield White Paper, which limited Jewish immigration and settlement, and was therefore seen by the Zionists as drastically reducing Britain's commitment to a Jewish homeland in Palestine. But before it could even come into effect, Passfield's White Paper was for all practical purposes abrogated by the MacDonald Letter, which annulled its principal features, thanks to Chaim Weizmann's skilful lobbying. The reality was that the Jewish population in Palestine increased steadily during the Mandate years – it rose from 12 per cent of the total inhabitants of Palestine in 1914 to 33 per cent in 1947 – and with it the foundations of the Jewish state were being progressively cemented and strengthened.

The chances of the Jews ever reaching demographic supremacy in Palestine were, of course, nothing but utterly unrealistic hallucinations, if only because the Arabs of Palestine enjoyed one of the highest repro-duction rates in the world. The future of the National Home would have to be built on the Yishuv's capacity for organisation and human development. And it was precisely in this sense that philo-Zionist high commissioners like Sir Herbert Samuel and Sir Arthur Wauchope were especially instrumental in enhancing the potentialities of the Yishuv. In the 1920s Herbert Samuel laid down the foundations of a consistent

British policy of concessions to the Zionists for infrastructure projects. Arthur Wauchope's term as High Commissioner in the 1930s was a golden age of Jewish immigration – with his active encouragement, 200,000 Jews, that is, double the number of those who had come since the start of the Mandate, arrived on the shores of Palestine – public works, economic prosperity and an extraordinary flow of Jewish capital.

Nor were the restrictions on land acquisition an obstacle the Zionists could not overcome. Throughout, the Arabs' incompetent leadership, their lack of purpose and national cohesion, proved to be a major ally of the Zionist enterprise. White Papers notwithstanding, Arab landowners ready to sell land to the Jews and to betray their own national cause were never in short supply. As no other than King Abdullah of Transjordan observed in his memoirs, 'The Arabs are as prodigal in selling their land as they are in ... weeping [about it].' The Zionists aimed at possessing the land as part of an irresistible drive at nation and state building, and the Arab landowners, among them key nationalist figures, some of them even members of the Supreme Muslim Council, helped facilitate the Zionist project. Lands were sold to the Jews by the noblest families among the Palestinians, the El-Husseinis, the Nashashibis, the Abdel Hadi family, the El-Alamis, the Al-Shawas and the Shukeiris, among many others.

The question of Palestinian collaborators with Zionism and later with the State of Israel is no anecdotal matter in the history of the struggle for Palestine. Arguably, without the assistance given by Palestinian collaborators to the Zionist movement, the entire map of Jewish settlements, and consequently that of the State of Israel, would have been substantially different. Palestinian Arabs helped the Zionist cause not only by selling land to the Jews, but also by actively assisting the British and Zionists in repressing the Arab Revolt, and later by collaborating with the Yishuv in the 1948 war. Entire sections of the Palestinian front during that conflict collapsed and capitulated, thanks largely to the work of collaborators. Conspicuously, however, many of the collaborators were not motivated by greed and lucre; they acted out of a political conviction that Zionism could not be defeated and a serious attempt to reach an accommodation with it was, therefore, called for. Important Palestinian families like the Nashashibis, the Slimans and the Tukans believed in a Transjordan option, and would indeed reach high positions in the Jordanian administration after the war. The phenomenon was so widespread that one is led to the conclusion that Palestinian nationalism was either not yet an unquestionable aspiration for all the Arabs living in Palestine, or that it simply meant a different thing to those who did not follow the leadership of the militant Husseinis. In many cases family relations, tribal loyalties and the link to the village rather than to an undefined 'national territory' proved to be stronger than the loyalty to an amorphous Palestinian territorial community. Many among the collaborators simply believed that they were defending the Palestinian national interest by refusing to second the Mufti's suicidal strategy of all or nothing.

No doubt the road to the Jewish state was paved not only with the advantages drawn by the Yishuv from the Mandate years, but also by the shattering and dissolution of the Arab community in Palestine. The Arabs of Palestine paid dearly for their challenge to British rule. They were left practically without leaders and representative institutions. The Arab Higher Committee was dissolved and all its leaders were sent into exile. The Mufti, the chief instigator of the insurgence and the embodiment of Palestinian nationalism, fled the country and left the Supreme Muslim Council, the focal point of Palestinian nationalism, leaderless and irrelevant. There is hardly a method of repression the Israelis would use in quelling the Al-Aqsa Intifada in 2001–5 that was not anticipated, even surpassed, by the British in their reckless, brutal repression of the Arab Revolt. Terrorists and guerrilla fighters were court-martialled and executed, their houses were blown up, collective punishments were applied throughout the Arab communities and the RAF razed whole villages to the ground.

The indiscriminate roughness of the repression brought the Revolt to an end but not before the mythology and the ethos of Palestinian heroism and resistance were firmly established in the collective mind of the defeated nation. The Palestinian revolt was an affair of lower classes. The upper classes and the institutional leaders either betrayed their cause by leaving on their own or were exiled by the British. But the imagination of the masses was fired and inspired by the popular heroes of the resistance, such as the Islamic charismatic fighter Sheikh Izzedin al Qassam, whose death in a shoot-out made him a nationalistic icon for future generations, Sheikh Farhan who confronted the British forces around Nablus until he was arrested and executed, Abu-Jildeh who managed to terrorise the northern parts of the country and, last but by no means least, Abd' el Khader el Husseini who was destined to become one of the more charismatic military leaders in the war for Palestine in 1948. As happened in the first Palestinian Intifada against the Israeli occupation (1987–91), the rebels also managed for a while to establish parcels of Palestinian self-rule and thus offer their followers the sense of pride that came with the destruction, however partial and symbolic, of the trappings of the colonial power.

The British were not alone in drawing their conclusions from the Arab Revolt. For the Yishuv and its leaders an entirely new phase in the struggle for a Jewish homeland in Palestine was now inaugurated. The message of the conflict with the Palestinian Arabs as a clash between competing, exclusivist nationalisms, not just a banal dispute with indigenous fellahin who could be easily bought off and evicted, that had started to penetrate the Zionist discourse in the wake of the 1929 riots became now an unequivocal reality for most, if not all, the leaders of the Yishuv.

As the Yishuv was gaining ground through immigration and settlement, and the dispossessed Arabs of Palestine were driven to despair and rebellion by the unstoppable Zionist élan, much of the intellectual and ideological debate on the 'Arab question' was nothing but an exercise in righteousness and self-delusion. It was now becoming patently clear to all that the clash between Zionism and the Palestinian national movement was bound to be decided by force. Chaim Weizmann, the embodiment of the diplomatic and moderate trend in the Zionist movement, would say to President Roosevelt in 1944, 'we could not rest our case on the consent of the Arabs.' Much earlier and less subtly, Berl Katznelson, the main ideologue of the mainstream Labour movement, had acknowledged in the wake of the 1929 Arab riots that 'the Zionist enterprise is an enterprise of conquest'. Precisely because they were not blind to the Arab dilemma, the more sober Zionist leaders departed from the inertia of self-delusion and political correctness. They understood, just as their Arab counterparts did, the irreconcilable nature of the contradiction between the objectives of the two national movements vying for the control of Palestine.

One of the first to realise the depth of the conflict was David Ben-Gurion. A leader of the Labour Zionists in Palestine and the future founder of the State of Israel and her first prime minister, Ben-Gurion was the leading voice of the Yishuv, the organized Jewish community in Palestine in the Mandate years, and later of the State of Israel until his final retirement from the premiership in 1963. In the 1920s he served as Secretary General of the Histadrut, the trade-union movement. In 1933 he became the director of the political department of the Jewish Agency, and two years later he assumed the chairmanship of the Agency, a position that was practically that of the 'prime minister' of the Yishuv. A man with a deep Messianic drive, he was at the same time a man of action, a pragmatic doer who believed that the redemption of the Jewish people could only be achieved through the creation of facts on the ground, a return to 'Jewish labour' ('*Avodah Ivrit*') and self-help. Historical rights mattered to him, of course, but more so the conviction that the land is possessed only by those who settle and work it. Like most of his contemporaries who came to Palestine in the 'second Aliyah' (immigration) in the first years of the century, Ben-Gurion was totally indifferent to the presence of the Arabs in Palestine and gave no thought to their living conditions or national aspirations.

But indifference to the fact that 'the Arabs of Palestine represent a mortal danger', as he put it in the wake of a violent incident between Jews and Arabs in Galilee in 1909, could not be maintained for long. True, Ben-Gurion frequently acknowledged the 'rights' of the Arabs, spoke of the role of Zionism 'to raise up the Arab masses from their degradation', and at some point he even suggested expanding the Jewish Yishuv to the empty Negev desert in order not to impinge on the Arabs. But the contradictions in his attitude were fast becoming irreconcilable. 'We did not come here to expel the Arabs', he said, 'but to build.' But building implicitly meant evicting and expelling. In the last analysis, he believed that the Arabs did not deserve to possess the land for they were 'incapable of reviving the land and restoring it from ruin'.

If early incidents between Jews and Arabs did not alert the leadership of the Yishuv to the challenge of the 'Arab question', the 1929 'riots' did. In the wake of the 1929 riots the leaders of the Yishuv had started to gauge the real meaning of the outburst of Arab rage. Ben-Gurion and Yosef Sprinzak were among the first to sound the alarm at what the latter defined as 'the renaissance of the Arabs'. A national movement was taking shape with its heroes and martyrs, and the Zionists took notice. Not too concerned with the subtleties of theoretical definitions, Ben-Gurion did not lose sight of the political challenge posed by the 1929 riots. 'Politically speaking,' he said, 'it is a national movement.' In 1933, during the Arab mass demonstrations throughout Palestine that were staged in protest against Jewish immigration, Ben-Gurion went a step further in identifying what he called an Arab 'political movement which must arouse respect'. It was then that the grim inevitability of a military showdown between the two national movements became clear to him, for they both desired the same thing: the land and a demographic majority. 'We both want Palestine, and this is the fundamental conflict,' he would explain to the Jewish Agency's Executive in May 1936. In 1938 Ben-Gurion even made the stunning acknowledgement that the entire presence of the Zionists in Palestine was 'politically' an aggression. The fighting, he said, 'is only one aspect of the conflict which is in its essence a political one. And politically we are the aggressors and they defend themselves.'

Ben-Gurion realised by then that war was inevitable, but as a cautious realist he also knew that an immediate war would undermine the, for now, successful policy of gradual growth and expansion of the Yishuv. In fact, for years Ben-Gurion preferred to deny the profound, intractable nature of the conflict, mostly for tactical reasons. He would engage in diplomatic contacts and contemplate compromise solutions he never really believed in only in order to consolidate British support for Zionism and postpone the inevitable war with the Arabs until the Yishuv was strong enough. Publicly acknowledging the national, insoluble nature of the conflict could inevitably have meant war and a premature showdown with both the Arabs and the mandatory power.

Ben-Gurion never really developed workable peace schemes. He only tried to buy time. It is hard to accept that he sincerely believed that the Arabs would endorse his plan for a Jewish–Arab Palestinian Common-wealth that established the principle that 'Palestine *belongs* to the Jewish people and to the Arabs who *reside* therein,' and put an emphasis on 'the moral worth of the Zionist enterprise' and on the 'justified' demand of the Jewish people for self-determination. Ben-Gurion's flirtation with a diplomatic solution to what, as he fully realised, was an intractable national conflict was in any case short-lived. As the riots of 1929, and more emphatically the Arab Revolt of 1936–9, made clear to him, war was inevitable. It was by then that the differences between Ben-Gurion, ever the gradualist and the pragmatic, and the maximalist Vladimir Jabotinsky, had become blurred, for Ben-Gurion endorsed, for all practical purposes, Jabotinsky's 'iron wall' doctrine. Arab despair before the Jewish pioneering and military élan would eventually bring the Arabs to terms with Zionism – such was now the conventional, bipartisan conviction. In the Zionist movement, patriotism and the endorsement of a military response were not the monopoly of the Right. The Arab Revolt helped to turn them into a bipartisan philosophy.

For both the Right and the mainstream Zionists, an immediate peace with the Palestinian Arabs was out of the question until their will to resist Zionism was totally broken. But peace was not necessarily desirable either, and it certainly was not the priority for the leaders of the Yishuv. Peace was not the objective, explained Ben-Gurion in a letter to the Jewish Agency's Executive in the early days of the Arab Revolt. He recognised, of course, that 'peace is indeed a vital matter for us', but, he insisted, it was only 'a means', and it became irrelevant if it was not accompanied by the complete and full realisation of Zionism. But then, of course, Ben-Gurion knew only too well that 'the full realisation of Zionism' in terms of territory and immigration meant that there could be no peace, for the Arabs would never reconcile themselves to such Zionist objectives. His conclusion was sober and blunt: 'A comprehensive agreement is undoubtedly out of the question now,' he wrote after his fruitless discussions with Palestinian leaders in the 1920s. His conclusion was not dissimilar to that developed by Jabotinsky, the founder of right-wing Revisionist Zionism, when he wrote in his iron wall article that only Jewish might could force the Arabs to 'acquiesce in a Jewish Eretz-Israel'.

Zionist democratic diversity did not mean that there was no common ground between the major segments of the movement. Initially, Ben-Gurion preferred an 'iron wall of workers', namely settlements and Jewish infrastructure, on Jabotinsky's call for an iron wall of military might and deterrence. In 1929, he even lashed out against what he defined as Jabotinsky's 'perverted national fanaticism', and against the Revisionists' 'worthless prattle of sham heroes, whose lips becloud the moral purity of our national movement...' Eventually, however, under the growing challenge of Arab nationalism and especially with the growth in the Yishuv of a collective mood of sacred Jewish nationalism following the Holocaust, the Labour Zionists, chief among them David Ben-Gurion, accepted for all practical purposes Jabotinsky's iron-wall strategy. The Jewish State could only emerge, and force the Arabs to accept it, if it erected around it an impregnable wall of Jewish might and deterrence.

'A Jewish Eretz-Israel' was something 'the Arabs' would, of course, under no conditions accept. But what became patently clear with the Arab Revolt was that it was now a struggle to the death, a war for individual and national survival between two antagonistic national communities vying for the same territory. All the well-intentioned or pragmatic ideas of the past about coexistence, a federal or a bi-national state were put to rest. It was now 'them or us'. The Arab Revolt was an authentic outburst of anger and frustration at the creeping ascendancy of the Yishuv that had just received a massive reinforcement of new immigrants driven by the gathering storm of Fascism and anti-Semitism in Europe. It was the threat of an expanding Zionism that nurtured the emergence of Palestinian nationalism and accelerated the decline into a dramatic military showdown between the two national movements.

The Jews would by then be far better prepared and ready for war than their enemies, if only because, driven by the sober conviction that the conflict was simply not susceptible to a political solution, they were quick to assume the inevitability of war and to endorse the views of those who wished to see a militarisation of the Yishuv.

The Zionists came to Palestine with idealistic intentions, but the Jewish state was to assert its birthright by the logic of force. An Israeli brand of militarism was now taking shape, whereby the militias of the Haganah – the clandestine armed forces of the Yishuv – and their young commanders practically imposed on the leaders the response to the new challenges. The years 1936–9 saw the emergence of the Israeli ethos of a nation in arms and the beginning of what would soon become the total integration of the military into the process of policy making, first in the Yishuv and later in the State of Israel, which still exists today. Throughout the Middle East and the Third World, for the military to impose their priorities they would have to stage a takeover that would do away with civilian rule altogether. In the case of Israel there would hardly ever be the need for the men on horseback to take over, for their solutions to the major challenges were either integrated into the political system when they were still in uniform, or they themselves enjoyed a peaceful, perfectly natural move to the highest political positions once they left the army. The militia commanders of the late 1930s and the field officers of the 1948 war would become the future ministers and prime ministers of the State of Israel.

A synchronisation between the military, 'activist' drive of the militia commanders in the Yishuv on the one hand, and the political leaders on the other, was now clearly developing. Such was the extent of the change that Chaim Weizmann, of whom Lloyd George wrote in his *War Memoirs* that 'his name will rank with that of Nehemiah in the fascinating and inspiring story of the children of Israel', voiced his estrangement from the homeland he had done so much to secure for the Jews. He was dismayed to see how, as he wrote in his autobiography,

> the negative traits against which I warned are now appearing: the old, traditional Zionist morality is being eroded, a tendency to militarism and an admiration of the martial ways, a tragic, useless and so unJewish flirtation with terror, the distortion of the pure, defensive role of the Haganah.

True, the civilian leaders first reacted to the Arab aggression with a policy of 'self-restraint' (*havlaga*). But *havlaga* could not last. First, it was Menachem Begin's Irgun that challenged the Yishuv's reliance on the goodwill of the British and Weizmann's 'Galuthic' diplomatic ways. The Haganah lost no time in following suit. An eccentric Bible-fanatic British officer, Orde Wingate, created the 'Night Squads' where the younger generation of Jewish fighters were taught to abandon their traditional defensive tactics in favour of bold, offensive reprisals against Arab villages. And through his 'Field Battalions' (*Plugot Sadeh*), created in 1937, a charismatic field officer, Yitzhak Sadeh, inculcated in the younger generation an ethos of war, struggle and military initiative. It was in units like these and under the inspiration of legendary commanders like Wingate and Sadeh that the two most emblematic field commanders of the 1948 war, Moshe Dayan and Yigal Allon, absorbed their vision of war and military Zionism.

The military way advocated by the younger generation was not just a matter of operational tactics. It was an entirely new political concept, whereby national aspirations could not be realised through traditional

Zionist diplomatic means or by way of political accommodation, but only through the use of military force. Convinced of the inevitability of an all-out war between Jews and Arabs for the possession of Palestine, the impatient young military leaders now wanted to extricate the movement for Jewish national liberation from the old evolutionary methods of the founding fathers.

But the military commanders went even further. In their aspiration to be those who would define the political objectives of the movement, they established the pattern for the future preponderant role of the military in the process of decision making in the State of Israel. The 'Avner Plan', prepared in 1937 by the Field Battalions, not by the politicians, was of course at the time utterly unrealistic, pure wishful thinking. But it nevertheless anticipated, and laid the ground for, what in 1948 would be the momentous Plan D, that is, a strategy of going far beyond the modest boundaries of the different partition plans and absorbing into the Jewish state typically Arab areas. The Avner Plan was, in fact, much more presumptuous than Plan D, for it also envisaged the conquest of the Galilee, the West Bank and Jerusalem. What this hectic military activity really represented, however, was that the ethos of the fighting youth was now being placed at the very heart of the new Zionist project.

That military force was now seen not just as a necessary evil, but also as a vital instrument for the shaping of a new national conscience, was certainly a far cry from the supposed heritage of the diaspora, where the Jews had gone, as it were, 'like sheep to the slaughter'. The young militia leaders represented the 'new man' of the Zionist revolution and, unlike the founding fathers who brought with them from the Galuth the millenarian fears of annihilation of a persecuted nation and seemed sometimes to carry with them the entire burden of Jewish history, the young Sabras' (native-born Israelis) way was that of self-confidence and certainty. Possessed by a sense of native ownership of the land they were born into, they harboured no doubts that they would prevail in the imminent war against the Arabs.

Havlaga, then, had its limits. Either in co-operation with the British or through the independent operations of Wingate's Special Night Squads and Yitzhak Sadeh's Field Battalions, let alone through the activities of the Irgun, the Jews started to respond. After the Arab Revolt was quelled – mainly, of course, by the brutal repression of the British – it was a new military offspring of the Haganah, the 'Poum', that led what became almost routine reprisals and collective punishments against Arab villages. Later, with the creation of the Palmach in 1941, a special elite unit made up of the cream of the youth of the new Jewish society in

Palestine, the ethos of offensive defence received a major boost. Adopted by the 'activist' Hakibbutz Hameuhad, which glorified the military way and maintained throughout its commitment to an 'unpartitioned' Jewish state in the whole of Palestine, the Palmach, whose members combined the duties of the warrior with those of the farmer, was supposed to be the model of a popular army that would realise through conquest and settlement Hakibbutz Hameuhad's vision of Greater Eretz-Israel.

The Zionists clearly enjoyed major advantages in the approaching conflict. Theirs was an essentially democratic movement, rich and diverse in social, cultural and political expressions, and formidably well organised in a modern, state-like structure. However vital, the military option was always to be accompanied by a diplomatic effort. The Zionist way of achieving the dream of Jewish statehood was a double-edged strategy, namely, a powerful military response and a subtle deployment of diplomatic skills.

Rarely in history has a national movement marched to the Promised Land, as the Zionists did, with such a brilliant display of diplomatic savoir faire and military skills. A keystone of Zionist diplomacy, Britain remained throughout vitally important for the consolidation of the National Home. The British connection, as well as the persistent drive of the future State of Israel for a strategic alliance with a Western power, reflected the inherently Western-orientated inclination of Zionism. The implicit assumption was that Israel could not, some also believed that it should not, peacefully integrate within the Arab Middle East. Wisely, even when taken aback by Britain's frequent retreats from its commitments to the National Home in the Balfour Declaration, the Zionists shunned open confrontation with the mandatory power. Not only mainstream figures like Weizmann and Ben-Gurion, but also the more radical leader of the Revisionists, Zeev (Vladimir) Jabotinsky, valued the alliance with Britain as a vital guarantee for the National Home. The pragmatic alliance with Albion, however perfidious Albion appeared to them, had to be maintained as long as this was possible. Facts on the ground and the consistent build-up of Jewish power were preferred to grandiloquent proclamations on the long-range objectives of Zionism, and to unnecessary and precipitated clashes with the mandatory power. And when an undesirable British idea was put forward, such as the initiative for an Arab–Jewish Legislative Council in Palestine, the Zionist Executive preferred to make the best of a bad bargain and negotiate a parity structure for the new body rather than reject its creation out of hand. The Zionists could always rely on Arab obsessive rejectionism to pull the chestnuts out of the fire for them. What was to become a pillar of Ben-Gurion's strategic thinking as the prime minister of the future State of Israel – never to operate without the support of a Western superpower – was discernible already at the point where the inevitability of a total war for Palestine became evident to him. Nothing haunted Ben-Gurion's mind more than an isolated Jewish Yishuv, or even independent state, at war with the Arab world without the support of a superpower.

The Zionist Western-orientated strategy was also a response to the cultural alienation of the Zionists from the Arab East. It was a cultural choice as much as a strategic inevitability. Ben-Gurion never pretended that Zionism was about the integration with the East. He was candid enough to write to the Arab nationalist, George Antonius, the author of *The Arab Awakening* (1938): 'We want to return to the East only in the geographic sense, for our objective is to create here a European culture … at least as the cultural foundations in this corner of the world remain unchanged.' Ben-Gurion was expressing the core essence of Zionism, not merely a personal view. There was no difference between his letter to George Antonius and the political philosophy of Max Nordau, Herzl's successor at the head of the Zionist movement, who had claimed that 'we intend to come to Palestine as the emissaries of culture and to expand the moral boundaries of Europe to the Euphrates.' Most of the leaders of the Yishuv knew very little of Arab civilisation and despised what they saw. In this respect – the condescending attitude to the Arabs – there was hardly any difference between Jabotinsky and Ben-Gurion. The Arab East represented to them fatalistic passivity, social and cultural stagnation, and political tyranny. And like most of his opponents among Labour Zionists, Jabotinsky was no friend of the idea of Jewish integration into the Arab Middle East. The future Jewish state was to be for all of them an offshoot of Western civilization in the stagnant and despotic East. To Jabotinsky, 'the Jews have nothing in common' with the East, and like Ben-Gurion he also held Oriental culture in contempt and disdain.

But the common ground that united Right and Left in the Yishuv should not obscure the bitter political rivalry that prevailed throughout between the Labourites under Ben-Gurion and Jabotinsky's right-wing Revisionists. At the root of the differences lay, as so often, a struggle for political hegemony, but the questions of substance that divided these two major strands of Zionist politics were considerable. It was not only that the Revisionists, who supported a bourgeois political economy, derided what Bert Katznelson, the socialist ideologue of Labour Zionism, called 'constructivism', that is, the politics of settlements, egalitarianism and the harnessing of the trade-union movement for the creation of material assets, health services and a physical infrastructure for the future Jewish State; they also challenged the gradualist and pragmatic political strategy of the Labourites. The latter refused to endorse Jabotinsky's emphasis on the integrity of Eretz-Israel that should include, according to him, both banks of the River Jordan. They also rejected his call for a public acknowledgement by the Zionist movement that full-fledged Jewish statehood and political sovereignty over the whole of Eretz-Israel was the unquestionable objective of the Zionist movement. The issues at stake were so central to the political identity of the two parties that, once his proposals were defeated by the Labourite majority, Jabotinsky decided in 1931 to lead the Revisionists out of the Zionist organization altogether. In 1935, the Revisionists seceded to found the New Zionist Organization, and a year later they took over an independent underground military organization, the Irgun Zvai Leumi (the National Military Organization).

The gradualist, cautious move of the Yishuv to statehood in the course of which the radical and unrealistic Revisionists were sidelined stood in stark contrast to the developments in the Arab camp. Obfuscated by an understandable sense of loss and dispossession at the hands of a well-organised Zionist community and its British protectors, the Arabs gave way to the most radical trends and leaders in their midst. They doomed their cause by targeting their struggle against their two powerful enemies at the same time: the Zionists and the British. The ascendancy of the Mufti in the 1930s to undisputed leadership at the expense of more moderate options – that of the Nashashibi clan, for example – paved the path to revolt and total war. The Arabs opted for very high stakes – doing away altogether with the Zionist project and confronting militarily the British Mandate – with inadequate resources. By the end of the Arab Revolt, Palestinian society was in total disarray, their communities in a state of disintegration, and their internal cohesion dramatically undermined by military defeat and by the collaboration of many, not least among the local elites, with the Zionist enemy. The Palestinians were to face the 1948 ordeal in a state of fragmentation and with no real absorbing capacity.

The war for Palestine in 1948 was lost by the Arab community ten years before it even began. The Arab Revolt had, of course, an understandable rationale behind it, namely, to force Britain to reverse her policies in favour of the National Home for the Jews, stop immigration and curtail the land acquisition by the Zionists. But the method and the evolution of the Revolt reflected rage and blind despair more than organisation or careful strategy. The result would be a resounding defeat for the Palestinian Arabs that would bring them to the ultimate débâcle of 1948 in a state of fatalistic disarray. The years between the Arab Revolt and the Naqbah of 1948 witnessed the dismemberment of the Palestinian community and the loss of their political autonomy to the extent that when they had to face the challenge of partition and war in 1947–8, they were no longer the masters of their own destiny. By then their cause would be usurped by the neighbouring Arab states. It was not until the emergence of the Fatah movement and Yasser Arafat's PLO in the mid 1960s that the Palestinians recovered the control of their own cause.

But it was definitely during the Arab Revolt that the Palestinian problem turned into a pan-Arab issue and the idea took root that the whole Arab nation was now threatened by Western imperialism, Zionism being its beachhead. From the Arab Revolt onwards, Palestine would become the convenient battle-cry for the entire Arab world, the cohesive glue of pan-Arab nationalism, the platform for mass hysteria in Cairo and Baghdad, Tunis and Casablanca, Damascus and Amman. So much so that in 1948 the Arab states were practically forced against their will to invade the newborn Jewish state 'for the sake of Palestine ...'

II Bisecting the Land or Zionism's Strategy of Phases?

The kingdom of David was smaller, but under Solomon it became an empire. *C'est le premier pas qui compte.*

> *Chaim Weizmann's reaction to the minuscule Jewish State proposed*
> *by the Peel Commission,*
> August 1937

Erect a Jewish state at once, even if it is not in the whole land. The rest will come in the course of time. It must come.

> *Ben-Gurion,*
> October 1937

If I weigh the catastrophe of five million Jews against the transfer of one million Arabs, then with a clean and easy conscience I can state that even more drastic acts are permissible.

> *Werner Senator, a non-Zionist member of the Jewish Agency,*
> 16 December 1944

Zionism is a political movement aiming at the domination of at least the whole of Palestine; to give it a foothold in part of Palestine would be to encourage it to press for more ...

> *The Arab Office: Evidence Submitted to the Anglo-American Committee,*
> March 1946

The borders of our state will be defined by the limits of our force.... The borders will be the fruit of our conquests.

> *Israel Galili, Chief of Staff of the Haganah,*
> 8 April 1948

Zionism is both a struggle for land and a demographic race; in essence, the aspiration for a territory with a Jewish majority. How to reconcile the drive for a Jewish state in historic Eretz-Israel with the reality of Palestine clearly not being, as some believed, 'a land without a people', but one with an irresistible Arab majority, is the essence of the struggle between the two national movements vying for supremacy, and even exclusivity, within the same piece of land. To bisect the land or to possess it all was the dilemma. In the end, as is being reflected in Ariel Sharon's policy today of unilateral withdrawal from densely populated Palestinian areas, it is the demographic concern that would prevail. No argument was more compelling for Zionism to trim its territorial ambitions than that of the demographic imperatives.

But 'separation' and 'disengagement', a powerful political platform in Israel during the Palestinian Al-Aqsa Intifada, is not a new panacea. It was born in the wake of the Arab Revolt when the exposure of the irreconcilable nature of the gulf between two conflicting national movements, both fighting for the same objectives, land and demographic superiority, swept away lofty dreams about coexistence, and shattered the belief in a bi-national, one-state solution, or in federal schemes of any kind. One overriding issue was now on the agenda: how to partition the land and separate the two communities.

As a matter of fact, separation was a natural condition in the development of the two national movements. Arab and Jewish societies had evolved along separate paths ever since the early days of Zionism. This was certainly the case during the vital Mandate years when the two societies were segregated along physical, institutional and developmental lines. The social services, the economic infrastructure, the educational system and the geographical boundaries of the Arab and Jewish communities were clearly defined. This was never the case, however, of an imposed South Africa style segregation by either side. Neither the Jews nor the Arabs were especially keen on having a mixed society in Palestine. A central ethos of the early Zionist enterprise, the principle of 'Jewish labour', was also instrumental in limiting the interaction between the two societies. Lofty dreams and platforms about Jewish–Arab coexistence notwithstanding, and in spite of the development of some bi-national spaces of co-operation and communal life, as Professor Ilan Pappe has indicated, the essential condition of life in Palestine was one of mutual exclusion. As in the case of Ariel Sharon's wall and that of the overwhelming support of Israelis for 'separation' in the wake of the Al-Aqsa Intifada, the violent reaction of the Arabs to the progress made by the Yishuv enhanced, if anything, the trend towards disengagement. The riots of 1929 and the Revolt of 1936–9 sealed the fate of the two communities to be segregated from each other.

The supporters of partition abandoned the illusions about the supposedly civilising role of Zionism and the paternalistic assumption that economic prosperity would eventually reconcile the Arabs to the Zionist enterprise. The Arab Revolt was a defining moment, a clash of national characters that could not be reconciled by economic subsidies and poetic hallucinations. The leaders of the Arab community were not even ready to discuss Weizmann's idea of restricting Jewish immigration as a way of calming down the Arab rage and disarming the Revolt. The rejection of his overture reinforced Weizmann's conviction that partition was the only feasible solution. He was not the first, nor the last, Zionist leader to despair of a negotiated settlement. Arab nationalism, he now explained, was inherently unable to contemplate a reasonable compromise with Zionism.

The panacea of partition in the 1930s and 1940s, just like that of separation and disengagement during the Al-Aqsa Intifada, was the outcome of fear, the offspring of despair, the consequence of a new conviction about the insoluble nature of the conflict. This was also the victory of Jabotinsky's iron wall. For both the Right that opposed partition and the Centre-Left that supported it now shared a common philosophy, that of the deterrence of Jewish might as the only tool remaining to coerce the Arabs into acquiescing with the Zionist project. Partition and separation were also fed and enhanced by the cultivation of the image of a brutal Arab enemy that was not susceptible to dialogue and compromise. The demonisation of the Palestinian national movement, combined with a profound sense of despair as to the chances of a political solution to what looked like a tribal, almost mythological conflict, was now the prevailing attitude among the leaders of the Yishuv. Yitzhak Tabenkin, the mentor of the 'activist' Hakibbutz Hameuhad, spoke about the Nazi-like brutality of the Arab riots. Berl Katznelson described a primitive Arab national movement whose genocidal plans against the Yishuv were embedded in a tradition of religious fanaticism and xenophobia, and in an Arab culture permeated with bloodlust.

As from the late 1970s Israel would always reject the admittedly ambiguous peace overtures of the PLO on the ground that they were part of a 'strategy of phases', the final objective of which was to take over the whole of Palestine and eventually do away with the State of Israel altogether. But the copyright for the strategy of phases might lie elsewhere: it was conceived by the leaders of the Yishuv in the mid 1930s; it was inherent in the notion they had of the real meaning of partition as the first stage to wider territorial accomplishments. By endorsing partition, as it was proposed by the Peel Commission in 1937, Ben-Gurion did not necessarily mean to relinquish the Zionist claim for the entire Eretz-Israel. The minuscule Jewish state proposed by the Commission could by no means solve the Jewish question or satisfy the minimal yearnings of Zionism. But, as Ben-Gurion put it, it 'can serve as a decisive stage along the path to greater Zionist implementation'. In Jabotinsky's concept, maximalist territorial solutions needed to be implemented outright; Ben-Gurion was a prudent gradualist who relied on 'the course of time'. The immediate task, as he put it in a letter to his wife in the summer of 1937, was that of establishing a Jewish state, however modest in its size, as a guarantee for Jewish immigration and as a possible springboard for future expansion. To his son Amos he wrote in October of the same year: 'Erect a Jewish state at once, even if it is not in the whole land. The rest will come in the course of time. It must come.'

It would come if only because, as he wrote, the Jewish state would have 'an outstanding army' that would ensure that 'we won't be constrained from settling in the rest of the country, whether out of accord and mutual understanding with the Arab neighbours or otherwise'. If endorsing partition would have meant 'relinquishing our historical rights over the whole land of Israel', he said in a speech in August 1937 to the Twentieth Zionist Congress, 'then I would reject the State'. The attitude of Chaim Weizmann, more moderate and always more measured in his words than Ben-Gurion, was not essentially different. To him as well the 'Peel state' was only the beginning. 'The Kingdom of David was smaller,' he said, 'but under Solomon it became an empire. *C'est le premier pas qui compte,*' he consoled the sceptics.

In other words, the defeat of the territorial drive by the demographic imperatives, which would be the core reason for the Israeli Right's flirtation with the idea of 'unilateral disengagement' in the wake of the Al-Aqsa Intifada, was not yet clear to the Zionist leaders in the 1930s, especially as the Peel Commission itself advanced a panacea that they were quick to embrace. Probably the most appealing article in the recommendation of the Commission was that about the 'forced transfer' of Arabs from the future Jewish state. To Ben-Gurion this was an 'unparalleled achievement'. It was 'the best of all solutions', according to Berl Katznelson. 'A distant neighbour', he said, 'is better than a close enemy.' Transfer was such an ideal solution that 'it must happen some day', he concluded. A strategy of phases, admittedly always vague and anything but an articulate plan of action, could only prevail if a solution could be found to the demographic problem. 'Transfer' was the magic formula.

The idea of transfer for the Arabs had a long pedigree in Zionist thought. Moral scruples hardly intervened in what was normally seen as a realistic and logical solution, a matter of expediency. Israel Zangvill, the founding father of the concept, advocated transfer as early as 1916. For, as he said, 'if we wish to give a country to a people without a country, it is utter foolishness to allow it to be the country of two peoples. ... One of the two – a different place must be found either for the Jews or for their neighbours.'

The idea of transfer was not the intimate dream of only the activists and the militants in the Zionist movement. A mass exodus of Arabs from Palestine was no great tragedy, according to Menachem Ussishkin, a leader of the General Zionists. To him the message of the Arab Revolt was that coexistence was out of the question and it was now either the Arabs or the Jews, but not both. Even Aharon Zisling, a member of the extreme Left of the Zionist Labour movement, who during the 1948 war would go on record as being scandalised by the atrocities committed against the Arab population, saw 'no moral flaw' in the transfer of the Arabs, although he avoided the term in favour of the euphemism of 'concentrating the development of national life'. 'In a new world order', he said, 'it can and should be a noble human vision.' But again, Ben-Gurion's voice had always a special meaning and relevance. At a Zionist meeting in June 1938 he was as explicit as he could be: 'I support compulsory transfer. I don't see in it anything immoral.' But he also knew that transfer would be possible only in the midst of war, not in 'normal times'. What might be impossible in such times, he said, 'is possible in revolutionary times'. The problem was, then, not moral, perhaps not even political; it was a function of timing, and this meant war.

However much they might have shared dreams of great territorial accomplishments, the Zionists would reach the vital showdown with the Arabs in 1947–8 as a movement deeply divided over the immediate territorial objectives of Zionism. Not everybody was ready to settle, even tactically and as a first stage, for the minuscule Jewish state proposed by the Peel Commission. Partition was opposed by all the radical wings of the Zionist camp. Hashomer Hatzair rejected it because it clashed with its socialist dream of a bi-national Arab–Jewish state; Tabenkin's Hakibbutz Hameuhad saw no reason to succumb to the pressure of Arab violence and relinquish the ethos of settling and conquering Eretz-Israel. As to the religious Zionists of the Mizrahi, the Eternity of Israel and the exclusive millenarian link of the Jews to Eretz-Israel meant that there was no room for partition.

Partition was, of course, utterly out of the question for Jabotinsky's Revisionists. Only after a Jewish majority on both banks of the Jordan was achieved, a full and unconditional possession of the land by the Zionists was reached, and an iron wall of Jewish might and deterrence was erected would the Arabs reconcile themselves with the existence of a Jewish state in their midst. Jabotinsky was nevertheless a statesman brought up in a European liberal, romantic tradition. His military phil-osophy conceived a political solution of sorts and a fair deal for the Palestinian Arabs both as individuals and as a national community. But more radical offsprings of his movement such as Brit ha-Biryonim (League of Outlaws), led and inspired by Abba Ahimeir and the poet Uri Zvi Greenberg, moved in the wake of the 1929 riots to a Fascist glorification of violence that ruled out any possibility whatever for an understanding between Jews and Arabs, let alone for a partition of the land between them.

The democratic diversity of the Yishuv was indeed impressive. The Socialist idealism and class solidarity with the Arabs that brought Hashomer Hatzair to reject the idea of partition was matched by the moralistic approach of left-wing, non-Zionist intellectuals who questioned the very ·legitimacy of the aspiration to Jewish statehood. Politically, Brit Shalom and its derivative in the 1940s, Ihud, represented, of course, no challenge to mainstream Zionism. But it did embody a trend persistent throughout the history of Zionism and the State of Israel of a radical, left-wing intellectual response to the powerful, and to them immoral, drive to Jewish statehood based on might and the dispossession of the Arabs. Led by luminaries like Ernest Simon, Gershom Sholem and Yehudah Magnes, they opposed the partition of the land and a Jewish separate state. Instead, they championed the right of the Arab majority to rule the country in a bi-national Arab–Jewish state. Not unlike the anti-Zionist religious orthodox who disputed the notion that Judaism as a religion needed a material Jewish state for its perpetuity, there was in the preachings of Brit Shalom a philosophical rejection of the very idea that Judaism as a civilisation needed political power for its survival. For Gershom Sholem, the scholar of Jewish mysticism, the Zionists represented nothing but a 'sect', an episode in the annals of Jewish history.

Partition would not be given to the Zionists on a silver platter; it had to be wrested by force from the British. So long as the British Mandate was instrumental in bringing Zionism closer to its objectives, one could justify collaborating with it. After the war this was clearly no longer the case. But timing was nevertheless of the essence, and the Zionist leaders were admirably careful in choosing the right moment for their total and irreversible divorce from Britain. Initially, and so long as the war against Hitler continued, the White Paper as such did not immediately alter the policy of the Yishuv, which still viewed Britain as the major strategic ally of the Zionist cause. However embittered and betrayed by the mandatory power, and however ready to embrace the military option, the mainstream leaders of the Yishuv knew that Britain's support was vital for the emergence of the Jewish state. Ben-Gurion's famous catchphrase that 'we will fight with the British against Hitler as if there were no White Paper; we will fight the White Paper as if there were no war' represented the wise and subtle balance of a movement bent on pursuing the drive for a

Jewish state without alienating itself from the concerns of the civilised world in its struggle for survival against Nazi Germany. And while the Mufti was busy compromising the international image and the fate of the Palestinian cause, striking sinister deals with Hitler and lending his support to the 'final solution', the Zionists wisely absorbed the severe blow dealt to them by the White Paper and resisted the temptation of adopting an unrealistic anti-British course of action. Rather, they pressed Britain to allow the Yishuv to join the Allies' war effort. Moreover, both the Haganah and the Palmah persisted throughout the war in their military collaboration with the British with whom they conducted joint military operations against Vichy targets in Syria and Lebanon. And more than 27,000 Jewish volunteers from the Yishuv joined the British army throughout 1942–4.

The insistence of the Zionists on an alliance with Britain did not mean that they were blind to the radical changes in the global balance of power, with America emerging as the major broker in the international system. The shift of focus of Zionist diplomacy from Britain to the United States in the early 1940s was a masterly exercise in strategic intuition and diplomatic skill. The May 1942 Biltmore Conference in New York was in effect the core of a Zionist political and public relations campaign for the heart and mind of America. Interestingly, it was Ben-Gurion, the man of action, not Weizmann, the brilliant diplomat, who was the first to grasp the meaning of the changing balance of world power. Weizmann continued to believe in traditional Jewish individual diplomacy mainly in Britain, while Ben-Gurion was quick to realise the opportunities offered to the Zionist cause by the American political culture where public opinion, Congress and, of course, the Jewish community could be exploited to help formulate a policy that was friendly to the Zionist cause.

The target of Zionist diplomacy was no longer Britain but the United States and international opinion. There was little hope of averting an open clash with the mandatory power now entangled in the conflicting pledges and promises to Arabs and Jews. And as happened frequently in the history of Zionism, the cause was enhanced by the Jewish catastrophe. It was the full truth and the awesome impact of the Holocaust of European Jewry, as it was exposed worldwide after the war, that served now as the platform upon which Zionist diplomacy could mobilise governments and international opinion in order to attain its major political objective, a Jewish state in Palestine. Once again, Jewish catastrophe was the propellant of the Zionist idea and a boost to its prospects. Britain could not resist the moral pressure created by the struggle of thousands of Holocaust survivors to reach the shores of Palestine. The harsh, even brutal, policy of the British against the immigration to Palestine of the survivors of the Holocaust was the platform upon which the Zionists succeeded in mobilising international opinion, mainly in America, and in uniting the Yishuv in the final showdown with the British. The Haganah organisers used as a matter of policy and tactics the suffering of the illegal immigrants crammed into broken old ships to further a clear political end. In the years 1945–8, 40,000 illegal immigrants landed on the shores of Palestine, but an even greater number, 51,000, were seized on the high seas by the British and taken to camps in Cyprus.

It was not only through the exploitation of the Jewish catastrophe that the Zionists defeated the British in America. They also played their diplomatic cards wisely. The decision of the Zionist Executive in August 1946 to depart from the Biltmore Plan and endorse the idea of partition was a brilliant move that a few months later received the support of the United States. America's endorsement of partition would be one of the main reasons that would force the British to refer the question of Palestine back to the UN.

This was a war Britain could not win, for its outcome was to be decided by public opinion. The British image was shattered throughout the world, especially in America. It was little surprise that the Anglo-American Committee of Enquiry into the conditions of the Displaced Persons Camps throughout Europe should have recommended the immediate absorption in Palestine of 100,000 Jews, a recommendation that Britain could by no means digest, for it contradicted its attempt to appease the Arabs. The British Labour Party, which in its 1944 platform went as far as endorsing the principle of Jewish majority in Palestine even at the price of a 'transfer of population' ('let the Arabs be encouraged to move out as the Jews move in ...'), was now as a government mainly concerned with rebuilding its bridges with the Arab world and protecting Britain's strategic position in the wider Middle East.

No other state in modern times was born with such a degree of international sympathy and guilt feelings as the Jewish state. But not only did Zionism now have the Jewish catastrophe as its major ally, it also possessed a formidable institutional infrastructure and a reliable military force. For all practical purposes, a Jewish state had existed for some time in all but name. The war being over, the British were in no condition to impose a settlement of their own. With the future of Palestine an international issue, the Mandate government was reduced to impotence. The British–Zionist clash was an experience that broke all the known patterns of colonial rule. It was under British protection that the Zionists built their power and state-like infrastructures. Now, in defiance of British rule, the Yishuv commanded an extraordinary and well-equipped military force of about 100,000 men. Exhausted by an unpopular war in Palestine,

a land British public opinion saw more as a liability than as a strategic asset, and harassed by Jewish terrorism on the one hand and by the Arabs' utterly unrealistic expectations on the other, the British government decided to refer the question of Palestine back to the UN.

UN Resolution 181 of 29 November 1947 partitioning western Palestine into a Jewish and an Arab state was a resounding victory for the Zionist undertaking and for the Jews' millenarian longing for statehood. It was the crowning achievement of one of the most brilliantly successful national enterprises of the twentieth century. The Zionists finally achieved the charter of international legitimacy that Herzl had established as the central objective of the movement from the moment he conceived it as a political enterprise. The Arabs were defeated by the Zionists' remarkable persistence and by their extraordinary capacity to combine military means with diplomatic savoir faire. The Zionists' bold creation of facts on the ground and construction of the institutions of the future state were now complemented by a skilful manipulation of the Jewish catastrophe, the Holocaust, in order to enlist international support for their cause. The prospects of Zionism were always fed and enhanced by unique encounters between global and local developments. The rise of Hitler to power, the consequent upsurge in Jewish immigration in the 1930s, the awesome impact of the Jewish Holocaust and the change in the global balance of power with America's ascendancy to world leadership were all historical opportunities that the Zionist leaders responded to in a masterly way. A sense of realism and the unique capacity of the Zionist mainstream leadership to respond to changing historical conditions made the Jewish state possible.

The effect of the Holocaust on the Yishuv and its leaders was to enhance the sense of national cohesion, as well as the conviction that the war for Palestine was now more inevitable than ever. This was no longer the time for self-delusive or righteous debates on the 'Arab question' or for far-fetched plans for a bi-national state. The 'Jewish question' excluded all other considerations. And since the obduracy of the Arabs in rejecting any compromise, and all and every plan of political accommodation, was patently clear to all, this became the time for sacred national and ethnic egoism. From Brit-Shalom Ihud to the Left-Poalei Zion and Hashomer Hatzair to some, admittedly not all, religious sectors that had opposed in the past the idea of partition, the clamour sprang for uncurtailed Jewish immigration and for a homogeneous, 'separate' Jewish state, however 'partitioned' and however small. Brit-Shalom Ihud was an interesting case in point. Out of a profound ethical conviction, Brit-Shalom warned that a Jewish state might inevitably imply the suppression of the Arabs of Palestine. And also because it never believed in the Zionist fantasy of a

Jewish majority in Palestine, Brit-Shalom had in the past sternly opposed the idea of a Jewish state and also the desire of the mainstream Zionists to partition the land between Jews and Arabs.

This was always the predicament of the Republic of the Philosophers: it responded to genuine moral anxieties and reflections, but it frequently failed to take into account the irresistible power of the historical process and that of human atavism and national will. Not only did Brit-Shalom's lofty ideas about Jewish–Arab coexistence in a bi-national state with the Jews as a minority find no meaningful echo among Arab nationalists, but also the rise of Nazism and the dramatic plight of European Jewry were soon to make them irrelevant. When faced with the apocalyptic dimensions of the Jewish catastrophe, the Holocaust, even Brit-Shalom Ihud moved to endorse first the necessity of demographic parity between Jews and Arabs in Palestine, and then, as 'a necessary evil', the idea of a Jewish independent state, that is the partition of Palestine. It was no longer the time for moral scruples or guilt feelings towards the dispossessed Arab population. This is how a Brit-Shalom Ihud, non-Zionist member of the Jewish Agency, Werner Senator, put it: 'If I weigh the catastrophe of five million Jews against the transfer of one million Arabs, then with a clean and easy conscience I can state that even more drastic acts are permissible.'

As for Hashomer Hatzair, the Marxist champions of Arab–Jewish fraternity and of the bi-national state, and those who had in the past placed in the hands of the Arabs the right to determine the scope of Jewish immigration, the significance of the Holocaust was that the rights of the Jewish people should now have 'moral priority over that of the Arabs'. The principle of partition and separation that had been moral and political anathema, for it clashed with the belief in a socialist Jewish–Arab state based on class solidarity, not on nationalist narcissism, was endorsed by Hashomer Hatzair in 1947, probably also under the inspiration of the Soviets, their patrons, who, eager to drive the British out of the Middle East, now supported the idea of partition. The Soviet Union made it easier for Hashomer Hatzair to reconcile their change of attitude with the cause of 'international progress', their humanitarian scruples with their Jewish nationalism.

But supporters and opponents of partition alike – Ahdut Haavoda and the Revisionists persisted throughout in their rejection of partition because they both believed in a Greater Jewish state, for which the indivisibility of the land was a vital condition – would soon realise that the borders of the future Jewish state would not be defined by ideological priorities, but through the logic of war that all knew was inevitable. In reality, and for all practical purposes, it was not the principle of partition that was in dispute; rather it was the scope and the physical dimensions of the 'separate' Jewish state that was at stake. As the Zionist project gained strength, and the Arab fears of dispossession turned into panic, war became inevitable. It was now clear that a Jewish state could only be created, as Tabenkin predicted, by imposing the will of the Jews on the Arabs, even if that meant the mass transfer of the Arab population. The Arabs helped defeat their case by obstinately rejecting even the most minimalist requirements of Zionism and they turned down all the initiatives advanced by the British for a political settlement. Zionism was to them a colonialist movement that needed eradication, not reconciliation.

The two communities, Jews and Arabs, were approaching their hour of truth because coexistence was simply beyond their will or capacity. On the Jewish side a mixture of fatalistic mistrust with a condescending attitude towards the Arabs accompanied the drift to war. To Chaim Weizmann, Arab nationalism proved to be nothing but a feudalistic hangover, a decadent offshoot of European nationalism. 'As a people, as a race', Moshe Shertok reflected, the Arabs could never reconcile themselves to the Zionist drive to possess Palestine. Ben-Gurion now saw the encounter between Zionism and the Arab world almost in the fatalistic terms of an insoluble clash of civilisations. 'We live in the twentieth century; they live in the fifteenth,' he said; 'we have created an exemplary society in the heart of the Middle Ages.' Even among some of the progressive minds of Brit-Shalom Ihud the stipulation was raised that in the case of a bi-national state being created, the Western powers would have to extend their protection to such a state lest the 'Fascist' tendencies of Arab nationalism and the Levantine culture of the Arabs should prevail.

However satisfied they might have been with the vital international legitimacy accorded to the principle of a Jewish state in Palestine, it is hardly conceivable that the leaders of the Yishuv thought of the minuscule state that was now created as the final territorial stage in the Zionist enterprise. True, unlike the Revisionists who did not mince their words in utterly rejecting the partition of Palestine as 'illegal' and in pledging allegiance to 'all of it', the Jewish Agency endorsed Resolution 181. It is impossible, of course, to predict what would have happened if the Arabs had not persisted in their self-defeating rejectionist pattern of behaviour. The course of history might have been substantially different. For by endorsing Resolution 181 the Yishuv practically agreed to a bi-national state in Palestine. The 'partitioned' Jewish state as defined by the Resolution consisted of an Arab 'minority' of 49 per cent of the total population. In a memorandum it addressed to the UN, the Jewish Agency even made an explicit pledge to the effect that the new state 'will not be Jewish in the sense ... that the Jewish community will be superior in status to other communities'.

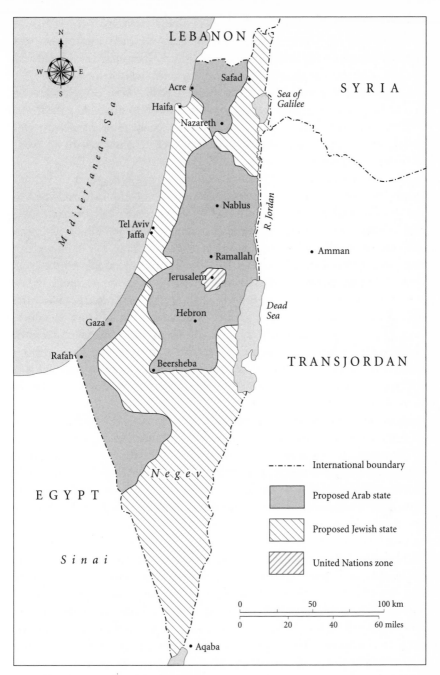

The United Nations partition plan, 1947

But this was nevertheless a half-hearted endorsement. The leaders of the Yishuv were happy neither with the provision that called for the creation of a Palestinian state nor with the clearly non-viable borders of the Jewish state, let alone with the exclusion of Jerusalem from it. The borders between the Arab and the Jewish states were a nightmare of points and lines of friction, of isolated areas lacking in viable contiguity; and, last but not least, a demographic absurdity characterised the proposed Jewish state where 500,000 Jews were supposed to coexist with an Arab 'minority' of close to the same size.

The endorsement of partition along the lines of Resolution 181 by Ben-Gurion was essentially a tactical move. 'Does anybody really think that the original meaning of the Balfour Declaration and the Mandate, and indeed, that of the millenarian yearning of the Jewish people, was not that of establishing a Jewish state in the whole of Eretz-Israel?' he had asked rhetorically in a speech to the People's Council on 22 May 1947. His acceptance of the principle of partition, he explained a week later, was an attempt to gain time until the Jews were strong enough to fight the Arab majority. And in early December 1947 – that is, a few days after the UN Resolution – he chose to hide his views behind philosophical reflections: 'There are no final settlements in history, there are no eternal borders, and no political demands are final. We shall still see great changes in the world.' A week later he pledged to Mapai's Central Committee that the borders of Jewish independence as defined by Resolution 181 were by no means final. It was then that Yigal Allon, who in the 1948 war was to be the most influential general and one whose impact in the definition of the objectives of the war was especially vital, said that 'the borders of partition cannot be for us the final borders ... the partition plan is a compromise plan that is unjust to the Jews. ... We are entitled to decide our borders according to our defence needs.'

The paradox of the winter of 1947 was that the Jews, who accepted Resolution 181 – the Jewish public acclaimed its endorsement by the UN with genuine outbursts of jubilation – were ready and well deployed to face a war should this be the outcome, and the Arabs, who rejected the Resolution out of hand and made no secret of their intention to subvert it, were not at all prepared for war. Ben-Gurion, who upon his appointment as the 'defence minister' of the Jewish Agency in 1946 made it clear that the time had now arrived for 'a showdown of force, a Jewish military showdown', had been for some time meticulously preparing for a war he was convinced, at least ever since the Arab Revolt, was inevitable. The Palestinians, who on 1 December 1947 made their views clear when the

Arab Higher Committee declared a general strike, were totally unprepared and poorly equipped for an armed conflict. Arab society had been crumbling from within ever since the brutal repression of the 1936–9 Revolt. Leaderless and decapitated of their traditional elites, deeply fragmented, respectful and frightened of the Yishuv's military power, and disorientated as to their real or achievable objectives, the Palestinians approached the imminent conflict and, as it turned out, their second catastrophe in a decade, in a state of disarray and fatalistic despair.

The Arab disaster of 1948 was that of a people that opted for high stakes – doing away with the aggressive Zionist presence in Palestine and with the 181 Resolution that legitimised it – with inadequate resources. In a debate at the UN on 16 April 1948 the Palestinian delegate explicitly acknowledged Moshe Shertok's allegations that the Palestinian Arabs had started the fighting and had no intentions of accepting a ceasefire. 'We do not deny that fact,' he admitted. But neither the Arabs of Palestine with the support of volunteer units from neighbouring Arab countries in the first phase of the war, nor the Arab armies that invaded Palestine in the wake of the British departure on 14 May 1948, proved to be problems an embattled but well-organised Yishuv, which stretched its energies and resources to the outer limits of its capacity, was not prepared to face.

The 1948 War – the Naqbah ('The Disaster') for the Palestinian Arabs, the War of Independence for the Zionists – started with the invasion on 15 May 1948 of the newly born State of Israel by the armies of Egypt, Syria, Lebanon and Transjordan. The war between the regular armies was preceded by a fierce civil war between the Jewish and Arab population, initiated by the latter as a violent rejection of Resolution 181. Already in the course of this first phase of the war, the Zionists managed to extend the boundaries of the Jewish state considerably beyond the partition lines of the 29 November 1947 UN Resolution. The second phase of the war, that between the regular armies, lasted until 7 January 1949, immediately after which armistice agreements began to be negotiated between Israel and each of the states that fought against her. The war consisted of three rounds of fighting separated by two UN-brokered truces; it ended with the victory of the incipient Jewish state over the invading Arab armies, and with its borders stretching further beyond the lines reached by the Yishuv at the end of the civil war phase. Ill prepared and poorly co-ordinated, the Arab armies were dragged into the war by popular pressure in their home states, and because their leaders each had his own agenda of territorial expansion. Securing the establishment of a Palestinian state along the lines of Resolution 181 was less of a motive for the Arab leaders who sent their armies to Palestine than establishing their own territorial claims or thwarting those of their rivals in the Arab coalition.

Ben-Gurion's initial defensive strategy of containment in the face of the onslaught of local Arab militias against Jewish settlements and access roads during the first phase of the war could not be sustained for long. Plan D, launched in March 1948, was not the first time the forces of the Yishuv went on the offensive. The aggressive defence ordered in December 1947 in the wake of the initial, even spectacular, success of Abd'el Khader el-Husseini's forces in defeating Haganah units and encircling Jerusalem, meant that the Haganah would now respond to Arab attacks with decisive blows against Arab villages and with the expulsion of their residents. High Commissioner Cunningham believed that it was this overreaction by the Yishuv that further escalated the conflict.

Clearly, however, Plan D represented a major shift in the war strategy of the Yishuv. In what was to become a typical Israeli war doctrine, the military forces of the Yishuv 'exploited the success' of the 'aggressive defence' of the winter and their evident superiority over the irregular Arab forces, and embarked now on a campaign aimed at a new definition of the borders of their state. For Plan D went beyond just securing the boundaries of the Jewish state as defined in Resolution 181. The initiative was taken to target Arab villages and cities, and to link to the Jewish state all the settlements that lay beyond the partition lines. These lines, it should be stressed, did not fully reflect the ethnic boundaries that had developed over the years. Some Jewish settlements were cut off from the borders of the Jewish state, while an Arab 'minority' of almost 50 per cent was 'trapped' inside the Jewish state.

The new war doctrine was not that new. It had its origins in the offensive mentality and practices as they developed in the Jewish militias during the Arab Revolt of the mid 1930s. The novelty now was not only in the scope of the conflict but in the policy that accompanied the military exploits. A pattern was established that would repeat itself throughout all the phases of the 1948 war and would become almost a rule of conduct in the future wars of the State of Israel: to turn down diplomatic initiatives for a settlement that did not respect the status quo created by military gains. The shift of the Haganah's strategy from containment to aggressive defence, then to a ruthless, successful offensive, unleashed a momentum of territorial expansion that the leaders of the Yishuv would not allow to be interrupted by premature diplomatic overtures. An American proposal for an unconditional ceasefire in early May 1948 and a British initiative for a truce in Jerusalem at about the same time were turned down by the Yishuv.

The 1948 war was not only an inevitable military showdown between Jews and Arabs. It also served to define the patterns of conduct of the new Jewish state and the internal balance between military and political considerations in the process of decision making, both in times of war and peace. A high degree of synchronisation, though, existed in 1948 between the drive of the military for conquest and expansion, and that of Ben-Gurion himself. Neither Ben-Gurion nor the military viewed the borders of partition as sacrosanct, and both wanted a Jewish state with as small an Arab population as possible. Ben-Gurion did not differ from Israel Galili, the Chief of Staff of the Haganah, who said on 8 April 1948 – during Operation Nahshon for breaking the siege of Jerusalem – that:

> We are fighting and we shall fight for all the lands that were possessed by the Jewish settlement so far. ... The borders of our state will be defined by the limits of our force. ... The political borders will be those of the territories that we shall be able to liberate from the enemy; the borders will be the fruit of our conquests.

But Ben-Gurion and Galili were essentially 'activists'. Moshe Shertok, a presumably more moderate statesman, did not really distance himself from this attitude. When, in a Cabinet meeting in June 1948, Ben-Gurion officially declared the death of Resolution 181, Shertok's response was fully supportive. We should not relinquish any of the territories taken over beyond the borders of partition, he said. This was 'a bitter necessity', he explained.

Every military plan that had been prepared ever since the late 1930s – the Avner plan, Plan B of September 1945 and a similar scheme of May 1946, and the 'Yehoshua Plan' that preceded Plan D – relied on the premise that the whole of Palestine was a single territorial unit that needed to be addressed as such in a future war. The borders of the Jewish state were defined by the logic and the dynamic of military operations. It was not Cabinet decisions that determined the borders of the new state, but military operations that were almost invariably proposed or initiated by the military commanders themselves, such as 'Harel' that consolidated Jewish control in Jerusalem, 'Hametz' for the conquest of Jaffa, 'Hiram' and 'Yiftah' for the control of the Galilee, 'Dany' where Ramleh and Lydda were taken over, and 'Yoav' for the inclusion of the Negev in the Jewish state.

'What are the borders of the new state?' wondered one of the ministers, Pinhas Rosen, at a meeting of the People's Directory on 21 May 1948, that is, a week after the Declaration of Independence. Ben-Gurion's reply was that 'everything is possible ... there is nothing a priori'. As a matter of fact, when independence was declared on 15 May the borders of the new state were already well beyond those of partition. Four out of the five mixed Jewish–Arab cities (Tiberias, Haifa, Safed and Jaffa) were by this time emptied of their Arab inhabitants, and more than a hundred Arab villages had been taken over.

This by no means meant, however, that the war was a smooth march to victory for the Jews, or that they were saved really existential dilemmas. The very decision of Ben-Gurion to go ahead on 14 May with the Declaration of Independence against the advice of some among the military, who feared they might not be able to contain a concerted invasion by the Arab armies, while overlooking the pressure from the United States, which wanted to prevent an all-out Arab–Jewish war, was the move of a leader who decided against all odds not to miss his and his people's encounter with history. However well organised the Yishuv might have been, a concerted Arab invasion and the slide to a total war was not exactly what its leaders expected. Rather, they thought in terms of a second version of the 1936–9 Arab Revolt, a new civil war between Jews and Arabs in Palestine. This should help to explain not only the popular fears but also the concern among the leaders. General Yigael Yadin explicitly warned the provisional government three days before it took the historic decision to declare independence that 'the advantage [of the Arab states] is considerable' in terms of arms and equipment. But 'one man of courage makes a majority', as Andrew Jackson had put it. Ben-Gurion was such a man when, with a very tight majority of six to four in the Provisional State Council, he went ahead with what many looked upon as a gamble.

A gamble it was not; a calculated risk perhaps. For hardly had the signatories of the Charter of Independence left the Tel Aviv Art Museum when the news came in that President Truman, against the advice of the State Department and largely in response to domestic political needs, extended US recognition for the new state. This – the tension between a presumably professional State Department and an always more politically driven White House, that came now to rescue the newborn State of Israel from miscarriage – was to become a salient characteristic of America's policy with regard to Israel. 'There are people [in] the State Department who have always wanted to cut my throat' was President Truman's reaction, as he confided to his diary, to an initiative of Secretary of State George Marshall in March 1949 to reverse America's recognition of the partition of Palestine into two independent states. The Soviet Union, which followed in Truman's footsteps and recognised the Jewish state, helped seal the fact that the Middle East now entered a new phase in its history that would no longer be dominated by British supremacy but by American–Soviet competition.

But external political support, however important, is not sufficient to win a war. The chances of Ben-Gurion's bold move prevailing were sustained mainly by the extraordinary advantages enjoyed by the Yishuv on the ground. The last British officials in Palestine were witness throughout the spring of 1948 to the emergence of a Jewish state in all but name alongside the total disarray of the Arab side. 'The machinery of the Jewish State now seems to be complete,' wrote Sir Henry Gurney, the last Chief Secretary of Palestine, on 22 April 1948. A week later he observed, 'no responsible Arabs to see', and that all the rich Arabs were leaving the country. It was 'Arab fecklessness at its worst, with black market exploitation and throwing of the blame on somebody other than themselves'. Ten days before the Tel Aviv Museum ceremonious declaration of the State of Israel, Gurney reacted to the mass exodus of the Arab inhabitants of Jaffa with the remark that the Arabs were behaving like 'rabbits'.

The invasion by the Arab armies did not necessarily mean that the Jews now faced superior Arab forces. The invading Arab armies were ill prepared for battle, and poorly equipped; they suffered from a total lack of co-ordination and very low motivation. Moreover, flamboyant rhetoric apart, the Arab leaders did not send sufficient forces to Palestine as they needed the bulk of their armies to protect their regimes back home from popular revolution or military takeover. At practically every stage of the war, except during the first weeks of the Arab invasion until the first truce, Israel was able to put together forces far superior to those of its enemies. It was none other than Ben-Gurion himself who recognised in a meeting of the Israeli Cabinet by the end of the war (19 December 1948) that 'this is not true' that it was a war of the few against the many. 'Though it sounds somewhat strange, we had then an army that was bigger than theirs,' he acknowledged on another occasion.[1] By the end of the war the formidable organisational capacity of the Yishuv, sustained by a unifying Israeli ethos of self-sacrifice and *'Ein Brerah'*, that is, the notion that defeat was not an option, was responsible for an extraordinary military mobilisation of about 17 per cent of the Jewish population, almost 100,000 men and women in arms out of a population of 650,000.

But however right the 'new historians' of the 1948 war are in questioning Israel's myth about the victory of 'the few against the many' – and as we just saw, the 'old historiography' was not entirely blind to this reality either – at the end of the day the Zionists won the war because they had an infinitely higher motivation than that of their enemies. The young conscripts of the incipient Jewish state knew that they and their families faced annihilation should they be defeated. This was by no means the

---

[1] Yoav Gelber, *Independence Versus Naqba* (Hebrew), Zmora-Bitan, 2004, pp. 12, 476.

kind of motivation of the invading Arab armies. The Arab rejection of Resolution 181, the civil war started by the Arab community in Palestine and the subsequent all-Arab invasion provided the Jews with the most noble motive in war: survival.

Collective psychology, national myths and the perception that a given group might have of its enemy have always been major factors in the decision to go to war and in the capacity of leaders to motivate their armies. The Arab–Israeli conflict is no exception. Defending the rights of the embattled Arab community in Palestine was perhaps a worthy undertaking, but it certainly was not the driving motive behind the Arab invasion. The Arab states were driven to war in great measure by the perception that prevailed in their societies as to the Jewish state and the threat it posed to the Arabs. The Arab invasion of Palestine in the summer of 1948 might have been ill conceived and poorly executed, but it was partly propelled by what was now becoming a powerful mobilising ethos, that of the Muslim struggle against this latest Jewish reincarnation of the Crusaders. As a Syrian author, Vadi'a Talhuq, explained in his book *A New Crusade in Palestine*, published in the spring of 1948 (that is, a few weeks before the Arab invasion), the volunteers of the 'Arab Salvation Army' in Palestine were the successors of the heroic young Arab fighters that flocked to Saladin's army in 1187 to repel the infidel armies of Richard Lionheart.

Another myth that was now manipulated in Egypt to justify the rush to war was that the new Jewish state with its kibbutzim and collectivist spirit was, in fact, as Egypt's Prime Minister, Nukrashi Basha, put it when he asked Parliament to declare war on Israel, an agent of 'atheism and nihilist Communism' in the region that threatened to subvert Arab regimes and societies. The outspoken support of the Soviet Union for the Jewish state gave, if anything, additional credibility to the argument. Paradoxically, the Jewish state was then at the same time both a Western capitalist beachhead in the region and a dangerous agent of international Communism, the two sins for which Hitler thought the Jews had to be annihilated.

The Arabs could not accept an alien Jewish state in an otherwise homogeneous Arab and Muslim Middle East. Arab representatives at the UN debate on partition mentioned explicitly the risk that the new state might break the physical and cultural Arab contiguity of the region in a way that would definitely stymie the grand design of Arab unity, as a reason for their rejection of Resolution 181. 'Israel is alien to, and different from, the Arabs in everything. Here, in the midst of the Arab ocean, Israel is bound to trigger disputes, instability and complications.' This was how Egypt's delegate to the Lausanne Peace Conference of 1949, Abd el-Munim Mustafa, would spell out the reasons for the fact that his country 'did everything [it] could to prevent [the] creation' of the State of Israel. The Jews were 'a racial and geographical obstruction between the Arab countries' and they needed therefore to be 'destroyed' was how an Arab writer, Mahmoud Azar Darwaza, put it in a book published in 1943 in Beirut (*The Growth of Modern Arabism*). Such was the degree of opposition to the idea of a Jewish state that Arab spokesmen even threatened openly to hold their Jewish populations as the hostages of the Arab–Israeli conflict. Heikal Pasha, Egypt's representative at the UN debate, warned the international community of a violent anti-Semitic reaction throughout the Arab world that might even lead, as he said, 'to the massacre of a large number of Jews' in Arab countries.

It was not uncommon for the Arab states to unite for rhetoric but separate for action. With a better trained army than that of his enemies, with a unified single command system and a clear sense of mission and objective among the troops facing the fragmented Arab armies of invasion, Ben-Gurion was able to lead his nation to victory, establish new borders for the Jewish state and lay the foundations of Israel's military doctrine for the years to come. He would always opt for an offensive strategy, for assuming the initiative – in the battles of the Ten Days (8–18 July 1948) Israel seized the initiative in a way that was not relinquished until the end of the war – and for targeting the Arab armies separately so as to be able to enjoy at every moment of the war a superiority in terms of men and equipment.

A major strategic debate in late September 1948 between Ben-Gurion and his generals, and within the government itself, was to have a crucial impact on the future shape of the State of Israel and its relations with the Hashemite kingdom. The debate was also important in the sense that it referred to an issue – that of the West Bank – that for years, until 1967, would remain in the minds of generals and politicians as 'unfinished business'. Ben-Gurion was never very happy with the understandings that had been reached with King Abdullah before the war and he pushed for the occupation of the West Bank, of biblical Eretz-Israel. But the military seemed at that stage to have preferred expanding the borders of the new state in the south, into the Egyptian front, and in any event the government defeated Ben-Gurion's initiative. This was for Ben-Gurion, as he put it, 'a cause for mourning for generations to come'. But he himself might have had second thoughts about the wisdom of the idea. Invading the West Bank might have not only triggered Britain to activate its defence treaty with Transjordan and intervene in the conflict. It could also have brought into the borders of the expanding State of Israel a massive Arab population it could by no means digest. The Negev desert was an empty space for expansion, and it was to the Negev that the main effort was shifted from the early days of October 1948 to January 1949. When the ceasefire came into effect on 7 January the entire Negev was in Israel's hands.

In 1948 the Palestinians became a disinherited people. They lost their land and saw the promise of a state of their own being thwarted by poor leadership, by the incompetence of the Arab armies and the selfishness and lack of purpose of their commanders, and by the overwhelming military élan of a Jewish Yishuv that for decades had been carefully preparing itself for this decisive trial.

But land, real estate and political independence were only one part of the legacy of the 1948 war; another was the chapter of human suffering, the ordeal of a nation. The war of 1948 was the Palestinian Naqbah, the Disaster, of which the dismemberment of the Palestinian community and the mass exodus of its members – around 700,000 of them – was the major tragedy.

The Israelis preferred to see the birth of the Palestinian refugee problem, as Ben-Gurion put it, as revealing 'with overwhelming clarity which people is bound with strong bonds to this land'. The Palestinian exodus was, then, that of a rootless community and was therefore the ultimate vindication of the Zionist claim of exclusive ownership of Eretz-Israel, of Jewish monopoly on the history of this land.

But Ben-Gurion's was the reflection of a nation builder, always focused on the need to cultivate an Israeli ethos of belonging, of settlement and of possessing the land. The Palestinians were not a rootless community. The truth of the matter was that holding fast to the soil of Palestine and resisting the eviction of their communities had been, throughout, the policy of Palestinian Arab leaders ever since the struggle acquired its national dimension between the two world wars.

The reality on the ground was at times far simpler and more cruel than that which Ben-Gurion was ready to acknowledge. It was that of an Arab community in a state of terror facing a ruthless Israeli army whose path to victory was paved not only by its exploits against the regular Arab armies, but also by the intimidation, and at times atrocities and massacres, it perpetrated against the civilian Arab community. A panic-stricken Arab community was uprooted under the impact of massacres that would be carved into the Arabs' monument of grief and hatred, like those of Dir Yassin, Ein Zeitun, Ilabun and Lydda; of operational orders like those of Moshe Carmel, the commander of the Carmeli Brigade in Operations Yiftah and Ben-Ami, 'to attack in order to conquer, to kill the men, to destroy and burn the villages of Al-Kabri, Umm al Faraj and An Nahar'; and by the mass expulsions during the Yoav Operation. In that operation, in the words of one of the Israeli soldiers, as quoted by Benny Morris, whose thesis about the birth of the refugee problem being not by design but by the natural logic and evolution of the war is not always sustained by the very evidence he himself provides, 'cultured officers ... had turned into base murderers and this not in the heat of battle ... but out of a system of expulsion and destruction; the less Arabs remained, the better; this principle is the political motor for the expulsions and the atrocities'.

Self-criticism in times of war was not to be an unusual trait in the history of Israel. Nor is it true that the 'official' Israeli historiography waited for the 'new historians' to acknowledge some, admittedly not all, of the more unpleasant aspects of Israel's conduct of the war. Yigal Allon and Israel Galili exposed and openly analysed in the *Book of the Palmach* in the early 1950s the story of 'Plan D'. And in 1973 Shaul Avigur, a key man in the security establishment, published the full plan in *The Book of the Haganah*. As a matter of fact, *mutatis mutandis*, as in the case of the so-called 'black legend' about the atrocities committed by the Spanish conquerors in South America that was first revealed and criticised by a Spaniard, Bartolomé de las Casas, before it became a trigger for the worldwide denunciation of Spain, it was the leaders of the Zionist Left who were first to sound the alarm. Aharon Cohen, the director of Mapam's Arab Department, confessed to being 'ashamed and afraid' at the 'deliberate eviction' of the Arabs. In July 1948 his leader, Yaacov Hazan, warned that 'the robbery, killing, expulsion and rape of the Arabs could reach such proportions that we would no longer be able to stand'. And another member of the party, Aharon Zisling, even exclaimed in November 1948 that 'Jews too have committed Nazi acts'.

It is not at all clear, as maintained by a conventional Israeli myth, that the Palestinian exodus was encouraged by the Arab states and by local leaders. Benny Morris found no evidence to show 'that either the leaders of the Arab states or the Mufti ordered or directly encouraged the mass exodus'. Indeed, Morris found evidence to the effect that the local Arab leadership and militia commanders discouraged flight, and Arab radio stations issued calls to the Palestinians to stay put, and even to return to their homes if they had already left. True, there were more than a few cases where local Arab commanders ordered the evacuation of villages. But these seemed to have been tactical decisions taken under very specific military conditions; they did not respond to an overall strategy either of the local Palestinian leaders or of the Arab states.

As a matter of fact, the leaders of the surrounding Arab states, who were reluctant to be drawn into the war, had no particular interest in the Palestinian exodus. For it was precisely that exodus that subjected them to an irresistible popular pressure for a war they were not exactly eager to join. The mass exodus was, however, inadvertently encouraged by the leaders of the Palestinian community when, in their eagerness to trigger the invasion of Palestine by the Arab armies, they blew up out of all proportion the atrocities committed against Arab civilians. The Arab armies came in eventually, but by puffing up the atrocities, local leaders such as Dr Hussein Fakhri Al-Khalidi, the head of the Arab National Committee in Jerusalem who gave explicit instructions to the Palestinian media to inflate the reports, helped enhance the magnitude of an exodus driven by fear and hysteria.

The first major wave of Arab exodus in April–May 1948, essentially in the wake of the Dir Yassin massacre that was perpetrated by Lehi and Irgun with the Haganah's connivance, and the unfolding of Plan D, might perhaps have taken the leadership of the Yishuv by surprise. But they undoubtedly saw an opportunity to be exploited, a phenomenon to rejoice at – Menachem Begin wrote in his memoirs, *The Revolt*, that 'out of evil, however, good came' – and be encouraged. 'Doesn't he have anything more important to do?' was Ben-Gurion's reaction when told, during his visit to Haifa on 1 May 1948, that a local Jewish leader was trying to convince the Arabs not to leave. 'Drive them out!' was Ben-Gurion's instruction to Yigal Allon, as recorded by Yitzhak Rabin in a censored passage of his memoirs published in 1979, with regard to the Arabs of Lydda after the city had been taken over on 11 July 1948. At this stage it was probably the unchallenged military superiority of the Yishuv and the consequent collapse of Arab morale that explains the psychosis of flight of a panic-stricken Arab community. Plan D, however, was a major cause for the exodus, for it was strategically driven by the notion of creating Jewish contiguity even beyond the partition lines and, therefore, by the desire to have a Jewish state with the smallest possible number of Arabs.

The debate about whether or not the mass exodus of Palestinians was the result of a Zionist design or the inevitable concomitant of war should not ignore the ideological constructs that motivated the Zionist enterprise. The philosophy of transfer was not a marginal, esoteric article in the mindset and thinking of the main leaders of the Yishuv. These ideological constructs provided a legitimate environment for commanders in the field actively to encourage the eviction of the local population even when no precise orders to that effect were issued by the political leaders. As early as February 1948, that is before the real mass exodus had started but after he witnessed how the Arabs had fled from west Jerusalem, Ben-Gurion could not hide his excitement. Never 'since the days of the Roman destruction', he said to a convention of his party, Mapai, was Jerusalem 'so completely Jewish as today. There are no strangers, one hundred per cent Jews.' Ben-Gurion did not have to issue particular orders for expulsion. Rather, he established the strategic-ideological framework of the war effort. 'Certainly there will be great changes in the composition of the population of the country,' he said in the wake of the Arab exodus from west Jerusalem and later from Haifa.

To Ben-Gurion the war was not just about the physical survival of a small Jewish state, it was about the conquest, the possession and the settlement of the land. Plan D was about enlarging the borders of partition and creating Jewish contiguity. And Operations Yoav and Hiram were conducted in the winter of 1948 when, for all practical purposes, Israel had won its war for survival and it now needed new lands and greater strategic depth. The Jews did not have to buy land any more, but to 'conquer it', as Ben-Gurion said to an official of the Jewish National Fund in February 1948. He also instructed that abandoned Arab villages needed to be settled by Jews even before the end of hostilities. Settling the land in a way that created Jewish contiguity and demographic superiority was not to be an enterprise to be executed after the victory. Rather, it was part of the war itself. Villages were destroyed, their populations either evicted or fled, and their lands were settled by immigrants or cultivated by kibbutzim in the course of the war itself. This is how Ben-Gurion put in April 1948: 'We will not be able to win the war if we do not, *during the war*, populate Upper and Lower, Eastern and Western Galilee, the Negev and the Jerusalem area.' And this, he understood, would be facilitated by the 'great change in the distribution of the Arab population', a euphemism Ben-Gurion frequently preferred to more blunt expressions.

Not only the physical boundaries of the new state were determined by the logic of military operations and without the political leaders always being privy to decisions made by Ben-Gurion and his generals; this was also the case with the eviction of the Arab population from areas taken over by the army. 'I spoke to Shkolnik about the question of the eviction of Arabs from some of our areas. He doesn't know a thing about this. Who then takes the decisions here?' wondered one high official. In the course of a discussion in the Histadrut's Executive Committee on 14 July 1948, all the participants, including a central figure in Mapai, Yosef Sprinzak, and Mapam's leader Yaacov Hazan, complained of being left in the dark as to who exactly took the decisions with regard to the eviction of Arabs. There seemed not to have been any precise political instructions, nor any Cabinet decisions. There was only an ideological predisposition, a mental attitude, a supporting cultural environment within which military commanders initiated or encouraged the eviction of the Arab population.

The expulsion of the Palestinian Arabs from areas taken over by the Israelis was to the military commanders a natural, perhaps even compelling, outcome of the drive to conquer and possess the land by military force. Yigal Allon, at times with Ben-Gurion's connivance, was a major promoter of the expulsion of Arabs from conquered areas. This was, for example, the case with Operation Yiftah in eastern Galilee that ushered in a major Palestinian exodus, and Operation Danny in Ramleh and Lydda – both under Allon's command – where about 60,000 Arabs were expelled. In a lecture delivered in June 1950, Yigal Allon had no scruples in admitting that 'the flight of the Arabs was a positive process. Moreover, our efforts to bring about the evacuation of areas of military importance from its hostile Arab population was not only unavoidable but also justified.' Allon definitely saw the 1948 war as a historic opportunity to change the demographic balance in Palestine and he complained that the opportunity was not fully exploited. He had defended the case for the occupation of the West Bank, a move that he knew would have entailed a massive transfer of Palestinians to the East Bank. But he was overruled by Ben-Gurion, mostly because of demographic concerns. The Prime Minister preferred now to divert the thrust of Israel's offensive to the strategically vital but sparsely populated Negev desert.

The army, however, played a major role not only in defining the borders of the Jewish state, and in the expulsion of refugees, but also in preventing their return after the end of hostilities. It was only after the practice had been established by the army that, on 21 July 1948, a special decision by the Cabinet made this into *ex post facto* official policy. A month later, another Cabinet decision institutionalised the policy of inheriting the abandoned Arab villages and lands, and settling them with Jews. There was hardly any opposition in the government to this decision. The Arab exodus was, as none other than Moshe Sharett had put it, 'a momentous event in world and Jewish history', and the Arabs, he said in a debate on 16 June, 'must get used to the fact that [their wish to return] is a lost cause'.

And indeed, this, Israel's formal rejection of the refugees' claim for return – a position that remains intact to this day – rather than the expulsion and the dispossession, is the real defining moment of the conflict. For the flight of refugees, even their dispossession, has through-out history always been a concomitant of war, and in many cases they were allowed to return once the hostilities ceased. The novelty this time lay in the refusal even to consider their return. The new state could by no means reconcile its existence and national development with the return of the dispossessed refugees, and this continues to this day to be a central bone of contention in the conflict. For the Palestinians it is a vital belief, a defining principle of their national identity, their unifying collective dream. For the Israelis it was and continues to be an anathema, utterly irreconcilable with the survival of the Jewish state.

Israel's victory in war has rarely produced bold or imaginative peace-making. As Nahum Goldmann, the life-long Zionist diplomat, put it, the victory in the 1948 war seemed to have vindicated the advantages of direct military action as against the Zionist tradition of negotiation and diplomacy. For a nation whose millenarian history was replete with persecution and humiliation, adaptation and compromise, a new way of action became available through military might and victory. In Nahum Goldmann's words, the new way was an invitation to 'cut through Gordian knots, and shape history by creating facts'.

The State of Israel was born in a storm of military superiority and was the product of the victory of power and national will that had no precedent in the history of the struggle of other nations for independence. Jewish independence was born out of the defeat of a Western superpower, Great Britain, the crushing capitulation of the indigenous Arab population and the almost unconditional rout of the invading Arab armies. As in Israel's future wars, nothing could stop the Israelis' military exploits and their territorial expansion but the outside pressure of the superpowers. It was because of British and American pressure that Ben-Gurion ordered General Allon to refrain from taking over the Sinai Peninsula, and it was Ben-Gurion's fear of British intervention that stopped him from proceeding with his plan to conquer the West Bank of the River Jordan and pose a threat to the Transjordanian Hashemite kingdom whose survival was guaranteed by an unequivocal British commitment. The 1948 war did not only usher in the birth of a state; it also resulted in the emergence of a regional superpower. It was, therefore, hardly a prelude to peace-making in the aftermath of the war.

But the hubris of victory was not exactly the predominant feeling when the war ended. This was to be the paradox of Israel's existence over the years, a sense of power combined with a no less genuine, ever present, almost apocalyptic fear of annihilation. There was a genuine sense of fatalism as to the prospects of ever reaching a settlement with the Arabs. That Israel became a state in the storm of war and amidst its total and unconditional rejection by the entire Arab world indicated to its leaders the road for national survival in the future: to live by the sword. Not even its military victory diminished Israel's mistrust in the willingness of the Arabs ever to come to terms with a robust Zionist presence in their midst. 'Even if we conquer the whole of the land down to the Jordan River,' wrote Ben-Gurion in his diary in the last days of the war, 'the Arabs will not accept us, for their fear will only increase and the war will continue.'

For many the war ended prematurely. Haim Guri, a poet of the 1948 generation and a major exponent of the spirit of the Labourite establishment at the time, wrote in 1950 about the sense of frustration of his generation for not having conquered the West Bank, 'the imprisoned spaces of our homeland'. 'The border', he wrote, 'has bisected our souls.' The unfulfilled dream of Greater Eretz-Israel meant that 'the time to rest has not yet come'. That the West Bank was now home for hundreds of thousands of Palestinian refugees who were evicted from their villages on this side of the newly established Green Line – the border that emerged between Israel and the surrounding Arab states from the war of 1948 – did not seem to trouble Haim Guri's mind. But this was consistent with a tendency inherited from the Yishuv years to ignore the existence of the Palestinians as a community and now to repress the memory of their plight.

This collective state of mind can perhaps be best exemplified by the Israelis' conventional perception of the 1948 war. The first phase of the hostilities prior to the Arab invasion, the civil war between the Yishuv and the local Arab community, was probably the fiercest and the one that posed the most dramatic challenge to the survival of both communities. But the popular idea of Israel's War of Independence as cultivated over the years ignored that particular part of the struggle against the Palestinians fighting for their lands and rights. It focused instead on the heroic stand of the tiny Yishuv against the invading Arab armies. The Israelis chose to repress the memory of their war against a dispossessed, *autochthonous* Palestinian community claiming national rights, and preferred the ethos of the struggle against *foreign* and supposedly superior invading Arab armies.

Israel as a society also suppressed the memory of its war against the local Palestinians because it could not really come to terms with the fact that its finest Sabras, the heroes of its war for independence and the role models of the new nation, expelled Arabs, committed atrocities against them and dispossessed them. This was like admitting that the noble Jewish dream of statehood was stained for ever by a major injustice committed against the Palestinians and that the Jewish state was born in sin. When the war was over the Palestinian problem practically disappeared from Israeli public discourse; it was conveniently defined as one of 'refugees' or 'infiltrators'. There was no Israeli–Palestinian conflict, hardly a Palestinian plight. This was submerged into one single issue: the Arab–Israeli conflict.

III   The Early Years: A Missed
       Opportunity for Peace?

Unless Israel can be brought to understand that it cannot have all of its cake ... and gravy as well, it may find that it has won Palestine war [*sic*] but lost peace. It should be evident that Israel's continued insistence upon her pound of flesh and more is driving Arab states ... to gird their loins for long-ranged struggle.

US Ambassador in Damascus,
19 May 1949

What do we need peace for now? Peace will only give you economic advantages and will consolidate and strengthen [your state]. Egypt does not need peace now. On the contrary, we are interested in not having peace in order to deny you the consolidation and the power [you need].

Abd el-Munim Mustafa, Egypt's delegate to the Lausanne Peace Conference,
July 1949

No member state is allowed to negotiate with Israel, sign with it a separate peace or any other political or economic agreement ...

Arab League resolution,
25 March 1950

New historians of the Arab–Israeli conflict, and some old historians as well, albeit with varying degrees of conviction, have maintained that a chance of peace between the newborn State of Israel and its Arab neighbours existed in the aftermath of the 1948 war. This chance, they add, was spoiled by Israel's intransigence and incapacity to seize the historic opportunity and nip in the bud a solvable dispute before it degenerated into an intricate and protracted conflict.

To do justice to these historians, however, they never thought that the task of peacemaking was that simple. There was a deep sense of humiliation throughout the Arab world following the resounding defeat at the hands of an entity they all saw as a colonial imposition. Nor were inter-Arab rivalries with leaders engaged in a selfish contest of land grab exactly conducive to a coherent Arab peace strategy. This, as well as the overwhelming military victory of Israel – as would eventually happen in the aftermath of the 1967 war – created in its leaders the belief that they could impose a settlement on their own terms and certainly not accept anything that did not legitimise the status quo created by the war, one the Arabs were adamant in rejecting. All these proved to be insurmountable obstacles.

In practice also, peace was hardly possible, given the already unbridge-able gap of legitimacy stemming from the rift between the more pragmatic Arab leaders and an Arab opinion boiling with hatred and rejection towards the 'Zionist entity'. Arab leaders were ready to settle for a compromise on the issue of borders, but not when it came to the problem of Palestinian refugees, the cohesive glue of pan-Arab politics from now on. An Arab consensus, much of it rhetorical but nonetheless paralysing, was quickly building up around the plight of the Palestinian refugees.

The assumption about the theoretical possibility of peace in the after-math of 1948 is totally out of tune with the very essence of the historical conditions as they existed at the time. A massive repatriation of Palestinian refugees would have clashed irreconcilably with the most vital and fundamental ethos of the new State of Israel, indeed with its very *raison d'être*, namely the consolidation of a Jewish state through the mass immigration of the survivors of the Nazi Holocaust in Europe and the uprooted and dispossessed Jews of North Africa and the Arab Middle East. To say, as some do – for example, Malcolm Kerr and Rony Gabbay – that peace might have been achieved had Israel agreed to admit large numbers of Palestinian refugees, is to miss the very essence of the Israeli project. No Israeli statesman, either in 1948 or in 2005, would conceive of peace based on the massive repatriation of Palestinian refugees as an offer the Jewish state could accept and yet survive. The ethos of Zionism was twofold; it was about demography – ingathering the exiles in a viable Jewish state with as small an Arab minority as possible – and land. For the victorious, incipient Jewish state in the aftermath of the 1948 war, peace was certainly desirable, but not at the price of sacrificing these two fundamental basics of the Zionist idea.

On *moral* grounds one could of course convincingly defend the case for the repatriation of refugees. But this was out of the question in a *historical* and *political* context, where a clash existed between an emergent Jewish state and its defeated enemies, for whom the repatriation of refugees was one way of hampering the growth and development of the newborn, yet intimidating, state against which they harboured under-standable intentions of revanche. At the Lausanne Peace Conference Israel eventually agreed to the repatriation of 100,000 Palestinian refugees, but this was almost by force of habit rejected out of hand by the Arabs as too little. Too little it might have been, but Israel made the offer only with the hope of getting relief from American pressure. The Arabs clearly missed an opportunity to call Israel's bluff. But this was to be a distinguishing characteristic of the Arab–Israeli tragedy. The minimal requirements of the parties for a settlement always fell disparately short of meeting each other's vital conditions.

When purely theoretical assumptions are brought down to the earth of real historical conditions there seemed not to have been much of a missed opportunity here, as Avi Shlaim, an outspoken exponent of the missed opportunity thesis, acknowledged in an admittedly early article in the *International Journal of Middle East Studies* (no. 27, 1995). Israel, he wrote, had in the period 1947–9 no Palestinian option or any other Arab option, and he realistically limited the notion of a missed opportunity to the Jordanian–Israeli track. King Abdullah, he wrote, 'was the only Arab head of state who was willing to accept the principle of partition and to coexist peacefully with a Jewish state after the dust had settled'.

Some old historians, Ben-Gurion's biographer Shabtai Teveth for example, who are bent on defending the Israeli case at all cost, miss the point when they argue it was Israel that made every effort to reach a settlement, only in order to be rebuffed by Arab rejectionism. This was clearly not the case. Peace was not a priority for Israeli leaders; settling the land and absorbing immigrants was. Willing peace and making it can be two entirely different things; the question is always the price one is willing to pay and Israel was clearly adamant in resisting any erosion of the territorial status quo that had emerged out of its victory. A dichotomous Israeli mindset that combined the hubris of military prowess with an ever-present fear of imminent catastrophe or even annihilation, and the Zionist ethos of the ingathering of the exiles and settling the land, were powerful forces of resistance to any territorial compromise. But peace also became a historical impossibility because of the illegitimate demands of the Arab leaders who, rather than sticking to the principles of partition as they were embodied in the November 1947 UN Resolution, themselves engaged in a selfish land grab at the expense of the territories allocated in that Resolution to the Palestinian state.

Major breakthroughs in history – peacemaking in the Arab–Israeli conflict is a case in point – were normally made possible only when bold and visionary leaders were sustained in their quest for such a course, and sometimes even forced to act, by the general readiness – ripeness, one might say – of their societies for dramatic change. This encounter between leadership and socio-political fruition did not exist between Israelis and Arabs in the period here under review.

No war lost by a humiliated Arab side has ever become the introduction to a peace Israel could consider reasonable, just as a war overwhelmingly won by Israel has hardly ever brought its leaders to be magnanimous in victory. Israel's peace initiative immediately after the end of the Six Day War – a proposal to withdraw from Sinai and the Golan Heights in exchange for full peace with Egypt and Syria – is an interesting and difficult case that will have to be looked into later in the proper context. What is undisputable, however, is that it took the recovery of Arab pride and the undermining of Israel's myth of invincibility in the Yom Kippur War effectively to pave the way for a still difficult and uncertain march to peace between Israel and Egypt; and it took Israel's reverse in the first Intifada and the psychological effects of the Gulf War on the Israeli home front to force Yitzhak Rabin finally to realise that the Palestinian problem is susceptible only to a political – not to a military – solution. These were the hard facts of life that paved the way to the Madrid Peace Conference and eventually to the Oslo accords.

In the aftermath of 1948, many of the prevailing conditions in the Arab world were anything but conducive to a peace that could be legitimate and durable: a chaotic inter-Arab system stricken by conflicting interests, rivalries and jealousies; and regimes at a crossroads in which their legitimacy was being questioned by the emergence of new social and political classes bent on reforming a decrepit, corrupt and failing order. In the case of Transjordan, not only was there a problem of isolation of that particular branch of the Hashemite dynasty from the rest of the Arab family, and hence of its necessity to adapt itself to the Arab consensus, but also the Palestinisation of the kingdom that was to be the inevitable outcome of the integration of what later came to be known as the West Bank to Abdullah's domains desperately narrowed the King's manoeuvring space for a separate deal with Israel.

Elias Sasson, a civil servant who was involved in every overt and covert peace negotiation with an Arab partner, was certainly no warmonger. Sasson was a peacenik *avant la lettre*, somebody who would always look for a compromise and courageously question the dangerous inertia of his superiors. A man who was brought up in the culture of the Arab East, and who knew how to appreciate Arab sensibilities and penetrate the Arab mind without ever being condescending or patronising, he also knew only too well that there was no real future for the new State of Israel unless it found a way to peace and reconciliation with its Arab neighbours. Yet he was not naïve, nor was he blind to the powerful instincts to reject the Jewish state that prevailed throughout the Arab world and to the hidden, sometimes also overt, intentions of its leaders when they called for peace.

In a sober and lucid memorandum he wrote to Moshe Sharett in September 1949, Sasson explained that it would be foolish to deny that it was the cherished dream of the Arabs to do away with the State of Israel altogether. Short of that, and not being capable of wiping her out of existence either immediately or in the more distant future, the Arab world had opted for a realistic strategy, he explained. This consisted of reducing Israel's size and strategic potentialities while at the same time preventing her from reaching anything approaching regional economic hegemony. Israel should be denied recognition and co-operation by her Arab neighbours. She needed to be constantly maintained in a state of military tension and alert, always depending on their goodwill. An accommodation with Israel, he explained, was not ruled out by the Arabs, but this would be possible only after a long period of test and trial. Israel was a state on probation; she would be accepted as part of the region pending her good behaviour.

Eventually, both Sasson and the Arabs he purported to interpret were proved wrong. It was not Israel's good behaviour, but rather its 'bad behaviour', as it were, as an invincible regional superpower – the war against which drained the Arabs of their wealth and resources and hindered their development while turning them into the tool of the cynical power politics of the superpowers – that would eventually produce a shift in the Arab strategy from confrontation to accommodation with Israel.

Much has been said and written on the assumed existence of two conflicting schools of policy making in Israel, the diplomatic, peace-orientated school headed by Foreign Minister Moshe Sharett, and the so-called 'activist' militant and even militaristic school headed by David Ben-Gurion. Such a division might have existed in the 1950s and even then it expressed itself more in Sharett's intimate reflections in his personal diary than in real life and actual policies. What is clear, however, is that the two-school theory is hardly detectable in the evolving story of the abortive attempts at peacemaking in the aftermath of the 1948 war. Israeli leaders were all essentially of one school. Bernard Henry Levy wrote about what he called *l'idéologie française*, the one common worldview shared by all French politicians of both Right and Left. By the same token one could speak of an *idéologie israelienne* to which both Ben-Gurion and Sharett subscribed. The difference in their approach was, as Abba Eban rightly put it, 'trivial to the point of being microscopic'.

Ben-Gurion was undoubtedly the all-powerful leader, the *pater patriae*, who formulated the grand strategies of the Yishuv and later the State of Israel. His was a pessimistic *Weltanschauung*. It was, we may recall, during the Arab Revolt of 1936–9 that he first realised the depth and magnitude of the clash between the Jewish and Arab national movements and subsequently lost any realistic hope of a peaceful accommodation. However, notwithstanding the convincing victory of 1948, Israel was to Ben-Gurion an intrinsically fragile entity surrounded by sworn, mortal enemies who could never forgive or forget their humiliating defeat. Hence his obsession with the idea of having a Western power as a strategic ally, or for joining NATO, and his quest in the fifties for an independent Israeli nuclear option.

Peace for Ben-Gurion was a commendable objective but never the first priority; in the best of cases it was a tool for the development and consolidation of the Zionist dream. But as far as Ben-Gurion was concerned, the purpose of consolidating Zionism could be reasonably well served also by the armistice agreements that were signed with the Arab states throughout the spring and the summer of 1949. A full-fledged peace agreement was therefore not only not vitally necessary, but could also entail risks, for it would inevitably require a territorial price Ben-Gurion was not ready to pay. Between the status quo without peace and peace without the status quo, Ben-Gurion opted for the former. And in any case, as he said as early as 1935 to Yehudah Magnes, the Rector of the Hebrew University in Jerusalem and a member of Brit Shalom, 'the difference between me and you is that you are ready to sacrifice immigration for peace while I am not.' This unequivocal scale of priorities would be repeated by Ben-Gurion in different ways throughout his years as the Prime Minister of the State of Israel. Moreover, he never made it a secret that he was not only unhappy with the borders of partition, he did not especially like those of 1949 either and would always harbour hopes for more comfortable borders.

He was likewise not especially fond of the initiatives aimed at reaching a peace settlement with Jordan or Syria, for he dismissed their capacity to lead the entire Arab world to a comprehensive reconciliation with Israel. The real strategic breakthrough he looked for was peace with Egypt, for solely Egypt, unlike the other Arab states, was, as he saw it, a 'non-artificial' nation and the only one that could change the fatalistic trend towards war and confrontation with Israel that prevailed in the Arab world.

Ben-Gurion's Egyptian orientation was to be endorsed by most of the prime ministers who succeeded him and was eventually vindicated by the Camp David peace accords between Anwar Sadat and Menachem Begin. The weakness of Ben-Gurion's argument, however, was that he nonetheless refused to pay a special price for peace with Egypt as well. Israel's borders were to remain practically untouchable. The deal he was ready for was essentially one of peace for peace, not land, let alone refugees, for peace.

Moshe Sharett was more forthcoming and flexible than Ben-Gurion in form but hardly in substance. Years later, looking back at the attempts at peacemaking in the aftermath of the 1948 war, Sharett contemptuously dismissed the 'illusive hopes' of those who spoke about a 'mutual misunderstanding' between Jews and Arabs, about 'common interests' and about 'the possibility of unity and peace between the two fraternal peoples'. Not only was Sharett, like Ben-Gurion and most of the leaders of Mapai, an enthusiastic advocate of the idea of the transfer of Palestinians to Transjordan as 'the crowning achievement, the final stage in the development of our policy', as he put it during a debate in Mapai's Central Committee in 1944, but he also, again like Ben-Gurion, would not accept any peace settlement with an Arab partner that did not respect the status quo created by the war. When, in 1948, Syria's strong man Husni Zaim came forward with what clearly looked like a most dramatic and far-reaching peace initiative, Sharett suggested responding with some creative diplomacy but with no concessions on the ground. And even in the case of Transjordan, where no major territorial concessions were required, Sharett would warn the enthusiasts on the Israeli side that peace with King Abdullah would mean 'burying for ever our dreams about Western Palestine'. In a very revealing speech after his retirement from politics in which he set out his essential political beliefs, Sharett challenged what he called 'the assumption that peace can be bought at the price of concessions'. He believed that the whole concept of concessions as an avenue to peace was a fallacy that needed to be 'utterly rejected'.

Hawks and doves alike, whatever this might have meant in the years following the War of Independence, could not conceive of the rejection of a peace proposal that required Israel to relinquish the Negev, as the Egyptians and the Jordanians wanted, as a missed opportunity, for such a settlement would not have allowed Israel to fulfil the core objectives behind her creation; and the Zionist ethos of absorbing immigrants and developing and settling the desert would have been subverted.

It is certainly true that, contrary to what the Zionists wanted us to believe when they propagated the myth about the Israeli David winning the day against the Arab Goliath with seven powerful invading armies at his disposal determined to throw the Jews into the sea, Israel won the 1948 war so conclusively precisely because her forces were larger and better trained than the poorly equipped and ill-commanded armies of her enemies. Yet the pessimism and the sense of immanent fragility that permeated the Israeli mind, and determined the attitude of suspicion at the Arab peace overtures – especially to what were seen as draconian conditions aimed at reducing Israel's size and potentialities in preparation for a second round – were nevertheless fully genuine. A mechanical, arithmetical approach to the balance of power in the 1948 war tells only part of the story. The battleground as such was never the only problem for Israel; it was the wider strategic context of a nation surrounded by an immense Arab hinterland that could afford, as indeed it did, one defeat after another, yet always recover and be ready for the next round. This was a luxury – losing a war – the Israelis were always genuinely, and one should also say rightly, convinced that they could never afford.

The mechanical approach to the balance of power misses the role of the state of mind, that of the crisis of the Jewish-Israeli conscience in the traumatic transition from Holocaust to statehood. It also neglects the impact that key battles, and some emblematic Israeli defeats in 1948, could have had on the Israeli psyche, that is, on the feeling that this was a nation living on a razor's edge. Such were the battles of Yad Mordechai, Nirim and Deganiah, the defeat of the Carmeli Brigade in Jenin, the capitulation and evacuation of the old Jewish quarter in Jerusalem, the defeat of the Israeli forces in the battle of Latrun in the winter of 1947–8, the assassination of fifty Jewish workers in the Haifa refineries in December 1947, and that of the physicians, nurses and faculty members of the Hebrew University on their way to Mount Scopus in April 1948, the massacre perpetrated by the Arab Legion in, and the subsequent evacuation of, the Etzion Bloc, the evacuation of all the children from the kibbutzim of the Jordan Valley, the conquest of Mishmar Hayarden and sizeable areas east of the international border by the Syrian army, the bombardment of Tel Aviv by the Egyptian air force and the loss in battle of 10 per cent of the country's population in a war in which 17 per cent of Israel's human resources had to be mobilised to repel the Arab invasion. In fact, the 'civil' half of the war, that is before the invasion of the Arab armies, proved in many ways to be more traumatic for the Yishuv. It was then that the Jews really felt they faced slaughter should they be defeated and that the survival of the incipient Jewish state hung by a mere thread.

Clearly, unlike in the aftermath of the 1967 war where Israel could by all accounts afford to be magnanimous in victory and advance far-reaching peace proposals thanks to its spectacularly improved strategic conditions, in 1949 Israel's victory did not relieve her from her sense of strategic vulnerability. With a width of 15 kilometres at her narrowest yet most densely populated belt, Israel's major cities were all within the range of Arab artillery. A population of 700,000 Jews who viewed the 150,000 Arabs in their midst as a fifth column to be ruled by a military administration was now submitted to a tight Arab economic boycott, to a virulent war of propaganda, and to a blockade of the Suez Canal and the Straits of Aqaba to her maritime traffic. To borrow an expression from Abba Eban, one might say that the Arab siege and boycott allowed Israel to breathe with only one lung.

In this state of affairs, and with such a national turn of mind prevailing among the population of the incipient State of Israel, the real question was not whether she would agree to a meaningful change in the territorial status quo that was reached after a war which, however clumsily it might have been waged by the Arab armies, was perceived by the Jews as one of self-defence, in exchange for peace. The possibility of peace, at least in the mind of the Israeli policy makers, in any case became redundant once the armistice agreements gave a legitimacy of sorts to the new borders. To the Israelis, the real question was not peace for land and refugees, but whether they would refrain from 'completing the job', as it were, and take over the whole of the West Bank down to the River Jordan, an idea that both Ben-Gurion and Moshe Dayan toyed with frequently in the aftermath of 1948, and political parties like Ahdut Ha'avoda and Herut advocated as a key item in their platforms. There clearly existed no political conditions whatever for a retreat from the status quo post bellum.

Initiatives for peace and contacts aimed at reaching some kind of accommodation between the parties were part of the relations of the Yishuv with the Arabs from the early days of the Zionist enterprise. At the crossroads between war and truce throughout the years 1946–51 the deluge of initiatives was especially impressive. All these, with the notable exception of the armistice accords, precisely because of their nature as interim agreements, failed to materialise into viable settlements either because of the fundamental reasons described earlier or because of specific reasons pertaining to each particular case.

Already during the war itself, or during a truce in the hostilities, sometimes the parties themselves and sometimes UN officials or the Western powers would initiate plans for a settlement. But as early as the summer of 1948 Israel responded to a British–American initiative calling for a return to the partition lines with Israel swapping the Negev for the western Galilee, with an unequivocal rejection. In her view the conditions for peace could never be the same after Israel's military achievements, when the source of the conflict, that is the plan for an independent Palestinian state, was ignored even by the invading Arab armies themselves. This fact would be officially sealed by the armistice agreements of 1949 when each of the Arab states would selfishly cater to its own territorial ambitions and conspire, as it were, to brush aside the interests of the Palestinians. The betrayal of the Palestinians by the Arab states was seconded by the international community. Neither the UN nor the superpowers were especially active in advocating the case for Palestinian statehood, or even that of their political rights. They treated it mainly as a humanitarian problem of refugees. The UN Palestine Conciliation Commission that put together the Lausanne Peace Conference in the spring of 1949 even refused to recognise the Palestinian Higher Arab Committee as a valid participant.

It was not surprising that the leaders of the Yishuv, always fearful and suspicious of the Arab-Muslim Middle East, should have seen the Christian Maronites of Lebanon as a natural ally, a cornerstone in a wider concept that would enjoy a long life in Israel's strategic thinking: the alliance of minorities, namely Jews, Christians, Druze, Kurds, Persians and Turks. Those in the Israeli system who believed that Israel would only be secure when she reached an accommodation with the Arab-Muslim majorities of the Middle East at the time lacked the political power to change the country's priorities. Nor were they sustained by the conditions prevailing among the Muslim majorities in the region. Their day would only come after the 1973 war, in the peace with Egypt, and after the first Palestinian Intifada and the Oslo accords.

In 1946, finally choosing between what Laura Eisenberg defined as taboo and temptation, the Maronites signed a secret agreement with the Jewish Agency that might explain why Lebanon's participation in the all-Arab invasion of Palestine in 1948 was nothing more than a token gesture to Arab solidarity. But this agreement did not turn into a full-fledged peace accord after the war because Christian Lebanon was either unwilling or too weak and fragile to risk dissociating itself from the Arab family and consensus. The 1946 agreement contradicted the National Pact upon which modern Lebanon was founded, a pact that asserted the 'Arab' character of Lebanon and its allegiance to the Arab League. This inherent tension between the Maronites' longing for special relations with Israel and Lebanon's Arab identity that prevented a peace agreement in the aftermath of 1948 was the same that would eventually turn the peace treaty that was practically imposed by the Israelis and the Reagan administration on President Amin Gumayel in 1983 into a dead letter.

But the truth of the matter is that neither in the aftermath of 1948 nor in 1983 did Israel have in mind a peace between equals with Lebanon. Rather, she thought of peace with conquest and annexation. In the early 1950s both Ben-Gurion and Dayan considered ways of subverting the Lebanese government, annexing the area south of the Litani river and making peace with a monolithic Christian Lebanon. Ben-Gurion would

.actually share his designs on Lebanon along with some other items in his grand strategy for the restructuring of the entire Middle East with his French allies whom he met at Sèvres in 1956 to prepare the Sinai campaign. Israel's invasion of Lebanon in 1982 might have looked like the sudden whim of a warmonger Minister of Defence, Ariel Sharon, but it was actually an operation embedded in a concept with a long pedigree and in Israel's mainstream strategic thinking from the very early years of the State.

It may be that today, after so many attempts at bilateral peacemaking have failed, the Israeli–Palestinian tragedy can only be susceptible to an international solution. But the record of international initiatives of peacemaking has been anything but edifying so far. Such was also the case with the Lausanne Peace Conference convened by the Palestine Conciliation Commission in late April 1949. The Conference only vindicated Israel's fears that whenever all the Arab delegations convened internationally their tendency would invariably be to assume radical positions that could by no means be assumed by Israel.

In peace as in war, a divided Arab side was in Israel's interest. To split the Arab family and deal separately with each of its members would always be her preferred pattern of negotiation. Even in the case of Lebanon and Syria where during the armistice talks Israel presumably had a keen interest in conditioning her withdrawal to the international border in Lebanon on Syria's pull-out from areas she had occupied east of the international border, Ben-Gurion nevertheless decided against such a linkage. In the 1970s Syria would succeed in restoring and consolidating the linkage in a way that would pose a major strategic challenge to Israel and prevent a separate peace deal with Lebanon. Israel's unilateral withdrawal from south Lebanon in the summer of 2000 needs to be seen as an attempt to cut off the linkage, do away with the Syrian strategic blackmail and deal separately with each country at a time.

The Arabs frequently defeated their own case by the absurdity of their demands. The Arab League proposal in Lausanne for a substantial repatriation of refugees and for Israel's withdrawal to even more modest borders than those proposed for the Jewish state in the partition plan was so absurd that not even the US, that had been bringing pressure to bear on Israel to the point of threatening to withdraw her recognition of the Jewish state if she did not sign the Lausanne Protocol of 12 May 1949 which confirmed the partition borders, was ready to endorse it.

In fact, the absurd positions presented by the Arabs in Lausanne allowed Israel to manoeuvre in such a way that she won relief from

American pressure, and created a sense of moderation and progress without having eventually to pay any tangible price. Israel's offer to admit 100,000 refugees, rejected out of hand by the Arabs as insufficient, its readiness to sign the Lausanne Protocol confirming the borders of partition – which neither the UN nor the superpowers were in any case ready to enforce – a proposal to conduct a referendum on the West Bank where the Palestinian Arabs could opt for self-determination, and Ben-Gurion's idea of annexing the Gaza Strip with its refugees as Israel's contribution to the relief of the plight of the refugees (an idea that eventually came to nothing), were all wise moves in creative diplomacy that allowed Israel to get away unharmed from the trap of Lausanne.

No other Arab party has ever matched the long record of political dialogue and the degree of strategic intimacy that Jordan had with Israel. Indeed, Israel and Jordan were, as one historian put it, 'the best of enemies'.

In the 1940s the platform for the strategic partnership between the Yishuv and King Abdullah was their common enemy, the Palestinians, whose embodiment was the Mufti (with King Hussein, the common enemy would be Arafat). Both the Zionists and the Jordanians had a shared interest in preventing the emergence of an independent Arab state in western Palestine. As early as 1946 an understanding to that effect was reached between the parties, again confirmed by them in November 1947. The Palestinians themselves, in what became a sad and self-defeating pattern of political behaviour, acted as the worst enemies of their own cause and did their utmost to prevent the creation of their state. But it is nonetheless intriguing that on the very eve of the UN's historic decision to partition Palestine into separate Jewish and Arab states, Israelis and Jordanians should have conspired to subvert the imminent plan and allow the King to take over Arab western Palestine.

Throughout 1948, however, King Abdullah gave a vivid demonstration of what would be in the years to come Jordan's strategic predicament. Jordan was torn by the difficult quest for balance between the temptation to come to an accommodation with Israel at the expense of the Palestinians and to have security guarantees against her enemies in the Arab world on the one hand, and the necessity not to lose her inter-Arab legitimacy by dissociating herself too openly from the Arab consensus on the other. This was certainly a most complex and dangerous exercise in diplomatic and strategic acrobatics. Paradoxically, to protect his deal with the Zionists, King Abdullah had to become, as it were, the leader of the all-Arab invasion of Palestine. He knew, as he put it to the commander of his army Glubb Pasha, that 'the Jews are too strong; it is a mistake to go to war'. If it was a mistake, he was condemned to commit it by Jordan's unique predicament, even if that meant suffering what a Spanish general had called during the Cuban War of 1898 against the overwhelming might of the United States, a 'splendid defeat'.

Israel wanted a peace settlement with Abdullah after the war if only because this responded to what would now become a persistent element in her strategy, namely 'to export', as it were, the Palestinian problem to the Hashemite kingdom. But neither Ben-Gurion nor Sharett was willing to pay a territorial price for such a peace.

Ben-Gurion's major concern, however, was that Jordan was too weak a link to the Arab world, too artificial an entity in order to have the necessary legitimacy to lead the entire Arab world to a comprehensive reconciliation with the Jewish state. Why should Israel pay a high price for peace with a state that could under no conditions become the vanguard for an overall settlement with the Arab world? To his diary Ben-Gurion would even confide that Jordan was such an artificial creation that she needed to be dismantled altogether and her territory split between Israel and the Arab states. Somehow he never really assumed the loss of the West Bank to Jordan and he kept resisting what he viewed as the 'ridiculous borders' established by the armistice agreement with Jordan.

In fact, as both Ben-Gurion and Sharett wondered throughout the second half of 1948, an independent Palestinian state in the West Bank might perhaps have been less of a threat to Israel than the annexation of the West Bank by a Jordanian state that might one day merge into a larger Hashemite kingdom with Iraq. If they both nevertheless came to terms with the option of the annexation of the West Bank by Transjordan, it was mainly because of their fear that an independent Palestinian state would be a springboard for an irredentist drive under Haj Amin al-Hussein's leadership. The irony was that, of all people, it was Ralph Bunche, the UN's Deputy Secretary General, who presumably should have defended the implementation of Resolution 181, who helped instead to convince the Zionist leadership to shelve the idea of an independent Palestinian state. It would be one led and inspired by the Mufti, he warned them, and would be a continuous source of friction and instability.[1] Israel's Jordanian option was clearly enhanced by Palestinian radicalism and by the opposition of both Israelis and Jordanians to Haj Amin el-Husseini's fanatic leadership. History hardly knows of a similar gap between the justice of a cause and the performance of the leadership that

---

[1] Efraïm Karsh, *The Falsification of Israeli History* (Hebrew), Hakibbutz Hameuhad, Tel Aviv, 1999, pp. 102–3.

embodied it. This, the failure of leadership, was throughout a major source for the calamity that had befallen the Palestinian people.

No peace with Jordan was not to Ben-Gurion a missed opportunity, but a sober strategic calculation that would eventually be vindicated by history. A strong and invincible Israel would force Egypt to make peace with her in the late 1970s in a way that would, for all practical purposes, neutralise the Arabs' military option and force a radical transformation of Arab strategy from war to a settlement through negotiations.

There were no great peace lovers, either Jews or Arabs, in this story of the quest for a settlement in the aftermath of the 1948 war. There were, however, little Bismarcks or Machiavellis, each looking for his own territorial conquest, for ways to outsmart his counterpart, or for a regional balance of power and deterrence. To Abdullah, a settlement with Israel would allow him to protect his flank while he annexed and digested the West Bank, and tried to execute his grand design of a Greater Syria under his leadership. An access to a Mediterranean port and economic advantages were seen by the King as an additional bonus of such a settlement. Abdullah preceded Sadat in his understanding that peace with Israel was also a way to a rapprochement with America.

But a deal was nevertheless missed. First, it was because of the absurd, even megalomaniac, conditions of the Jordanians. They wanted the southern part of the Negev, the Gaza Strip, Lydda and Ramlah and the Arab neighbourhoods of Jerusalem.[1] Then, when they scaled down their ambitions and were ready to settle for a 150-metre-wide safe and sovereign passage from Hebron to the Mediterranean, a condition Israel acquiesced to in a meeting in the presence of the King himself, and the Principles of a Territorial Settlement were ready for signature, it was the Jordanians, not the Israelis, who got cold feet and proved unable to deliver. The King simply could not overcome the opposition of his own government to such a deal.

The Israelis might have been tough negotiators, but the dysfunctionality of the Jordanian political system was now the major obstacle to a settlement. A situation was emerging in Jordan where the King's legitimacy for striking a deal with Israel was being seriously undermined by a supposedly patriotic, pan-Arab, philo-Palestinian and pan-Islamic government. As it turned out, the annexation of the West Bank extended the borders of the Hashemite kingdom but, by Palestinising the kingdom and shifting the emphasis of Jordanian politics to a pan-Arab sensibility

---

[1] Itmar Rabinovitch, *The Road Not Taken: Early Arab–Israeli Negotiations* (Hebrew), Maxwell-MacMillan-Keter Publishing, Jerusalem, 1991, p. 106. Rabinovitch's own source is *Documents on Israeli Foreign Policy*, Jerusalem, 1986, edited by Yemima Rosenthal, vol. IV, May–December 1949, p. 636.

towards the plight of the Palestinians, it diminished the King's power and capacity to continue being the undisputed autocratic leader he had been thus far.

On 17 February 1950 the King made a last-ditch attempt to salvage something from the wreckage of his peace strategy with Israel by proposing a non-aggression pact. This was a brilliant move, for it could unleash a dynamic leading to a possible peace deal in the future. It also implicitly meant Israel's recognition of Jordan's annexation of the West Bank. The agreement could likewise allow Israel to claim her first political breakthrough with an Arab state and a crack in the Arab economic boycott. There were even some provisions in Abdullah's proposal that could satisfy the Palestinians by opening judicial channels for refugees to reclaim their abandoned property in Israel. The Israeli Cabinet ratified the agreement at its meeting of 22 February, with Foreign Minister Sharett praising the 'psychological' importance of the document.

But it was again the Jordanians, not the Israelis, who failed to deliver. Abu al-Huda's government got cold feet and unilaterally changed both the title and the content of the agreement.

It was now becoming clear that the Palestinisation of the kingdom and the rift between the King and a no longer docile political class had emerged as an insurmountable obstacle to an Israeli–Jordanian settlement, however modest its provisions. Abdullah could not allow himself the political luxury of being exposed as a yielding king in conflict with a patriotic pan-Arab government. Moreover, the structural changes that were now taking place in the expanded kingdom changed the King's priorities. At stake were the stability of his throne, perhaps even the very survival of his kingdom and the chances of ending its isolation in the Arab world, where he was portrayed as the puppet of British imperialism and an ally of the Zionists at a time when the seeds of a new and more radical brand of Arab nationalism were spreading throughout the region. These were now for Jordan certainly more vital concerns than a deal with the Zionists that in any case fell far short of a full-fledged peace agreement.

The annexation of the West Bank by Jordan proved to be a prelude to the perpetuation of the conflict. The opportunity for a 'blitz peace' operation, if there ever was one, had clearly vanished. The King's defeat in his show of force with his government was more than just a local political dispute. It signalled to the entire Arab world that the end had come to the attempts, however hesitant, to reach peace with Israel. The traits of the Arab–Israeli dispute as we would know them in the coming years, namely a protracted, intractable conflict, were at an advanced stage of development.

Jordan now safely returned to the Arab fold and assumed the discipline imposed on its member states by the Arab League, which in its meeting of 25 March 1950 decided that 'no member state is allowed to negotiate with Israel, sign with it a separate peace or any other political or economic agreement. ... Any state that would fail to respect these conditions would be automatically expelled from the League.' Abdullah's consolation was that in exchange for turning his back on Israel he got a tacit acceptance from the Arab world for his annexation of the West Bank. This and Jordan's armistice agreement with Israel were for all practical purposes tantamount to a death sentence for the idea of a Palestinian independent state.

The Syrian story was indeed extraordinary. Husni Zaïm, a man on horseback, staged a *coup d'état* on 30 March 1949 and immediately came forward with a breathtaking peace initiative. His proposals included a separate peace with Israel, full economic co-operation and even a common Israeli–Syrian army that would allow the new allies to become the masters of the Middle East. And, if this were not enough, the strong man from Damascus would later propose to absorb in Syria 300,000 Palestinian refugees provided the US would finance their resettlement and make available to Syria additional economic aid.

Israel's response was initially formalistic – Ben-Gurion's instructions were not to proceed to any peace negotiations before Syria had agreed to Israel's terms for an armistice, that is, her withdrawal to the international border – and then practically dismissive. Ben-Gurion even thought of resuming the military offensive in order to drive back the Syrians east of the border. This was exactly the pattern of gunboat, coercive diplomacy he had used with the Jordanians through Operation Uvdah (Operation Fait Accompli) that expelled the Jordanians from the southern Negev, while the armistice talks were still being conducted, and forced Abdullah under the threat of an ultimatum to relinquish the Wadi Ara area.

Nonetheless, once Ben-Gurion had his way and the armistice agreement was signed with Syria on 20 July 1949, Israel was ready to resume the contacts for a peace settlement with the Syrian regime. However, Israel's peace strategy remained unchanged. The instructions given to the Israeli negotiators not by the hawkish Ben-Gurion but by his supposedly dovish Foreign Minister, Moshe Sharett, were as strict as ever: 'Not even a hint should be given to the Syrians of the possibility of border modifications along the Jordan River or in the Lakes. On the contrary, it needs to be made clear to them that no such modification can be contemplated.' It is inconceivable that Zaïm could have agreed to a settlement on such a basis; it offered him no legitimacy whatever for a separate deal with the Zionist enemy.

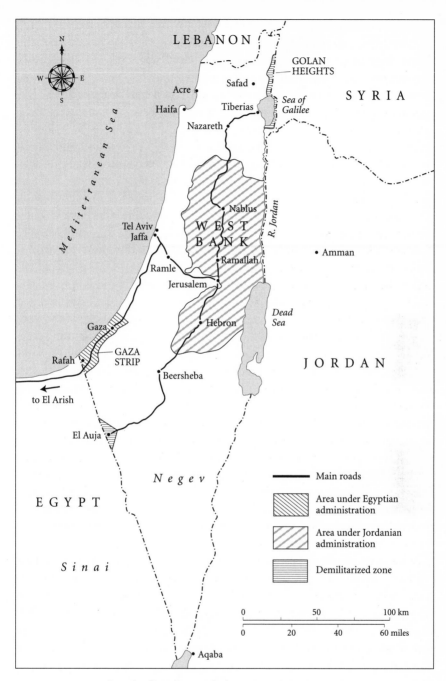

Israel after the armistice agreements, 1949

But the whole enterprise was anyway not relevant any longer. Once the armistice agreement was signed, a formula was found for the demilitarised zones and the threat of a renewed war removed, both Israel and the US lost interest in the Syrian track. By mid August Zaïm and his Prime Minister were overthrown from office and later executed.

Clearly, Husni Zaïm was the only Arab leader who was ready in those years to cross the barrier of hostility with Israel in such an extraordinarily imaginative and bold way. Israel did not respond. Reasons abounded, some of them solid and valid. Of course, there was always Israel's sanctification of the territorial status quo post bellum, and in this case also the imperative of preserving the country's water resources, that is the Zionist core ethos of land and water. But there was also a deep mistrust of the nature of a regime born of a *coup d'état* that could hardly be expected to legitimise in Syria, let alone throughout the Arab world, such an extensive peace settlement with Israel.

The proposed Syrian deal was much more far-reaching in its provisions than the Jordanian proposals, but the gap of legitimacy that derailed the chances of a settlement was even more dramatic in the Syrian case. 'Farouk is probably the man who represents Egypt, but who the hell is Zaïm?' exclaimed Ben-Gurion in front of the American Consul General in Jerusalem. There was not much trust either in the hallucinatory and far-fetched ideas of a corrupt, megalomaniac and unreliable officer who, additionally, was a Kurd and seemed to be out of tune with the prevailing nationalist currents of opinion in Syria and throughout the Arab world. In fact, it was precisely Zaïm's divorce from nationalist and pan-Arab sensibilities that eventually brought about his downfall. As was the case in the dichotomous relations between the peace seeker King Abdullah and his nationalist ministers Rifaï and el-Huda, Zaïm's Foreign Minister, Adel Arselan, a far more genuine representative of the deeper currents in Arab nationalism, opposed his leader's peace overtures and denied them a vital fig leaf of legitimacy.

One needs also to resist the temptation of referring to Zaïm as a Syrian Ataturk or the visionary statesman that Anwar Sadat was. Husni Zaïm was neither. In his short-lived rule of hardly four months he did not exhibit much of the spirit of a reformer. And, unlike Israel's peace with Egypt in the 1980s, it is totally inconceivable that a peace deal with Zaïm would have outlived the assassinated dictator.

Ben-Gurion expressed what would become a cornerstone in Israel's strategic thinking when in December 1949 he said to the American ambassador in Tel Aviv that 'Egypt is the key to peace in the Middle

East' and the gate to the Arab world. This was truly the case, but at no point in the contacts that started during the war could Egypt's territorial ambitions be reconciled with Israel's insistence on keeping her war gains.

Arab nationalism was still anything but a dominant force in Egypt. That her commitment to the Palestinian cause was still far from being irreversible could be seen in the very debate that took place in the Egyptian Upper House on the eve of the Arab invasion of Palestine. 'A whole desert separates us from Palestine,' explained Ismaïl Sadqi, a senior statesman who had served twice as prime minister, when he defended the case for not joining the war. 'Peace and internal reforms need to be our priorities,' he said in the parliamentary debate where the war was discussed. To join an all-Arab war for Palestine was by no means what the Egyptian parliament was eager to approve. Eventually, the war was a one-man decision, that of King Farouk, who himself was more concerned with curbing the aspirations of the Hashemite monarchy in Palestine than with the plight of the Palestinian people. 'We were not thinking about the problem of Palestine,' recalled Zakaria Mohiedin, a young officer about to go to war (he would later be Egypt's Vice-President). Uppermost in the Egyptians' minds, he said, 'was how to get rid of British colonialism in Egypt'.

If there was a missed opportunity it was in the incapacity of Israelis and Egyptians to curtail their conflict before the 1948 war had irreversibly immersed Egypt in the Palestinian imbroglio and made it the leader of what would soon become an all-Arab crusade against Israel. It was not the Palestinian problem that dragged Egypt to war, it was the war that dragged Egypt into the Palestinian problem. In fact, when Egypt's Prime Minister at the time, Mahmoud Fahmi el-Nukrashi Basha, asked the Egyptian parliament to declare war on Israel, he did not dwell on the Palestinian issue as the main reason. Israel's Socialist ethos, he said, was what made the Jewish state a threat to Egypt and to other Arab regimes. The man who took the decision to go to war, King Farouk, was the same man who led the resistance to reconciliation after the war. True, with the first setbacks on the battlefield the King made some hesitant attempts towards a separate settlement with Israel. But this was mainly as a tactical device to stave off imminent defeat, a defeat that would soon be sealed by Operations Yoav and Horev in the south, not in search of a real peace. Kamal Riad, Farouk's emissary, was candid enough, surprisingly, to explain to his Israeli counterparts in the autumn of 1948 the rationale behind his mission as being an attempt to curb Israel's expansionist schemes.

However, once Egypt's immediate war concerns were over and the armistice agreement was signed, Egypt lost interest in an urgent deal with

Israel. Contacts continued in Lausanne and beyond, but the Egyptians were now only looking for a truce that would allow them to prepare for a second round. These were the guidelines that Abd el-Munim Mustafa, Egypt's delegate in Lausanne, received from his superiors in Cairo:[1]

> Egypt needs to look as if it weighs seriously every peace proposal, for international opinion is not yet prepared to accept renewed hostilities. Time is in Egypt's favour, and we need to persist in our military preparations; time, however, is not yet ripe for a decision to go to war.

Mustafa himself turned out to be an eloquent exponent of the core cultural and strategic dilemmas of the Arab–Israeli conflict, and of the civilisational clash between Zionism and Arab nationalism. 'What do we need peace for now?' he asked his Israeli counterpart in Lausanne, Elias Sasson. 'Peace', he added, 'will only give you economic advantages and will consolidate and strengthen [your state]. Egypt does not need peace now. On the contrary, we are interested in not having peace in order to deny you the consolidation and the power [you need].' The Arab world, and Egypt in particular, realised then that Israel was becoming a fact of life, however undesirable. Therefore, as Mustafa put it, the Egyptian and Arab strategy from now on should be that 'Israel does not become too big or too strong, or too populated'. 'Egypt', he said, 'would not feel secure when four million Jews, all educated, all with a drive for initiative and all permeated with a sense of self-sacrifice, would live on its borders.'

Mustafa might not have been the embodiment of Egypt at the time, but he was clearly not very far from expressing the essential attitude of the policy makers in Cairo then and in the years to come. 'Peace is out of the question' was Muhammed Hassanin Heikal's expression of the Arab mood in the aftermath of the 1948 war. Non-belligerency was the most the Arab world was ready to think of and even this, as he noted, was extremely controversial. Both Abba Eban and Gideon Rafael, not exactly the most militant among Israeli officials, concluded in February 1950 that, when it came to Egypt, there was not that much of a missed opportunity for peace. 'In these conditions,' they reported to their superiors, 'there is no chance whatever for a settlement with Egypt.'

The first years of the Egyptian Free Officers in Power were essentially no different. The initiative this time was Israel's and it was fairly bold. But the secret channel between Ziamah Divon and Abdel Rahman Sadeq,

---

[1] This extraordinary document and other revealing reflections by Mustafa are quoted by Professor Itamar Rabinowitz in his *The Road not Taken: Early Arab–Israeli Negotiations* (Hebrew), Jerusalem, 1991, pp. 156–62.

Nasser's personal envoy, that was to operate in Paris for almost two years, led nowhere. Soon Ben-Gurion lost patience with what he rightly saw as Egyptian procrastination and tactics aimed at winning American support through Israel's good services without paying an irreversible price in terms of a binding settlement.

Indeed, peace with Israel was not exactly what Nasser was looking for, although he was not interested in war either. The Free Officers wanted time and stability in order to promote their reforms and advance key national objectives such as driving the British out of Egypt and getting economic assistance from America. Latent contacts with Israel on a low level served these purposes perfectly well. The contacts continued well into Moshe Sharett's premiership (1952–5), but the crisis of the 'Affair' brought them finally to a halt. An abortive attempt by Israel's intelligence services to derail Egypt's rapprochement with the West by acts of sabotage against British and American institutions inside Egypt, the Affair terminated Sharett's peace moves. 'We will not negotiate in the shadow of the gallows,' explained Prime Minister Sharett when an Egyptian tribunal decided to execute two of the Israeli agents in that infamous affair. The executions made it politically unsustainable for Sharett to pursue the talks. Although he had been kept in the dark by the security establishment about the entire business, he simply could not allow himself to remain indifferent to the popular rage following the executions.

The avalanche of infiltrations from the Gaza Strip, Israel's retaliatory incursions, Ben-Gurion's return to the Ministry of Defence, and the IDF's spectacular Gaza Operation on 28 February 1956 signalled the countdown to the Sinai war. In 1955 the Western powers had made a last attempt to prevent the drift to war by their Project Alpha, a joint British–American peace initiative that required Israel to give up the whole of the Negev or part of it, and accept the repatriation of a substantial number of refugees. Eventually Egypt, which was not ready to settle for anything less than the whole Negev, and Israel, which refused to consider any territorial concessions whatsoever, jointly shared the responsibility for derailing this initiative.

But the really intriguing thing about Alpha is how, seven years after Israel's War of Independence, the Western powers still did not fully appreciate the depth of Israel's refusal even to consider territorial concessions, and the absurdity of the Arab demands.

There was, of course, an inherent contradiction in Ben-Gurion's attitude to peace deals with Arab leaders. He dismissed as corrupt and unreliable leaders like Zaïm, Farouk and Abdullah. But as it turned out, he was not especially forthcoming either with strong leaders like Nasser who had the vision of reformers and modernisers. This was because he now feared such leaders might improve their countries' potentialities and pose a threat to Israel. With such leaders he would rather prepare for war, as he did from the moment he returned to the Ministry of Defence in February 1955.

Israel, and this was true on all fronts, was ready for a peace based on the status quo, both territorial and demographic, on deterrence and on her military edge. 'Peace for peace' was the formula. The Arabs, especially Egypt, wanted peace with an Israel that was reduced to its 'natural size' – both geographically (by its return to the boundaries of the 1947 partition) and in terms of its military and economic potential – and ceased to be a threat to its neighbours. These were stipulations that were utterly irreconcilable in the conditions prevailing at the time.

Wars in the Middle East have frequently served as a prelude to peace, or at least have triggered attempts to reach a settlement. Such was certainly the case in the Yom Kippur War that led to Israel's peace with Egypt and the first Intifada that ushered in the Oslo accords. It was also true of the 1948 war. But although only armistice borders emerged from that war, these would prove nonetheless to be the accepted and internationally legitimate borders between Israel and her Arab neighbours. Moreover, it is these very borders that were then rejected by the entire Arab world, which have now become the Arabs' condition sine qua non for peace with Israel.

It was, then, the Arabs who were not ready in the early years to accept the fact of Israel's existence within the borders of 1948. It took thirty years of conflict, wars, destruction and desolation, but especially the conquest by Israel of additional territories in the 1967 war, for the first Arab leader to come forward with an unequivocal offer of peace based on the borders decided by the 1948 war and, no less important, this time Israel responded.

IV   The Rise and Fall of the Third Kingdom of Israel

This is going to give us the possibility of living here.

Ben-Gurion to Major Ariel Sharon, the Commander of the
Kybieh operation,
15 October 1953

We speak of the second round that will come. But, we are already in the second round ... and, in this battle, God forbid that we should fight within our own borders.... We must be ready to fight back beyond our borders.

General (Res.) Yigael Yadin addressing the Histadrut's
Executive Committee,
10 January 1955

We are a generation of settlement, and without the steel helmet and the gun's muzzle we will not be able to plant a tree or build a house ... That is the fate of our generation.... To be prepared and armed, strong and resolute, or else our sword will slip from our hands and the threads of our lives will be severed.

Moshe Dayan's eulogy for Roi Rutenberg,
April 1956

Yotvata, or Tiran, which until fourteen hundred years ago was part of an independent Jewish state, will revert to being part of the Third Kingdom of Israel.

Ben-Gurion's cable to the Seventh Brigade on the last day of the
Sinai Campaign,
5 November 1956

The road to the Sinai Campaign of 1956 was paved by the realisation of both Arabs and Israelis that peace, and the necessary concessions it required, was not a realistic option. Israel's paranoiac sense of siege and its inbred tendency to assert its military superiority on the one hand, and the Arabs' irresistible choice of inertia and boycott and the comfort of inflammatory rhetoric on the other, brought about the breakdown of the precarious truce that had followed the 1948 war.

Israel's War of Independence was not for a moment seen by the leaders of the new state as heralding an era of peace. That a 'second round' was inevitable was almost public knowledge, let alone that such was the working premise of most of the leaders, first and foremost of Ben-Gurion. To him, as he said when presenting to the Knesset a new 'Security Law' on 19 August 1952, Israel was living in a state of 'armed peace,' and he warned against the illusion and the danger of a 'false peace' with the Arab world. The new nation made out of immigrants from all corners of the world had to be shaped and galvanised as a nation in arms, a people in uniform, a fully mobilised society. The army, Ben-Gurion taught, should be the vital agent of nation building. When initiating military reprisals against the neighbouring Arab states, he would frequently consider not only the need to inspire and motivate the army, but also to boost the morale of the new immigrants through the exploits of their army. The notion of a nation living on a razor's edge between war and a precarious truce became a collective state of mind, a philosophy of life. 'Security' was definitely elevated to the status of the sacred cow of the young Jewish state.

But the psychosis of a second round was not an exclusively Israeli obsession; it was fed by the Arabs' uncompromising hostility. It was widespread throughout the entire Arab world as well. The incipient Jewish state was not allowed any relief by its Arab neighbours from economic boycott, incendiary propaganda, military threats, the blockade of its maritime roots and a worldwide campaign aimed at isolating and ostracising it.

The military reprisals conducted by the Israel Defence Force (IDF) throughout the 1950s were normally triggered by infiltrations of Palestinian civilians who crossed the borders, mostly driven by economic or social reasons, and sometimes by acts of terrorism perpetrated against Jewish border settlements. The cycle of infiltrations and reprisals against the neighbouring Arab states accused by Israel of standing behind the infiltrators became almost routine. It allowed the IDF's military superiority to be displayed in a way that Israel expected would serve as a deterrence to its enemies. In many cases, however, the scope of Israel's response to the infiltrations tended to be disproportionate. Such was certainly Moshe Sharett's view. After the Kinnereth Operation of 11 December 1955 – a major Israeli onslaught on Syrian positions, allegedly as a response to Syrian interference with Israeli fishing in the Lake of Galilee – he confided to his diary that 'again we see a blood lust and a provocation to war. This operation was preceded by no killing of Jews.'

As it turned out, the reprisals did not serve as a deterrent or a brake on the slide into open war, but rather as a prelude to it, a catalyst to an all-out confrontation. Conspicuously, this is how both General Dayan, as the IDF's Chief of Staff, and Ben-Gurion, albeit always qualifying and tempering his drive for a pre-emptive war with the caution of the statesman, wanted it to be. Egypt was seen by both as being propelled to war by its charismatic leader, Gamal Abdel Nasser. Nasser's aspirations were to unite and lead the entire Arab world under the banner of his own particular brand of pan-Arab nationalism where Israel played the role of an alien Western implantation that needed to be eradicated if the Arabs were to recover their pride and redeem their rights. Both Dayan and Ben-Gurion believed that launching a pre-emptive strike before Egypt became too strong was an existential necessity for Israel.

In the early 1950s, however, neither Egypt nor Jordan had a policy of encouraging infiltrations from their territory. Of course, they had no love for the Jewish state, but they preferred not to instigate an Israeli military response, let alone a total war, so long as they were not ready for the inevitable second round. In fact, King Hussein, who ascended the throne in May 1953, indicated that he wanted to follow in the footsteps of his grandfather and conduct a strategy of peaceful coexistence with Israel.

But Ben-Gurion's was essentially a strategy of pre-emptive war. He took the bellicose rhetoric of the Arab leaders at face value and not only prepared for the inevitable war but also did not discard precipitating it, so that it could be conducted on Israel's terms. He led an 'activist' line, one that assumed that sooner or later the Arab states would unite in a war aimed at wiping the State of Israel out of existence. To survive in such an unmerciful environment, Israel would have to be able constantly to deter and intimidate her neighbours. They must be brought to assimilate the notion that they had no chance in battle and that a strong Jewish state was there to stay.

There was, presumably, a different line, more diplomatic and conciliatory than that of Ben-Gurion and his disciples. Moshe Sharett, the Foreign Minister and from 1953 to 1955 the Prime Minister in place of Ben-Gurion who had announced a temporary retirement, represented it.

But as it emerged from the history of the 1948 war and its aftermath, this two-school theory has been overemphasised by some historians. Sharett had neither the stamina and the sense of leadership needed to confront the activist school in the army and in the Ministry of Defence, nor the ability to stand by his own principles in moments of trial. He failed, for example, to prevent the unlawful works for the diversion of the River Jordan, which caused a confrontation between Israel and the international community. Chief of Staff General Moshe Dayan, politically inspired and backed by Ben-Gurion from his retirement in Kibbutz Sdeh Boker, was the motor behind Israel's affront to its northern neighbours and to international law. Eventually, it was not Sharett's leadership but the overwhelming pressure from the two superpowers, the United States and the Soviet Union, as well as that of the Security Council, that forced Israel to interrupt the project. One did not have to belong to the 'moderate school' to succumb to such overwhelming international pressure. The activist Ben-Gurion would do just that when faced, in the wake of the Sinai Campaign, with brutal Soviet–American pressure for Israel's pull-out from the peninsula.

Moshe Sharett's deficient leadership could not inspire confidence among his potential Arab interlocutors. His weakness was such that Ben-Gurion's years of temporary retirement in Kibbutz Sdeh Boker did not mean that his policies went on leave with him. Ben-Gurion was, for all practical purposes, Israel's Prime Minister *in absentia*, one who ruled by proxy through his disciples back in the government. Not only was Sharett incapable of controlling his Chief of Staff Dayan, he was also outmanoeuvred by Defence Minister Pinhas Lavon when the most notorious of all reprisal operations, the attack on the Jordanian village of Kybieh on 14 October 1953 following the assassination of an Israeli woman and her two children – the IDF left behind sixty-five civilians dead, most of them women and children – was decided without even notifying Prime Minister Sharett. Sharett was also left in the dark – 'I'm Prime Minister, and I don't know anything about it' – when the defence establishment activated a Jewish spy cell in Egypt to sabotage that country's rapprochement with the West. Known as 'The Affair', it became an international scandal that was to haunt Israel's political system for years. The message to Nasser was unequivocal: Sharett was too weak to impose his will on the military and there was no point in holding secret peace negotiations with him. He was not a leader who could deliver.

The activists led Israel into a course of action that was more in line with that of a Yishuv, that is, a revolutionary national entity seeking to establish facts on the ground by outwitting the colonial mandatory power, than with that of a state that was expected to abide by international norms of behaviour. Moshe Dayan never denied that he intended the cycle of violence to spark a full-scale war. And if war was nevertheless avoided, the display of Israel's military superiority would certainly, he believed, discourage the Arabs and nip in the bud any hope they might have harboured of destroying Israel. Israel needed to live by her sword, such was the existential philosophy of this most political of Israeli soldiers. This is how Dayan would put it in his typically eloquent style, in his elegy at the funeral of Roi Rutenberg, a kibbutz member of Nahal-Oz murdered by Arab infiltrators in April 1956:

Let us not be afraid to see the hatred that accompanies and consumes the lives of hundreds of thousands of Arabs who sit all around us and await the moment when their hand will be able to reach our blood. Let us not avert our gaze, for it will weaken our hand. That is the fate of our generation. The only choice we have is to be prepared and armed, strong and resolute, or else our sword will slip from our hand and the thread of our lives will be severed.

This was fully in tune with Ben-Gurion's philosophy that the international community mattered to a very limited degree. What was really important was the lesson that operations such as that of Kybieh would teach the Arabs of the region. They would now respect Israel's ruthlessness in battle and would, it was hoped, be intimidated. Far less eloquent and poetic than his disciple Dayan, Ben-Gurion meant the same thing when he said to the officer who commanded the Kybieh operation, Ariel Sharon, that 'this is going to give us the possibility of living here'. Self-defence and self-reliance rather than 'the preposterous and totally unfounded and baseless illusion' that an outside force would protect Israel was Ben-Gurion's philosophy as he now spelled it out.

Few politicians in Israel's history have succeeded in working closely with the military without succumbing to their priorities. Pinhas Lavon is a good example. He was a thoughtful and moderate politician who, as minister of defence, was transformed into an indomitable hawk. He was quick to adopt the military ethos of power, and he even developed a confrontational strategy of his own. His analysis was that, given the strategic edge that oil gave to the Arab world and the consequent policy of appeasement of the West towards the Arab states, peace could only be given to Israel in most adverse and unfavourable conditions. Israel, as he explained in a meeting of his party, Mapai, on 15 April 1954 and later made abundantly clear in his autobiography, needed therefore to avoid a settlement, and stay the course of confrontation and possibly war, in order to improve the strategic environment in her favour before she agreed to peace with the Arab world.

Admittedly, the hawks in Israel operated against the background of an unstable strategic environment, and a dangerous Middle East where very tangible threats were building up around the Jewish state. But it was also true that Prime Minister Sharett's unconvincing struggle against Ben-Gurion's disciples had no chance whatever, not only because he himself, indeed like Ben-Gurion and the activists, was not ready for a peace deal that did not respect the territorial status quo created by the 1948 war, but also because there was no real Arab partner ready to depart from the rejectionist line established by the Arab League. However much

Ben-Gurion's disciples looked like warmongers, the threats they responded to were not just the product of their wild imagination. These were, indeed, times of an increased sense of isolation and strategic vulnerability for Israel. In 1954 the United States started to supply Arab states in the region with weapons as part of a strategy aimed at creating an anti-Soviet Arab axis around countries such as Egypt and Iraq.[1] Britain's decision to pull out her forces from the Suez Canal was also interpreted in Israel as likely to enhance the strategic links between the Arab world and the West. It was believed that Britain would now provide Egypt with weapons as a way of preserving their influence in that country. Convinced of Egypt's intentions to go to war sooner or later, the Israelis interpreted Britain's pull-out as the removal of a vital buffer between Egypt and Israel, and hence as a potential avenue to war.

As in the immediate aftermath of the 1948 war, peace was simply not an option in the run-up to the Sinai Campaign. If anybody harboured any doubts as to the feasibility of an Egyptian–Israeli settlement, these were dispelled when Operation Gamma, an American mediation between the parties that lasted from December 1955 to March 1956, was wrecked by the immobilism and adamant rejection of any compromise ideas by both Nasser and Ben-Gurion. Nasser would only negotiate on the basis of the 1947 partition lines and Israel would not consider anything that went beyond very minor border modifications. It was like a trip back in the time machine to the all too familiar positions of the parties in the immediate aftermath of 1948. Nothing had changed but the tragic fact that the hour of the much spoken about second round was approaching.

True, as Anita Shapira observed,[2] Menachem Begin's speech at the College of National Security in the summer of 1982, where he defended Israel's invasion of Lebanon in the name of a philosophy of 'war of choice', was the first time that a Zionist leader had openly preached war as an instrument of policy making. But Lebanon was clearly not Israel's first war of choice. Three decades earlier, admittedly in a different setting, Israel definitely pushed for a war of choice with Egypt without, however, exposing in public its full intentions or rationale. Ben-Gurion and Dayan engaged in wars of choice of their own, but they were far less given to ceremonious declarations than Begin. They certainly lacked his sense of drama when presenting their case for war. In fact, in an attempt to present his Lebanese adventure as a link in a long chain of strategic thinking, Begin himself acknowledged in his war of choice speech that

---

[1] Avi Shlaim, *The Iran War*, Penguin Books, London, 2000, pp. 104–5.
[2] *Land and Power, The Zionist Resort to Force, 1881–1948*, Oxford University Press, 1992, p. vii.

neither the 1956 Campaign nor the 1967 pre-emptive strike were wars of 'no choice'. 'In November 1956 we had a choice. ... In June 1967 we again had a choice,' he said to his audience of high-ranking officers. Nasser in 1967, he explained, deployed his army in Sinai in a way that 'did not prove' that he was really about to attack Israel. 'We must be honest with ourselves. We decided to attack him.' And such was also the case in 1956. Ben-Gurion then summoned the chief of the opposition to tell him that 'we are going to meet the enemy before it absorbs the Soviet weapons'.

The way to the 1956 war was preceded by Israel's drive to deter her enemies and pre-empt real, and sometimes exaggerated, threats through a persistent policy of force and confrontation led by her military establishment. Not all were strictly military operations. Such was, for example, the case of the notorious 'Affair'. Operations such as the fiasco of the Affair, or the hijacking of a Syrian civilian aircraft ordered by Lavon in order to force the Syrians to release five Israeli commandos that were arrested on 8 December 1954 while conducting an intelligence operation deep in Syrian territory, seriously compromised the already precarious international standing of the Jewish state. According to Sharett, in a candid speech in the Knesset on 17 January 1955, the dilemma was to be 'a state of law' or 'a state of piracy'.

Sharett was 'raising a generation of cowards' – this was Ben-Gurion's way of announcing his official return on 21 February 1955 to the helm of Israel's military system as the new Minister of Defence. Ben-Gurion lost no time in asserting his leadership. A week later he ordered Operation Black Arrow against positions of the Egyptian army in Gaza, in retaliation for the assassination by infiltrators of an Israeli bicycle rider, leaving behind thirty-seven Egyptian soldiers dead. Whether or not the Egyptians were now officially behind the wave of infiltrators from Gaza might be open to debate. To Ben-Gurion this was a secondary consideration. Nasser's drive to pan-Arab leadership was bound, sooner or later, to pose an existential threat to Israel, and the Egyptian *rais* needed to be disciplined and reduced to his natural size before it became too late.

But the Gaza operation had the opposite effect. Rather than cutting short Egypt's commitment to a war strategy, it enhanced it. A military humiliation is a luxury a military regime can ill afford without putting at risk its stability and perhaps even its very survival. The argument is not implausible that the Gaza operation changed the Egyptian posture from one of indifference or half-hearted attempts to curb the infiltrations into one of active support and encouragement. A new phase of terrorist attacks by squads of fedayeen from the Gaza Strip was now unleashed. By dealing a blow to Nasser's prestige precisely at a time when the

Egyptian leader was engaged in a difficult attempt to meet the challenge to his regional leadership posed by the Western-orientated Baghdad Treaty, and by exposing in such a humiliating way the incompetence of his army, the Gaza operation served to shift his regime from whatever emphasis it might have had on internal reforms and economic development to a hasty build-up of a military option with the help of the Eastern bloc.

The Middle East was about to become the playground of the two major superpowers, and Israel's humiliation of Nasser was one reason, among others, that accelerated the rush of Egypt into the arms of the Soviet Union. The pattern was now being established in the Middle East whereby the Soviet Union and its allies would become the exclusive providers of a war option to any Arab side in conflict with Israel and in a state of estrangement and alienation from the West. Nasser's arms deal with Czechoslovakia in September 1955 meant that the Arab–Israeli conflict had fallen into the only logic that could perpetuate it indefinitely, that of becoming the tool of the bipolar competition in the Middle East.

It is true that the conflict existed before superpower competition and, as we can see today, it still persists after the fall of the Soviet Union. But the struggle for mastery in the Middle East by the two big powers blocked the possibility of a major peace breakthrough for years. Conspicuously, Egypt's peace with Israel in 1979 started as a bold bilateral move behind the back of the superpowers. The Madrid Peace Conference of 1991, the Oslo accords of 1993 between Israelis and Palestinians, Israel's peace with Jordan a year later, and the most serious attempts to reach an Israeli–Syrian settlement throughout the 1990s were all possible only after the collapse of the Soviet Union.

But Ben-Gurion was not to be deterred by Egypt's war preparations in autumn 1955. On the contrary, the case for a pre-emptive strike was, if anything, becoming stronger in the aftermath of the Gaza operation. In late March 1955 he had proposed in practice to conquer the Gaza Strip and annex it to Israel in response to an Egyptian attack on a settlement of immigrants in the Negev. And when the Cabinet turned down his proposal he suggested officially calling off the armistice agreement with Egypt. The infiltrations and the blockade of the Canal to Israeli maritime traffic had made it a farce, he said, and Israel should recover her freedom of action. But, a keen supporter of the territorial status quo produced by the 1948 war, Prime Minister Sharett was still just able to defeat what he rightly viewed as an unwise move to unilaterally and officially abrogate the only agreement that gave an international legitimacy to Israel's borders.

When it came, however, to the vital question of safeguarding Israel's freedom for independent military action, there was no significant disagreement between Sharett and Ben-Gurion. However much they both yearned for a defence treaty with the United States that would guarantee Israel's borders, would deter the Arab states and perhaps even compel them to come to a peace settlement with the Jewish state, both Ben-Gurion and, admittedly less outspokenly, Sharett refused to accept John Foster Dulles's conditions for such a treaty, namely that Israel should refrain from her independent defence policy at the centre of which was the pattern of reprisals. Self-defence and self-reliance were to remain key components in Israel's strategic doctrine of offensive defence. It was fully consistent with this doctrine, as it was developed by Ben-Gurion in the 1950s, that in the early 1980s Ariel Sharon did not mourn President Reagan's decision to abrogate America's Strategic Understanding with Israel as a reprisal for its annexation of the Golan Heights. He feared that such an understanding might hinder his plan to invade Lebanon.

Israel's doctrine of offensive defence did not necessarily call for territorial expansion; it was essentially a pre-emptive concept. Though changing and expanding Israel's borders was not a priority, however, it nevertheless remained a dream, an aspiration waiting for the right conditions. Both General Dayan and Ben-Gurion spoke more than once throughout 1955 of the need to annex southern Lebanon up to the Litani river and to turn the rest of it into a friendly Christian state. In terms that almost fully anticipated Menachem Begin's and Ariel Sharon's adventurous Lebanese enterprise of the early 1980s, Moshe Dayan even proposed to buy, with money, a Maronite officer, and conspire with him on the division of Lebanon between Israel and a Maronite state.

But the main objective was Nasser's Egypt. According to Ben-Gurion, this was where the main threat to Israel lay. Destroying Nasser's regime and toppling him was for Ben-Gurion a central strategic objective. And as from November 1955 when with Moshe Sharett's resignation he was once again Prime Minister, he would focus his energies on that vital objective. The way was now open to a pre-emptive war against Egypt, and the momentum for war was such that, with their leader gone, even key members in the 'diplomatic' school such as Abba Eban and Gideon Rafael joined the activist bandwagon and abandoned their efforts to stop the drift to war. Toppling Nasser's revolutionary regime was the objective, war the means. Such was now the common view throughout the Israeli system.

Though fully subscribing to the pre-emptive conception and unquestionably confrontational in his attitude to Egypt – on his first night as Prime Minister, on 2 November 1955, he approved one of the biggest and boldest incursions against Egyptian positions in al-Sabha that left fifty Egyptian soldiers dead – Ben-Gurion was nevertheless more attentive to wider strategic and political considerations than his Chief of Staff. His hope of acquiring weapons from the United States, for example, caused him to vacillate over whether or not to approve Dayan's drive to take over the Straits of Tiran, an idea that the government eventually turned down. He was likewise haunted by the spectre of Israel being isolated and having to fight for her survival without the support of a Western ally. He wanted a pre-emptive war, but he nevertheless wavered in search of the right timing and the proper conditions.

The right conditions were for Ben-Gurion first and foremost the availability of a major Western ally. The drift into the Sinai Campaign was indeed determined by the outcome of a power struggle within the Israeli system as to the strategic orientation of the Jewish state. Ben-Gurion and his men, especially his deputy at the ministry of defense, Shimon Peres, and the army's chief of staff, General Moshe Dayan, did not believe in the possibility of an accommodation with the Arab world. They came to the conclusion that the US would not allow Israel a free hand in its war with the Arabs, nor would she make available to her the weapons needed to sustain a strategy of permanent war. The only option was therefore a military alliance with one or more major European power. In a far cry from positions he would champion in the 1990s, Shimon Peres fought vehemently against the idea of Israel's integration into the Middle East. Israel's link to the region, he used to say, was only geographical. Like his master Ben-Gurion, Peres maintained that Israel was doomed to live in a state of permanent war with the Arab world, and needed therefore to disengage both culturally and politically from the Middle East by forging an alliance with Europe. As Shabtai Teveth, Ben-Gurion's biographer, put it, the objective of having an alliance with the major European powers was so dear to Ben-Gurion and his circle that they were ready to pay for it with a war. The Sinai Campaign was such a war.

Ben-Gurion could not have planned it this way, but the international uproar unleashed by Operation Kinnereth of December 1955 and the unanimous condemnation of Israel by the Security Council helped advance the option of an alliance with France. By cutting short a possible change in America's position in favour of supplying arms to Israel, a supply that in any case would have had conditions attached that Israel could not have accepted, the Kinnereth Operation signalled the shift of Israel to a French orientation. Ben-Gurion never abandoned the hope of securing American arms supplies, but he also definitely looked for the friendship of a Western power that did not demand unacceptable conditions in exchange.

A second round required a Western ally and the almost inevitable choice was now France. An alliance with France was in these conditions by definition an alliance for war. It also meant clear victory for the defence establishment over Moshe Sharett's conceptions and his attempt to accommodate Israel to the requirements of an American orientation. Sharett's resignation in June 1956 and his replacement as Foreign Minister by Golda Meir removed a major hurdle to the French connection, and allowed Ben-Gurion a much freer hand, both within the party and in the government, to make his views and policies prevail.

The French alliance was not the result of a romantic, idealistic friendship, as it has sometimes been portrayed. It was a matter of *realpolitik* that was born in a moment of grace when the crude interests of the two parties, France and Israel, seemed to coincide. The Algerian revolt was a vital concern for France in the mid 1950s, one that had far-reaching internal consequences as well. Not only was the conventional assumption that Nasser's brand of popular Arab nationalism was a major inspiration to Algerian nationalism, but also that the rebels were being materially assisted by Egypt. An Israeli blow to Egypt, or any Israeli success in preventing Nasser from diverting his energies to North Africa, the French believed, would undermine and cripple the Algerian revolt. Israel's interest was as simple as it was obvious. By pursuing her objective of toppling Nasser and his regime, she would at long last gain the strategic asset – an alliance with a Western power and a lavish supply of weapons – that first Zionism as a movement and later the State of Israel had always yearned for.

Essentially, the alliance was one between the defence and military establishments of the two countries. As from the summer of 1956 an understanding was reached that in exchange for French arms to Israel, the two countries would work to curb Nasser's pan-Arab activities and undermine his regime. In effect this meant a French guarantee to secure Israel's military superiority in the Middle East and, as it turned out, French generosity was so abundant that it also included offering Israel the facilities for developing a nuclear option.

Nasser's was the case of a charismatic Arab nationalist whose zealous pan-Arab drive, and his determined attempt to free his country from the dominance of Western imperialism and to get rid of the last vestiges of the British military presence in Egypt, brought him to a fatal collision with the West and eventually into the arms of the Soviet Union as the competing pole upon which he could rely to advance his revolution. That the Americans committed a major blunder by turning down Nasser's request to finance his most spectacular infrastructure project – the Aswan High Dam – was an additional blow that pushed him even further away from the West. On 26 July 1956 Nasser nationalised the Suez Canal, a severe blow to British and French economic and strategic interests. This in its turn triggered a British–French–Israeli war conspiracy aimed at toppling him.

The sealing of the plot at the Sèvres Conference was to Ben-Gurion like a dream come true, an operational alliance with two Western powers to topple a leader about whose intentions he had no doubt whatever: to dominate the entire Arab world and unite it in a war of extinction against an isolated State of Israel.

A realist and a pragmatist, Ben-Gurion was also a leader who harboured in his heart powerful Messianic dreams and grand territorial designs. His private dreams were not only of a defensive nature. Ben-Gurion was a man of grand strategic visions. An aspiration he always had was to reshape the map of the Middle East in a way that would guarantee Israel's existence as a hegemonic regional power and change the entire political environment around it. Strangely and embarrassingly, he confided his regional grand strategy to his new allies at Sèvres. This consisted of the partition of Jordan between Iraq and Israel, of Israel's annexation of southern Lebanon and the creation of a Maronite state in the north, and of the freedom of navigation being secured by Israel's control of the Straits of Tiran. His plan also included replacing Nasser with a pro-Western leader who would make peace with Israel. However sceptical and dismissive his new allies were of his grand schemes, Ben-Gurion was convinced that a successful war against Egypt would unleash a dynamic that would sooner or later change the Middle East according to his plan.

On 29 October, Israel's army invaded the Sinai peninsula in conjunction with a French and British attack along the Suez Canal, and in a matter of days achieved a crushing military victory on an Egyptian army that was hastily withdrawing across the Canal. By 5 November, the entire peninsula was under Israel's occupation. The performance of the French and the British was far less edifying, however. They were both forced by Soviet and American pressure to interrupt their offensive and retreat from the Canal area in disgrace.

The sin of hubris is frequently a concomitant of victory. This was clearly the case with Israel's crushing military triumphs. The 1956 victory unleashed a sense of nationalistic, even Messianic, euphoria not entirely dissimilar to that which would later be produced by the lightning victory of the Six Day War. 'Military historians will still have to investigate the wonders of the secret of the IDF's exploits in such a short war,' Ben-Gurion now declared. Moreover, he lost no time in recalling, in a speech to the Knesset, that a Hebrew kingdom did exist as far as the island of

Tiran 1,400 years ago.[1] And Mapai's mouthpiece, *Davar*, chose to refer to the new conquered lands of the Sinai Desert as 'liberated territories'. 'Gaza', it wrote, 'has returned to our borders and will now be a city in Israel.' Indeed, in a message he sent to the 9th Brigade in Sharm el Sheikh on the last day of the war, Ben-Gurion spoke ecstatically of the revival of the 'Third Kingdom of Israel' (the First was King Solomon's kingdom in biblical times and the Second lasted from the sixth century BC to the destruction of the Second Temple by the Romans in 70 AD), and asked the soldiers to 'extend your hands to King Solomon'. His territorial appetite was now clearly being aroused. The war, whose proclaimed rationale was that of destroying the bases of the fedayeen, became suddenly a voyage into Jewish history and a campaign to recover millenarian certificates of ownership.

But the euphoria could not last long, and the unrealistic Messianic hallucinations of an Israeli leadership that lost any sense of proportion and any touch with reality were cut short by overwhelming international pressure. The combination of a brutal Soviet military warning and American political and economic pressure, to the degree of threatening to allow Israel's expulsion from the UN, brought Ben-Gurion back to his senses. He realised how, driven by the elation and the drunkenness of the moment, he had misread the international set-up and grossly miscalculated Israel's chances of imposing her will. It was now back to his worst-case scenario, his ultimate nightmare: an Israel standing alone, isolated and threatened militarily and economically by the entire world community, with the two superpowers leading the international onslaught on his embattled nation. He agreed to give in, almost unconditionally, and to declare unceremoniously the end of Israel's short-lived 'Third Kingdom'.

Military victories do not always translate into political gains and the lesson to Israel for the future was that if her military successes were not to be lost she could not afford to be denied the support of the United States. Such support would also be necessary to deter Soviet intervention on the side of its humiliated Arab clients. This was exactly the difference between the 1956 campaign and the 1967 war, where Israel was allowed by America to keep her territorial gains as a bargaining card in future peace negotiations. In 1956, however, Ben-Gurion's grand strategy was utterly defeated because it only had the support of two colonial powers in decline.

---

[1] Why 1,400 years? After all, Jewish independence was destroyed by the Romans in 70 AD. Ben-Gurion despised the chapter of Jewish life in the Diaspora, and he preferred to arbitrarily shorten what to him was a sad and disgraceful part of Jewish history by artificially extending Jewish sovereignty in Palestine until its occupation by the Arab invaders in the seventh century.

In the Arab world a leader defeated, and even humiliated, by what could be described as a sinister conspiracy of Zionists and Western imperialists would always be more popular than the peacemaker, who is inevitably forced to make concessions and would be seen as yielding. The story of Nasser as opposed to that of Sadat is a case in point. Not only was Nasser not toppled, but his prestige was boosted as the champion of the Arab world and the nations of the Third World in their struggle against Western colonialism. Israel's image as a beachhead of the imperialistic West in the Arab Middle East received its ultimate proof and vindication. If there ever was a chance that Israel could be admitted into the Middle East family of nations, her alliance with two decadent colonial powers in a war against a most popular Arab regime, which had fired the imagination and inspired the dreams of liberation and emancipation of the masses throughout the Arab Middle East and beyond, gave it a fatal blow.

There was a lesson for France and Britain, too. Analogies can sometimes be odious and are invariably imperfect. But it may be illustrative to draw a comparison between the Suez war and the American–British invasion of Iraq in 2003. In both cases two Western powers grossly exaggerated the threat posed by an Arab leader, went as far as defining him as a new Hitler and launched a pre-emptive war in order to remove him from power. They did this against the advice of their other Western allies and without UN approval in a way that created a very serious rift within the West itself. In both cases the war ended in a fiasco for the Western actors and with their international prestige severely undermined. In both cases a severe blow was also dealt to the position of the members of the war alliance in the Arab Middle East. For France and Britain, 1956 signalled the end of their strategic presumptions in the region. America's overwhelming might could still help it salvage its position in the region from the wreckage of the Iraq war, though this will certainly require a change of policies and, no less important, of style and discourse. But the bitterness and the high degree of popular rage it left behind is a legacy that will not be easily forgotten. It will continue to feed and inspire Islamic terrorism in the region and beyond. Moreover, as in the case of France and Britain with Egypt, Iraq in 2003 saw the birth of America's pre-emptive strategy, but also its demise. After the fiasco that accompanied the Iraq war it is extremely difficult to see how a domestic and international legitimacy could be found in the future for such a pre-emptive strike to be repeated.

For Israel, however, not all was bad news. Just as Nasser was able to turn his resounding military débâcle into a major political victory, so Israel drew from her Sinai adventure non-negligible assets. However isolated it might have looked to her neighbours, the IDF's outstanding military performance would now turn Israel into the undisputable hegemonic military power in the region and would serve as the ultimate deterrence against any illusions of an Arab nation challenging the existence of the Jewish state. Moreover, as a price for a withdrawal she had no other option but to undertake, Israel gained the demilitarisation of the Sinai peninsula that would now serve as a buffer with its sworn enemies in the south. The conditions for Israel's pull-out from Sinai meant that the Egyptians were forced to stop entirely the infiltrations from Gaza and do away with the fedayeen bases in the Strip, and last, but certainly not least, to open the Straits of Tiran to Israeli navigation in a way that any future Egyptian blockade could be legitimately viewed by Israel as a *casus belli*.

It could not exactly be said of Israel's Sinai Campaign that, as the English seventeenth-century poet George Herbert put it, 'he that makes a good war makes a good peace'. The war was not that 'good', nor did it usher in a 'good peace'. Yet though it appeared at first as a tactical achievement but a strategic calamity for Israel, nevertheless it ushered in a decade of truce on her Egyptian border and a much needed respite from the tensions of war, which enabled the continuous absorption of immigrants and unleashed the economic energies of Israeli society into years of spectacular growth and national self-confidence.

V The Jewish Fear and Israel's Mother of all Victories

Israel is the cancer, the malignant wound, in the body of Arabism, for which there is no cure but eradication.

Cairo Radio,
1963

The danger we face is one of complete destruction.

Levi Eshkol upon assuming office,
1963

If Israel embarks on an aggression ... the battle will be a general one and our basic objective will be to destroy Israel.

President Nasser's speech to Arab trade unionists,
26 May 1967

Nobody ever said that we are an army for preventive wars ... I do not accept that the mere fact that the Egyptian army is deployed in Sinai makes war inevitable. ... We are not alone in the world. ... Are we to live all our lives by the sword?

Levi Eshkol addressing the Army's General Staff,
27 May 1967

We have restored Arab honour and renewed Arab hopes ... we are now ready to confront Israel. ... We are now ready to deal with the entire Palestine question.

President Nasser's speech at the National Assembly,
29 May 1967

The clash between Jewish fears and Arab warlike rhetoric is always likely to produce a fatal chemical reaction. Throughout the 1960s, both Arabs and Israelis let their national complexes and the built-in contradiction between their respective political cultures lead them, almost against their own will, into a mental and strategic deadlock from whose grip only war could save them. At stake were not, of course, only misperceptions about the real distance between rhetoric and intentions, but also a struggle for the control of the rules of conduct in the region. The principles that defined the precarious truce that was established after 1956 had to be preserved at all cost. The Arab challenge to these principles was a threat to Israel's vital philosophy of deterrence that could not be allowed to prevail.

The Arab–Israeli clash of perceptions and interests took place against the background of a Middle East strategic reality that had radically changed in the wake of the Sinai Campaign. The war represented a major turning point in the structure of the Arab–Israeli conflict. The grip of the Western colonial powers on the region was severely undermined and their capacity to articulate a common policy with the United States in the Middle East was crippled. The stage was set for a robust penetration of the Soviet Union into the politics of the region, while the US was inevitably drawn into the vacuum left by France and Britain. The conflict was intricate enough without the global dimension it now acquired; with it, the Middle East became the chessboard of the two major powers and the Arab–Israeli conflict a tool in superpower competition, with the Soviet Union offering the Arabs a war option to counter Israel's military hegemony and America's increasing support for the Jewish state.

Defeated and humiliated, Nasser was in no mood for compromise with the Jewish state in the aftermath of the war. But he was sober enough to realise that a 'third round' was not an immediate realistic option. His new strategy, backed by his soaring popularity as the champion of Arab nationalism against the Zionist and imperialist conspiracy, was that of turning the Israeli problem into a pan-Arab enterprise and enhancing pan-Arab unity with the Palestinian issue as the cohesive glue. 'Palestine supersedes all differences of opinion,' he would say during the Cairo Arab League Summit of 1964, a central resolution of which would be that of creating the Palestine Liberation Organisation. It was not to be an Israeli–Egyptian dispute any more, but an all-Arab struggle, with Palestine as the battle-cry, the mobilising banner, against the Zionist state. Indeed, whether or not Arab states would be ready to let their territory become the springboard for Fatah incursions into Israel – incursions that, as it turned out, served as a major catalyst for the Six Day War – would become a vital test of loyalty to the cause of pan-Arabism.

By pushing Palestine to the forefront of the struggle against the Jewish state, Nasser radically changed the parameters of the conflict. Now it was no longer just a border dispute between sovereign states, and one that was susceptible to a rational solution, but a conflict of an almost mythological nature over the plight of the Palestinians and their 'inalienable' rights, where hardly any room for compromise could exist. It is from this perspective that Sadat's peace initiative, in the wake of the Yom Kippur War, needs to be understood. To make peace he needed to extricate Egypt's conflict with Israel from the paralysing hold of the Palestinian dilemma into which Nasser had locked it and bring it back to the realm of rationality as a solvable border dispute between two sovereign states.

The lesson for Israel was that the dreams of territorial expansion, which many in the Israeli system saw as the unaccomplished tasks of the 1948 war, would have to be shelved for now. The superpowers would not allow Israel to build her security on the modification by force of the territorial status quo. Therefore the view that the 1949 armistice lines were a status quo to be consolidated became a necessity imposed by the new international conditions. The notion was being assumed and digested in Israel that the territorial phase of Zionism was over and a doctrine of deterrence, not war and conquest, preferably with the backing of an alliance with the Western powers, was developed as the strategy best adapted to cope with the new challenges.

Notwithstanding the French alliance and its extraordinary benefits for Israel, Ben-Gurion remained obsessed with the need for a strategic association with the United States. For only America could curtail what he now viewed as the major new strategic threat facing Israel, namely, the forceful penetration of the Soviet Union into the Arab Middle East. Just as in the early 1940s he had been quick to gauge the change in the global balance of power, and subsequently opted for shifting the focus of Zionist diplomacy from Britain to the United States, so now he realised that the Sinai Campaign had not only exposed but also enhanced the bankruptcy of the old colonial powers, Britain and France. In the early 1940s he needed America to facilitate the creation of the Jewish state. Now she was needed to secure its *survival* and prosperity.

A man with the passion and the look of a biblical prophet, Ben-Gurion was at the same time a most practically minded politician. He never let his tendency to engage in prophetic visions and grand designs divert him from the leader's obligation to set an example and advance a workable solution to the nation's dilemmas. He was the architect of Israel's transition from Yishuv to statehood and the father of its war doctrine. His theatrical retirement to a life of simplicity and pioneering dedication in the Negev desert was his way of preaching the Zionist ethos of making the desert bloom through personal example.

Ben-Gurion was driven by an unyielding conviction about the singularity of the Jewish people and its capacity to create a state that is unique in its qualities. But this required a departure from the old ways of diaspora life. Zionism was to him a rebellion against the tragic course of Jewish history that had alienated the Jews from their land and from the habits of sovereign existence. The diaspora was to him both the chronology and the geography of national perdition. He therefore aspired to shape the new nation on the legacy, and continuity, of the Hebrews' sovereign life in biblical times. The kings and prophets of Israel were his heroes and role models.

Like Lenin, who made every value subservient and secondary to the revolution, Ben-Gurion was a revolutionary obsessed with one single idea: the creation and consolidation of the Jewish state. Hence his decision in the 1920s to transform his national vision from the Marxist-driven reliance on the working class to an emphasis on 'the people', 'the nation'. 'From class to people' was from now on his platform. To secure the cohesion of the old-new nation, and cement the links holding together all the diverse ethnic groups that made the state he had created in 1948, Ben-Gurion needed to make his peace with Jewish history.

Conspicuously, in his earlier Socialist phase Ben-Gurion focused his attention mainly on cultivating the pioneering ethos in those areas of Palestine that best represented the culture of the new, secular, working-class society. The Jordan Valley and the Valley of Izrael, the Galilee and the Lake of Galilee, and kibbutzim like Deganiah and Kinnereth were then far more central to his Zionist vision than 'Jewish' sites such as Jerusalem, Safed and Hebron, or holy shrines like the Temple Mount and Rachel's Tomb. But his momentous shift from class to people, that is, his embrace of an almost Jacobin idea of the state, reshaped his attitude to national symbols with a Jewish meaning. His struggle in 1948 for Jerusalem, a city he had earlier almost ignored, and his decision to declare it (in December 1949) as Israel's capital against the advice of those who feared the reaction of the international community, were bold reflections of the transformation of his vision of Israel as a state now inspired by, and united through, Jewish memory.

The evolution of Ben-Gurion's attitude towards the Holocaust from startling indifference to a pedagogic embrace was an additional reflection of his endorsement of a new brand of Israeli nationalism, one that did not rely solely on the secular pioneering ethos, but was also linked to the long, tortuous chain of Jewish history. Throughout the 1950s, years of military trial and mass immigration of the survivors of the Holocaust and the dispossessed and uprooted Jews from the Arab world, Ben-Gurion realised how difficult it was to forge a new nation only through the ethos of the melting pot and *Israeli* (as opposed to *Jewish*)-centred values such as the army, the charms of the Sabra and the settlement of the desert. He was forced to resort to the most awesome tragedy of Jewish history in order to find a unifying factor that would forge into one nation the young *Israeli* generations and their *Jewish* brethren, that mosaic of diverse ethnic groups that flocked en masse to the young state.

The kidnapping of Adolf Eichmann and his subsequent public trial in 1961 was Ben-Gurion's attempt to establish a link between the new state and the saddest chapter of Jewish history in the diaspora. The victims of the Holocaust were no longer 'human dust' and 'slaughtered cattle' as they were portrayed in the past, and the Holocaust was not just the symbol of how the Jews went 'like sheep to the slaughter', but also the scene of untold acts of Jewish heroism. Through the Eichmann trial Ben-Gurion 'nationalised' the Shoah and its victims, and absorbed them into a new *Israeli–Jewish* unifying national ethos.

An instrumentalisation of the Shoah it certainly was, but Ben-Gurion, the nation builder, had only one paramount idea in his mind, that of securing the survival of the Jewish state, to which all other considerations were subservient and secondary. This was exactly the same idea that had brought him in the early 1950s to one of the most controversial and divisive decisions he ever made, one that was seen by many as a premature endorsement of the 'new Germany' in exchange for reparations. Rehabilitating Germany, even if prematurely, and bitterly splitting the nation, was a price he was ready to pay in exchange for reparations that he deemed vital for the development of the country and for the absorption of the mass of displaced Jewish immigrants.

By cultivating the perception of Israel as an embattled Jewish ghetto under siege rather than the regional power that it was, Ben-Gurion helped to create the psychological conditions for the Six Day War. The creation in February 1958 of the United Arab Republic – a merger between Egypt and Syria – increased, if anything, his existential fears. Israel's military prowess was never sufficient to calm the old man's holocaustic anxieties. When in 1967 Nasser deployed his army in the Sinai peninsula, neither he nor Ben-Gurion, by then out of office, wanted a war. But the Israeli national psyche, as it was shaped over the years by the discourse and the policies of the government in Jerusalem, could not but interpret Nasser's moves as part of a strategy of extinction against the Jewish state. Ben-Gurion's successor and Israel's Prime Minister during the 1967 war, Levi Eshkol, inherited and expressed the same holocaustic sentiments. 'The danger we face is one of complete destruction,' he said upon assuming office in 1963.

Whether in times of war or during intervals of truce, Israel was unable to extricate herself from her mental ghetto or, worse, from her Holocaust complex. Ben-Gurion's frenetic political moves were the child of a mind troubled by the burden of Jewish history and by a fatalistic interpretation of Israel's regional dilemma. His fears of a weakened and isolated Israel in the middle of a hostile Arab ocean made him restless and obsessively given to apocalyptic reflections. His attempt to make America share his predicament and entrust her with the mission of being the ultimate guarantor of Israel's existence ended, however, in frustration. He was denied the qualitative leap in Israel's relations with the United States that his successor, Levi Eshkol, would achieve. Eisenhower's America preferred to rely on the Arab world, not only because of oil, but also because of her conception that the Arabs were central to any reliable strategy aimed at curbing the Soviet threat.

That the big leap to a full-fledged alliance with the West was denied to Ben-Gurion became the context that produced the new doctrine of the 1960s, the 'Alliance of the Periphery'. Ben-Gurion's fatalistic pessimism with regard to the possibility of ever reaching a settlement with the Arab countries bordering on Israel was an additional rationale of the new doctrine. The idea was to break the siege of hostility of the neighbouring countries by an alliance with those in the outer circle of the Middle East, that is, non-Arab countries such as Iran, Ethiopia and Turkey, countries that did not have any particular dispute with the Jewish state and were themselves in varying degrees of tension with their Arab neighbours. The myth of Israel's military power, her resourcefulness in economic and agricultural matters and an exaggerated perception about her unique capacity to lobby, and influence, American policy combined to make the Israeli connection especially attractive to these countries.

The Alliance of the Periphery had an impact in boosting the morale of the embattled nation and in producing tangible benefits for the Jewish state. But it fell short of vindicating the grand designs of its founders, who wanted to see Israel turn into the axis of an American-backed regional alliance against Nasser's aspirations to forge a strategic alignment of Arab, Islamic and African states. The objective of convincing the West to see Israel as the leader of an alternative regional alignment and, hence, as a strategic asset was not achieved.

Israel's achievements were, nevertheless, not negligible. Diplomatic relations were established with Turkey and Iran in the aftermath of the 1948 war, a strategic partnership was built with the two countries, and throughout the 1950s the triangle Israel–Iran–Turkey shared an active anti-Nasserite and anti-Soviet agenda, while Israel's intimate relations with Haile Selassie's Ethiopia were supposed to help undo Nasser's African ambitions. The 1950s and early 1960s were also the honeymoon years of Israel's relations with black Africa. Her pioneering ethos and technological qualities captivated the minds and hearts of African nations, and helped to erode the image of Israel as a beachhead of the colonialist West in the midst of the emerging Third World. The strategic and technological resourcefulness of the Jewish state in its attempt to break the siege imposed on it by a hostile Arab world was the reflection of an admirable determination to acquire manoeuvring space for the assertion of Israel's qualities in her struggle for survival.

It was to become one of Israel's major strategic dreams, that of being able to develop the space to manoeuvre for an independent, imaginative foreign policy not necessarily linked to, or conditioned by, the paralysing constraints of the protracted Arab–Israeli conflict. But this could never really be achieved. The centrality of the Arab–Israeli conflict in Israel's international relations could not be diluted, not by joining Eisenhower's anti-Communist regional alliance, nor through the strategic partnership with Reagan's America in its fight against the Soviet 'empire of evil', nor yet during President Bush's global war against terror. The capacity of the Arabs to maintain their pressure on Israel and to keep alive the interest of world opinion and foreign governments in the plight of the Palestinians made the Israeli quest for evading the consequences of the conflict, either through periodic wars or by the forging of alternative regional alignments, such as the Alliance of the Periphery, into a futile exercise. The Alliance was a creative attempt to escape the constraints and the consequences of the Arab–Israeli conflict. It certainly gave a breathing space to the embattled nation and opened new strategic horizons for Israel's foreign policy. But it could not change the main focus of national energies on the Arab–Israeli conflict, nor did it spare the Jewish state from being condemned to overstretch her resources in order to tackle the challenges posed by her immediate neighbours.

The British and American military intervention in Lebanon and Jordan, aimed at curtailing any adverse repercussions for the West's strategic interests following Abdul Karim Kasim's 1958 revolution that shook the pro-Western Baghdad Treaty, offered Israel an additional opportunity to press for a more solid alliance with Britain and the United States. However, Ben-Gurion's hopes of exploiting the new regional conditions and Israel's role in safeguarding the interests of the West in order to advance his dream of an anti-Nasserite, pro-Western regional strategic alliance with Israel at its centre were again frustrated. The United States would not endorse Israel's Alliance of the Periphery, and Britain turned down Ben-Gurion's approach for a formal alliance. A selective supply of arms from Britain and a verbal American commitment to the 'integrity and independence of Israel' were the best he could wrest from the Western powers for his help in salvaging Hussein's pro-Western throne.

Ben-Gurion's existential fears were indeed of an extraordinary magnitude and intensity. He accorded almost mythological dimensions to the threat posed by Nasser, and he dreaded a confrontation with the Soviet Union while Israel lacked solid guarantees from a Western superpower, or an organic alliance with Nato. This explains Ben-Gurion's outright capitulation in the face of a brutal Soviet threat in August 1958 that 'ominous' consequences might follow if Israel continued to challenge Soviet interests in the region. He immediately ordered the suspension of British military flights to Jordan over Israel's airspace. He would not expose Israel to a possible retaliation by the Soviet Union while the West denied him formal security guarantees.

Lack of superpower guarantees, an almost apocalyptic fear of physical annihilation, the threat of a Nasserite Middle East bent on the destruction of Israel, a fatalistic pessimism as to the chances that the Arab world would ever reconcile itself to the existence of a Jewish state in its midst and the ever-present Holocaust complex, was the context for Ben-Gurion's quest for a credible nuclear option. The nuclear option could also be seen as a protest against, or an alternative to, America's reluctance to accord solid and unequivocal conventional guarantees to Israel's existence and incorporate it into an organic regional alliance. Indeed, there were those in the Israeli political system who wanted to use the Dimona nuclear reactor as a way of pressuring America into securing Israel's conventional capabilities.

Israel's ultimate strategic deterrence, its nuclear ambiguity, proved to be a brilliant move. Not only did it serve as a major deterrent, but it should not be minimised either as one of the considerations behind President Sadat's decision to make peace with Israel. It was also a factor that encouraged President Kennedy to start laying the ground for what would later become an unwritten alliance between America and Israel. Concerned by Israel's nuclear strategy, the President wanted to help move the Jewish state away from its dangerous flirtation with a nuclear option by increasing its sense of security through the supply of conventional weapons. Kennedy was the first American president to commit himself not to allow the balance of conventional power in the Middle East to change against Israel. In the summer of 1962 a qualitative leap in America's relations with the Jewish state came with his decision to supply ground-to-air Hawk missiles to Israel. Later that year, he defined America's relations with Israel as similar to the 'special relationship' she had with Britain and he made it clear that an unprovoked Arab attack on Israel would trigger America's military intervention.

But Ben-Gurion's fear of a Nasser-inspired Arab strategy for the destruction of Israel could not be abated. Kennedy's good intentions and his evident sensibility to Israel's needs were not sufficient to make redundant Israel's nuclear strategy. The refusal early in 1963 of the Egyptian *rais* to meet Ben-Gurion in order to try to find possible common ground for a settlement on the one hand, and the trilateral Arab confederation (Egypt, Syria and Iraq) established a few months later

(17 April 1963) with the commitment for the liberation of Palestine as a key item in its constitution on the other, only confirmed his worst nightmares. He wrote to Kennedy that he was no longer sure that the State of Israel 'will continue to exist after my life has come to an end'. Ben-Gurion was possibly magnifying the threats to Israel in order to get weapons from America. But at the same time, his was the mind of a troubled Jew who could never trust the Arabs or the international community. A formidable military might always coexisted in Israel with a sense of Jewish vulnerability. *'Shimshon der Nebechdeiker'* ('Samson the nebbish') is how Levi Eshkol would later define the Israeli psyche; it certainly characterised the dichotomy in the minds of the founding fathers.

Ben-Gurion oscillated frantically from a strategy of deterrence to the politics of hysteria. He bombarded world leaders with dramatic appeals for an international commitment to the independence and territorial integrity of all the states in the Middle East. Whatever territorial dreams he might have harboured in the past, he was now a keen champion of the status quo. To him, the territorial phase of Zionism was over and the safety of Israel within the borders of 1949 was his exclusive concern. Only the full demilitarisation of the West Bank and a formal defence treaty with America could set his mind at rest. But such a change of emphasis by the United States would have meant too radical a departure from the established American policy of carefully catering to its strategic interests in the Arab world.

Ben-Gurion retired permanently to Sdeh Boker, a kibbutz in the Negev desert, in the summer of 1963, a man exhausted by the struggles and intricacies of Israel's internal politics, but also a prophet of rage who remained convinced to his last day that Israel's physical existence could not be taken for granted. To him the Jewish state, notwithstanding its qualitative military edge, remained under immanent and imminent threat of extinction.

Israel's security doctrine as it developed following the Sinai Campaign, where Israel was forced by international pressure to relinquish conquered territories, was essentially one of deterrence and the prevention of war. The acquisition of new territories was no longer a strategic objective for it became a standing invitation to international pressure. The Six Day War into which Israel was dragged by the hyperactivism of her army and the subsequent occupation of new lands was therefore, as General Rabin himself admitted when he said that 'I got Israel into trouble because of a number of mistakes I committed', a strategic failure. The army's over-reaction to real or imaginary threats, and especially its reprisals against the Syrians in the years preceding the war, went far beyond the intentions of the government. Moreover, the army itself never intended to escalate the conflict and turn it into an all-out war. It simply blundered by producing strategic responses to tactical challenges. The Samu operation in Jordan, and the use of the Air Force against the Syrians in April 1967 as a reprisal for terrorist incursions into Israeli territory, escalated the conflict beyond what anyone in Israel, including the army, wanted. The civilian government failed, not for the first or last time, in exercising proper control over the armed forces. The stunning victory of 1967 should not obscure the fact that the IDF failed to achieve the real strategic objectives inherent in its own security doctrine, namely the prevention of war and the defence of the status quo. In their assessment that Nasser would not ultimately go to war, Israel's Intelligence services gave the army too wide a manoeuvring space in its policy of reprisals on the Syrian front, thus allowing the delicate line separating deterrence from escalation and total war to be crossed. The army got the nation 'into trouble', to use Rabin's expression, and Israel went into a war it never wanted to wage, and it occupied territories that were not included in any pre-planned 'war objectives'.

It was a paradox or an irony of history that the change at the head of Israel's government from the apocalyptic and fatalistic style and policies of the prophet of rage that was Ben-Gurion, to the more conciliatory approach of the good-humoured, warm-hearted Levi Eshkol eventually signalled the beginning of the countdown to the 1967 war.

To be sure, neither Eshkol nor his Chief of Staff, General Yitzhak Rabin, was a warmonger. Both shared the view that Israel needed no additional territories and could fulfil all the objectives of Zionism within the 1949 boundaries. Moreover, although he did not altogether freeze the Dimona reactor, Eshkol clearly departed, to Ben-Gurion's dismay, from the old man's hyperactive nuclear policy in favour of a more conventional emphasis. And it was precisely this calculated shift that enabled Eshkol to reach a qualitative improvement in relations with America. The first Israeli prime minister to be officially invited to the White House, Eshkol received a historic commitment from President Johnson to the territorial integrity of Israel and secured an additional conventional arms supply from America. The new Prime Minister was also able to establish, for a while, peaceful neighbourly relations with King Hussein, to the degree that the latter even agreed to depart from the Arab position and acquiesce with Israel's plan of diverting water from the Lake of Galilee to the Negev desert through a National Water Carrier, the construction of which had started as early as 1959.

But Israel nevertheless contributed to the logic of war. The slide to war was enhanced by her almost inbred incapacity to resist the temptation of the use of force, and by the inability of her military intelligence to appreciate the nuances in Nasser's position, that is, his difficult strategy of striking a balance between rhetoric and intentions. The Water War in the north left the Israeli military establishment with the impression that a general war was only a matter of 'when', not 'if'. The conventional wisdom in Israel's military establishment was that only by asserting her military deterrence could she still avert a general war.

But not unlike the case of the descent to war in 1956, the coming of the Six Day War was, if anything, precipitated by Israel's assertion of her military deterrence and by her frequently disproportionate policy of retaliation. In an amazing interview given by Moshe Dayan to Rami Tal of *Yedioth Aharonoth* in 1976, he made the stunning confession that at least 80 per cent of the clashes with the Syrians in the years that preceded the 1967 war were initiated by Israel. The IDF clearly provoked the Syrians into confrontations in order to change unilaterally the status of the demilitarised zones, teach the Syrians a lesson and humiliate their regime, as in the dogfight over Damascus in April 1967 that ended with the loss of six Syrian MiG aircraft. Dayan was candid enough to admit in that interview that 'the operations and the actions of Israel increased the fear among the Arabs' and enhanced the chances of war. The humiliation that Israel dealt to the Syrian regime by frequently flying her aircraft over Damascus was a trigger to further escalation.

Nor was Jordan spared Israel's policy of swift and disproportionate retaliations. Such was the case of the Samu Operation in November 1966. After insistently pointing at Damascus as the source of all evil, Israel suddenly and massively retaliated against Jordan in response to a local, relatively minor incident. A typical case of the feebleness of the politicians when confronted with the army's tendency to dictate the scope and nature of military operations in a way that sometimes created new and unplanned political realities, Samu was a disproportionate operation that stood in stark contradiction to Israel's official commitment to the stability of Hussein's regime. Israel publicly humiliated and betrayed an Arab leader so far careful to stay aloof from the war rhetoric and practices of his Syrian neighbours in the north, and pushed him into the fold of the Arab war camp. The King could not but interpret Samu as the genuine reflection of Israel's persistent dream of completing the task started in 1948 and occupying the whole of the West Bank down to the River Jordan.

The Arab–Israeli truce was too precarious to resist a lurch to war that was being quickened by mutual misperceptions, exaggerated fears, overreactions to real or presumed threats and the rhetoric of war, even when it was only that, rhetoric. The resurgence of the Palestinians' struggle against Israel under the guidance and support of the Arab states created, as always, a fertile ground upon which the rhetoric of war flourished and sabre-rattling overflowed. The Arab League summit of January 1964 in Cairo went down in history as the first official all-Arab gathering to call for Arab military preparations in order to create the conditions 'for the final liquidation of Israel'. The decision to divert the headwaters of the River Jordan in Syria and Lebanon – a United Arab Command was created to protect the project and prepare for war – and create the Palestinian Liberation Organisation under Ahmad al-Shuqayri's chairmanship were understandably perceived in Israel as part of an overall Arab war strategy against the Jewish state. The task of liberating Palestine from 'Zionist imperialism' was reiterated in the Alexandria Arab League summit later that winter, and pledges were made by the League's members to mobilise their resources against the Zionist enemy.

Regardless of whether or not the Arabs were capable of defeating Israel or, indeed, if they were actually ready to mobilise their resources for an all-out war in an operational way, became almost secondary to the perception that developed in Israel that the Arab–Israeli conflict had now entered an entirely different phase. To Israel, the decisions taken by the Arab League in Cairo and Alexandria could no longer be dismissed as traditional, shallow, nationalist rhetoric. Nor could she allow the Syrians to win the war for the water in the north. By carrying water from the Lake of Galilee to the Negev, Israel was not infringing any water rights of her Arab neighbours, and the Arab decision to divert the sources of the River Jordan was legitimately interpreted by her as an act of war. Eshkol, in the past a director general of Israel's national water company Mekorot, for whom water was a vital pillar of the Zionist pioneering ethos, could not afford to lose that particular war. Israel mercilessly thwarted the Arab efforts. Water was a nationalistic totem in Zionism and the Arabs knew it.

But the truth of the matter was that the Arab admission, at the Casablanca Arab League summit in September 1965, of defeat in the Water War, and Nasser's insistence that the attempts to divert the River Jordan be interrupted, meant that Egypt recognised that the Arabs were not yet ready for war and he badly wanted to prevent an escalation to an all-out war with Israel.

War oratory and summit resolutions laying the ground for war preparations were, paradoxically, as far as Nasser was concerned, an attempt to prevent the slide to war rather than hasten it. Nasser's war rhetoric concealed a hidden agenda. The Cairo Summit was to him the ideal all-Arab platform against Israel that could allow him to extricate his army from the quagmire of Yemen without losing face. His was the strategy of a rope dancer trying to strike an impossible balance between his pan-Arab warlike policies and his refusal to be dragged to war with Israel. He had made clear, in a public speech in Port Said on the eve of the Cairo Summit, that he did not want war. 'For', he said, 'I would lead you to disaster if I were to proclaim that I would fight at a time when I was unable to do so. I would not lead my country to disaster and would not gamble with its destiny.'

Nasser's exercise in strategic jugglery was astonishing indeed. As late as 1966 he still toyed, even if tactically, with the possibility of reaching a settlement of sorts with Israel. He allowed Egypt's Head of Non-Conventional Weapons Projects, General Azm al-Din Mahmud Khalil, to conduct negotiations in Paris with the head of the Israeli Mossad, General Amit, on a reduction of tension between the two countries. General Amit was even invited to Cairo for that purpose, a visit that Prime Minister Eshkol eventually thwarted, either out of fear for General Amit's life or because he was suspicious of Nasser's intentions. There was nothing sinister about those. Essentially, they were the same that he had tried to advance in his contacts with Ben-Gurion, namely, to reduce the tension with Israel in exchange for American economic assistance to Egypt. Nor is it at all clear that the Egyptian–Syrian defence treaty of November 1966 was Nasser's way of encouraging the Syrians in their war policy. The opposite might be true. The Egyptian *rais* might have believed that such a treaty would calm Syria's fears of Israel and divert its energies away from the dynamic leading to confrontation.

But the tragic logic of the Arab–Israeli conflict was frequently one of misperceptions, almost invariably fed by the irresistible penchant of the leaders for a warlike rhetoric even when their real intentions might have been more benign. This was always the dilemma and the paradox of Arab politics: how would the leaders reconcile their proclaimed intention to do away with the Jewish state with their fear and respect for its military power? How to placate and control the 'Arab street', which the leaders had incited with bellicose language against Israel, without actually going to war against her? How to vindicate their support for the 'liberation of Palestine' for which they created the PLO and allowed their countries to become the springboard for Fatah operations against Israel, yet resist being manipulated into war by the Palestinians? Arab leaders managed to manoeuvre themselves into an insoluble conundrum, a trap of their own making.

King Hussein's predicament proved to be even more serious than that of Nasser. In his case it was the very existence of his kingdom that was at stake. He did not want to be dragged into war, but was too weak to resist the tide. As much as the supposed threat posed by Israel, it was actually the pressure of Fatah and the PLO that put in jeopardy the stability of the Hashemite kingdom. For the PLO, liberating Palestine also meant overthrowing the Hashemites' 'colonialist rule'. The King harboured no illusions as to the ultimate rationale of the PLO's presence in Jordan, namely, as he explicitly wrote to Nasser, 'the destruction of Jordan'. Caught between the pressure of the Arab states, especially that of his northern neighbour Syria, and the challenge to the stability of his regime posed by the Palestinians, war was for Hussein almost the only outlet from an agonising dilemma. If Israel did not destroy him, he gathered, his Arab 'brothers' would.

The paradox of Arab policy could not be sustained for long. The Arab League summits created instruments of war – in January 1965 the Fatah, with active Syrian backing, launched its first attack against the National Water Carrier – and unleashed a virulent propaganda campaign against Israel without being especially enthusiastic about actually going to war. Egypt and Jordan were clearly unwilling to be dragged in by Fatah's provocations and refrained from any active support for the PLO in its war against Israel. Admittedly, this was clearly not the case with Syria, especially after the Ba'ath Party seized power in Damascus in February 1966. A popular war for the liberation of Palestine, an active encouragement for Fatah's incursions into Israeli territory and an attempt to turn, against Nasser's intentions, the United Arab Command into an instrument of war against Israel – this was now the official policy in Damascus. Zionism and imperialism were perceived as the twin brothers that had conspired to dispossess the Arab nation. It was a question of identity for the Ba'ath regime to focus its struggle against both. The liberation of Palestine became the main axis of Syria's domestic, regional and international policies. The plight of the Palestinians was born out of the sins of these two satanic enemies of Arab nationalism: Zionism and imperialism. The struggle against both was the very *raison d'être* of the Ba'ath regime. Syria's warlike rhetoric and its active support for Fatah units operating from its territory against Israel were vital defining elements for the new regime in Damascus. Israel's threats of retaliation could not change or abate Syria's twin commitments to fight 'Zionism' and 'imperialism', especially when from 1966 the Soviet Union, in a cynical drive to take positions in the region while the United States was presumably bogged down in Vietnam, started actively to encourage the warlike policies of her clients in Damascus.

When it came to Syria, the Israelis were not free from complexes either. Eshkol's aide-de-camp, General Lior, noted that Rabin's threat stemmed from what he called the 'Syrian syndrome', the obsession of the

IDF and its chief commander with the Syrian enemy and their tendency to overreact to the Syrian threat. The present author can bear witness to the fact that any young Israeli soldier who served in a crack unit along Israel's northern front in those days was subjected to a persistent indoctrination as to the Syrian threat. One day, we knew, what was then called the 'Syrian Heights' would have to be taken over.

Recently published documents provide abundant confirmation that in the years before 1967 Yitzhak Rabin intentionally led Israel into a war with Syria.[1] Rabin was determined to provoke a war with Syria not because he wanted to acquire additional territories for Israel – 'the problem is not to conquer but to hold', he said in August 1966 – but because he thought that this was the only way to stop the Syrians from actively supporting Fatah attacks against Israel. As a professional soldier he knew that it was easier to deal with a regular army like the Syrian than a guerrilla war. 'To defeat [guerrillas] is one of the most difficult military problems,' he admitted to his officers in October 1965. Rabin magnified the effect of the Palestinian attacks on Israel, turning what was essentially a tactical nuisance into a strategic challenge. Fatah, he told the General Staff, 'could be the match that will set the big fire alight'.

And when retaliations and verbal threats failed to deter the Syrians, Rabin made it clear that his intention was to provoke the Syrians into an all-out war. In December 1966 he wrote to General Zvi Zamir, Israel's military attaché in London: 'an escalation with Syria is not against Israel's interest, and in my view there is no better time than now for a confrontation with Syria. I prefer to go to war rather than allow this continuous harassment, especially if the Syrians persist in their efforts to facilitate the activity of Fatah on our border.'

Rabin believed, wrongly as it turned out, that Syria could be deterred and its regime even toppled under the pressure of Israel's threats and show of force. Another miscalculation was his assumption that the Ba'ath regime would fail in its attempt to enlist Egypt's support for a war against Israel. But Syria was adamant and unyielding. Its Prime Minister, Yusuf Zuayyin, responded to Rabin's public call for war with a defiant attitude. 'We are not resigned to holding back the Palestinian revolution,' he said. And in order not to leave any doubt, he added that Syria will 'set the area afire, and any Israeli movement will result in a final grave for Israel'.

Instead of curbing the enthusiasm of his Arab allies for war, Nasser was dragged by them to a fatal showdown with Israel. It was the Syrians who successfully lured Egypt into a trap and Nasser to his downfall.

---

[1] Yemimah Rosenthal (ed.), *Yitzhak Rabin, Prime Minister of Israel. A Selection of Documents from His Life*, Jerusalem, 2005.

Jordan's dilemma was an additional burden on Nasser's conscience. Following the Samu Operation, Radio Amman ridiculed Nasser for his 'empty rhetoric' of Arab solidarity against Israel, while Jordan was left alone to bear the brunt of Israel's military might. Eventually, as Moshe Dayan himself explained, the nature and scale of Israel's reprisals against Syria and Jordan posed a very serious challenge to Nasser's leadership position in the Arab world. Unwilling as he certainly was to be dragged to war, he could not afford to neglect the defence of his image and prestige in his own country and throughout the Arab world. The 'train of escalation in the entire Arab region', as Dayan put it, left Nasser no option but to lead the anti-Israeli tide with the hope that he could control it and tame it when necessary. It turned out, however, that this was like riding on the back of a tiger.

Jews and Arabs have a special reverence for the past. But they are also fatally trapped in its lies. The Arabs' struggle against the Crusaders, as embodied in the mythical figure of Saladin, was not just an important chapter in Arab history but, as Professor Emmanuel Sivan has shown, a fundamental source through which Egypt's modern national consciousness, and its role within the wider Arab nationalism, was shaped. The largest and most powerful Arab country, Egypt was bound and destined to assume a leadership position in the struggle against the contemporary reincarnation of the Crusaders, the Western imperialists and their Zionist clients. Saladin was adopted in Egypt as 'the hero of the Egyptian Jihad'.

This pan-Arab, Nasserite ethos that drew its inspiration and historical legitimacy from Saladin's exploits received an extraordinary boost in Egypt's official propaganda in the aftermath of the Sinai Campaign precisely because a parallel could be drawn between Saladin's days and the present. In both cases a sinister coalition of Zionists and imperialists, the modern Crusaders, as it were, joined forces in order to invade and possess Arab lands. The very profile of Israel further enhanced her image as a Crusader state in the Arab perception. It was a state that relied on religious claims, it consisted of immigrants from Europe, it was conceived and built on ethnic and religious precepts, and its artificial existence was being sustained by a combination of external support and technological superiority. But, also like the old Crusader state, Israel had major weaknesses that doomed it to perdition: a lack of internal cohesion given its ethnic diversity, and a tiny, strategically vulnerable space that would not stand a massive Arab onslaught.

'Almalek Alnasser' ('The Redeeming Ruler'), Saladin's official title, was probably a welcome coincidence for the millions in Egypt and throughout the Arab world who viewed Gamal Abdel Nasser as a modern reincarnation of the mythical hero of Muslim history who defeated the Crusaders and liberated Jerusalem. The popular yearning for a modern Saladin could be understood, as was explained by an Egyptian biographer of the hero of the battle of Hitin published in the aftermath of Egypt's defeat in the Sinai Campaign, because the conditions of Saladin's rise were similar to those now faced by the Arab world. Then, as now, the deep divisions within the Arab family served to facilitate the penetration of the European imperialists, and paved their way to grab and occupy Arab lands. And, as then with Saladin, so luckily now in the figure of Gamal Abdel Nasser, the sacred historic mission of repelling the invaders and redeeming the dignity of the Arab peoples had found the right, providential leader to execute it.

Providential perhaps, but trapped in his own contradictions nonetheless. Gamal Abdel Nasser was the victim of the nationalist hysteria he himself had unleashed throughout the Arab world. A modern Saladin who came to redeem the honour of the Arabs trampled underfoot by the contemporary successors of the Crusaders, he could not stem the tide of war that was the natural consequence of his very style of leadership and of the expectations of the Arab masses he himself had nourished. Instead, he was condemned to surf to his downfall on the waves of his own popularity. Like a cyclist who must keep pedalling in order to maintain his balance, Nasser had to feed daily the enthusiasm of the masses if he was to survive politically. Not only were his image as a Messianic saviour and his pride being challenged by Israel's disproportionate reprisals against his Arab brothers, the Syrians and Jordanians, but the stability and perhaps the very existence of his regime were also at stake. He came to face the challenge posed by Israel as a frustrated dictator who had failed in his Yemen adventure, and his entire shift of strategy to the Israeli–Palestinian situation was in the first place a device to distract public attention from his failures in Yemen, and from the troubled domestic front where the revolution was not exactly delivering. How could he now afford to keep still while his Arab allies were being punished by Israel for supporting the Palestinian resistance and their official media was ridiculing him as a coward?

Nasser's deputy, Field Marshal Abd al-Hakim Amer, was neither a brilliant strategist nor a field commander of any weight. But Nasser seemed to have had a soft spot for a man whom General Gamassi, the architect of Egypt's successes in the Yom Kippur War, dismissed in 1978 in a conversation with Israel's Defence Minister Ezer Weizmann as an incompetent captain who had been promoted to general without any qualifications whatsoever. Amer's was the idea that the way out of Nasser's predicament was through the removal of the UN forces (UNEF) from Sinai, the massive deployment of the Egyptian army in the peninsula, and the closure of the Straits of Tiran to Israeli maritime traffic. By not resisting his deputy's unrealistic assumptions about the capacity of his army effectively to challenge the IDF, impose Egypt's political conditions, and 'force Israel to respect Arab and Palestinian rights', as he himself put it, Nasser offered the Israelis a *casus belli* on a silver platter.

Anwar Sadat quoted Nasser in his autobiography as saying that closing the Straits meant that 'war will be 100 per cent certain'. But up to the very eve of the war Nasser hoped he could avert it and win politically, without having to fight. In what looked more like a move of political blackmail his forces poured into Sinai without clear strategic objectives or precise tactical missions. General Rabin himself admitted that all this was nothing but 'a demonstrative move'. Egypt was definitely not ready for war and Nasser did not want a war. 'He wanted victory without a war,' as Abba Eban preferred to put it. He allowed himself to be caught in the dynamic of war not because he believed, unlike Amer, that Egypt could win, but because he knew his regime would not survive the pressure of Arab opinion if he failed to lead and if he persisted in resisting the calls from Syria for a common front against Israel. And when it nevertheless became clear, as indeed none other than the Egyptian Chief of Staff, General Fawzi, acknowledged, that, contrary to Syria's and the Soviet Union's allegations, Israel had concentrated no forces on the Syrian border and Damascus was not under imminent threat of attack, Nasser could not withdraw his army from Sinai without losing face. He might even have been tempted to believe that the fact that Syria was not under immediate threat meant that he could get away with his bravado and consolidate his leadership of the Arab world without paying the price of war. But Nasser was the hostage of the military adventurism of the Syrians and in Syria it was the very identity of the regime that was at stake.

Unlike the Syrian Ba'ath or Nasser's brand of popular nationalism, the essentially conservative Hashemite monarchy was not founded on social mobilisation or nationalist hysteria. Hence war and conflict for Jordan were not an inherent, built-in necessity for survival. But just as in the case of his grandfather Abdullah, who was forced to lead the Arab war coalition against Israel in 1948 in order to safeguard the legitimacy of his regime within the Arab family, so Hussein in 1967 was the hostage of the inherent weakness of a kingdom sandwiched between powerful radical Arab states and subject to accusations of betrayal from the Palestinians. For both, grandfather and grandson, the agonising dilemma was the same.

It was either to risk a war with Israel, with the possibility of a disgraceful defeat in which he would lose the West Bank, or to be crushed by Arab pressure and Palestinian subversion and lose his entire kingdom. In 1967 Hussein preferred the first option. In 1973, after he had already lost half his kingdom, he opted for the second alternative and stayed out of the Yom Kippur War.

The almost fatalistic convergence of all the actors in the region into a war nobody, except perhaps the Palestinians, really wanted was enhanced by the ambivalent position of the superpowers and, in the case of the Soviet Union, a position that was clearly irresponsible and adventurist. A regional conflagration with its possible global ricochets was probably not what the Soviets could have wanted. In fact, once Nasser closed the Straits of Tiran and war became a tangible possibility, the Soviets would awkwardly preach a diplomatic solution and try their best to dissuade Nasser from going to war. High tension, not necessarily war, even if fuelled by false alarms and distorted information about alleged massive Israeli forces deployed on the Northern Front, was clearly a Soviet objective. They believed that an opportunity was there to consolidate their alliance with the Arab world, especially with Syria, and replace America, now in any event bogged down in the quagmire of Vietnam, as the hegemonic power in the region.

In Israel the road to war was paved by a genuine existential fear, a legacy of the Ben-Gurion years, which always led to perceiving crises in apocalyptic terms and reacting only according to worst-case scenarios. For the military, however, the psychosis of annihilation was not the rationale for war. Rather, it was the fear that a diplomatic compromise or an American-led international fleet that would break the Egyptian blockade would shatter beyond redemption the IDF's deterrence and with it Israel's entire security doctrine, and consolidate the image of Israel as a nation at the mercy of the goodwill of the West.

That Israel finally opted for a pre-emptive strike also needs to be understood in the context of the built-in tension in the Israeli system between the 'Israeli' military and the 'Jewish' civilian power, with the former almost always having their way in dictating the nation's strategy and its response to evolving crises. On 12 May 1967 Chief of the General Staff Rabin openly called for a wide operation to overthrow the Ba'ath regime in Damascus, a threat that only fuelled the crisis and vindicated Soviet allegations about Israel's aggressive intentions. Prime Minister Eshkol was quick to reprimand his Chief of Staff for his bellicose rhetoric. Nor was the restless General spared Ben-Gurion's ire. From his seclusion in the Negev desert, the Old Man had been following the evolving crisis with awe. Precisely because he shared the military's assessment that the closure of the Straits threatened to vitiate all the achievements of the Sinai Campaign and could soon turn into a question of 'national survival' – this was Rabin's expression – Ben-Gurion saw all his old fears coming true: Israel was now surrounded by an all-Arab coalition aggressively supported by the Soviet Union, without being able to rely on an alliance with, or security guarantees from, a Western superpower. Ben-Gurion accused both Eshkol and Rabin of this ominous strategic blunder.

Eshkol's was the voice of wisdom and prudence that was desperately running out of arguments. He valiantly resisted the army's call for war almost against all odds. That neither the British nor Israel's French allies were more forthcoming than the Americans only increased his anguish. He saw how the West turned its back on Israel, refused to deter the Arabs on her behalf and left her alone to face an agonising dilemma: capitulation or a war that he, Eshkol, unlike his generals, did not want.

In the crisis of the summer of 1967 Eshkol faced an army command whose arguments for war were becoming increasingly convincing. The government's reluctance to launch a pre-emptive strike while the West was turning its back on an embattled Israel simply vitiated the argument about Egypt's inability to win a war. For Nasser's potential victory lay not in the capacity of his army to prevail on the battlefield, but in the bankruptcy of Israel's deterrence as a regional superpower, should the Egyptian *rais* be allowed to get away with his act of strategic blackmail. The patience of the generals exploded when even after the government had heard Abba Eban's report of the non-committal position of the Americans, it still decided to give diplomacy yet another chance and ordered the release of 40,000 reservists. Even Eshkol's loyal aide-de-camp, General Lior, could no longer understand the embarrassing lack of resolve of his Prime Minister.

The heroic insistence of Eshkol and the doves in his government on giving diplomacy a chance was becoming desperately indefensible. The army's position and the case for war were clearly enhanced by the frustrations that accompanied the diplomatic option. De Gaulle was now about to formulate a new policy for France in an attempt to heal the wounds of the war in Algeria and build bridges with the Arab world, and he would not let the 'arrogant' and trigger-happy Israelis spoil his strategic shift. The British were ready to participate in an international convoy that would open the Straits for Israel, but they waited for America's leadership. And America wavered. She was not ready to provide any guarantees or commitments. Nor was her half-hearted attempt to put together an international convoy especially successful. Israel's almost hysterical appeal to the United States to declare that any attack on Israel was equivalent to an attack on the US was met by what Abba Eban defined, after his meeting with Lyndon Johnson, as the 'rhetoric of impotence' of 'a paralysed president', paralysed probably also by his mounting troubles in the Vietnam quagmire. For all practical purposes, the political achievements of the Sinai Campaign lay in shambles.

What divided the Israeli elite in its response to the rapidly evolving crisis was not just the old traditional rift between the military and the civilians. A deep cultural and political cleavage surfaced between the young, Israeli-born generals, all self-confident, bold, proud of the formidable military machine under their command, and contemptuous of the 'Galuthic' and 'submissive' ways of the older generation on the one hand, and the diaspora-born politicians who, haunted by Holocaust memories and fearful of international isolation, resisted having to depart from the old politics of diplomatic Zionism on the other. 'It is very difficult to create a state, but very easy to lose it' was the response of Minister of Finance Pinhas Sapir to the generals' impatient call for war. 'I am prepared to fight but not to commit suicide,' said Haim Moshe Shapira, the leader of the National Religious Party. The radical transformation of this party from a conservative position before the war, to the politics of Messianism as the party of the settlers in Judaea and Samaria after the war, tells a great deal of the story about the meaning of the Six Day War in the life and politics of Israel.

Whether a military *coup d'état* was then a real probability is highly doubtful, but the possibility was nevertheless being aired in open discussions between the generals, as General Ariel Sharon was later candid enough to admit. Dr Ami Gluska revealed in his book, *Eshkol, Give the Order!,*[1] that on two occasions (28 May and 2 June) Sharon suggested to Rabin the possibility of, as he said, 'locking up the members of the government in an adjacent room' and 'seizing power in order to make a decision to go to war'. This was a step, he said to the Chief of Staff, that 'the army can take without the government'. Rabin apparently took Sharon's wild suggestion as simply the expression of anxiety and did not think for a moment that it was a proposal for concrete action. But of one thing there can be no doubt, as Sharon himself confessed in his candid revelations to the history department of the army: this was 'the first time that a situation emerged where such a thing [a *coup d'état*] can happen, and will be well received [by the public]'.

Eshkol's was the voice of caution and diplomatic serenity that was overwhelmed by the fever of war in times of mounting public hysteria. He did not give in easily, however. His response to the restless generals in a meeting at the war headquarters on 27 May, as recorded by his aide-

---

[1] (Hebrew) Tel Aviv, 2004.

de-camp, should go down in history as a remarkably courageous expression of a different political philosophy from that of the army:

> Nobody ever said that we are an army for preventive war.... I do not accept that the mere fact that the Egyptian army is deployed in Sinai makes war inevitable.... We are not alone in the world. The very term 'deterrence' calls for patience.... I know this enrages those of you who were brought up all their life on concepts of attack and war. But we spoke of deterrence, and deterrence doesn't necessarily require action. ... I never imagined that if an Egyptian army is deployed near our border this inevitably means that we must wake up in the middle of the night and destroy it.... Are we going to live all our lives by the sword? ... You wanted a hundred more aircraft? You got it. You also received the tanks you asked for. You received everything that is needed to win a war if a war becomes necessary. You did not receive all these weapons in order for you to say that now that we are ready and well equipped to destroy the Egyptian army, we must do it....

In reality, Eshkol's response to the Egyptian threat was the voice of reason and sober statesmanship in front of an army that had lost its nerve. It was the government, not the army, that showed courage and exhibited iron nerves while resisting the enormous strategic pressure on Israel. It was Eshkol's insistence on exhausting all diplomatic possibilities that eventually prevented Israel's surprise attack being seen by the international community, especially the United States, as sheer aggression, and made it a legitimate war of self-defence. The generals claimed to have lost their trust in the government. But how did they expect the politicians to trust *them* after the intelligence services had so colossally failed to predict Nasser's moves and intentions, their Commander-in-Chief, Yitzhak Rabin, had physically collapsed under the weight of pressure and lay in bed for almost two days, and they had all been exhibiting since the beginning of the crisis behaviour that can only be defined as hysterical, for they kept changing their war plans every day?

Moshe Sharett in the 1950s and Levi Eshkol in the 1960s were tragic anti-heroes, the champions of moderation in an era of militaristic excitement and in a political environment never too friendly to ideas of appeasement and to the politics of restraint. At the end of the day, the moderates proved to be prophets without honour for, eventually, Israel's shift from war to peace would not depend on them. It would be the result of a change of attitude by the hawks, Menachem Begin, Moshe Dayan, Ezer Weizmann and Yitzhak Rabin. It was only when the latter reached the conclusion that the price of immobilism was higher than the sacrifices required for peace that the road was paved for an accommodation with Egypt in 1979 and with the Palestinians in 1993. But – and this also needs to be affirmed – in every case where peace breakthroughs were made by the hawks and the strong men – the peace with Egypt and the Oslo accords with the Palestinians – it was not as a result of their initiative, or because they had a sudden divine revelation urging them to make peace, but as a compelling response to an Arab strategic move. Without the Yom Kippur War, an essentially Clausewitzian war with a political purpose initiated by President Sadat, Begin and Dayan would never have come to terms with the imperative of total withdrawal from Sinai and the peace with Egypt would not have occurred. Nor would Yitzhak Rabin, the oppressor of the Intifada as Minister of Defence in Shamir's Cabinet, have made his radical shift from war to peace if it were not for the effects of the Gulf War on the morale of the nation, and his own realisation that the Intifada, the Palestinians' Yom Kippur War, could not be quelled by military means.

The real *coup d'état* was finally staged by the Israeli civil elites, not by the generals. Powerful political and social forces joined the chorus of protest against a government that was now being presented by most of the press as utterly inadequate to lead the nation in these times of trial. General Moshe Dayan's political friends in RAFI, the splinter party created by Ben-Gurion in the early 1960s, continued to harass Eshkol's government throughout the crisis leading up to the war. Acting as the main spokesman of RAFI, Shimon Peres adopted typically paradoxical positions. He castigated Eshkol for his weakness when faced with the Egyptian threat, but at the same time he warned against going to war, and was the prime mover in the attempt to replace Eshkol with Ben-Gurion. The Prime Minister was rapidly losing his legitimacy as the leader of the embattled nation at a time when the public sense was of an approaching holocaust. Hysterical public opinion and the mounting pressure by the media and the upper classes combined to break Eshkol's resistance. The public call for a government reshuffle with Moshe Dayan, the hero of the Sinai Campaign, as the new Minister of Defence, was irresistible. The liberal *Haaretz* echoed the people's voice, but especially the mounting discontent and agitation among the social elites, when it wrote on 29 May that 'Eshkol should make way for a new leadership'. And, in what General Lior defined as 'a mini *coup d'état*', on 1 June 1967 Moshe Dayan joined the newly formed National Unity government with Menachem Begin and his right-wing Herut Party for the first time in a coalition with their bitter rivals from Mapai. The die was cast. The strategic decision to go to war was now a reality. The timing was just a tactical question to be decided by Dayan and the army.

True, at the end of May a last attempt at international mediation was made by both the UN's Secretary General and the Americans. Nasser was not negative and he presumably did not reject the idea of 'a breathing space' in which 'peaceful traffic' would be allowed in the Straits. He was ready to send his deputy to Washington to discuss such an avenue to a possible compromise. The American Secretary of State, Dean Rusk, would later write in his memoirs that 'we had a good chance to de-escalate the crisis'. Whether an agreement could eventually have been reached is nevertheless extremely doubtful. What was certain was that Dayan's appointment and Israel's irrevocable decision to strike cut short this last-minute peace overture.

At such a late stage in the crisis Israel's most fundamental defence doctrine did not allow room for a diplomatic initiative. Her deterrence was already seriously undermined and an agreement reached through mediation or arbitration would not have redeemed it. For Israel to opt for such a solution would have been an inconceivable departure from her security philosophy and practices as they had developed ever since the 1930s. Israel, as Dayan had put it in his elegy to Roi Rutenberg in April 1956, must always be 'strong and resolute, or else our sword will slip from our hand and the thread of our lives will be severed'. The doctrine was one of offensive defence and Dayan was now there as Defence Minister to implement it.

War and peace in the Middle East, however, could never be dissociated from superpower politics. Interestingly, Egypt's dilemma in 1967 resembled Israel's predicament in 1973. Just as Israel considered striking first in the hours that preceded the Egyptian onslaught on the Bar-Lev Line in 1973, the possibility of Egypt launching a pre-emptive strike against Israel was seriously contemplated by the Egyptians once Nasser unleashed, through the closing of the Straits, the tide of war. In both cases the pre-emptive move was discarded because of the fear of losing the support of the friendly superpower. Golda Meir feared that America would not come to Israel's rescue if she struck first; and Nasser was explicitly warned in 1967 by Prime Minister Alexei Kosygin, through Egypt's Minister of War Shams el-din Badran on a visit to Moscow, that 'We, the Soviet Union, cannot give our consent for your pre-emptive strikes against Israel. ... Should you be the first to strike, you will be the aggressors ... we cannot support you.'

The Soviet intention throughout the crisis was to intimidate rather than to kindle the fire. In the war of nerves between the United States and the Soviet Union in the days leading to war, the Soviets were the first to blink. If the State Department was engaged in a last-ditch attempt to produce a diplomatic solution, the White House was not. It moved in the first days of June to a position that Israel could safely interpret as a green light to a pre-emptive strike. The President lost any hope of a diplomatic solution and confessed he was unable to put together the international convoy. Meir Amit, the head of the Mossad, who was sent in the first days of June to bring home to the Americans Israel's call for arms, diplomatic support and the need for them to neutralise the Soviet threat to Israel in case of war, came back convinced that a change of attitude had taken place in Washington. At no time was he warned by his hosts against starting an attack.

Amit's report to the Cabinet on the American position and the news of the imminent deployment of Iraqi forces in Jordan completely disarmed the opponents of war in the government. Wisely, Prime Minister Eshkol still remarked that 'nothing will be settled by military victory. The Arabs will still be here.' But the die was cast. The biggest offensive in the history of the Middle East was unleashed in the early hours of 5 June 1967.

The immediate reasons that led to war can be detected in the chain of events as they developed from the moment that Nasser decided to deploy his army in Sinai in clear violation of the spirit of the post-1956 settlement. But on a deeper level the entire crisis was fed and fuelled by perceptions and fears, by Israel's concern for her military hegemony as the basis of her existence in the midst of a hostile Arab world and by irrational Arab military moves, the reflection of the tragic gap in Arab behaviour between rhetoric and practice, between dreams and reality.

On the Israeli side, though always complaining of the backwardness of Arab societies as being the reason for their incapacity to make peace with Israel, there also existed a deep, and never really fully acknowledged, undercurrent of satisfaction at this state of affairs, and hence a hidden apprehension prevailed at the possibility that the Arab world might be reformed and modernised. The Israeli leaders, who in the aftermath of 1948 dismissed peace overtures on the grounds that the Arab leaders were corrupt, illegitimate rulers who could not be taken seriously, were equally suspicious of popular would-be reformers of the calibre of Gamal Abdel Nasser, even when he was ready to engage in peace moves, admittedly always hesitant and ambiguous. On the eve of the Sinai Campaign, Ben-Gurion was candid enough to confess to his diary that:

I always feared that a personality might arise such as arose among the Arab rulers in the 7th century or like [Kemal Ataturk] who arose in Turkey after its defeat in the First World War. He raised their spirits, changed their character, and turned them into a fighting nation. There was and still is a danger that Nasser is this man.

The Sinai Campaign was not unrelated to this Israeli instinct, shared at the time by both France and Britain, to curtail the life of a popular nationalist regime bent on recovering 'Arab dignity' by confronting what in the Arab perception were the twin threats of Zionism and imperialism. In 1956 as well as in 1967, Nasser threatened Israel's military supremacy, hence, according to the prevailing military doctrine, her very existence. Should he be allowed to prevail and win a political profit for his aggressive moves, Israel could no longer intimidate her neighbours and would lose their respect in a way that was tantamount to losing her ability to survive in a region that rejected the very legitimacy of her existence. Muhammed Hassanin Haikal, Nasser's confidant, was not entirely wrong when he defined the 1967 crisis in the following terms:

[Egypt] succeeded for the first time, vis-à-vis Israel, in changing by force a fait accompli imposed on it by force. ... To Israel, this is the most dangerous aspect of the current situation: who can impose the accomplished fact and who possesses the power to safeguard it?

Israel's war aims were always an ambiguous matter, with the objectives almost invariably – such was clearly the case in 1948, 1967 and in Lebanon in 1982 – being dictated by the inner, evolving dynamic of the war, or autonomously by the generals, and sometimes even by field commanders on the ground. Initially, of course, the Six Day War was not about the acquisition of new territory; it was a defensive war Israel was forced to launch in order to break the siege imposed on her by a military alliance of three Arab armies. But recovering Israel's deterrence, destroying the Arab military machine that had reduced Israel to apocalyptic fears of annihilation, and perhaps even overthrowing radical regimes such as Nasser's in Egypt and the Ba'ath in Damascus, were reasonable, albeit not always acknowledged, war aims. The government, however, never set specific goals for the war. The objectives that developed from the military dynamic of war were later assumed by the politicians as faits accomplis. Practically all the initial premises upon which the politicians, including the Prime Minister and his Defence Minister, expected to conduct the war were made irrelevant by the commanders and by the natural logic of a war in which the enemy's collapse allowed Israel to acquire an empire almost by absence of mind.

The new empire was born also out of the confusion and the inconsistent behaviour of Israel's leaders, as clearly emerges from Michael Oren's invaluable narrative of the war. Moshe Dayan was a case in point. Surprisingly, he positioned himself throughout the war as a voice of reason and moderation, a brake on the military's activism. He initially warned that he would court-martial any officer who went as far as reaching the Suez Canal. He also did his best to avoid a war with Jordan and be caught up on two fronts. He likewise warned against the international repercussions of going into the Old City of Jerusalem, and did not conceal his fears at the possibility of direct Soviet involvement in the war should Israel take over the Golan Heights from Syria. Dayan's obsession with avoiding having to fight on what was now a third front and risk a clash with the Soviets was such that he even went to the extreme of proposing that the Israeli settlements in the Hulah Valley, whose continuous shelling by Syrian artillery was the presumed rationale of those who lobbied for taking over the Golan Heights, be moved miles away from the range of the Syrian artillery. Never before had a Zionist military leader dared utter such heretical proposals.

A man of contrasts and unresolved paradoxes, a war hero who was also the son of Zionist pioneers who settled the land to create political facts and define the borders of the Jewish Yishuv, Dayan now defended the case for not attacking Syria with the stunning argument that Israel could not tell the Syrians 'that their border should be moved just because we have set up settlements close to it'. He also defied another sacred Zionist idea by airing the suspicion, confessed in an interview with Rami Tal in *Yedioth Aharonoth* (published posthumously on 27 April 1997), that the settlers in the Hulah Valley had lobbied the government to take over the Golan Heights out of sheer agrarian hunger. They simply wanted to acquire more land in the Golan.

But in all these cases Dayan's typical ambiguity, his notorious lack of firm convictions and his frequent changes of mind on the one hand, and the logic of military expediency, not design, in front of an enemy whose lines collapsed with vertiginous rapidity on the other, defined the limits of Israel's territorial gains. In the east, Hussein should bear the responsibility for unleashing the irredentist drive of the Israelis in Judaea and Samaria – most, if not all, the architects of Israel's 1967 stunning victory were the military commanders of 1948, some of whom later referred to the West Bank as the 'unfinished business' of that war – for Israel did her utmost not to provoke the Legion and pleaded with the King, to no avail as it turned out, not to initiate an attack.

In the case of the Golan Heights, it was not only the collapse of the Syrian army and the powerful lobby of the settlers in the north that changed Dayan's mind. Here it was the Prime Minister who positioned himself as the driving force behind the offensive. A moderate who did his utmost to prevent the war, Levi Eshkol succumbed, like most of his ministers, to the lure of territorial expansion made possible by the rout of the Arab armies. A former director of Mekorot, Israel's water company, as well as a former minister of agriculture and development, Eshkol could not resist the opportunity of acquiring in the Golan Heights land and water for the Zionist project. Typically, Eshkol now saw the chance, at long last, of taking over the sources of the River Jordan in the Banias. 'Eshkol was eager to conquer the Golan Heights, and there was no way to dissuade him,' noted his aide-de-camp. But General Lior also pointed out the underlying motive behind the offensive in the north. It was again the notorious Syrian complex – 'the Syrian syndrome' as he called it – of the Israelis, especially of their army, that this most outspoken and staunch enemy of Israel should not go unpunished and 'parade in victory', as Eshkol put it in a Cabinet meeting, while Egypt, Jordan and even Iraq had been humbled.

The war in the north was an extremely dangerous exercise in brinkmanship. More than on any other front the Syrian Golan Heights put to the ultimate test the Soviet Union's commitment to the Arabs and the credibility of her strategic designs in the Middle East. On the Golan Heights Israel humiliated both the Syrians and their Soviet patrons, and the latter responded with brutal, unambiguous threats of military action. No clear-cut commitment by the United States was offered to Israel, but the Americans could not afford to allow the war to end because of a Soviet military threat. The movements of the Sixth Fleet in the eastern Mediterranean helped neutralise that threat, and the swift collapse of the Syrians allowed the superpowers to save face by shifting their rivalry and competition to the diplomatic arena.

A new Middle East emerged from Israel's breathtaking victory and the Arabs' abject defeat. At the price of half his kingdom and of Israel's annexation of the holy city of Jerusalem, Hussein had gained legitimacy in the Arab world and a new lease of life for his throne. The humiliated champion of pan-Arab nationalism, Nasser, had lost the Sinai peninsula with its strategic assets, as well as the control of the Suez Canal to Israel's overwhelming might.

A new empire was born in the Middle East with the flag of the Star of David being hoisted from the River Jordan in the east to the Mediterranean Sea in the west, from Kuneitra in the north, forty kilometres from the capital city of Damascus, to the Suez Canal in the south-west and Sharm el Sheikh in the far south. With 42,000 square miles conquered in a blitzkrieg, if ever there was one, in which the ratio of casualties between the parties was 25:1, Israel now controlled an area three and a half times its original size. The Arab armies, and indeed the Arab nation, lay defeated and crushed under the haughty feet of a Jewish superpower.

To the annals of serial catastrophes that had befallen the Arabs ever since the emergence of Zionism, in which the 1948 Palestinian Naqbah, the ruthless reprisals of the IDF throughout the 1950s and the rout of the Egyptian army in 1956 stood as sad landmarks, a new tragedy was now added. But in a typical exercise of denial, the Six Day War débâcle was described as a 'disaster', as 'God's will', or, according to the Big Lie theory invented by Nasser and Hussein, as the outcome of a concerted British–American attack on the Egyptian forces. In either case the Arab leaders and elites could not be expected to be accountable. The Arabs were not being defeated by the superior Jewish state, nor were the Israelis responsible for knocking out the entire Egyptian air force in a matter of hours. The idea of a sinister Anglo-American conspiracy with Israel was conceived to help mollify public opinion and preserve the stability of the defeated Arab regimes. Just as in 1956, Nasser managed again to reap a political victory from the jaws of military defeat. It would only be after the Arab armies had recovered their pride in the 1973 war, in large measure thanks to Israel's own sin of hubris and a disproportionate sense of superiority, that a more honest assessment of the meaning of 1967 would be allowed in the Arab world, especially in Egypt.

VI *Sedanlaghen* – The Sin of Hubris and its Punishment

We are awaiting the Arabs' phone call.... If anything bothers the Arabs, they know where to find us.

Moshe Dayan,
12 June 1967

The entire nation was exalted and many wept upon hearing the news of the capture of the Old City.... The sense of salvation and of direct participation of every soldier in the forging of the heart of Jewish history cracked the shell of hardness ... and released ... spiritual emotion ...

Yitzhak Rabin's address at the Hebrew University,
28 June 1967

... the principle that what has been taken by force cannot be regained by anything but force is a sound and correct principle in all circumstances ... this basis is clear and definite in UAR policy: no negotiations with Israel, no peace with Israel, no recognition of Israel, and no deals at the expense of Palestinian soil or the Palestinian people ...

Gamal Abdel Nasser, Cairo University,
23 July 1968

We have fought for the sake of peace.... Our enemy has persisted in his arrogance and stupidity not only over the past six years, but ... since the Zionist state usurped Palestine.... We might ask the Israeli leaders today: Where has the theory of Israeli security gone? ... I add, so they may hear in Israel: We are not advocators of annihilation, as they claim.... Our war was not for aggression, but against aggression.

Anwar Sadat,
16 October 1973

'We are awaiting the Arabs' phone call. We ourselves won't make a move. We are quite happy with the current situation. If anything bothers the Arabs, they know where to find us.' This was how Moshe Dayan haughtily and disdainfully spelled out, in an interview with the BBC on 12 June 1967, his understanding of Israel's victory in the Six Day War. It was an expression of hubris in victory for which Israel was to pay dearly. Her orgy of political drunkenness and military triumphalism blinded the eyes of her leaders from seeing the *real*, not the *Messianic*, opportunities that her lightning military exploits opened for her. The opportunity was missed to turn the tactical victory in war into a major strategic victory for Zionism that could have made the Six Day War into the last major war of the Arab–Israeli conflict, and an avenue to a settlement with at least part of the Arab world. The truth of the matter was that when the Arabs finally called, Israel's line was either busy, or there was no one on the Israeli side to pick up the phone.

The interval between the two wars – 1967 and the Yom Kippur War – emphasised once again a central feature of the Arab–Israeli conflict. Israel's military victories and the Arabs' humiliating defeat could never be the prelude to peace. Israel's siege mentality, her ever-suspicious attitude of the Arabs' final intentions, even when they lay defeated under her feet, her dreams of an improved territorial deal in search of total security, and her incapacity to resist this inbred proclivity towards a policy of faits accomplis, a legacy of the patterns of the Yishuv's struggle for land and immigration, clearly prevented the victory of 1967 from becoming a prelude to magnanimous creativity in peacemaking.

It took the recovery of Arab pride and a serious setback for Israel in 1973, as well as the national trauma and collective soul-searching that followed, to make the Israelis and their leaders ripe for compromise. But as frequently happens in history, ripeness as such is not sufficient. An Itzhak Shamir or a Golda Meir might have missed the unique rendezvous with history that was to be made possible after the Yom Kippur War. It was the combination of the conditions created by that war together with leaders of courage and vision – Menachem Begin, Anwar Sadat and Jimmy Carter – that made the difference.

The defeat of the Arab armies in 1967 was the prelude to a fundamental transformation of the Arab–Israeli conflict that was either misread or overlooked by Israel's leaders. As in the aftermath of 1948, a settlement through diplomatic means was put on the agenda once again. But unlike the early years, this time the settlement was being conceived by the Arab states on the basis of the very borders they had then rejected, those of 1948. 'Removing the traces of aggression' was an Arab policy no longer applied to Israel's conquests in 1948, but to the lands it occupied in the 1967 war. That for the first time new, auspicious premises for a possible Arab–Israeli peace were established was due, however, not only to the psychological impact of the war, but also to the gradual ascendancy of the United States to a hegemonic position in the region at the expense of the Soviet Union, whose weapons and military doctrine also lay defeated in the battlefields of the Sinai desert and the Golan Heights. But it was the Israeli side that proved desperately slow in seeing the real meaning of her military victory; namely, the surprising legitimacy it gave to the 1948 borders as the basis for a final settlement with her Arab neighbours.

The change in the structure of the conflict did not end there. The Six Day War proved to be the prelude to the vigorous reappearance of the Palestinian national movement as a major independent actor in the politics of the region. The Palestinians, the absentees of the last twenty years, now emerged from oblivion to make their voice sound louder and clearer than ever before. The collapse of the Arab armies and the eagerness of the Arab governments to recover their lost territories, preferably by diplomatic means, once again relegated the Palestinian problem to a secondary position in Arab strategy. This, in its turn, forced the Palestinians to assume full responsibility for their cause. The plight of the Palestinians would now come back to the fore. But this time the organisations representing them, which since the end of the Arab Revolt had been a tool controlled and manipulated by Arab governments, asserted their autonomy and developed their own independent strategy for the liberation of Palestine. An entirely new front for Israel to deal with – military as well as political – emerged in the form of a new assertive and combative PLO with a plethora of guerrilla and terrorist militias under its command.

To the Israelis the 1967 war brought both grandeur and moral and political decay. Israel's swift victory in the Six Day War changed not only the geo-strategic map of the Middle East and consequently the parameters of the Arab–Israeli conflict; it also transformed the national mood in Israel in a way that made peace an especially difficult endeavour. The nationalist intoxication reached dangerous heights to the degree that this 'mother of all victories' was now being interpreted as a Messianic, providential salvation. Caught up in the euphoria of the moment, a whole nation and its leaders lost touch with reality and fell in love with the new, unexpected real estate stretching from the River Jordan in the east to the Suez Canal in the south-west, from Mount Hermon in the north to Sharm el Sheikh in the south. The distinctions between past and present, between mythology and reality, history and nationalistic exaltation became so indistinct that even *Haaretz*, a supposedly enlightened newspaper which during the war had published 'recipes for victory cakes for the soldiers', wrote on 8 June 1967, the day Jerusalem was conquered by a brigade of paratroopers:

The glory of past ages no longer is to be seen at a distance but in, from now on, part of the new state, and its illumination will irradiate the constructive enterprise of a Jewish society that is a link in the long chain of the history of the people in its country ... Jerusalem is all ours. Rejoice and celebrate, O dweller in Zion!

Of all the new land it was, of course, Judaea and Samaria that particularly awakened the Messianic instincts in the Israeli mind. 'I didn't know that the fighting there would release such powerful emotions hidden inside me,' exclaimed a young fighter pilot while flying over Bethlehem, Hebron and Jericho. 'We are fighting', he said, 'on our historic homeland.'

If this was the age of Divine Redemption, as an influential school of politico-religious fundamentalists believed, then Eretz-Israel needed to be settled, certainly not negotiated away. The disciples of Rabbi Zvi Yehudah Kook in the religious Bnei Akiva youth movement, an offspring of the until very recently sober and temperate National Religious Party that would soon succumb to a fetishist infatuation with the new territories, used the name of a remote biblical era to start settling Judaea and Samaria through a policy of pre-emptive moves, that was, moreover, to be tolerated by Labour governments. The land had now become an idol that needed to be possessed and settled by force. In a stark rebellion against the long history of Jewish powerlessness, the religious settlers in Judaea and Samaria elevated Zionism's resort to force from a compelling necessity into a religious reverence for power. Rabbi Menachem Drukman, a spiritual and political mentor of Gush Emunim (the Block of the Faithful), spoke of 'Jewish tanks' as 'holy vessels', 'ritual articles'. Labour governments were powerless to resist a *Zeitgeist* that gave popular legitimacy to what was now an irresistible bacchanalia of passions inspired by nationalist cult images, fundamentalist ardour, and a Jewish religion that became indistinguishable from an almost pagan cult of holy sites and dubious shrines. The Jewish people did not need to wait for the fullness of time to witness the coming of the Messiah. A new interpretation of Maimonides' concept of the Messiah and Messianism was advanced to support the claim that the miraculous re-encounter of the Israelis with the biblical lands of Judaea and Samaria was the ultimate proof that *this* was indeed a Messianic age. The religious settlers and their spiritual mentors believed it was a commandment of God to settle all the land of Israel and that only thus could the Jewish people be redeemed.

The religious-political fundamentalism that gained strength in Israel during and following the Six Day War did not require European or other foreign sources; its roots were entirely indigenous. Political-religious Messianism, with its violent challenge to democracy in the name of a total, uncompromising religion, now became one of the major threats to political stability. The eminent historian Yaakov Talmon named this phenomenon a 'new religion'. This was a concept calling for an absolute identity between politics and religion. In Gush Emunim and in other extremist nuclei among yeshiva students, a *Weltanschauung* developed based on a total, enveloping sanctification of reality; a mystical realism according to which politics is not the province of the possible, but a space for the application of eternal truths. That cognitive form of Messianic Zionism – in the European context, Talmon spoke of 'Messianic nationalism' – was no more than the assignation of a social and political meaning to theological truths, or ways of thinking. Uriel Tal found in this structure aspects of what he called 'political theology', a concept rooted in St Augustine's *Civitas Dei* (City of God), that is a political community, in the sense of the *polis*, bearing divine status. Uriel Tal did not even hesitate to draw structural analogies between Gush Emunim's political theology and Nazism's sanctification of political articles of faith.

The founders of 'political theology' in Israel, who unwittingly found themselves adopting one of these great distortions of Western culture, would have been horrified at the thought of there being any identity between them and any European heritage whatsoever. Indeed, the struggle against Western culture filled their entire world. The wars of Israel, to them, were a method of purifying the soul; the physical conquest of the Land of Israel would be followed by the conquest of impurity. Western heritage, including democracy as an exotic import from the Gentiles, was for them the greatest of impurities. This, then, was a dogmatic, rigidly governed system incapable of digesting the principles of human and civil rights, as, by its very nature, this total concept of time and space left no room for tolerance. Tolerance is not exactly a biblical message and the history of Orthodox Judaism was essentially one of alienation from the world. The fundamentalist settlers of the Block of the Faithful wanted it to remain that way.

The mood of religious and nationalistic exaltation was not confined to religious fundamentalists or to what Amos Elon defined as secular Khomeinis like Elyakim Haetzni, the founder of Kiryat Arba. The 1967 victory reflected such a shift in the national mood from a state of panic and holocaustic fatalism to nationalistic euphoria that even sectors of the non-Zionist Orthodox community joined in the chorus of Messianic hallucinations. 'This is not natural victory but a magnificent miraculous revelation as in the days of our exodus from Egypt,' wrote Agudat Israel's *Hamodia* on 7 June 1967 in response to the very first reports from the battlefield. More important in its political implications, the new politico-religious exaltation also took over many who belonged to the very core of Israel's Socialist, Labourite culture. A man not especially prone to religious reflections, Chief of Staff Rabin could not hide his emotions at the liberation of Jerusalem. In a lecture at the new campus of the Hebrew University on Mount Scopus, with the sublime landscapes of the Judaean desert at his feet, he embarked on a voyage through Jewish history and invoked the dream of redemption coming true: 'The countless generations of Jews murdered, martyred and massacred for the sake of Jerusalem say to you, "comfort ye our people; console the mothers and the fathers whose sacrifices have brought about redemption."' Dayan was more practical. 'We have returned to our holiest places', he said, 'in order not to part from them ever again.' At the UN, Foreign Minister Eban proclaimed 'the glorious triumph of the IDF and the redemption of Jerusalem'.

The writers and thinkers close to the Labour culture joined in the choir of Messianic chauvinism. In fact, they accorded it an intellectual legitimacy. This was true, for example, of the novelist Haim Baer, whom Amos Elon quotes as saying that the war had proved that peace was unnecessary and even dangerous. Tension and existential danger, he said, served a useful role, for they gave 'backbone and unity' to the nation. Others, like Aharon Amir, now a member of the Movement for Greater Eretz-Israel, a body created and inspired mostly by Labour Party intellectuals, spoke about Israel's 'manifest destiny' to become the hegemonic power in the Middle East and the saviour of all the minorities in the region, from the Maronites in Lebanon to the Copts in Egypt and the Kurds in Iraq. One of the most embarrassing and extraordinary hallucinations was that of Haim Guri, another icon of the Labourite culture, who invited the Gentiles of the world to come to Israel, convert to Judaism, marry 'our pretty daughters' and have their own daughters 'find here men worthy of the name', and then 'partake in the wonderful adventure of building Eretz-Israel'. In the words of General Bar-Lev, the new Israeli nationalistic macho-ism acquired an especially vulgar expression. 'We have screwed every Arab country,' he said.

The case of Nathan Alterman is especially interesting. The poet of Israel's resurgence as a nation and a close friend of all Labour leaders, Alterman used to confess that for him the secular, hedonistic city of Tel Aviv was the most genuine expression of the New Israel, and he liked to define himself first and foremost as a 'Tel Avivian'. But he now confessed that the encounter with Eretz-Israel changed his life and joined the founding group of the Movement for Greater Eretz-Israel. The war, he said, 'blurred the differences between the State of Israel and Eretz-Israel'. This was the first time 'since the destruction of the Second Temple that Eretz-Israel was in our hands', he exclaimed, and warned that any initiative to give it away would be tantamount to another 'Munich surrender'. 'Munich' was a common currency invoked and manipulated by Israeli politicians and intellectuals, normally of the Right, in order to express the duty of the Jewish state not to follow in the footsteps of the appeasers by selling out territory and values under either the pressure of well-wishing friends or the blackmail of staunch enemies.

Another vital myth which shaped the Israelis' collective mentality was Masada. In its obsession to erase the memory of the diaspora, Zionism resuscitated the longing for the First and Second Kingdoms of Israel, the golden ages of Hebrew sovereignty. In this context the heroic defence of Masada, the last bastion of the rebels against the Roman legions of Titus, was cultivated as the expression of a nation's unyielding struggle for freedom, a stark contrast with the presumably sheeplike obedience with which the diaspora Jews went to the slaughter. 'Never again shall Masada fall!' was the ethos to be inculcated into the new generations.

But even such a central constituent myth of Zionism as Masada underwent a transformation under the impact of Israel's 1967 lightning victory. An essentially secular myth, Masada was overwhelmed and eventually defeated by the Messianic, fundamentally religious ethos of the Temple Mount that was born in the wake of the liberation of Jerusalem in 1967. Young recruits who in the past climbed to the awesome heights of the Masada fortress overlooking the Dead Sea to swear allegiance to the flag would from now on perform the same ceremony in front of the Wailing Wall in the heart of the Jewish Quarter of the Old City. After all, did not Moshe Dayan, the legendary Minister of Defence, promise that now that 'we have returned to our most holy places ... we shall never leave them'? As a myth, Masada will die hard, but its transformation after 1967 was one more expression of the fact that the Messianic passions unleashed by the 1967 victory were definitely eroding the nation's secular ethos.

The leadership of the Labour Party showed itself entirely incapable of stemming the tide of nationalistic exaltation; rather, it preferred to ride on it. The religious settlers in Judaea and Samaria claimed to have inherited the pioneering vitality of the secular Socialist founding fathers of Israel that was abandoned by the new Labour movement. Labour, now essentially driven by a bourgeois mentality and led by a conservative nomenclature, looked with admiration, even with an inferiority complex, at the pioneering élan of the young religious settlers and was too feeble to find the will to resist their drive.

It was, however, the figure of Defence Minister Moshe Dayan that became the embodiment of the Israeli mind and policies in the years following the Six Day War. In a fair reflection of Dayan's extraordinary influence on Israeli life and politics in those years, Abba Eban once said that a majority in the government that did not include Dayan was like not having a majority at all. Already during the war, Dayan had encouraged and facilitated the flight of about 200,000 Palestinians to Transjordan. 'We want to create a new map,' he said immediately after the war to his advisers and as his aide-de-camp, General Aryeh Braun, recorded, this required encouraging the transfer of the Palestinian population. Dayan was of course not alone in his eagerness to see as many Palestinians as possible cross the River Jordan to the East Bank. He certainly was not out of tune with the Chief of Staff, Rabin. 'We have created the conditions for those who want to flee to do it', Rabin told the ministerial committee for security. The reason, he explained, that the Allenby bridge on the River Jordan was not blown up by the army was in order not to hinder the flow of Palestinians to the East Bank.[1]

By establishing a policy of total economic subservience to, and dependence of the territories on, Israel and by continuously reducing the living space of the Palestinians to serve the agrarian hunger of the Israelis, Dayan aimed to achieve just that. He was a major exponent of the policy of creeping annexation of the West Bank that all the governments, right or left, subscribed to after 1967. It was as if he saw here the opportunity to complete the job that was left undone in 1948. This helps explain why the government's peace guidelines of 19 June 1967, which established the conditions for peace on the basis of the restitution of occupied territories, advanced no territorial compromise for the West Bank. These, the hills of Judaea, Hebron and Jericho, Anatot and Shilo, were, as Dayan put it, the 'cradle of the nation' and they could not be traded.

It was reflective of the general mood in the country that, although less given than Dayan to biblical rhetoric, Foreign Minister Abba Eban, a consistent exponent of dovish positions in Eshkol's government, coined the expression that called Israel's old borders with the West Bank 'Auschwitz borders', which needed to be substantially modified. Israel needed, he said in the immediate aftermath of the war, 'a better security map, a more spacious frontier, a lesser vulnerability'.

Not all, however, was nationalistic euphoria on the Israeli side. Inklings of statesmanship were not entirely lacking. As early as the third day of the war Yigal Allon alerted his colleagues in the Cabinet to the fact that the way the war was evolving offered a 'historic opportunity' to make peace with the entire Arab world. He then believed, wrongly as it turned

[1] Yemimah Rosenthal (ed.), *Yitzhak Rabin, Prime Minister of Israel. A Selection of Documents from His Life*, Jerusalem, 2005.

out, that the first candidates for a peace deal were the weaker links in the Arab world, namely Jordan, Lebanon and Morocco. Prime Minister Eshkol tried initially to resist the tide of annexation and advanced the idea of Palestinian autonomy in the West Bank. The possibility that Israel would annex two million Palestinians seemed to him like a nightmare to be avoided at all costs. A pragmatist and a realist, Eshkol was throughout a man of moderate views, albeit unfortunately not one of assertive leadership. Even in a moment of ecstasy, such as when Colonel Motta Gur's paratroopers stood at the gate of the Old City of Jerusalem and everybody started to experience Messianic hallucinations, Eshkol was there to inject a dose of sober realism. 'Even if we conquer the Old City we will have to pull out from it sooner or later,' he said to his ministers.

But just as he had been incapable of stemming the drift to war, Eshkol failed to curb the politics of Messianism during the war and the creeping annexationism in its aftermath. He supported Israel Galili's call for settling Jews in the Old City even before the war had ended. Moshe Dayan shared Eshkol's autonomy concept for the West Bank, but he saw it as part of a federation with Israel, not as a fully separate autonomy. But in any case Dayan was so erratic in his capricious changes of opinion that one could never know what exactly were his positions. The tragedy was that on these matters his views counted more than those of the Prime Minister, for he was to be the all-powerful architect of a relationship of total dependence and subservience of the Palestinians to Israel and her economy.

The Six Day War reopened the dormant debate on the territorial objectives of Zionism. True, on 19 June 1967, in a moment of grace and political lucidity, the National Unity government agreed on policy guidelines for the future of its relations with Syria and Egypt. The aim would be to reach full peace agreements with these two Arab countries on the basis of Israel's withdrawal to the international borders, and the subsequent demilitarisation of the Sinai and the Golan Heights. Jordan and the West Bank were conspicuously left out of the peace equation. There, as Menachem Begin noted, 'it was decided not to decide'. Ideas about Palestinian autonomy were raised, but no decision was taken. Autonomy, Begin certainly understood, could lead to statehood, and Prime Minister Eshkol, as he made clear on different occasions, did not rule out such a possibility altogether. He did not fight, however, to turn his intuition into an official policy of his government. The risk of autonomy developing into statehood was to be precisely Begin's concern in the future peace talks with Egypt at Camp David. How to downscale the autonomy deal and sterilise it so that it could never usher in a Palestinian state was Begin's obsession at Camp David and beyond.

Israel and the occupied territories, 1967

But was there on 19 June 1967 an Israeli peace overture towards Syria and Egypt? Did the Israeli Cabinet end its deliberations on that day with a decision to convey concrete peace proposals to its Arab neighbours along the lines that were discussed in the Cabinet, or perhaps ask the American administration to do so on its behalf? Notwithstanding Abba Eban's insistence that this was indeed the case, there seems to be no solid evidence to corroborate his claim. No formal peace proposal was made either directly or indirectly by Israel. The Americans, who were briefed of the Cabinet's decision by Eban, were not asked to convey it to Cairo and Damascus as official peace proposals, nor were they given indications that Israel expected a reply. At its meeting on 19 June the Israeli government developed policy guidelines; it did not discuss a peace initiative, nor did it ever formalise it as such.

Israel's sin in the aftermath of the war lay in her total misunderstanding of the conditions that were created by her victory. She developed, therefore, no reasonable strategy as to the best way to turn her military supremacy into a political tool and use her exploits in the battlefield in order to change the nature of her relations with the Arab world. Instead, she fell back conveniently on the politics of immobilism and faits accomplis. There was no Israeli peace initiative, and there was no credible and thoughtful response to the initiatives coming from others. In fact, the first to understand the meaning of the new conditions created by the war were, surprisingly, the local Palestinian leaders throughout the West Bank and, conspicuously, also junior Israeli officials. The latter bombarded their superiors with peace proposals ranging from a limited Palestinian autonomy to a full-fledged Palestinian state, without getting any real feedback from them. It is more than a mere curiosity, it is also a reflection of what a defining moment the Six Day War was, and how radical the transformation of both the political map and the collective attitude of the Israelis to the biblical lands of Judaea and Samaria, that among the officials who proposed a Palestinian state along the Armistice lines of 1949 were Professor Yuval Neeman, later to become the leader of a staunchly right-wing party ('Thyah'), and General Rehavam Zeevi, later to be the founder of 'Moledet', a party that championed both annexation and the mass transfer of the Palestinian population from the West Bank. In the immediate aftermath of the war, Zeevi was still lucid enough to warn that 'an Israeli military rule in the territories will only widen the gulf between Israel and the Palestinians in the West Bank'. Palestinian dignitaries, such as could be defined as pro-Jordanian and others who were less so, exhibited a hectic political activity, initiated ideas and made concrete proposals for a settlement with Israel. It was Israel that was confused, overwhelmed by her victory and disorientated as to the right political course she should take. Israel was being short-sighted; she vacillated and hesitated between contradictory approaches. Certainly shocked by the rout of the Arab armies, the Palestinian local leaders were nevertheless quick to get back on their feet, assume responsibility for the destiny of their people and plead for a peace deal with Israel. The scope of political restlessness among the local Palestinian leaders from Aziz Shehadeh, hardly a friend of the Hashemite monarchy, to Anwar Nusseibeh, an ex-minister of defence in Jordan, was such that Arab governments had to warn them, through their official press, against betraying the common Arab cause.

There is, of course, much reason to doubt whether, even if formalised as an official peace proposal, the Arabs would have accepted the government's peace guidelines as the platform for a full-fledged peace agreement with Israel. Israel's shortcomings notwithstanding, the Arabs were by all accounts not yet ready for such a deal. The proof is that a more unequivocal American overture along the same lines as the Israeli Cabinet's decision would soon be turned down by the Arabs and their Soviet patrons.

The Arab League summit in Khartoum in late August 1967 reflected the difficult dilemmas in their camp. They were now in the midst of a painful transition, albeit inevitably full of ambiguities, to a new phase in their attitude to Israel. The old anti-Zionist rhetoric did not fade away, of course. But the buds of a readiness to contemplate a tactical accommodation with Israel could nevertheless be detected. True, Israel's withdrawal from the occupied territories needed to be unconditional, they insisted. A comprehensive peace agreement with the memory of at least three successive military débâcles – 1948, 1956, 1967 – still fresh in their minds was utterly out of the question. Khartoum might not have been an entirely rejectionist summit, as Professor Yoram Meital has shown in an excellent article, but it nevertheless sealed the fate of Israel's peace guidelines of 19 June. No recognition of Israel, no negotiations and no peace with it – the notorious three nos of Khartoum – were seemingly somewhat less categorical than they sounded. But Israel was in no mood to enter into a Talmudic interpretation of the fine print in the protocol and the resolutions of the summit.

And the fine print was that Nasser and Hussein did, indeed, lead the summit against the more radical positions of the Palestinians and the Syrians to an acknowledgement that the immediate recovery of the occupied Arab lands through military means was utterly unrealistic. Therefore, the diplomatic option needed to be given priority. King Hussein proved to be a man of his word. In his meeting in London on 2 July 1967 with Levi Eshkol's emissary, General Chaim Herzog, he had pledged that if he failed in the Arab summit to reach a common Arab position for peace, he would go it alone and negotiate with Israel. In Khartoum, he fought for his approach and got the green light from his Arab counterparts, admittedly mainly thanks to Nasser's backing. Khartoum was, then, probably the first time in its history that the Arab League contemplated the principle of a political solution to the Arab–Israeli conflict.

It did so, however, for strictly tactical reasons and the lack of an immediate military option. Nasser's lucid analysis was simple: should the Arabs wait until they were ready to defeat Israel, the Israelis would by then 'Israelise' the territories and make their recovery practically impossible. The Arabs' hesitant flirtation with the diplomacy of peace had its limits, however. First, they made it clear that, should they fail in their peaceful attempt 'to remove the traces of aggression' *on their conditions*, they would then have gained the international legitimacy necessary to move to the military phase. Second, the Arabs expected to recover their lost territories without having to negotiate with Israel, recognise it and make peace with it. Nasser would not even pledge non-belligerency in an unequivocal way. 'The price of non-belligerency', he said to Secretary General of the Soviet Communist Party Leonid Brezhnev, 'will turn our defeat into a double defeat.'

Though Nasser positioned himself in Khartoum as the hesitant initiator of what could become a dramatic change in Egypt's strategy, a formula potentially palatable to Israel of a full separate peace with each of its Arab neighbours was not yet ripe in his mind. It would have to wait for Sadat. But Nasser clearly signalled the beginning of a road that would be taken by Sadat in a much more assertive and unambiguous way, as early as 1971–2, that is, even before he had recovered Egypt's pride in the Yom Kippur War. Sadat would then rely on the most surprising and encouraging legacy of Khartoum, and one that was to strike deep roots in the Arab discourse in the coming years. The Arab call that was led by Nasser for the elimination of the 'traces of aggression' referred to the lands occupied in 1967 and could therefore be implicitly interpreted as an oblique recognition of the borders of 1948. And this was indeed to be the unequivocal deal proposed by Sadat: 'all the land', meaning the borders of 1948, for 'all the peace'.

A system founded on the principles of reform and the vindication of Arab rights, Nasser's regime could not afford the luxury of allowing the consequences of military defeat to degenerate into an unbearable status quo. Khartoum was Nasser's attempt to reconcile the irreconcilable: his need to reach the truce required for carrying through his regime's deal of reform, and to win back the lost Arab lands without offering peace to Israel in return, on the one hand, with Israel's utterly unrealistic expectations for a full peace in exchange for only a partial withdrawal from occupied lands and without fully addressing the Palestinian question, on the other. This was a circle that could by no conceivable means be squared.

It was out of the question that the euphoric Israeli government – Nasser spoke in July 1968 of an 'enemy drunk with victory' – would give away the occupied Arab lands without negotiations, without winning Arab recognition and in exchange for an ambiguous state of non-belligerency rather than a full peace treaty. Israel's interpretation of Khartoum was not entirely implausible when she claimed that war, not peace and mutual recognition, remained the Arabs' strategic priority. In any case, Nasser did not wait too long before despairing of a political process. 'We must be the ones to liberate our land by the force of arms,' he declared in February 1968. It is evidently true that in those years Israel committed a fatal blunder by succumbing to a chauvinistic state of mind and assuming the haughtiness of the all-powerful victor. But nor were the Arabs then ripe for an overture that would cut short the dangerous slide into another war. They turned down President Johnson's 19 June ideas for a settlement,[1] ideas that were not essentially different from those that were approved by the Israeli Cabinet on the very same day. To Israel's *Sedanlaghen*, – 'the smile of Sedan', to use the expression reflecting Prussia's sense of arrogant superiority over France following its victory at Sedan in 1871 – the Arabs responded with an attitude that was understandably perceived by Israel as an attempt to wrest from her the territories gained in a just war of defence but without even extending to her recognition, let alone peace.

The slogans of Khartoum served as a convenient pretext for those in Israel, including the ministers who had voted for the 19 June peace guidelines, who harboured private dreams of a meaningful readjustment of the country's borders on all fronts. Israel lost no time in withdrawing her peace guidelines. In response to what she interpreted as Khartoum's rejectionist resolutions, Eshkol's Cabinet cancelled its 19 June decision and announced that any future peace settlement would have to satisfy her needs for 'secure borders', a new euphemism for the rejection of the 4 June 1967 lines. And it was only when this euphemism was embedded in the language of a UN Security Council Resolution that Israel was ready to endorse it. The constructive ambiguity of the November 1967 Security Council Resolution Number 242, which called for peace based on the restitution of 'territories' instead of 'the territories', allowed Israel to claim that the borders would have to be modified on all fronts as a condition for peace and gave manoeuvring space to her post-war diplomacy.

---

[1] Michael Oren, *Six Days of War. June 1967 and the Making of the Modern Middle East*, Oxford University Press, New York, 2002, p.324.

Resolution 242 was the result of the need to find a formula that would reconcile Israel's unrealistic expectation to have full peace for less than all the territories, and the Arabs' drive for a full restitution of land in exchange for a watered-down state of non-belligerency.

Not unlike Henry Kissinger in 1973, President Johnson's advisers in 1967 assumed that a war in the Middle East was not inherently bad for the cause of peace. A crisis is always an opportunity, for it has the potential of loosening rigid patterns and opening new doors, as Under Secretary of State Eugene Rostow put it. His brother Walt Rostow, a special adviser to the President, suggested on the very first day of the war a post-war settlement based on 'trading Israel's newly acquired territories for Arab concessions'. The concept of 'land for peace', which was to have a very long life indeed in Middle East peacemaking, was born on the very day that Israel started to extend her territory beyond the Armistice lines.

'An overall settlement' was what President Johnson had in mind when he made public his peace plan – the first in a long series of abortive presidential attempts to solve the core issues of the Arab–Israeli conflict – on the very day, 19 June, that Israel approved her own peace guidelines. The President's was a platform that called for the restitution of occupied lands on the basis of the recognition of the territorial integrity and the independence of all the states in the region, freedom of navigation and a solution to the Palestinian refugee problem. Coinciding as it did with the essentials of the Israeli peace guidelines, both Prime Minister Eshkol and Foreign Minister Eban could not but react with a forthcoming attitude. But the presidential concept of land for peace was rejected out of hand by the Arabs and their Soviet patrons. Nor was the reduction of the Palestinian problem to an issue of refugees especially palatable to the Arabs, let alone to the Palestinians. The Soviet and Arab position was as simple as it was utterly unrealistic and of course understandably unacceptable to both Israel and the United States: withdrawal with no conditions, a simple return to the old status quo ante bellum.

Neither of the parties to the conflict was especially happy with Resolution 242's oblique and foggy formulas, least of all the Palestinians, whose problem was reduced in the Resolution to that of the humanitarian plight of refugees. The PLO's outright rejection of 242 was an additional manifestation by the Palestinians that their struggle would from now on be independent of the Arabs' diplomatic strategy. The Palestinians were about to disengage from the status of a tool in the hands of the Arab states to that of an independent subject in the history of the Middle East. As from the Palestinian débâcle of 1936–9 and later the 1948 Naqbah, the Palestinians had lost their independence as a national movement.

They disappeared from the regional arena as autonomous players. The 1967 war, the defeat of the Arab armies with their consequent loss of a credible military option in the foreseeable future, and the relegation by Resolution 242 of the Palestinian problem to the margins of peacemaking in the region, signalled the beginning of a new phase in the history of Palestinian nationalism.

Levi Eshkol, the Prime Minister who led Israel in the Six Day War, was a good-humoured man of compromise and dialogue, and was an unlikely figure to be put in the position of the heroic leader in times of war. He was not pretending when he humbly confessed to Lyndon Johnson, in his visit to the President in Texas, that 'I have no sense of boastful triumph, nor have I entered the struggle for peace in the role of victor'. But he nevertheless failed in the aftermath of the war to improve in any meaningful way the chances of a settlement with the Arab world. Eshkol strongly supported Palestinian autonomy in the West Bank, and did not even rule out Palestinian statehood and sovereignty or, alternatively, a deal with King Hussein based on border modifications in the West Bank. But he nevertheless succumbed to a policy of creeping annexation. It is revealing that General Sharon, then busy moving Israel's military training camps to the West Bank, should have advised a key military analyst to refrain from criticising Eshkol because, as he said, 'it is in Israel's interest to have today a weak prime minister' (*Haaretz*, 19 November 2004). Incapable of stemming the nationalistic tide, and falling back on diplomatic immobilism after the Khartoum Summit, he died in February 1969 without leaving a clear peacemaking legacy.

Israel was wrong to assume that she could acquire new lands and have peace at the same time. But the Arabs had an illusion of their own: to get back their territories without offering peace in return. Nasser's persistent search for a national and pan-Arab purpose, and the belief of the Ba'ath in Syria that only through direct confrontation with Israel could the lost territories be recovered and the problem of Palestine be settled, fed the cycle of Arab rejectionism and Israeli inertia. The Israelis' hubris and the Arabs' sense of humiliation proved to be a fatal combination. Tragically, far-sighted leaders were a scarce commodity in the immediate aftermath of 1967.

Levi Eshkol's successor, Golda Meir, was to make things even worse. She was a self-righteous, intransigent and stubborn iron lady who turned political inaction and righteousness into a system of government. Her unwillingness to question the position of the complacent military, and the support she received from her close relations with President Nixon, who was more concerned with the task of curbing the Soviet penetration into the Middle East than with the need to advance an Arab–Israeli peace, made her premiership one of almost inevitable decline towards war. Mrs Meir stated her policy from the outset and stuck to it to the bitter end: Israel would not withdraw to the 1967 lines and no Israeli soldier would budge from his actual position unless this was done in the framework of a peace agreement.

But President Nasser would not allow Israel to impose her will and her strategic priorities. Egypt's March 1969 large-scale offensive against Israeli positions along the Suez Canal marked the beginning of the War of Attrition, in which Nasser tried to prevent the Israelis turning the Canal into their de facto border with Egypt. Egyptian tactics were aimed at wearing Israel out in a static war and through heavy artillery bombardments. This was not the kind of war that the Israelis were used to. Political constraints, however, ruled out what Israel would have otherwise done given its military doctrine of offensive defence – counter-attacking to capture the east bank of the Canal. Instead, Chief of General Staff Chaim Bar-Lev opted for the erection along the Canal of a line of fortifications that immediately bore his name. But Israel soon realised that she could not allow herself the luxury of a static, inconclusive war where the Egyptians had an evident edge in manpower and in their capacity to sustain casualties. The result was an escalation that led to the use of Israel's air force first as a 'flying artillery' against Egyptian positions and later against strategic targets deep inside Egypt.

As expected, Golda Meir was not to be deterred by the war. She did her utmost to thwart William Rogers's initiative of December 1969 that called for Israel's withdrawal to the international border with 'minor modifications'. That the plan required Egypt only to make a 'specific commitment to peace' rather than agree to a full-fledged peace treaty was a serious blunder of US Secretary of State Rogers, which served as an additional reason for the government to announce its 'unqualified rejection' of his plan. Israel saw the plan as an attempt by the two superpowers to impose a settlement at a time when the War of Attrition started by Egypt along the Suez Canal was developing, at least in its initial stages, into yet another defeat for the Egyptian clients of the Soviet Union. That the State Department and the White House, with Henry Kissinger as the architect of the President's foreign policy that put a greater emphasis on curbing the Soviets than on disentangling the Arab–Israeli imbroglio, were clearly speaking with two voices made it easier for Golda Meir to derail the Rogers plan.

But the truth is that the plan was born dead and again, there were two to this tango of steadfast rejectionism. Egypt had already brushed aside

Gunnar Jarring's mediation with its refusal to contemplate a 'peace treaty' with Israel. In its response to the UN envoy it even brought back from oblivion UN Resolution 181. Nasser also turned down the Rogers plan out of hand. He would not accept a separate peace with Israel, nor the demilitarisation of the Sinai peninsula. Nasser simply would not consider peace on the basis of a military defeat. His major concern at that point was not how to negotiate a reasonable compromise with Israel, but how to acquire sophisticated weapons from the Soviet Union in order to erase the impact of the 1967 defeat.

Nasser's rejectionist attitude, his success in blackmailing the Soviets into supplying him with new weapons and the subsequent collapse of the Rogers initiative led directly to the Sovietisation of the War of Attrition. By January 1970 there were already 40,000 Russian military advisers in Egypt. For all practical purposes, this would lead to Israel's defeat in the War of Attrition, for the Soviet SAM anti-air missile system was eventually deployed along the Canal and Israel was forced to interrupt her air raids against strategic objectives deep inside Egypt. The battle for the Bar-Lev Line had suddenly become an almost existential dilemma of an all-out war against the Soviet Union that, notwithstanding some morale-boosting successes of Israeli pilots in dogfights against their Soviet counterparts, Israel could of course not afford.

Civil protest at times of war was not exactly an Israeli tradition. War was always perceived as an *Ein Brerah*, a last resort that the nation could always identify with. The War of Attrition was the first to break that pattern of almost total coincidence between the war front and the home front. Golda Meir's politics of immobilism undermined the popular conviction about the inevitable necessity of war. Moreover, the heavy price that Israel was now paying in terms of casualties along the Canal started to erode the Israelis' complacent mood of invincibility. For the first time in Israel's history, waves of popular protest against the dangerous political inertia of the government were unleashed by key segments of society. Notwithstanding her newly acquired empire, 1967, as the War of Attrition proved, did not change the essentials of the Arab–Israeli dispute as a conflict between a besieged, small Jewish state, whose Achilles heel has always been her limited capacity to resist casualties, and an immense Arab ocean whose human resources were infinite. Two years after her stunning 1967 victory, Israel looked again like an embattled nation, trapped in her own contradictions and immersed in a deep moral crisis.

Malkat Ha-ambatia (*The Queen of the Bath*), Hanokh Levine's play staged at a Tel Aviv theatre in 1970, was the loudest and most articulate expression of the young generation's despair with a war that never ended and with the politicians and generals incapable of departing from the logic of war. In the play, the fallen soldier questions the nation's traditional mythology of heroism and sacrifice. Addressing his father, he says:

> And don't say that you made a sacrifice,
> Because the one who made a sacrifice is me,
> And don't talk high words any more,
> Because I'm already lower than low, Father.
>
> My dear Father, when you're standing at my graveside
> Old and very solitary
> And you see how they inter my body in the dust,
> Just ask my forgiveness, Father.

What a far cry from the nationalistic exaltation that overtook the entire nation in the aftermath of the Six Day War! Would the politicians respond to the growing yearning for peace of the younger generation?

Definitely not. The Queen of the Bath, Prime Minister Golda Meir, was candid enough to admit in an interview with *Newsweek* magazine, at a time when it was not entirely beyond human capacity to detect the possibility of another general war if the policies of obstinate immobilism persisted, that, as a leader, she was not necessarily driven by the spirit of the statesman, but by 'complexes'. 'It is true, we have a Masada complex, we have a pogrom complex, we have a Hitler complex,' she said to *Newsweek* a few months before the Yom Kippur surprise onslaught of the Egyptian army against the Bar-Lev Line. It was this 'Masada' psychology of never yielding and never compromising, embodied in the person of the Prime Minister, which more and more people now believed had made their leaders miss one opportunity after another of breaking the cycle of wars.

Israel refused to draw the necessary military and political lessons from the War of Attrition. Its insistence on only two options – either full peace with a partial withdrawal or an untenable status quo – was a recipe for an inevitable drift to war. As in the aftermath of 1948, Israel was now ready to enter negotiations only on the basis of the status quo post bellum. But with Nasser's sudden death of a heart attack on 28 September 1970, at the age of 52, a new Egyptian leader, Anwar Sadat, emerged who would radically change the parameters of the conflict. It is true that Nasser had started to shift Egypt's policy towards the Jewish state from war towards an attempt to reach a political settlement. Yet it would be up to his successor to start a new era of peacemaking in the region.

Initially, Israel was unimpressed by the change of leadership in its southern border. Jarring was explicitly told in February 1971 that Israel 'will not withdraw to the pre-June 1967 lines'. But Israel's blunder became more clearly apparent when President Sadat for the first time in the history of the conflict committed Egypt, in his response to Jarring's questioning, 'to enter into a peace agreement with Israel'. Sadat's commitment can be seen as a belated response to Israel's peace guidelines of 19 June 1967 or as a correction, as it were, of the notorious three Khartoum nos. The tragedy was that by now the Israeli government had drifted yet further to the right.

Israel's short-sightedness becomes even more unpardonable when one realises that her leaders were fully aware of the boldness of Sadat's move. Both Golda Meir and Moshe Dayan were forced to acknowledge the revolutionary change in Egypt's position. In an interview with the London *Times* the Prime Minister admitted that Sadat was 'the first Egyptian leader to say that he was ready to make peace'. Dayan believed that this was an entirely new situation that called for a 'careful assessment', one that was never made. In fact, Sadat's response to Jarring went even further: it indicated that Egypt wanted an Israeli withdrawal from all the occupied Arab lands, but it did not link Egypt's readiness for peace with the withdrawal from other fronts. Sadat was in effect anticipating the premises upon which he would strike a *separate deal* with Israel at the Camp David summit.

Mrs Meir's Cabinet did not rise to the dramatic challenge posed by Anwar Sadat. In the same interview where she recognised the boldness of Sadat's reply to Jarring, the Prime Minister continued to insist that Israel 'must have' Sharm el Sheikh, that Egypt 'could not return' to Gaza, and that the Golan Heights and much of the West Bank, including united Jerusalem, must remain under Israel's control. She also took the liberty on another occasion to say that 'Sharm el Sheikh is of absolutely no use to the Egyptians'. It would take the trauma of the Yom Kippur War for Israel to make peace under the same conditions Mrs Meir now so haughtily rejected. The Middle East is not an arena where opportunities can be missed without punishment. An opportunity that is not taken when it appears will never be repeated under the same conditions.

In his desperate attempt to stem the tide leading to war Sadat can claim to be the first to introduce into the politics of peacemaking in the Middle East the concept of interim agreements, of a piecemeal process. In February 1971 he proposed a partial Israeli withdrawal from the Canal that would then be opened to international traffic as a first stage leading to the implementation of Security Council Resolution 242. This meant abandoning the (for now) impossible final agreement track in favour of a philosophy of interim settlements that would help build the necessary trust between the parties, as a prelude to a final settlement.

Sadat's move also meant that he was the first Egyptian president fully to appreciate that peace with Israel would need the good offices of the United States, and would therefore require an Egyptian diplomatic revolution, that is, a shift from a Soviet to an American alliance based on the recognition of America's ascendancy to the position of the major broker in the politics of the Middle East. A reliable peace diplomacy, then, required improved relations with America and, in due course, perhaps even a strategic partnership with her. Sadat was thus clearly signalling the strategy that would eventually bring him to make peace with Israel at Camp David. The Soviet Union, he understood, could offer the Arabs the tools for war, but only the United States could deliver Israel. A stark departure from pan-Arab Nasserite conceptions, it was not surprising that Sadat's revolutionary shift of strategy should have been opposed by Nasser's old guard. Ali Sabri, the Secretary General of the regime's official party, the Arab Socialist Union, and a group of old ministers in Nasser's governments were now either purged or resigned voluntarily following Sadat's peace offer of February 1971.

But Golda Meir's intransigence derailed this last initiative as well. It is difficult to imagine a greater gulf than that which existed between the resourceful peace strategist, the compulsively creative and far-sighted visionary statesman that was Sadat, and the trivially immobile government led by Mrs Meir. The Prime Minister would not agree to the deployment of Egyptian forces on the eastern bank of the Canal and she would not accept the provision that the interim agreement should be a step leading to the implementation of Security Council Resolution 242. In fact, Mrs Meir wanted Egypt's commitment to end the state of belligerency with Israel already in the framework of the interim agreement, and prior to any Israeli commitment with regard to the nature of the final settlement, a position that not only Egypt but also Israel's American allies thought unreasonable. In the winter of 1971 Israel was clearly responsible, and Golda Meir must take the principal part of the blame, for the subversion of a unique opportunity for peace.

The rejection of his last overture signalled for Sadat the beginning of the countdown to war. In May 1971 he signed an agreement with the Soviets, where the latter committed the necessary military assistance in order, as it were, to do away with the 'consequences of Israeli aggression'. And when he later found that the Soviets were reluctant to allow him to go to war and, moreover, looked to him to be conspiring with the Americans to freeze the 'no war no peace' situation, Sadat did not hesitate, in July 1972, to expel the Russian military advisers from Egypt. But as frequently happened in those years of military and political drunkenness, Israel misinterpreted Sadat's move. What was to him a stage towards war was interpreted by Israel as Egypt's abandonment of the military option.

It was clearly Israel that did not miss an opportunity to miss an opportunity in those years of dramatic change in Egypt's strategic thinking from confrontation to peacemaking. It was Israel's fatal mistake to assume that since the Arabs did not have a military option they would be forced to come to an accommodation on her terms. But Egypt was then what Henry Kissinger himself had defined in his study of Metternich's Europe as a revolutionary power, that is, a power that was so clearly unsatisfied with the status quo that it would do anything, including go to war, to undo it. Egypt as a nation and especially its intellectual elite, was boiling with national frustration and humiliation that could only be cured by a war against the arrogant Israelis. 'Should your military intelligence have read Egyptian poetry after 1967 you would have understood that the 1973 war was inevitable. Every good intelligence officer must read poetry.' This was the lesson the Israeli poet Haim Guri was taught in 1977 by the Egyptian intellectual Hussein Fawzi.

But the Israelis were blind and drunk throughout. 'We never had it so good,' declared Israel's complacent Prime Minister during her visit to Washington in March 1973. A month later her Defence Minister declared from the top of the awesome summit of Masada – a site that always drew from the Israelis the most hallucinatory, Messianic and even suicidal instincts – that 'a new state of Israel with broad frontiers was born'. Israel was taken over by 'a climate of exuberant self-confidence that began to border on fantasy', as Abba Eban would put it. Such a state of mind was, of course, an impossible introduction to peace.

The West Bank, unlike the Egyptian front, was not yet ripe for a total war or for its Palestinian equivalent, Intifada. But Israel's annexationist policies in Judaea and Samaria, and the vacuum of leadership in the Palestinian territories, only enhanced her drive to produce faits accomplis. One might recall that as early as July 1967 Eshkol contemplated an autonomy deal for the Palestinians that he did not rule out, as he confessed to a meeting of his party, even ending up in statehood. He spoke in the Cabinet of 'the creation of a movement for an independent state in the West Bank'. But he was not sufficiently resolute in advancing his peace insights, nor were the local Palestinians approached seriously with an Israeli proposal they could not refuse.

Israel's tragic mistake was not to realise that it was precisely her direct rule over the Palestinians that was more likely to unleash Palestinian nationalist sentiments and do more to strengthen the movement for Palestinian independence than the careful, albeit always fragile and precarious, balance between the Transjordanian and the Palestinian identities that the Hashemite kingdom had laboriously managed to maintain since its annexation of the West Bank. Defeated and humiliated by Israel, the Arab states lost, for the moment, their will to fight the Zionist enemy. The PLO thus became the vanguard of the Arab struggle against Israel. As soon as the war was over, the PLO started to stage guerrilla operations throughout the West Bank and Gaza. In July 1968 a new form of Palestinian terrorism was inaugurated with the hijacking of an El Al jet to Algiers. During the autumn and winter of that same year a car bomb exploded in Jerusalem, Tel Aviv's central bus station was attacked and El Al passengers were the target of a terrorist squad at Athens airport.

An entirely new phase in the struggle for Palestine was now inaugurated with the PLO definitely succeeding in dragging Israel into a total war on a global scale. On 27 December 1968, in response to the PLO's operation in Athens, the IDF stormed Beirut's international airport and destroyed fourteen jets belonging to Arab companies. Typically, the scale of the attack ordered by Dayan and executed by the army was larger than that approved by the government. The West Bank and Lebanon were to be the immediate battleground of what was clearly becoming a dirty war. Fatah struck roots throughout the occupied West Bank and dragged Israel into a war that is still going today.

The Karameh Operation of March 1968 – a massive Israeli incursion into the East Bank of Jordan where bitter clashes took place against both Fatah units and Jordanian regular forces that ended with serious setbacks for the IDF – was a major watershed in the Palestinians' struggle for international recognition. The performance of the Palestinians under Arafat's command on the battlefield of Karameh – which coincidentally means 'honour' in Arabic – was to have far-reaching consequences. A victory of sorts for the Arab side at a time when the memory of the humiliating rout of the Arab armies was still so fresh in everybody's mind, Karameh symbolised the rise of the PLO to prominence. Arafat now became a pan-Arab hero, and his picture occupied the front page of every major newspaper and magazine in the West. To the Arabs he succeeded where Gamal Abdel Nasser had failed, for he was able to inflict on the image of the arrogant Israelis more harm than all the Arab armies combined. Karameh also taught the Israelis that, although it was clear that the PLO had failed to stir up a popular rebellion in the Palestinian territories, a new kind of war was now being waged against them. It took Israel decades to realise that it was a war that could not be won by military means. It was only susceptible to a political solution.

However, the attitudes and the political conditions that prevailed in the aftermath of the 1967 war did not offer the necessary environment for the kind of political solution that the parties would start to conceive only after they had exhausted so many other ways that failed. Nor were the misperceptions that Israelis and Palestinians continued to have of each other exactly conducive to an accommodation. Nationalistic mythologies have always been bad advisers for an era of peace, though they certainly were powerful engines in times of war. Both the Israelis and the PLO were now busier fuelling the engine of the conflict than in devising credible ways to its solution.

The new combative PLO of the late 1960s was profoundly inspired by the FLN's struggle against French rule in Algeria. The implication was that the Zionist occupation would be dismantled by exactly the same type of popular armed struggle that had forced the French out of Algeria and brought about the evacuation of more than a million European settlers. For the Palestinians and their supporters in the European Left the Algerian case was also an exemplary illustration of the nature of Zionism as a colonial movement. The argument was that Zionism's rule, like France's occupation of Algeria, was based on the brutal repression of the local population, the control of the country's natural resources and manpower by a foreign minority, cultural and racial discrimination of the occupied nation, and the existence of a whole system of economic and physical segregation. And just as the defeat of the French was made inevitable, among other reasons, by their demographic decline, so the Israelis were likewise doomed to lose the demographic race.

Not until the emergence of the PLO as the formidable enemy that it became did the Israelis seriously awaken to the Palestinian dilemma. For years they had repressed the existence of a national Palestinian problem. Now, in the early days of their occupation of the West Bank, the same attitude persisted. It was as if they had come to an empty land where only their memory and their religious yearnings mattered. The autochthonous Palestinian population, hundreds of thousands of them refugees of the 1948 war, was still non-existent as a people with an inalienable right to the land it inhabited, let alone as a nation with political rights. It is difficult to find a more poetically powerful expression of the Israelis' disregard for the Palestinian presence in Palestine than Naomi Shemer's verses in her 'Jerusalem of Gold'. Written just before the 1967 war, it became a kind of unofficial anthem of the exalted nation in her hour of victory, in her re-encounter with the old landscapes of Eretz-Israel and with her holy capital, Jerusalem. Naomi Shemer wrote how 'The market place is empty and no one visits the Temple Mount of the Old City'. The tens of thousands of Arabs living and moving about those sites and flocking daily into the alleys of the Old City were 'no one' and the market place was 'empty'. Only a Jewish presence mattered, for only the Jews could make the market 'full' or 'crowded'.

The Palestinians acted as the mirror image of their Israeli enemies. They also conveniently shared in the sin of ignorance and disregard. Not exactly poetic, but powerful nevertheless, was the affirmation of the PLO's Palestinian National Covenant that denied any Jewish link to Palestine and any claim to being 'a nationality with an identity of its own'. Rather than acknowledging an authentic, powerful and resolute movement of national liberation that in 1948 was strong enough to win the day against the invading Arab armies and shatter into pieces the entire Arab community in Palestine, and in 1967 had defeated three powerful Arab armies and completed in the West Bank the 'unfinished job' of 1948, the new Palestinian leadership continued to negate the evidence of Israel's existence as a nation and preferred to assume the Nasserite pan-Arab discourse. Israel and Zionism exposed the extent of the failings and incompetence of Arab leaders and societies in their inability to match the capabilities of the Jewish state. It was therefore convenient to portray her through colonialist metaphors as an artificial Crusader state doomed to extinction, or as a local version of the French *pieds-noirs* in Algeria.

Israel aspired to have the best of all worlds in the West Bank: to control security down to the River Jordan and grab land for settlements and for strategic purposes without having to bear the brunt of ruling directly over the Palestinian population. This was the essence of the Allon plan – to have as much land as possible with as small a number of Arabs as possible – launched as early as 26 July 1967. Although never formally endorsed by the Israeli Cabinet, it became for all practical purposes, at least until the Right came to power in 1977 and unleashed a wild policy of settlements in densely populated Palestinian areas, the accepted map of Israel's security, and of her settlement priorities in Judaea and Samaria.

No Palestinian could be found to subscribe to such a scheme and no docile local leadership was ready to negotiate a watered-down autonomy along the lines of the Allon plan. This was how the so-called Jordanian option was born. It was an attempt to sterilise the Palestinian problem by 'Jordanising' it on Israel's terms, that is, by handing over to Jordanian rule only the areas that were initially proposed for Palestinian autonomy.

Notwithstanding the numerous contacts between Israel's leaders and King Hussein, however, and even a degree of intimacy that developed between them, the Jordanian option as conceived by the Israelis existed only in their mind and imagination. It never had the slightest chance of being accepted by the King. The Israelis wanted him to pull the chestnuts out of the Palestinian fire for them and to launder, as it were, their occupation of sizeable parts of the West Bank; but he would not lend himself to being their collaborator. Hussein's response to the Allon plan was clear-cut: 'wholly unacceptable'. For him it was all or nothing. Israel's proposal to explore the prospects of peace with her neighbours on the basis of established facts, of a new map – *A New Map, Other Relationships* was indeed the self-explanatory title of a book written in the late 1960s by Moshe Dayan – had no chance whatever of being accepted by a legitimate Arab partner.

In formulating her policies and addressing diplomatic initiatives, Golda Meir was flanked by a most powerful political triumvirate. Moshe Dayan, Yigal Allon and Israel Galili – the last was the mastermind behind the Galili document that established the major guidelines for Israel's creeping annexation of the West Bank – were the most authentic representatives of the Zionist Labourite ethos of land, settlements and security. Like Ben-Gurion, they wanted to explore avenues for peace, but again as in his case, peace was not their strategic priority, which was that of developing and consolidating the Jewish state. At that point they failed to assume what another Labourite general with the same mental profile, Yitzhak Rabin, would not assimilate until twenty-five years later, namely that peace, even when generous and magnanimous in terms of territorial concessions, should be a central pillar of Israel's security. They preferred still to rely on the traditional tools of the Zionist enterprise: land, water, Jewish immigration and military might.

Dayan and Allon were the prodigious sons of the generation of Israel's founding fathers. They were brought up on the notion of striking roots in an ever-expanding Yishuv and of standing fast against the Arab enemy. Deeply immersed in the biblical roots of Jewish nationhood – *Living with the Bible*, another book written by Moshe Dayan, was one of the most authentic expressions of his politico-religious, sometimes even pagan and erotic love story with Eretz-Israel – they both believed in the immanent right of the Jewish people to the totality of Eretz-Israel. Born into the farming culture of a moshav (an agricultural settlement), they would frequently speak of Judaea and Samaria almost in terms of real estate. They championed the Israelis' right 'to buy' land and 'settle' it, the way Jews had done throughout Palestine since the First Aliyah in 1882. They were ministers in a sovereign state, but could not abandon the revolutionary political culture of the Yishuv where outsmarting the British occupier and outwitting the local population were a philosophy of life. Nor could they betray their mentality as soldiers and settlers.

Allon and Galili were members of the most activist and militant kibbutz movement – Hakibbutz Hameuhad – the spiritual mentor of which was, one should recall, one of the most curious figures of modern Zionism, Yitzhak Tabenkin. Tabenkin was a kind of secular rabbi, an ideologue whose speeches and writings were almost tantamount to religious commandments for his disciples. He was an exponent of the unyielding belief in kibbutz Socialism as much as he was committed to the undisputable right of the Jews to all of Eretz-Israel. Hakibbutz Hameuhad was also the cradle where the Palmah – the Yishuv's elite storm battalions – was born. In the 1940s Allon was the Palmah's mythological commander. Although a moderate of sorts when it came to producing ideas for accommodation with the Arabs – the Allon plan was an example – Allon was more emotionally and philosophically attached to the ethos of settlements than any politician on the right. This is why he would vote in the Knesset against the clauses in the Camp David accords with Egypt that required Israel to dismantle the settlements of northern Sinai.

Dayan was a different kind of man. Unlike Allon, he detested party discipline. Free of political loyalties or firm convictions, he was loyal only to himself. Although a brilliant general in 1948, Allon never became a charismatic leader and he was incapable of stirring popular emotions. But Dayan had a magnetic influence on the Israeli mind. He was for the Israelis not just another politician, not even another brilliant military mind in a country that excelled in producing them; he was the idealised epitome of their collective profile, the ultimate new man of the Zionist revolution. He was a man of contrasts who lived by the sword but who at the same time was able to be resourceful as a statesman, as he would prove during the peace talks with Egypt at Camp David. There, the life cycle of an extraordinary individual was closed, that of a man of paradoxes, a symbol of military prowess who could be a statesman at the same time.

Dayan's creativity and originality, his endurance and charisma turned him into a hero of Israeli youth, the reflection of the mystical forces that gave a purpose to their lives. They felt attracted by Dayan, yet at the same time rejected by him, a man who never suffered from an excess of love for others. He was the prince of Israeliness, the proud *sabra*, a role model. But he was also a textbook cynic. He knew how to manipulate the tribal nerves of two generations of Israelis. Nor was his charisma always put at the service of a good cause. In the interval between 1967 and the Yom Kippur War it served to legitimise the status quo and drive Israel into yet another war. It is impossible to conceive the peace agreement with Egypt without him, but equally impossible to write the history of Israel's wars without the man with the black eyepatch. He was the architect of Israel's strategy of pre-emptive war in the 1950s and the accomplice of Golda Meir in her steadfast rejection of peace opportunities prior to the 1973 war.

Author Amos Oz found in Dayan a true poet of the experience of those Israelis whose lives had been lived amid wars and eulogies for the dead. War and death were the recurring themes in Dayan's language. He was the war hero on a permanent quest for death. Hence his passion for the eulogy. His speech at the funeral of Roi Rutenberg, who was riddled by bullets at the Gaza Strip, can be compared with Pericles' eulogy to the fallen soldiers of the Peloponnesian War. At the same time he displayed a sense of pessimism when he hinted that the gates of Gaza might prove to be too heavy a burden on Roi's generation, as if he doubted the ability of that generation of Israelis to emulate their biblical forefathers. Dayan's Hebrew was soaked to the point of obsession with the absurd charm of death. His funereal nostalgia was undoubtedly the most important trait of his tormented soul. He himself was not unaware of this sense of tragedy and death in his personality, for he wrote in his autobiography, 'My name, Moshe, was born in sadness; I was named Moshe after the first pioneer who fell in the defence of the Kibbutz Degania, where I was born.'

Politically, Dayan lacked strong convictions; he always kept all options open even when they were mutually exclusive. As minister of defense in 1967 he wanted to destroy the Egyptian army, but he opposed the occupation of new lands. Peace was not possible, he maintained, and there was no sense therefore in acquiring territorial bargaining cards for peace. The occupation of Arab lands, he warned, would only subject Israel to international pressure without advancing the cause of peace. This may explain why Dayan became the champion of the status quo after the war and, unlike Yigal Allon, refrained from initiating any peace plans. But, in a typical Dayan paradox, he allowed his policy of status quo in the occupied territories to drift into one of practical annexation. Dayan believed in resistance and permanent war, not in peace. His existentialist philosophy, as he spelled it out in an interview to *Maariv* (30 November 1970), was that 'the only peace negotiations are those where we settle the land and we build, and we settle, and from time to time we go to war'. Peace with the Arabs was to him nothing but 'words for land'. He preferred, as he said to *Yedioth Aharonoth* (4 March 1977), 'life with the Arabs without a peace agreement'. Paradoxically, his best way to show that peace was not an option was to discard the local Palestinian leadership as an interlocutor for peace negotiations, thus implicitly enthroning the PLO as the sole representative of the Palestinian people. As early as 1968 he said in a radio interview that Fatah was a movement of national liberation; he even compared it to the Vietcong. Dayan's PLO option was not advanced as an avenue to peace, but precisely in order to make the point that there was no way that Zionism and the Palestinian national movement could be reconciled with each other.

Dayan was a solitary man, creative, distant and alienated. He served as a minister under Golda Meir and Menachem Begin, and was never especially fond of either. However, he appreciated Golda Meir's charisma and authority. Dayan was not short of dialectic abilities to impose his ideas, but he always left the most important decisions in the hands of others, in this case of Meir and Begin, thus avoiding responsibility. He was resourceful and creative, but he would hardly ever fight for his ideas. Strikingly, the founding fathers of the state always found it in them to forgive him. All of them were diaspora Jews, unable to resist the charm of this latest dashing mutation of the Jewish genius.

A lone wolf, Dayan had many admirers, but was quite incapable of establishing profound relationships with another human being. Instead of his natural environment of Israeli politicians and military men, he preferred the company of Arab peasants and shepherds, who for him represented a primary feeling, a deeply rooted human landscape. He was able to strike up a more frank and open conversation with an Arab shepherd of the Izreel Valley than with any of his Israeli peers. Dayan had an honest appreciation of the Palestinian guerrillas and even of the terrorists among them: in many he admired their courage and perseverance. He had no respect for the Palestinians who collaborated with the Israeli authorities. Nor was he impressed, however, by the intellectuals of the Israeli Left who claimed to be tormented by the moral sins of Israel's occupation of the Palestinian territories. He was much more at ease with the memory of the founding fathers, the pioneers of Ein Harod and Nahalal: 'I saw their wrinkled faces, I saw the old faces of my mother and her friends in their final years, faces withered by the cruel sun, and I saw their legs in the mud of the valley...'

Dayan was buried in Nahalal, an agricultural settlement, cradle of the Israeli pioneer co-operative movement. He had asked his wife Rachel not to mourn him and politicians not to write his eulogy. Nihilist and pagan, for him the Bible was not an ethical document, but the aesthetic and mystic expression of the link between past and present; until the end, Dayan refused to be reconciled with Orthodox Judaism: 'I am not concerned at all about what history will have to say about me. There is nothing beyond death, only the worms.'

But the sad end reserved for all mortals was for Dayan more than a decade away when he served as Golda Meir's accomplice in creating the conditions that led eventually to the Yom Kippur War and in brushing aside the challenge posed by the Palestinian response to the Israeli occupation. Anchored in the politics of inertia, Dayan, Golda Meir and the rest of Israel's leaders failed to gauge the real meaning and consequences of the Six Day War.

The next watershed in the history of the Middle East would be the making of an Egyptian leader. Israel's hubris, her sterile peace diplomacy and the notorious 'conception' according to which the Arabs lacked a military option, left Sadat with no alternative but war.

If the Yom Kippur War was a surprise, it was not because Sadat did not give sufficient indications that once his peace overtures had been turned down he would go to war. The overconfident Israelis simply did not take him seriously. In April 1973, he told *Newsweek* in the most explicit terms possible that he was getting ready for war. 'The time has come for a shock,' he stated; 'everything is now being mobilised in earnest for the resumption of the battle, which is now inevitable.' But in Israel, Dayan dismissed the Egyptian threats. His was the view that the Arabs were almost congenitally incapable of winning a modern war. He addressed the General Staff in the summer of 1973 with an analysis of the balance of forces that ruled out an Arab attack, but also with a reflection on the 'moral, technical and educational backwardness' of the Arab soldier. At about the same time General Rabin wrote in an almost identically dismissive vein of the Arabs' congenital weaknesses in modern warfare: 'The Arabs have little capacity for co-ordinating their military and political action.'

Uri Bar-Joseph[1] advanced a rather reductionist answer to the question of who was really responsible for the fatal blunder that led to Israel being taken by surprise in October 1973. He lays the entire burden of responsibility on General Elie Zeira, the head of Military Intelligence, for failing to assess the available information and alert the political leaders accordingly. Dr Bar-Joseph practically exonerates Mrs Meir and her Minister of Defence by arguing that leaders can be expected to act only on the basis of the information that is available to them, and in this case their intelligence services failed them. But the question is certainly broader, and it needs to be seen in the context of the 'conception' that was cultivated by the politicians, and of the social environment prevailing after the 1967 victory. The politicians fully shared in creating and encouraging a national mood of complacency that percolated into the military system as much as it was influenced by it, thus paving the way for the success of the Arab exercise in tactical deceit.

Sadat was practically forced to go to war by the dismissive attitude prevailing both in Israel and in the United States towards Egypt and him personally. There was no other way he could be taken seriously. His peace overtures were defeated not because they lacked merit as such, but because Egypt was perceived as not having a war option to back them.

---

[1] *The Watchman Fell Asleep: The Surprise of Yom Kippur and its Sources* (Hebrew), Zmora-Bitan, Lod, 2001.

Henry Kissinger admitted in a later interview with Ahron Bregman and Jihan El-Tahri that he thought of Sadat 'as a character out of *Aida*. I did not take him seriously. He kept making grandiloquent statements but never acted on them. ... Frankly, I thought he was bluffing.' Kissinger implicitly advised the Egyptians that only by starting a war would they be given credence. 'I cannot deal with your problem unless it becomes a crisis' was Kissinger's reaction to an Egyptian last-ditch attempt to avert a war by advancing a proposal for a comprehensive settlement with Israel that was conveyed to him in February 1973 by Foreign Minister Hafiz Ismail.

The Israelis were wrong to assume that the Arabs would start a war only when they had a chance of winning it, which is why Mrs Meir overlooked an explicit warning by 'the best of Israel's enemies', King Hussein, ten days before the war, that an Egyptian–Syrian offensive was imminent. But Sadat's strategy did not aim at military victory. His was a political move made by military means. His was to be a political war, a classic Clausewitzian move that complemented his peace strategy, his quest for a settlement. Sadat never expected to defeat Israel. All he wanted was to unleash a political process by shaking Israel's complacency and forcing the superpowers to reactivate the search for a settlement. So eager was Sadat to begin a political dialogue through the good services of the United States and reach an alliance with her that, as Henry Kissinger related in his book of documents on the Yom Kippur War (and Vietnam), *Crisis*, he lost no time, as early as the first day of the war, in contacting Kissinger. Sadat then betrayed both the Syrians, who never saw this as a political war – they fought for the 'liberation of the Golan Heights' pure and simple – and his Soviet patrons, who were by then still busy enlisting the support of the other Arab states for Egypt's war effort. Sadat was so convinced of his strategy that he spelled it out in unambiguous terms to his military commanders. 'If you can get back ten centimetres of the Sinai, I can solve the problem,' he told them, as General Saad el-Shazly, Egypt's Chief of Staff, later recalled.

It was indeed the combination of the unexpectedly good performance of the Arab armies in the early stages of the war, Israel's psychological setbacks and the diplomatic skills of Henry Kissinger, who knew how to use and manipulate the military impasse in order to produce an exclusively American-sponsored political process, that made the 1973 war into the major watershed that it was.

VII   Begin's 'Capsule Theory' and
Sadat's 'Separate Peace'

The arrogant enemy lost its equilibrium. ... The wounded nation restored its honour.

President Sadat's speech,
16 October 1973

I have not come to you to seek a partial peace ... I tell you we welcome you among us. ... This in itself is a tremendous turning point, one of the landmarks of a decisive historical change ...

President Sadat's speech before the Knesset,
20 November 1977

It is a frightening proposition that someone's solution to the problems in the Middle East might be a single bullet dispatched to the heart of Egyptian President Sadat as the PLO's predecessors did at Al-Aqsa Mosque to King Abdullah.

Menachem Begin's speech at the Knesset,
28 December 1977

[Sadat] did not give a damn about the West Bank.

William Quandt, President Carter's Middle East adviser at the
Camp David summit,
September 1978

We are fighting the Camp David plot.

Yasser Arafat,
19 November 1979

Ben-Gurion's fear that an Egyptian leader might emerge who would be an Arab version of Ataturk and seriously challenge the myth of Israel's invincibility was vindicated in the figure and performance of Anwar Sadat in 1973, not as Ben-Gurion had assumed in that of Nasser. Sadat, who used to be dismissed by Israelis and Americans alike as Nasser's lapdog, emerged out of the 1973 war as a bold, imaginative world leader. He would dramatically change the parameters of the Arab–Israeli conflict, create the conditions for the unbelievable – namely, a peace agreement between the Jewish state and Egypt, the leader of the Arab world – and shake beyond recognition the balance of influence in the region between the two superpowers.

The Yom Kippur War (known as the 'October War' on the Arab side) that began as a combined Egyptian and Syrian attack on Israel was a brilliant exercise in strategic deceit. Taken by surprise, the Israelis suffered in the first days of the war one military setback after another. In an impressive performance and before Israel could regain her balance, the Egyptian forces overran the Israeli positions on the Bar-Lev Line and occupied a ten-mile-wide strip of land along the eastern bank of the Canal. Simultaneously, the Syrians managed to advance deep into the Israeli-occupied Golan Heights. Israel eventually recovered from the surprise and initial shock, and in a brilliant counter-offensive its forces crossed the Canal, and encircled and cut off the Egyptian Third Army on the east bank. By the end of the war, Israeli forces were within a hundred kilometres of Cairo. 'The road from Damascus to Tel Aviv is the same that leads from Tel Aviv to Damascus,' boasted a relieved Defence Minister Moshe Dayan when, in the last day of the war, his forces stood 25 kilometres from the Syrian capital. Militarily, Israel's heroic response in the second part of the war was certainly no less impressive than the Arabs' performance in the first stages of the war, and in terms of casualties and material losses the Arab side suffered considerably more than the Israelis. But the real meaning of the war for Israel lay in the moral and psychological setback that it represented. Never before had the Arabs succeeded in inflicting so many casualties and material damage on Israel (2,838 dead and 8,800 wounded as well as severe losses of war material). And another humiliating precedent: dozens of Israeli prisoners parading humbled, handcuffed and blindfolded for the entire Arab world to see and rejoice at. These were images that had never been seen before by an Israeli public always used to what General Bar-Lev had called in 1967 'quick and elegant' victories.

'The spirit of October', as Osama El-Baz, President Sadat's national security adviser, defined it, meant that the illusion of the Israelis about their invincible military prowess was shattered. 'We have proven ourselves their equals, both intellectually and practically,' he wrote in *Al-Ahram*'s weekly magazine on the twenty-fifth anniversary of the war. Having 'restored its honour', as Sadat explained in a speech in the middle of the war, Egypt was now ready for peace. Sadat's strategic war put Israel off balance and destroyed the famous 'conception' whereby time was in her favour. Now, Israel was forced to consider making peace not on the basis of her unchallenged supremacy, but on that of the most profound crisis of confidence ever known by the Jewish state, a crisis triggered in its turn by the most traumatic setback ever suffered by its legendary defence forces. Israel's military power – and this was a message to the Americans as well – could no longer ensure regional stability. By an act of force Egypt had asserted her own agenda and compelled Israel to enter a peace process with the now more than ever vital purpose of getting Egypt out of the war cycle in the Middle East.

Enamoured with her notorious 'conception', Israel seemed to have abandoned after 1967 her traditional emphasis on a settlement with Egypt as 'the gate to the Arab world', as Ben-Gurion used to put it. Now, both Rabin as Israel's new Prime Minister in 1974 and his successor, Menachem Begin in 1977, were forced to change fundamentally Israel's position to a more conciliatory approach in order to recover in a credible way the strategy of taking Egypt out of the conflict. They knew that this might not assure that the Arab–Israeli conflict would know no more wars, but should such a war nevertheless erupt, its nature would be substantially different from a war with Egypt's participation. The time had come to depart from Golda Meir's devastating legacy of righteous rejectionism and start responding to Egypt's territorial requirements for peace. Humbled and psychologically shaken, Israel was forced to change the rhetoric of supremacy and haughtiness for the policy of accommodation and compromise.

Indeed, in the first military disengagement agreement signed on 18 January 1974 between Israel and Egypt, Sadat achieved what he had planned and failed to get from Israel in his February 1971 initiative, that is, an Israeli withdrawal from the Canal that explicitly created a linkage with 'a lasting peace in accordance with SCRs 242 and 338'. Moreover, the disengagement agreements on both the Syrian and the Egyptian fronts were reflective more of the Arabs' military successes than of Israel's final victory.

This was not only due to American pressure, but also to that of an agitated and enraged Israeli public opinion that would not allow its failing government to miss yet another opportunity for a settlement. A salient characteristic of Israeli democracy had traditionally been the conformism of public opinion with the broad national objectives and with the security and foreign policy premises established by the nation's governments. The year 1973 saw the eruption of popular protest movements, whose far milder origins had appeared already during the War of Attrition, with a scope and vigour previously unknown in Israel. Such movements would from now on act as the watchdog of governments wavering in their task of seeking peace. The 1973 war signalled the emergence of public opinion and popular pressure as a central player in the process of policy making in Israel.

The military disengagement agreements also signalled the unequivocal confirmation of the ascendancy of America's power in the Middle East. The Geneva Peace Conference on 20 December 1973 was a grandiloquent occasion, where each party delivered its traditional script, predictably leading to nowhere. But it was the Soviet Union's participation in the conference in the role of a co-sponsor that Henry Kissinger was especially unhappy with. He had no intention of bringing the Soviet Union into the politics of peacemaking in the Middle East. On the contrary, he wanted to use the peace process in order to undermine the Soviets' position in the region.

Nor did he believe in the feasibility of a dramatic leap from war to a comprehensive peace agreement. He found the alternative in a not entirely new concept, for it was anticipated by Sadat during his hectic peace offensive prior to the war, a step-by-step process that would create a sense of progress and mutual trust before the agonisingly tough questions of the final agreement were addressed. Driven by a pessimistic philosophy about the nature of international relations, and hence by a possibilist attitude to conflict resolution in the Arab–Israeli dispute where he did not believe that the parties were yet ripe for the most painful decisions, Kissinger institutionalised in the politics of peacemaking in the region a concept – interim agreements – that would have a very long life indeed.

It was now clear to every Arab government in the region that only America was capable of delivering Israel, and they needed therefore to extricate themselves from the Soviet Union's grip and reconcile themselves with an American-led peace diplomacy if they wanted back their territories. This would be true of the PLO as well. The origins of the PLO's future change of strategy in favour of a two-state solution in Palestine need to be traced back to the 1974 disengagement. A change of strategy became an even more vital necessity for the PLO after September 1975. For America's pledge to Israel in the second disengagement agreement of September 1975 that it would not recognise, or deal with, the PLO unless it had radically modified its policies and renounced terrorism would eventually serve as a catalyst for the PLO to do just that – modify its policies – in order to join the American-sponsored peace process.

Yitzhak Rabin, an architect and hero of the Six Day War who succeeded Golda Meir as Prime Minister, was a novice, an inexperienced politician who was to be outmanoeuvred frequently by his then hawkish Minister of Defence, Shimon Peres. He also proved to be incapable of controlling the hardline lobby of the National Religious Party and that of his own colleagues in the government, Allon and Galili, all of whom pressed for a policy of creeping annexation in the West Bank.

The definition and control of Israel's policymaking has always depended on the power struggle between the two leading politicians of the ruling party. Such was the case when Ben-Gurion and Sharett vied for political supremacy in the 1950s, and such was also the case of the bitter rivalry between Peres and Rabin after the latter was preferred by the Labour Party leadership in 1974 as Golda Meir's successor.

Persistent, obstinate and proverbially patient, Peres was second to none in his talent for political manoeuvring and manipulation, 'an indefatigable master of subversion', as Rabin would later put it in his memoirs. He lacked the irresistible charisma of his political friend Moshe Dayan, but like him he was never committed to immoveable principles. Peres made up for his lack of popular appeal by an extraordinary capacity for accumulating political power. He never accepted Rabin's leadership, and throughout the latter's first term as prime minister he challenged him on almost every policy issue. He vehemently opposed, for example, the interim agreements with Egypt and Syria as representing 'territorial concessions without a valuable political compensation'. The man who in the 1990s practically invented the concept of a piecemeal peace process with the Palestinians, challenged Rabin in the early 1970s by utterly rejecting the concept of interim agreements and by persisting in his notion about an unsolvable Arab–Israeli conflict that doomed Israel to live eternally on its sword and under the protection of a balance of fear and nuclear deterrence. The prophet in the 1990s of a philosophy of a New Middle East of economic integration and democracy – he even suggested that Israel join the Arab League – Peres spoke in the 1970s of Israel's security as depending on the Arabs remaining backward and under-developed. He dismissed as empty talk any call for Israel's integration in the region. The architect of Israel's strategy of nuclear ambiguity, Peres substituted for Jabotinsky's Iron Wall his own concept of a 'nuclear wall'.

As a matter of fact, the Shimon Peres of the 1990s was never really the political 'dove' that he pretended to be – years after he was granted the Nobel Peace Prize for the Oslo agreement he was still opposed to the idea of an independent Palestinian state – but as Rabin's minister of defense in the 1970s he positioned himself as an undisguised 'hawk'. While Prime Minister Rabin was busy fighting the Block of the Faithful as a 'cancer in the body of Israeli democracy', as he defined it in his memoirs, his minister of defense continued looking for ways to please these fanatic exponents of the idea of Greater Eretz-Israel. It was Peres who allowed 'The Block' in 1976 to settle illegally, and against the prime minister's wishes, in 'Kadum' (Sebastia), thus inaugurating a pattern of settlements expansion through fait accompli. In a speech in Tel-Aviv on 24 January 1976 (*Haaretz*, 25 January 1976), Peres explained the rationale behind his position. 'It is beyond my understanding why it is allowed to settle in Judaea and not in Samaria. Jews have a fundamental right to settle everywhere.' 'What kind of a peace is this that prevents 15,000 Jews from living beyond the Green Line?' he later said in a Cabinet meeting. And he added: 'Such a peace would be a farce. The injustice that we are doing the Arabs by confiscating their land pales against the injustice they did to us by denying us peace for so many years.' Shimon Peres proposed to create wide settlement blocks in the Jerusalem area down to Maale Adumim and in what later became the city of Ariel deep in the occupied West Bank. 'I do not see how we can deny an Israeli passport-holder the right to settle wherever he wants,' he concluded in what Yehiel Admoni, the head of the settlements department of the Jewish Agency who kept the record of that Cabinet meeting, called 'a stunning performance' (*Yedioth Aharonoth*, 29 April 2005).

Peres lost no opportunity of deriding Rabin's concept of peace based on territorial compromise. 'We should not succumb to the view of all kind of advisers who want to convince us that we should go back to a state the width of whose ribs is between 14 to 16 kilometres', Peres declared. It was precisely in order to sabotage the option of a territorial compromise with the Palestinians that Mr Peres lent his support to the settlers' movement. He believed that the solution lay in what he liked to call 'a functional compromise', namely a joint Israeli–Jordanian control over the West Bank. 'If I have to choose between splitting the land or dividing the power over it, I prefer the latter,' he said (*Yedioth Aharonoth*, 13 July 1975). For all practical purposes, Shimon Peres was the champion of a bi-national Jewish–Arab state. In one of his many books of memoir – *Now Tomorrow* (*Kaet Mahar*) – he wrote that it was impossible 'to reach peace by giving up part of the land. It is my belief that the right way to reach peace ... is through the creation of a new political structure, not by means of again bisecting the land ...'

Rigid, systematic – 'too cautious', according to Ben-Gurion, who denied him the post of Chief of Staff – and slow in detecting the new trends in the Arab world, Rabin, who definitely looked for a territorial compromise on the West Bank, was nevertheless unwilling to encourage the movement for change, and a two-state solution to the Israeli–Palestinian conflict, that had hesitantly started in the PLO in 1974. Arafat's desperate ambiguous formulae always made it easy for Israel to ignore him. That Rabin failed to respond to the variable winds of change in the PLO was not perhaps a major sin. The problem was that he left a dangerous political vacuum in the territories by his insistence on a Jordanian option that did not exist. For like his predecessors, Rabin offered King Hussein nothing he could not resist. Rabin would not agree to the King's demand for an interim agreement in the West Bank based on a military disengagement along the Jordan Valley. Had the Israeli government accepted starting a peace process with Jordan along lines similar to those it had conducted with Egypt, it might have curtailed, or certainly slowed down, the ascendancy of the PLO in the territories. Left empty-handed from his endless secret meetings with Israeli leaders, Hussein could not prevent his diplomatic defeat at the Arab summit in Rabat in October 1974 that enthroned the PLO as 'the sole legitimate representative of the Palestinian people'.

In Rabin's defence one should say, however, that although he clearly was not, at least initially, the most imaginative and bold of peacemakers, for him to opt in 1974 for a deal with the PLO would have been not only an act of political suicide but also a move entirely out of tune with the national mood. There was no psychological or popular readiness for such a step. In his second term as Prime Minister Rabin finally opened negotiations with the PLO and he was then certainly acting as a visionary leader in times of transition. But he was also operating in conditions that were riper for such a move and, notwithstanding the severe political obstacles he had still to surmount, in 1993 he acted within a somewhat safer political environment than that which existed in 1974.

Rabin was a soldier who became a statesman, a military man who had the courage to respond to political challenges that were not susceptible to military solutions. In 1948, and later in 1956 and 1967, he still believed that a massive expulsion of Palestinians from the West Bank could solve Israel's Palestinian predicament. 'It will not be a humane solution, but war has never been a humane business', he told Ben-Gurion in 1956. Yet, as the documents recently released reveal,[1] in the immediate aftermath of the Six Day War he was surprisingly quick to appreciate the new reality and the need for the creation of a Palestinian state. On the eve of his departure to Washington as Israel's ambassador to the United States, he proposed to Prime Minister Eshkol the creation of a Palestinian state. 'This is the only manoeuvring space that we possess', he explained. 'The premise should be that we should not cut off the Palestinians in the West Bank. We are not going to expel half a million Palestinians.' To annex the West Bank to the state of Israel, he then warned, would mean creating an apartheid state or, as he put it, a 'South African' situation.

The paralysis on the Jordanian–Palestinian front meant that the only real peace option lay on the southern front and it was there that Rabin will go down in history for setting the stage, and establishing the conditions, for a future Israeli–Egyptian peace. The peace with Egypt

---

[1] Yemimah Rosenthal (ed.), *Yitzhak Rabin, Prime Minister of Israel. A Selection of Documents from His Life*, Jerusalem, 2005.

signed at Camp David in 1979 would have been inconceivable without the ground-breaking disengagement agreements so meticulously negotiated by Rabin. It was clear to him and to the American mediators that a leap to a final settlement between the two countries was beyond human capacity and probably beyond the capacity of Israel's polity to digest.

Rabin negotiated the second disengagement agreement in his characteristic style: rigid, systematic and obstinately careful with the details and the fine print. He even risked a confrontation with his American allies who threatened, as President Ford put it, 'to reassess' America's relations with Israel. But Rabin's insistence on what he believed to be vital concepts – he wanted, for example, Egypt's commitment to non-belligerency in return for Israel's partial withdrawal – eventually paid off. The agreement stipulated that 'the conflict between the parties and in the Middle East shall not be resolved by military force but by peaceful means' and that 'they undertake not to resort to the threat or use of force or military blockade against each other'. Such conditions did not sound especially reasonable when Golda Meir presented them in response to Sadat's 1971 initiative. But Rabin's case was entirely different. Not only was he now the Prime Minister of a country that had just emerged from a most traumatic surprise attack by two Arab armies but, unlike his predecessor, he was also ready to pay a heavy territorial price. And, no less important, he was ready to accept the linkage between the interim agreement and the final settlement.

From Israel's perspective the second disengagement agreement was a precursor of the future peace with Egypt also in the sense that it was accompanied, like the Camp David accords, by what amounted for all practical purposes to a strategic alliance with the United States. This included lavish American military and financial assistance, and two political commitments, deemed by the government of the day to be vital, according to which America would not recognise or deal with the PLO and would likewise reject any attempt to base future peace negotiations on any UN resolution other than 242.

Rabin's dramatic achievements in Disengagement II with Egypt meant, however, that the peace diplomacy on the other fronts was doomed to paralysis. For Israel's bilateral memorandum with the United States stipulated that the disengagement agreement was a separate deal between Israel and Egypt and not necessarily a step towards a comprehensive settlement in the Middle East. In a way, Rabin not only established the groundwork for Begin's peace with Egypt but also defined the nature of that future peace agreement as a separate settlement, one that was independent of the state of the conflict between Israel and other Arab parties. In Disengagement II Rabin acted as an authentic disciple of

Ben-Gurion, who saw Egypt as the main enemy that needed to be the first to be neutralised, for it was also the gate to the entire Arab world. With Disengagement II Rabin could claim to have reached a major objective of his premiership: a solid start to a peace settlement with Egypt, a strategic understanding with America, and a much needed respite for Israel to recover from the trauma of the Yom Kippur War and be ready to face the final stages of the peace process with Egypt from an improved military and strategic position.

Not many observers of Israeli politics could have guessed that 17 May 1977, the day Menachem Begin, the leading hawk of Israeli politics and a political outcast who had led for so many years a vociferous, but ineffective, opposition against the Labourite establishment, came out of the wilderness and ousted the Labour Party from office would mark the acceleration of the peace process with Egypt, not its demise.

But indications of Begin's ambition not to be an ephemeral episode in Israel's history could be detected immediately upon his coming to office. The incorporation into his government of the two most illustrious disciples of Ben-Gurion, Yigael Yadin and Moshe Dayan, the latter clearly anxious to erase the record of his blunder in the Yom Kippur War and leave his mark in history as a peacemaker, reflected Begin's desire to acquire the legitimacy that only Ben-Gurion's name could give him. But Begin aspired also to go beyond the legacy of the founder of the State of Israel and re-create, as it were, the Jewish state in his reformed image as a leader of historic achievements. Begin, who had resigned from the Eshkol government because of his rejection of Security Council Resolution 242, lost no time on coming to power in announcing his acceptance of that same Resolution as the basis for the Geneva Peace Conference, where he also agreed to participate. Thus Begin departed from the traditional objection of Israeli governments to international peace conferences where Israel always ran the risk of being isolated and manoeuvred into a trap by the Arab delegations and their Soviet patrons. Moreover, during his first visit to the White House, Begin indicated his willingness to make a significant withdrawal from Sinai and a more modest redeployment on the Golan Heights for the sake of peace with Egypt and Syria respectively. Maybe not a very spectacular overture, but a fair start nonetheless. On one crucial point – Judaea and Samaria – Begin never bluffed or played tactics. He made it clear to President Carter that he would in no circumstances allow Judaea and Samaria to be transferred to non-Jewish sovereignty.

Begin was thus positioning himself as the most eloquent and committed exponent of what could perhaps be defined as the 'capsule theory', namely the drive to reach a settlement with the surrounding Arab states that would 'capsulate', as it were, the West Bank and with it the Palestinian problem in an environment of binding peace agreements between Israel and the surrounding Arab states. This, Begin believed, would allow Israel to exercise her full control of Eretz-Israel, yet deny the Palestinians the possibility of again triggering an all-Arab war against her.

In many ways Begin thus became the initiator of an Israeli structure of peacemaking that would be endorsed and followed by practically all his successors. All of them – Rabin in his second term, Peres, Netanyahu and Barak – would follow in his footsteps. However much they might have differed from Begin's position on the West Bank, they all nevertheless assumed the premise that the Palestinian problem was so intractable, perhaps even insoluble, that they preferred to strike a deal with Syria, even if that meant paying the full and heavy territorial price on the Golan Heights, exactly as Begin did in Sinai. They also aspired to 'capsulate' the Palestinian problem, prevent it from triggering a regional war and eventually reduce the price for its solution when the Palestinians would finally join the negotiating table.

When it came to the Begin–Dayan government this also meant the unceremonial burial of the so-called Jordanian option. For this required a territorial price on the Palestinian front that neither was ready to pay. They both preferred to build on Ben-Gurion's legacy: once Egypt is taken out of the war cycle and an all-Arab war against Israel is thus ruled out, territorial concessions to assure stability on other fronts might no longer be that vital.

The Egyptian–Israeli conspiracy for peace was born out of a common view as to the right mechanism of peacemaking; both Israel and Egypt preferred the bilateral track to a cumbersome Geneva international format. Potential mediators and midwives in an Arab–Israeli peace were never in short supply. As early as August 1977, Begin and Sadat started their discreet flirtation, first through the good offices of President Ceauşescu of Romania and then, a month later, in a secret meeting under the auspices of King Hassan II of Morocco between Foreign Minister Moshe Dayan and Egypt's Deputy Prime Minister Dr Hassan Tuhami. Sadat did not believe that a Soviet–American co-sponsorship of the peace process would bear the political fruits he wanted. He could see his fears vindicated already in a joint declaration of the superpowers that, to his dismay, endorsed the Israeli interpretation of Security Council Resolution 242 when it spoke of 'withdrawal of Israeli armed forces from territories occupied in 1967'. And as to Begin, he was not yet ready to digest the concept of 'the legitimate rights of the Palestinian people', one of the central premises upon which the Geneva Conference was to be convened.

Deep in his heart, Sadat knew that he was embarking on a track leading to a separate peace with Israel. Begin might have been bluffing or playing tactics when he resisted the possibility of a full withdrawal from Sinai, and he might have been just bargaining when he opposed having to dismantle the settlements in the north of the peninsula. But Judaea and Samaria, as both Sadat and Carter were soon to realise, were the almost theological core of Begin's political philosophy and worldview as a Jew and as an Israeli. Recovering Sinai, Sadat would shortly understand, would only be possible through a deal with Israel that could not allow for a formula on the West Bank that would fully satisfy the Palestinians or the Arab family as a whole. Hence his peace with Israel would essentially have to be a separate peace.

Sadat's peace overture was born out of deep political convictions and a sober strategic analysis of the regional balance of power. It was clear to him that Israel was a nuclear power that had proved to be unbeatable even in a conventional war on two simultaneous fronts. For Egypt to persist in her military efforts to wrest from Israel the territories and a fair deal for the Palestinians, Sadat understood only too well, would only end up draining her resources and condemning her people to misery, poverty and backwardness. In fact, when Egypt went into the Yom Kippur War she was already in a practical state of bankruptcy. Sadat made this clear to his advisers a week before the war when he confided to them, as General Gamassi relates in his war memoirs, that Egypt was unable to pay her debts to the banks. Anis Mansour, Sadat's semi-official mouthpiece in the Egyptian press, was his master's voice when he wrote that 'the war has embittered everyone's life. The war has denied home, street and livelihood. ... Peace will bring prosperity for all.'

For Israel, Egypt was the gate to the Arab world; for Egypt, Israel was the introduction to America. The alliance with the United States was such a vital objective for Sadat that one may rightly wonder what came first in his strategy, peace with Israel or an alliance with America. Had he been able to reach an American alliance without peace with Israel he might have opted for that. When in 1974 General Gamasy questioned Sadat's flexibility in the disengagement talks with Israel, the *rais* calmed him down: 'Don't forget, General, we are talking here about peace with the Americans!' Only peace with Israel, Sadat understood, could bring him the vital American aid that was needed for Egypt's reconstruction. In his vision he was embarking on a major strategic and diplomatic revolution in Egypt's priorities and alliances. This meant moving away from the military dependence on the Soviet Union in favour of turning Egypt into America's main ally in the Arab world. He was determined not to let all his vital objectives be frustrated and subverted by the petty technicalities of labyrinthine international conferences or the need of the two superpowers to reconcile their differences at Egypt's expense.

Another shift implicit in Sadat's strategy was that of keeping Egypt's distance from the hollow, but costly, rhetoric of pan-Arabism. He could not allow the whims of the Arab leaders he so despised to thwart his grand designs for Egypt and the region. Weary of inter-Arab politics and tired of the high price Egypt had paid for the Palestinian cause, Sadat now wanted to move away from Nasser's pan-Arab ambitions and the excessive focus on the question of Palestine towards an emphasis on Egypt's role as a power at the strategic crossroads between two continents, Asia and Africa. With the Soviets consolidating their strategic positions in Ethiopia, Libya, South Yemen and Madagascar, and with the mounting tensions on Egypt's borders with Libya and Sudan, Sadat was driven by an urgent need to shift his strategic priorities from the Arab–Israeli conflict to more vital concerns. Conspicuously, his departure from the old Nasserite inertia of an all-out confrontation with Israel was to be reflected also in the realm of symbols surrounding the regime. Unlike his predecessor, Sadat denied any pan-Arab meaning to the annual celebration of the Free Officers' Revolution (23 July) which Nasser had established as 'Al' Id elkumi' (The Pan-Arab holiday). And as early as 1971 Sadat signalled his intention to embark on a strategy of 'Egypt first' by changing the name of the Republic from 'The United Arab Republic' to that of 'The Egyptian Arab Republic'.

Sadat's assessment about the decline of Nasserite pan-Arabism into irrelevance as a valid strategy for the Arabs needs to be seen also in the context of the failure of the Arab oil embargo. By 1977 the euphoria that had overtaken the Arab world with the sudden and dramatic rise of the power of Arab oil was fading away without the perverted wealth in terms of petrodollars acquired by the oil dynasties in the Gulf having borne any tangible political fruits for the Arabs. The palpable sense of excitement and defeats avenged throughout the Arab world that had accompanied the use of the oil weapon ended in bitter disillusionment.

Not unlike Yitzhak Rabin when he decided in 1993 radically to shift his peace strategy and go for a settlement with the PLO in Oslo, Sadat was also deeply disturbed by the rise of Islamic fundamentalism throughout the region. He went to Jerusalem to change the parameters of the Arab–Israeli conflict because, again like Rabin in 1993, he detected a narrow window of opportunity that, if missed, would only turn out to be a prelude to a decline of the region into yet another futile, but even more devastating, cycle of wars. He would, of course, continue to champion the Palestinian cause as an Arab consensus and sometimes also as a fig leaf of legitimacy for his own Egypt-focused foreign policy. But he would not let this prevent Egypt from advancing her own particular interests. Essentially, and for all practical purposes, Sadat had now embarked on a path leading to a separate peace with Israel.

But if a separate peace this would have to be, then the Geneva Conference was clearly not the forum Sadat needed to impress. He had to storm the mind of the Israeli people and its leaders with his vision. He needed to go, as he put it in a stunning speech to the Egyptian parliament on 9 November 1977, 'to the end of the earth', to the Knesset in Jerusalem, where he would captivate the imagination of the Israelis and, indeed, of the world.

Sadat's spectacular initiative took everybody by surprise. Begin was wise to respond generously. But interestingly, the American administration was clearly taken aback by, and was anything but happy with, a move that threatened to isolate the Egyptian President in the Arab world and undermine the prospects of the Geneva Conference as it was conceived by the two superpowers. In a stark departure from Kissinger's concept of a Pax Americana that would exclude the Soviet Union, the Carter administration wanted to confront the parties with a joint Soviet–American position on the peace terms and in practice establish an American–Soviet condominium in the Middle East. Curiously, Sadat's initiative responded to, and reflected, a joint Israeli–Egyptian challenge to President Carter's peace strategy and philosophy.

The Americans had their concept of a superpower-led peace process, but Sadat was determined to impose his own strategy, neutralise the Soviets and directly reach out to the Israelis. He believed in the psychological impact of his astonishing initiative, for he understood the complex Israeli psyche. Through his visit to Jerusalem he expected to banalise the nature of the Arab–Israeli conflict from being about the right of Israel's existence to a struggle about negotiable and solvable interests between legitimate sovereign states. For this is exactly the point – that of mythological, mutually exclusive rights of existence, conflicting historical narratives and religious claims of ownership – where the Palestinian–Israeli tragedy is stuck to this very day to the extent of making it practically insoluble. Through his visit to Jerusalem, President Sadat shook the Israeli siege mentality and gave psychological living space to an otherwise claustrophobic nation in the midst of a hostile Arab world.

One lesson and legacy of Sadat's initiative is that in highly protracted conflicts where deep emotions and historical hatred are involved, when almost every conceivable diplomatic formula has been tried, the shock of a visionary, generous and imaginative step is likely to open new and untold paths to peace. For the major problem in the Arab–Israeli conflict, as in many other intricate collisions throughout history, has always been the incapacity or unwillingness of leaders to conduct a peace policy that is not supported by what looked at the time like the legitimate, and frequently paralysing, consensus prevailing in their respective societies and polities. Leaders, more frequently than not, act as the hostages of the socio-political environment that produces them instead of shaping it. Anwar Sadat gained a privileged place in history and achieved immortality the moment he fled from the comfortable prison of inertia, and from the pseudo-solidarity and hollow rhetorical cohesion of Arab summits.

On the Israeli side of the equation, rarely has a diplomatic demarche aroused such a degree of popular enthusiasm and almost unqualified generosity as that displayed by the Israeli people and its government towards the Egyptian leader and his people, Israel's most formidable foe since 1948. The Sinai peninsula – three times the size of Israel, the unexpected source of a crucial self-sufficiency in oil and a vital space of strategic depth for a country whose width is the length of a main boulevard in a European capital – was to be given back to its owners with practically no opposition within Israel. Admittedly, though, this was achieved only after the difficult truth had percolated the minds of the decision makers that there was no conceivable way they could have both peace and territories. The test of statesmanship did not end with Sadat's dramatic leap into the future. It had yet to be met by Menachem Begin at almost every juncture down a most tortuous road to peace.

Arguably, only a political hawk who was also a man with a sense of drama, a political romantic with a keen eye to the judgement of history, of the kind of Menachem Begin, whose other advantage was that he had no Begin in opposition, could have responded in such a total way to Sadat's initiative. There is room for reasonable doubt as to whether the rigid and petulant Golda Meir would have gauged the real meaning of Sadat's peace initiative. Begin rose to the occasion and, with a sense of theatrical *mis-en-scène* highly typical of him, invited the Egyptian President to speak before the Knesset in Jerusalem in what was undoubtedly one of the most extraordinary events known in contemporary history or in international diplomacy.

The host in Jerusalem of Israel's arch-enemy, Menachem Begin was now approaching the dramatic zenith of his long and singular political life. His was a long life of deprivation, political marginalisation, persecution and imprisonment, underground activity and finally power. His ideological roots can be found in his fervent admiration for the Italian Risorgimento; his closest political mentor, Zeev Jabotinsky, popularised among his followers the tradition of the Italian national struggle. From his political idol Begin inherited his love for the right word, the gesture, the 'style'.

Begin had no rival as a brilliant orator, occasionally sarcastic and often populist. Despite his humble family background, he developed a style and gestures that seemed to be inspired by the manners of the Polish aristocracy, and by the aesthetic, poetic tradition of Polish nationalism. 'Dignity' was what Jabotinsky's disciples claimed to have contributed to Zionist politics.

Begin was born on 16 August 1913, in Brest-Litovsk, then a part of Poland (currently Belarus). He studied in a Hebrew school where he learned flawless Hebrew; later on, he went to a Polish high school and studied Law at the University of Warsaw. His father instilled in him Zionist fervour and a dislike of the Socialist way to national fulfilment. A fervent anti-Communist, it did not take him long to challenge the Soviet system. In 1940 he was sentenced to eight years' imprisonment in a Russian labour camp, but was released one year later when the German offensive against the Soviet Union forced Stalin to seek support even among Polish prisoners. Begin immediately joined the Polish army in exile under the command of General Władysław Anders and arrived in Palestine not as a Zionist leader, but as a trooper in that unit. But he soon abandoned the already irrelevant cause of Polish nationalism and joined the underground struggle against British rule. The deaths of his father and brother at the hands of the Nazis only served to reinforce his faith in the fight for the Jewish homeland.

As head of the Irgun, Begin stood out as a charismatic leader of unquestionable authority. Humiliated and persecuted by the Labourite establishment, he remained throughout uncompromising in his strategy that Jewish independence was not to be achieved by political means, but by force and terror. Irgun's strategy was rejected by the mainstream Zionist movements to the extent that the Haganah prosecuted its members and handed them over to the British forces. Persecuted by Jews, Arabs and the British alike, Begin reached the end of the war for independence as a political and social outcast. Sentimental and always given to theatrical gestures, he would describe his life in the following melodramatic terms:

> All those who have followed the story of my life know that I have not been pampered by destiny. I have suffered hunger and pain, and have often seen death up close. But I have never been able to cry, even though, as we learned in our struggle against the oppressor, sometimes it is necessary for blood to replace tears, whereas on other occasions, the tears must replace the blood.

From 1949 until his rise to power in 1977, Begin was the leader of what seemed to be an eternal opposition with no hope of ever reaching power.

Despite this, he never changed his ideas, even though that might have provided a road into government. He withstood the frustration of his followers for many years; he took Ben-Gurion's sarcasm against him with dignity and persisted unabated in what looked like a quixotic battle against the hegemony of the Labourite establishment, and for what then appeared an utterly outlandish notion, the dream of Greater Eretz-Israel. He would not give in to rivals or followers. The Six Day War in which Israel regained the biblical territories of Judaea and Samaria was a historic moment that proved vital for Begin's subsequent access to government, for it changed the national mood in favour of the mythologies of the Israeli Right and away from the conservative positions of Labour. But even before the war, Begin had successfully brought his party, Herut, to the centre of the Israeli political conscience when he entered into an alliance with the General Zionists, a respectable bourgeois party at the centre of the political spectrum. The party of the outcast, Herut, had thus become that of the respectable nationalist bourgeoisie, an alliance that lay at the roots of the Likud Party as it was to be forged in the aftermath of the Yom Kippur War. It was that newly acquired bourgeois respectability combined with Begin's irresistible appeal for the social outcasts of Israel, the Oriental lower classes, that would eventually bring him to office and break the long monopoly of the Labourites on power.

As Prime Minister, Begin's most outstanding achievement would be the signing of the historic peace treaty with Egypt. But this would not mean that he had abandoned his lifelong commitment to Eretz-Israel. That he eventually accepted total withdrawal from Sinai and carried out a traumatic dismantling of all the settlements in the peninsula concealed an intimate personal agenda – giving up Sinai in exchange for not having to do the same with the far more emotionally and strategically significant territories: Judaea and Samaria. Indeed, it was his lack of willingness to enforce Palestinian autonomy – as he would commit himself to do in the Camp David agreements – in Gaza and the West Bank, which would lead two of his closest collaborators to resign, the Minister of Foreign Affairs Moshe Dayan and the Defence Minister Ezer Weizmann. At Camp David, Begin would come to the outer limits of his capacity for peacemaking.

Probably Begin's biggest frustration was not having been the one who declared the independence of the State of Israel in May 1948, a historic privilege that befell his arch-rival, David Ben-Gurion. He did not even take part in the ceremony. Curiously, one of his younger ministers in 1977, Moshe Katsav, now President of the State of Israel, even proposed at the time that Begin be allowed to add his signature to the original Declaration of Independence of 15 May 1948. That, to a great extent, explains Begin's actions as Prime Minister. He now positioned himself as the second creator of the state. Ben-Gurion named the newly created state 'Israel'; Begin was always reluctant to use that name. He preferred to refer to 'Eretz-Israel'. Ben-Gurion created Tsahal, the Israel Defence Forces; Begin referred to the 'army', never to 'Tsahal'. Ben-Gurion created a state based upon the cultural and political supremacy of the European Jews; Begin was the greatest defender of the cause of the Israelis of Sephardi-Oriental origin. In fact, his coming to power in 1977 was the result of an alliance of outcasts: Begin the political outcast and his party on the one hand, and the cultural and social outcasts, the Oriental Sephardi Israelis on the other.

It may well be that the Beginism of the 1970s and 1980s was no more than a vulgar parody of Jabotinskyan 'glory'. Transmuted into cheap demagogical populism, it enlisted the Israeli proletariat in a cultural and political protest against the historic enemy of revisionism, the Labour movement. With Begin, the Likud relied on a culture of primitive mass democracy, on a longing for traditional values of family and nation, as have other populist, quasi-Fascist movements in situations of crisis in Europe, ever since World War One. The model was not new; its application in Israel only waited for the right conditions. These eventually came into being at a time when those who had immigrated during the 1950s to Israel from North Africa and other Arab countries became politically mature and self-aware enough to rebel against the 'Bolshevik' establishment of the Labour movement. From the paradise of the diaspora they had been uprooted, yet the paradise of Socialism promised by the Labour movement was beyond their grasp. By posing a populist, softly religious and nationalist challenge to the mostly unconvincing rhetoric of humanitarian universalism of the Left, Begin succeeded in mobilising the popular and dispossessed classes against the sins of the arrogant Labourite establishment. Detached and uprooted, they fell prey to the charms of the populist, traditionalist and paternalist Likud. Neither the fiction of Israeli Socialism, nor the empty rhetoric of Ben-Gurion's successors in the Labourite establishment extolling the universal values of social justice and equality, could blind the masses any longer. Begin now offered them an alternative illusion.

As for the old ideological guard of Begin's party, Herut, the peace that their leader would make with Egypt, the traumatic evacuation of the settlements in the north of the peninsula, and the difficulty of reconciling their dream of Greater Eretz-Israel with their liberal traditions would throw them into a political blind alley. Jabotinsky's was a *Weltanschauung* which drew fully from two opposing streams in the European heritage: on the one hand a romantic and military nationalism, which descended to Fascistic depths; on the other, characteristics of liberal democracy according to the best tradition of the Italian Risorgimento and American democracy. This overlapping was at the very core of the identity crisis and the political rift in the hearts of many of Jabotinsky's disciples, who would have liked to see an extensive, expanded Eretz-Israel, but understood, at the same time, that such a Greater Eretz-Israel, with more than two million Arabs living in a state of inferiority within its borders, could never be liberal. Jabotinsky bequeathed to his movement two contradictory branches of the European heritage – proto-Fascism and liberalism – which could not be resolved. This is why the political options proposed by Jabotinsky's disciples in Judaea and Samaria were doomed to failure. Greater Eretz-Israel was a project that could never prevail.

'Ninety per cent of the conflict is psychological,' Sadat would say on his visit to Jerusalem and he was not wrong. He captivated the mind and the imagination of the Israelis in a way that no Arab leader has ever been able to match. And having thus 'solved' with his visit, as it were, 90 per cent of the conflict, he apparently managed to wrest from Begin the remaining 10 per cent when the Prime Minister deposited with him, in their private meeting after the official dinner in Jerusalem, the pledge of a full withdrawal from the Sinai peninsula.[1]

Sadat's initiative was about an Israeli–Egyptian separate peace. His expectations on the Palestinian front were far harder to satisfy, as he might have known when he made his decision to come to Jerusalem. He could not be so naïve as to believe that his journey to Jerusalem would open all the gates to a comprehensive Arab–Israeli settlement and convince a right-wing Israeli government to make the painful concessions required for a settlement with the Palestinians. Sadat, of course, insisted in his Knesset speech that he had not come to Jerusalem in search of a separate peace. Palestinian and Arab Jerusalem were central to his concerns, he explained. To make his point more strongly he later walked barefoot through the gates of the Old City and prayed in the Al-Aqsa mosque where a generation earlier another Arab peacemaker, King Abdullah of Jordan, had been assassinated for breaking the Arab consensus of war to the end against the Jewish state. To further pursue his search for a Palestinian cover to his peace overture, Sadat subsequently convened an international conference in Cairo in mid December in what turned out to be an awkward and clearly unsuccessful attempt to promote an

[1] Moshe Dayan, *Breakthrough: A Personal Account of the Egypt–Israeli Peace Negotiations*, Weidenfeld & Nicolson, London, 1981, p. 91.

overall regional peace with the Palestinian issue at its centre. But at the same time he accelerated his efforts towards a bilateral understanding with Israel. True, Tuhami would insist in his second meeting with Dayan in Morocco in early December on Egypt's conditions for a Palestinian deal, but Dayan could read in Tuhami's subtext an Egypt desperately searching for a way to square the circle and get concessions for the Palestinians, even if these were to be essentially rhetorical, that could legitimise an Egyptian–Israeli separate peace.

Very few in the Arab world had much love for Arafat or for the PLO, 'the cancer in our midst', as King Hassan of Morocco defined it in his December meeting with Dayan and Tuhami. Years later this author would personally hear from the King, in his meeting with him in his Rabat palace in January 1993, similar harsh descriptions of Arafat and the PLO, an organisation he then confided to me had outlived its historical role and was becoming an obstacle to peace that needed to be dismantled. The King also related to me the advice he had given to Arafat's deputy, Abu-Mazen, that the PLO should disband and allow the local Palestinian leadership in the territories to assume the responsibility for dealing directly with Israel. When I later reported my conversation with the King to Prime Minister Rabin he could not conceal his embarrassment, for it was precisely at that time that an Israeli team was negotiating in Oslo with a PLO delegation what later became known as the Oslo accords.

Sadat had no higher regard for Arafat and the PLO than King Hassan. His weariness with the Palestinians exploded into open rage when in February 1978 the chief editor of *Al-Ahram* and a personal friend of the President, Yusuf al-Sibai, was assassinated in Cyprus by a Palestinian squad, admittedly belonging to Abu Nidal's splinter group, not to the PLO. To Sadat this was one more proof that Egypt was mortgaging its future for the sake of a people – 'pygmies' and 'hired killers', as he put it to Israel's Defence Minister Ezer Weizmann – who did not deserve Egypt's sacrifices. Sadat knew that the PLO had been campaigning throughout the Arab world to undermine his peace initiative and he confided to Ezer Weizmann that, 'I have excluded the PLO from my lexicon. By their behaviour they have excluded themselves from the negotiations.' Moreover, as he said to Weizmann, Sadat no longer believed that a comprehensive Israeli–Arab settlement was possible. Nor did he think that a Palestinian state could or should necessarily emerge from these negotiations. He even seemed to be endorsing a traditional Israeli vision for a Palestinian settlement when he said to Weizmann that a kind of Israeli–Jordanian condominium in the territories might be a reasonable solution.

Such seemed to be Sadat's eagerness to reach a separate settlement with Israel, and such was his estrangement from the PLO and the 'ungrateful Palestinians' that the Americans were genuinely concerned that, to secure for Egypt the recuperation of Sinai, Sadat might abandon altogether his defence of the Palestinian cause. They feared that this might isolate him even further in the Arab world and put in serious jeopardy his entire peace initiative. But they did not have to worry. Sadat was fully aware of his constraints within the wider Arab family. And however ungrateful the Palestinians might have been, he was compelled to advocate their case and look for a formula that might reconcile Egypt's interests with the defence of the Palestinian cause.

But it was not only Sadat who, in his quest for a separate agreement with Israel, was desperately looking for a Palestinian deal to salve his conscience. Begin, too, was trapped in the same predicament. The result was the autonomy plan for the Palestinians, which he submitted to President Carter during his visit to Washington in mid December 1977. A rather bizarre, syncretic scheme that drew its inspiration from the legacy of the Habsburg polyglot empire, and from Jabotinsky's principle of 'to the Arabs as individuals, everything; to the Arabs as a people, nothing', it proposed an autonomy for the Palestinians not as a people, but as individuals with no authority on the land and the space they inhabited. It also contained some of the ingredients of an Israeli–Jordanian condominium, for it gave the Palestinians the choice between two nationalities, Jordanian or Israeli. The plan was to allow Begin the best of all worlds; it postponed the debate on the final status of the territories until the separate peace with Egypt was concluded and it denied the Palestinians any trappings, or hopes, of statehood.

The attempt by the two leaders to overcome their respective constraints and reach out to each other's requirements was difficult enough. But no less formidable a barrier was the differences in their styles of leadership and in their attitudes to the process of peacemaking. These differences were a major reason for the fact that in the months following Sadat's visit to Jerusalem it looked as if his dramatic initiative was about to fade away into one more missed opportunity in a series of so many. Sadat came to his peace initiative out of a wide strategic vision aimed at disengaging Egypt from the Arab–Israeli conflict and building a partnership, perhaps even an alliance, with the United States. The vision was so revolutionary and appealing that Sadat believed it would rapidly dissolve the obstacles and allow him to conquer peace in a storm. He discovered, however, that Begin was a retail dealer bent on bringing his lofty dreams for peace down to the earth of complex realities and divergent expectations where they got lost in legalistic formulas and in the tactics of cautious gradualism. Sadat wanted from Israel an unequivocal commitment to

Palestinian self-determination, a condition that made of the Begin–Sadat Ismailya summit at the end of December a resounding failure, and of the meeting in mid January 1978 in Jerusalem of the Israeli–Egyptian political joint committee a political scandal, with Begin patronising in an utterly embarrassing way the Egyptian Foreign Minister Muhammad Ibrahim Kamel. This in turn forced Sadat to dissolve the military joint committee in Cairo and threaten Israel with an end to the process.

As General Avraham Tamir, the head of Israel's delegation in the joint military working group in Cairo, made clear in his memoirs, the Egyptians left their Israeli counterparts in no doubt as to Sadat's disposition for a separate peace as long as a declaration of principles providing for Palestinian self-determination was agreed upon and Israel's full withdrawal from Sinai was accepted. But Begin refused to accept the fact that he should pay for Sadat's visit to Jerusalem with such expensive Palestinian currency. The stalemate in the process now threatened to degenerate into open conflict. And if this were not enough, in order to placate his critics in his own party, the Prime Minister started to fall back on old positions and traditional rhetoric: he would not dismantle the Sinai settlements, he said he would not relinquish Israel's political and military control of the West Bank, and he would not let the Palestinians have a choice of statehood after the five-year interim phase of autonomy.

But regardless of Begin's positions and however creative and forth-coming some of them certainly were, Sadat was interested in a diplomacy of brinkmanship – this included a threat to resign or cut short the whole peace initiative and return to the Arab fold and consensus – in order to draw the Americans into a massive and robust mediation. It is otherwise difficult to understand why Sadat dismissed a major shift in Israel's position at the Leeds Castle Conference in July 1978, where Dayan produced a radical alteration in Israel's position and agreed to discuss the issue of sovereignty in the West Bank after the five-year transition stage. In his memoirs Dayan defined the Leeds Castle Conference as 'a milestone in the peace negotiations and a moment of truth'.[1] But what for a moment looked like a more promising bilateral Egyptian–Israeli dynamic was cut short precisely because Sadat wanted it that way. He wished to move the process to a stage where America would start delivering Israel. The invitation of President Carter to the parties in late August 1978 to come to a peace summit at Camp David was a clear victory for Sadat's tactics of brinkmanship.

That the dramatic encounter between two extraordinary political figures like Begin and Sadat should not have been allowed to decline into another

---

[1] Avi Shlaim, *The Iron Wall*, Penguin Books, London, 2000, pp. 370–1.

failure had much to do with the leadership of President Carter and with the concept of peace developed by his administration. Carter possessed one curious advantage as a peacemaker: he knew very little of the complexities, the intricacies and the nuances of the Arab–Israeli conflict. He knew even less about the Israeli–Palestinian imbroglio and about the degree of hostility that existed between Israel and the PLO. It was precisely this healthy innocence, one might say, which proved to be such an asset for the President in the titanic task that he took upon himself. His was a bold, simplistic, yet at the same time extremely effective, approach that shocked his Israeli interlocutors with the revolutionary peace recipes that he put forward without even bothering to consult them. Others might have tried to untie carefully and laboriously the Gordian knot of the conflict; Carter preferred to cut it pure and simple.

But this was not all; Carter had yet another vital advantage. A rare bird among American politicians, and especially among residents of the White House, he was not especially sensitive or attentive to Jewish voices and lobbies. A Southerner who moved in a social milieu that was free of Jewish acquaintances, and whose constituency was not the typical one of a politician on the East Coast where the Jewish vote and the issue of Israel were always so central to the political discourse, Carter did not hesitate to criticise Israel publicly, threaten her and even put pressure on her. As it turned out, it was this kind of president – George Bush in the late 1980s is another case in point – who was ready to confront Israel head on and overlook the sensibilities of her friends in America that managed eventually to produce meaningful breakthroughs on the way to an Arab–Israeli peace.

Unlike Nixon, who was obsessed with global power politics and grand strategic designs, and contrary to Kissinger's policy of using the Arab–Israeli peace process to drive the Soviet Union out of the Middle East, Carter was a peace missionary and one especially sensitive to the plight of the Palestinians. He had expected to reach peace through an international conference in full co-operation with the Soviet Union and with the participation of both Syria and the PLO. Now he was ready to assume the new rules of the game as they were virtually imposed by Sadat. Carter was the first president ever to commit the United States to the notion of a 'Palestinian homeland', as he put it.

Nor did Carter make any secret of his view that peace would require Israel's withdrawal to the 1967 borders and the creation of a Palestinian state. In his joint Aswan declaration with Sadat on 4 January 1978 he would also subscribe, to Israel's dismay, to an entirely new language for an American president with regard to the Palestinian problem: 'There must be a resolution of the Palestinian problem *in all its aspects*. The solution must recognise *the legitimate rights of the Palestinian people* and enable *the Palestinians to participate in the determination of their own future.*' Succumbing to Sadat's tactics of brinkmanship, Carter would a month later invite the Egyptian President to Washington where they would issue yet another declaration at least as shocking to the Israelis as that of Aswan. This time the statement was that the Israeli settlements were illegal and an obstacle to peace, and that SCR 242 was applicable, contrary to Begin's assumption, to all the fronts, that is, to the West Bank as well.

Neither Begin nor Dayan realised the scope of the changes that were required in Israel's traditional positions in the wake of Sadat's initiative. Nor did they appreciate the degree of commitment of the international community to the 1967 borders and to a fair deal for the Palestinians. They were, of course, aware of the need to make concessions, even big ones. But it took the almost Messianic commitment of President Carter and the most assertive and robust involvement of the United States to save the process from collapse and to force the parties to shoulder the formidable price of peace.

'None of us believe we have much of a chance to succeed,' confided Carter to his advisers when he invited the parties to the Camp David presidential retreat for a peace summit. But nevertheless it was a fairly well-calculated risk he took. By now he had realised the obvious: Sadat needed face-saving formulas on the Palestinian issue, while Begin, though clearly sincere and unyielding in his position with regard to Judaea and Samaria, was only bargaining on the conditions for what he assumed would have to be a total withdrawal from Sinai. Security arrangements and guarantees would settle the differences over Sinai. In very broad lines, Carter could see the contours of an agreement when he invited his guests to Camp David.

The success of the Camp David summit of September 1978 was not, of course, a foregone conclusion. Menachem Begin arrived with two objectives in mind: to make peace with Egypt and to keep Eretz-Israel for generations to come. Sadat shared the first objective but disputed the second. The status of the West Bank, Gaza and Jerusalem, as well as the future of the Sinai settlements, were the major hurdles on the way to an agreement.

The task ahead was still formidable, for Carter's guests were miles apart in their states of mind. Yes, they, like their host, were religious men who believed in destiny and in being chosen for this almost metahistorical, providential mission. But one, the Egyptian leader, was eager to see America deliver an obstinate Israel without always being sufficiently aware of the limits of America's capacity to twist Israel's arm. And the other, Begin, whose unquestionable drive for a settlement was tempered by his view of himself as a man cast in the almost biblical role of the champion of the destiny of his millenarian people, a destiny that should not be negotiated lightly. Fearful and suspicious of an American–Egyptian conspiracy, he came to Camp David in a defensive mood and determined to resist being outmanoeuvred into an Egyptian–American trap.

In the last analysis, however, the key to the success or failure of such a formidable enterprise as peacemaking between two states at war, with so many emotions and dire memories involved and when so many seemingly intractable issues were at stake, depended on the calibre of the leaders. The distance between failure and success was bridged by the leaders' sense of statesmanship, by their ability to rise to the challenge and take difficult decisions that departed from ideas they had been preaching all their lives. It was the unique encounter between three courageous peacemakers that made the Camp David summit into a gamble worth taking, and the peace between Israel and Egypt into a dream that came true.

Camp David produced an agreement on the basis of a fairly simple formula and a set of quid pro quos. Egypt would waive its condition that Israel should subscribe in advance to the exact nature of a final settlement in the West Bank and Gaza, and it would also agree to full normalisation of its relations with Israel, whereas Israel would consent to withdraw to the international border in Sinai, dismantle the settlements in the northern part of the peninsula, as well as its air bases in Egyptian territory. For all practical purposes, Carter was forced to endorse Begin's structure of peacemaking: the Sinai in exchange for Israel's freedom to assert her priorities in the West Bank and Gaza.

But in spite of Sadat's concessions on the Palestinian issue and Begin's adamant defence of Israel's rights in Judaea and Samaria, the Palestinian document agreed upon at Camp David was nevertheless a most revolutionary platform, for it contained all the fundamental principles and components that would eventually constitute the foundations of the 1993 Oslo accords. It established a five-year autonomy plan as a transitional stage to a final settlement, the negotiations about which would start three years into the first stage. Moreover, concepts that would be so central in the Oslo process such as a Palestinian 'full autonomy', Israel's withdrawal in the West Bank to 'specific military locations' and the creation of a 'strong Palestinian police force' were all laid down at Camp David. True, the word self-determination was avoided – incidentally, it would also be avoided in the Oslo accords – and the final stage was defined as peace between Israel and Jordan. But truly historic expressions of very far-reaching consequences were introduced into the language of the Israeli–Palestinian peace process.

It was Menachem Begin, not a left-wing radical, who subscribed at Camp David to such non-Jabotinskian concepts as these: 'a recognition of *the legitimate rights of the Palestinian people and their just requirements'*, 'the resolution of the Palestinian problem *in all its aspects'* and *'the Palestinians will participate in the determination of their own future'*. Moreover, not only did Begin agree to discuss the return to the territories of the displaced Palestinians who left the West Bank during the Six Day War, but he also consented to reopen the 1948 chapter, that is, to negotiate 'the resolution of the 1948 refugee problem'. And if all this were not enough, Begin succumbed to Carter's pressure and agreed to 'Resolution 242 in all its parts', thus implicitly also endorsing the Resolution's preamble about 'the inadmissibility of the acquisition of territory by war', and its possible applicability to other Arab fronts as well.

It was nevertheless clear that none of the leaders – Carter, Sadat, Begin or, for that matter, Hussein – wanted this platform to lead to an independent PLO Palestinian state that could be a destabilising agent at the service of Soviet interests. They expected the local Palestinian leadership to come forward and seize the opportunity that was now offered for a transitional autonomy, since for all practical purposes the new platform debarred a unilateral annexation of the territories by Israel.

It was a capital sin that the Palestinians should have rejected such a golden opportunity to join the Camp David process at a time when the West Bank was still practically free of Israeli settlements. This was a major missed opportunity by the Palestinian leadership. What was proposed to the Palestinians at Camp David, to use Oslo terms, was to turn the whole of the West Bank into Area B, that is, an area of Palestinian administrative rule and Israeli responsibility for security. Today, twenty-five years after Camp David and twelve years into the Oslo process, the Palestinians have hardly 20 per cent of the West Bank as Area B.

Israel's leaders were never willing to give away territorial assets. When they eventually did, it was always as a last resort and because they were forced to do so either by the Arab side or by international pressure. In the aftermath of the Camp David accords, the Palestinians failed to do what they wisely did in 1988, namely call Israel's bluff and join the peace process before Israel's occupation of the West Bank had created an irreversible reality. Begin was the last man on earth to take lightly the meaning of words such as those he endorsed at Camp David (the 'legitimate rights of the Palestinians'). At Camp David he fought for every word in the text. That the Palestinians did not call his bluff and instead engaged in a struggle against what Arafat himself called 'the Camp David conspiracy' only facilitated the putting into practice of Begin's grand designs on the West Bank.

It is difficult to understand what exactly Sadat's critics in Egypt and throughout the Arab world expected him to achieve if a reasonable compromise and not an unconditional capitulation by Israel was to be the outcome of the summit. The two 'frameworks' agreed upon at Camp David contained all the ingredients of a possible comprehensive peace in the region. The leaders could always, of course, try to subvert the process. Begin, for example, would continue to assert Israel's rights in the West Bank. But a different attitude of the Arab world, and the Palestinians in particular, could have changed the course of future events. Instead, Egypt, where there were also substantial objections to the accords – General Gamassi criticised the agreement for breaking the Arab strategic cohesion and allowing Israel to absorb the West Bank – was expelled from the Arab League, while the Palestinians, always tragically wrong in interpreting historical crossroads, dismissed the accords as 'a conspiracy against the Palestinian people'.

It is true that Begin, like Gamassi, believed that Israel had won the battle for the West Bank; but this was nevertheless not exactly so. As it turned out, Israel's peace with Egypt was only formally a separate peace. In practice, its ups and downs would always be directly dependent on Israel's performance in the Palestinian track. Peace between the two countries would remain through a cold peace. At times it looked like no more than a non-belligerency agreement. Indeed, the major achievement of Camp David remained unchallenged and that was Begin's and Sadat's commitment of 'no more war, no more bloodshed' between the two countries.

On the last night of the Camp David summit on the Palestinian issue in the summer of 2000, the present author stood with President Clinton in his cabin, Aspen, waiting for Arafat's response to the President's latest proposals on Jerusalem. Clinton was in a desperate, gloomy mood. I tried to encourage him by proposing that this should not be the end of his efforts. 'Don't forget', I told him, 'that after Camp David I, Carter still had to spend eight long months of tough negotiations and go through crises that threatened to destroy the entire process, in order to broker a final peace treaty between Egypt and Israel. You could do the same,' I said to the President.

'Unfortunately, I do not have these vital eight months' was the President's response. In a few weeks the presidential primaries would be over and in November, four months after our conversation in the President's Camp David residence, the American people would elect a new president.

These were not exactly the considerations that troubled President Carter's mind. But nevertheless formidable difficulties still lay ahead.

Problems such as how to reconcile Egypt's peace with Israel with its commitments to the Arab world; the linkage between the bilateral peace treaty and the Palestinian track that should not have existed according to the letter of the accords, but was now reintroduced by Sadat under internal and Arab pressure; and the timing of the establishment of diplomatic relations between the parties were some of the problems that threatened to derail the entire process.

Menachem Begin did not make life easier for the American President now desperately shuttling between Cairo and Jerusalem. The Israeli Prime Minister did not have insurmountable opposition at home. But he, or rather his conscience, was his own opposition. In order to calm it down he now had to prove that he, who had betrayed his pledge not to dismantle settlements, would not allow this to become a precedent for the West Bank. He would enhance the building of new settlements in Judaea and Samaria and he would block any possibility of the Palestinian autonomy ushering in a Palestinian state.

Eventually Sadat would give in to Begin's attritional tactics, for the Israeli leader was in a clearly advantageous position. Begin operated under no special pressures or constraints. This was not the case for Sadat who, isolated and harassed by Arab opinion and leaders, and fearful that the fundamentalist challenge that had just received a boost by the Iranian revolution might prevent him from collecting the reward for his Jerusalem adventure, desperately needed a deal; or for Carter who, approaching the end of his presidency and haunted by the spectre of the Iranian revolution that threatened to undermine America's position in the Middle East, needed to save the record of his presidency from a disgraceful failure. And if William Quandt, a privileged witness of the Camp David process, is to be trusted and Sadat, as he put it, 'did not give a damn about the West Bank',[1] there was no reason for Carter to fail in his endeavour. Begin had his way. Sadat waived his demand for a linkage between the Palestinian autonomy and the final status of the territories and, on 26 March 1979 in Washington, he signed a full and, at least formally, separate peace agreement with Israel.

---

[1] William Quandt, *Camp David, Peacemaking and Politics*, Washington, DC, 1986, p. 296.

VIII   The Road to Madrid

Operation Peace for Galilee is not a military operation resulting from the lack of an alternative.

Menachem Begin's speech at the National Defence College,
8 August 1982

The State of Palestine ... rejects the threat or use of force, violence and terrorism against its territorial integrity or political independence, and also rejects their use against the territorial integrity of other states.

Palestine National Council: Declaration of Independence,
15 November 1988

Israel [must] lay aside, once and for all, the unrealistic vision of Greater Israel. ... Reach out to the Palestinians as neighbours who deserve political rights!

Secretary of State James Baker, speech to AIPAC,
22 May 1989

The real aim of the treacherous American aggression [against Iraq] is ... to destroy Palestine ... and make way for three million Russian Jews in a Greater Israel stretching from the Nile to the Euphrates.

Arafat's reaction to the Gulf War,
January 1991

The time has come to put an end to the Arab–Israeli conflict.

President George Bush's speech,
6 March 1991

Camp David shifted the politics of the Middle East from the discourse of war to that of peacemaking. Notwithstanding the many crises that still lay ahead, among them a major war in Lebanon and the Palestinian uprising in the occupied territories, the question in the Arab world was no longer how to wipe Israel out of existence, but at what price an accommodation, if never a warm reconciliation, could be reached with her. Throughout most of the period leading from Camp David to the Madrid Peace Conference in October 1991, Israel was led by one of the most conservative and hardline prime ministers in its history, Yitzhak Shamir, the Golda Meir of the 1980s, who adamantly resisted any move or compromise. Yet not even he could prevent additional cornerstones in the architecture of Israeli–Arab peacemaking being laid down. Arafat's Algiers declaration of November 1988 and the subsequent recognition of the PLO by the Reagan administration was one such major cornerstone of the future peace process.

The ascendancy of the United States to a hegemonic position in the Middle East, accompanied as it was by the decline of the Soviet Union and Egypt's withdrawal from the cycle of Arab–Israeli wars, combined to bring home also to the PLO the message that only by assuming reasonably moderate positions could it be accepted by the United States as an interlocutor the way Egypt was and consequently be admitted to the peace process. Shamir's delaying tactics notwithstanding, the modalities for an international peace conference and the conditions for its convocation would gradually be created. Most of the concepts that would later be introduced into the Oslo accords, whose origins can be found in the Camp David agreements, would be developed further. The architects of Oslo would not act in a conceptual void. They had a legacy to build upon and much of it, surprisingly, was built in the Shamir years, albeit much against his will.

Ever since the start of superpower competition in the Middle East, the Arab–Israeli conflict evolved around a combination of global and local conditions that were not exactly conducive to a settlement. Bipolarity condemned the conflict to oscillate between paralysis and decline. It was therefore the momentous transformation of the structure of international relations and of the global balance of power that came about with the collapse of the Berlin Wall in 1989 and the subsequent dissolution of the Soviet Union, which served as the trigger for an entirely new phase in the history of the conflict. For the first time the opportunities started to overshadow the risks.

At Camp David, Begin reached the limits of his career as a peacemaker. Once the peace treaty was concluded he did all he could to derail the talks for Palestinian autonomy. His appointment of Interior Minister Yosef Burg as his chief negotiator for the talks conveyed the message that for Begin, Judaea and Samaria was not a foreign policy matter but an internal Israeli problem. The autonomy negotiations thus became a sheer waste of time. The conflicting interpretations of the parties as to the principles of the proposed autonomy were simply irreconcilable. Nor could the Egyptians be expected to be especially helpful in reconciling the plans of the Israelis with the national dreams of the Palestinians. For once they had satisfied all their aspirations and got back all their land, they had no incentive to draw the anger of the Palestinians and further to alienate the other Arab states by making additional concessions at the expense of the Palestinians and against their will. The Israelis who struggled to reach a final agreement with the Palestinians in the year 2000 can bear witness to the fact that Egypt's policy after Camp David was characterised, to the Israelis' distress, by an adamant refusal to be seen as the arm twister of the Palestinians. Nothing haunted the Egyptians more than arousing the Palestinians' enmity and facing the domestic consequences of such a 'sell-out' and 'betrayal' of the Palestinian cause.

The resignation of Foreign Minister Dayan in favour of a staunch Revisionist, Yitzhak Shamir, and that of Defence Minister Ezer Weizmann in favour of another hardline member of Herut's old guard, Moshe Arens, signalled the end of the era of peacemaking under Begin's leadership. The two newcomers to the government had also voted against the Camp David accords. Begin now decided to retreat to his mental ghetto. It was clear that the autonomy talks were nothing but camouflage behind which a quadrumvirate of hawks – Begin, Shamir, Arens and Sharon – joined the settlers of Gush Emunim in a renewed drive of settlements expansion throughout Judaea and Samaria.

Begin would not bargain over Judaea and Samaria. But Israeli rejectionism, as was frequently the case throughout the Arab–Israeli conflict, when not triggered by the Palestinians in the first place was certainly encouraged by them. The National Guidance Committee, a council of Palestinian notables in the territories, was created with one exclusive purpose, that of undermining and boycotting the autonomy talks, whatever their final objective might have been. The narrow window of opportunity that existed in 1967 for Israel to reach a deal with a local Palestinian leadership was now closed and sealed. In 1967, with Israel's stunning victory still fresh in their mind and with the PLO still too weak to dictate the Palestinian agenda in the occupied territories, the local Palestinian leadership was eager to engage in peace talks with Israel. But Israel then preferred the politics of confusion and ambiguity. Now, thirteen years later, the PLO held the unchallenged monopoly of Palestinian politics and there was no chance whatever that any local leadership would be allowed to negotiate with Israel a watered-down autonomy plan, or any peace plan for that matter.

When Begin brought the peace process to a halt he knew that he could rely on the strategic gains he had made through his peace with Egypt. He had taken Egypt out of the war cycle and he could rest assured that the collapse of the autonomy talks would not lead to war. The 'capsule theory' was vindicated. He would now also be free to destroy the Iraqi nuclear reactor and to invade Lebanon in order to do away with the military and political challenge posed by the PLO, which since its expulsion from Jordan in 1970 had established an autonomous mini-state of its own in that country. Begin was free to realise his real political *Weltanschauung*. Sinai, the price he had paid for recovering his freedom on the other fronts, was never the religious-political credo for a disciple of Jabotinsky that Judaea and Samaria were.

But there was also a bright side to the story as it unfolded in the aftermath of Camp David. The fundamental truths of the Palestinian–Israeli dilemma were clearly laid down at Camp David, and the road map for its solution was established, waiting for the right leadership and the appropriate conditions to build on them. Egypt's abandonment of the option of war would sooner or later leave the Syrians and Jordanians no choice but that of joining the peace process. And the new threat that had now emerged, Islamic fundamentalism with Khomeini's Iran as the revolutionary agent of its regional expansion – it is important to note that the fundamentalist officer who assassinated Sadat during a military parade on 6 October 1981, the eighth anniversary of the 1973 war, did not do it because of Sadat's peace with Israel but because of his Western tendencies; the assassin did not once mention Israel during his trial – would help bring together Israel, the Arab regimes and the United States in a joint effort to move from war to peacemaking and regional stability. Destroying Israel was no longer an option. From now on the question was not if, but how, to make peace with Israel; it was not whether or not to accept the Jewish state, but at what price and on what conditions.

This – the price of peace – was not a minor problem, of course, especially when it came to Syria's demand that Israel should pull out from the strategically vital Golan Heights, and to the Palestinians' drive for an independent state in Gaza and the entire West Bank. Egypt was a different matter. The reservations in Israel at the high territorial price that was paid to Egypt were not political or strategic. Rather, they were embedded in the national psyche of a nation living in an existential state of territorial claustrophobia. There was a broad national consensus in Israel for peace with Egypt in exchange for all the land. But there was nevertheless a widespread sense of a loss of space, of the geographical horizons that were desperately narrowing for the Jewish state. Its citizens had abruptly to come to terms with the reality that they were no longer a nation at the centre of an empire. Now it was back to the claustrophobic mentality of the Jewish ghetto. The novelist Aharon Megged reflected the feelings of many when he expressed his profound sorrow for the loss of

Mount Sinai and the abandonment of 'the desert to the wind, the sun and the dead'. Expressing a widespread sentiment, Haim Guri mourned the loss of Sinai: 'Farewell, great expanse of land extending to the horizon,' he wrote. 'Farewell, ancient memories.'

However, notwithstanding the widespread frustration at the cold nature of the peace with Egypt, second thoughts and a revisionist strategy towards the settlements were never a realistic option. The question was whether Israel and especially her leaders were now ready to pursue the peace process on other fronts and assume the inevitable price of trimming even further Israel's 1967 empire. Begin's second government was to give an unequivocal answer to the dilemma.

Once he reached his second electoral victory in June 1981 and formed his government, clearly a right-wing Cabinet with Ariel Sharon as Defence Minister and Yitzhak Shamir as Foreign Minister, Begin's policy looked more and more like an attempt to test the limits of Egypt's commitment to its peace with Israel. He laid down in no ambiguous terms the dominant principle of his post-Camp David policy. Upon presenting his second government, he assured that 'Western Eretz-Israel is entirely under our control', and pledged that 'it will never again be divided. No part of its territory will be given over to alien rule, to foreign sovereignty.'

Begin could draw inspiration and support for his relegation of the peace process to a secondary position from his strategic partnership with the new Reagan administration. Reagan's obsession with Soviet and Communist threats meant that the Memorandum of Understanding on Strategic Co-operation signed with Israel in January 1981 would focus on the common Soviet threat rather than on advancing the prospects of an Israeli–Arab peace. This suited the Begin government very well. It became a recurrent pattern in the relations between right-wing governments in Israel and conservative administrations in the White House that would be repeated in the Bush–Sharon partnership in fighting global terrorism in the wake of 9/11. It consisted of jointly concentrating on wider regional and global threats while relegating to a secondary priority the need to create and exploit opportunities for an Arab–Israeli peace.

Israeli right-wing governments after Camp David would always look for ways to submerge or dilute the centrality of the Palestinian dilemma into wider regional or global challenges as the safest and most legitimate way of avoiding paying the unbearably high price of peace. It is, of course, true that the Soviet Union, the constant guarantor of an Arab war option, was a major impediment on the way to peace; and its disappearance would eventually pave the way for the Madrid Peace Conference. But it is no less true that the existence of the Soviet Union, just like the global threat of terror later, was used by the Israeli Right and by Republican administrations in Washington as a pretext for paralysing the peace process or relegating it to secondary status.

But it is one thing to relegate the peace process and another to use America's umbrella in order to be defiant and manifestly provocative as Begin proved to be when, two months after he had signed the Strategic Memorandum with the United States and in a clear departure from his commitment at Camp David to Security Council Resolution 242, he announced the annexation of the Golan Heights. Begin's move was so bold and unexpected that it forced the Reagan administration to react by temporarily freezing the Strategic Memorandum. Though the crisis was manageable and temporary, it served as a warning to Israel. With the unilateral abrogation of a signed agreement, Israel experienced for the first time in its relations with America the taste of political, economic and military sanctions.

Conspicuously, in a way that was consistent with Israel's security doctrine of maintaining at all cost her freedom for independent military action, Defence Minister Sharon did not mourn the abrogation of the memorandum. Not unlike Ben-Gurion, who in the 1950s was reluctant to have a defence treaty with America that threatened to limit Israel's freedom of independent action in security matters, Sharon, who was already planning a major operation in Lebanon, feared that the Strategic Memorandum might curtail Israel's freedom in dealing with the PLO in Lebanon.

Begin's intention was to signal through his move on the Golan the limits of the peace process, namely that Israel's withdrawal from Sinai should not be seen by her neighbours as a precedent for other fronts. By pulling out from Sinai, Begin intimated, Israel had fulfilled the territorial aspects of Resolution 242 and no more withdrawals could be contemplated in future peace deals. From now on it would have to be 'peace for peace', not 'peace for land'. Likewise, the annexation of the Golan was Begin's way of testing the commitment of Egypt's new President, Hosni Mubarak, to Israel's concept of a separate peace.

But where Begin really tested Egypt was in his Lebanese adventure. Israel's invasion of Lebanon in the summer of 1982 was prompted by a number of far-fetched and unrealistic strategic objectives. In the background was always Ben-Gurion's dream, fully shared by Begin, of an 'Alliance of Minorities' with the Maronites of Lebanon. But the major objective was that of eliminating the military and political challenge posed by the PLO, which as a result of Israel's Litani operation in 1978 had fundamentally changed its deployment in Lebanon from a plethora of dispersed terrorist squads to a powerful standing army in control of much of the country. Destroying the PLO's infrastructure in Lebanon as well as dismantling the last remaining Palestinian springboard in an Arab country for the military struggle against Israel, was the immediate operational objective of the war. But the architects of the invasion had far wider ambitions. They believed that the defeat of the Palestinians in Lebanon would trigger a mass exodus of Palestinians to the East Bank of the River Jordan, which in turn would bring about the collapse of the Hashemite dynasty and the Palestinisation of the kingdom in a way that would allow Israel a free hand to assert her rule in Judaea and Samaria. Israel also believed that her victory in Lebanon would create a new political order in that country with an undisputed Christian hegemony. Lebanon would then be forced to make peace with Israel, and expel the Syrians in a way that would amount to a radical change in the entire strategic balance in the region.

Israel was encouraged to include the expulsion of Syria from Lebanon in her war aims by a fundamental change in America's position. The Carter administration had acquiesced to Syria's presence in Lebanon as a stabilising force in the chaotic Lebanese puzzle. The new Reagan administration believed that the withdrawal of all 'foreign forces' from Lebanon was a condition of inter-ethnic reconciliation and regional stability. In Israel, Sharon's strategy was also different from that defended by the Rabin government. Like Carter, Rabin acquiesced in Syria's presence in Lebanon as a stabilising force, but only so long as she respected Israel's red lines, namely did not deploy her forces too close to the Israeli border, refrained from keeping strategic weapons such as anti-aircraft missiles and did not interfere with her fight against the PLO. As to the Christians, Rabin agreed to help them help themselves, that is, without engaging the IDF in fighting on their behalf. But Sharon's decision to send planes against the Syrian forces during their battle in Zahlah against the Christians in the spring of 1981 provoked the Syrians to a breach of Israel's red lines by deploying land-to-air missiles in Lebanon in a way that made a direct clash with them virtually inevitable.

America's change of attitude to the Lebanon situation did not necessarily mean that she gave Israel a green light to invade that country, as Sharon would later claim. Secretary of State Alexander Haig should have known that Israeli politicians are not especially sensitive to nuances and understatements when he used unnecessarily ambiguous language in his conversation with Sharon. The American administration was very keen to prevent a war and indeed it sent to the region its special envoy, Philip Habib, in a last-minute attempt to avoid it. But Israel *wanted* a war and there was nothing that could stop her. The PLO gave her the necessary excuse by its continuous shelling of its northern villages, and the Begin–Sharon tandem used the shooting of Shlomo Argov, Israel's ambassador in London, by a splinter group of the PLO, as the final pretext. Israel had grand designs in Lebanon and Sharon, as his close aide General Avraham Tamir recalled in his memoirs, was determined from the outset to launch a much wider operation than that which the government was ready to approve.

How and why was this transformation of Menachem Begin from peacemaker to the commander-in-chief of a disgraceful war in Lebanon achieved? It can only be explained by his realisation that in his peace with Egypt he went too far in his concessions on the Palestinian issue and came dangerously close to losing Judaea and Samaria altogether. Now, in Lebanon, he detected what he wrongly believed was a window of opportunity to recover what he had almost lost at Camp David. And there was always Ben-Gurion's memory to haunt him. Through his peace with Egypt he had proved to his Labourite detractors that he could succeed where they had failed: removing Egypt from the war cycle. Now he wanted to have his own war and correct another major failure of the Labourites by modifying what Abba Eban had called Israel's 'Auschwitz borders'. Asserting Israel's rule in Judaea and Samaria was his way of both being loyal to his political credo as a Revisionist and of accomplishing the task that was left unfinished by his Labourite detractors in 1948.

But there was yet another clue to Begin's Lebanese adventure. He really perceived himself as a God-sent vindicator of the legacy of the Holocaust. Not only would he not allow another holocaust against the Jewish people, he would also teach a lesson of humanity to those hypocritical Christian European countries that had exhibited a criminal indifference to the plight of European Jews during the Second World War. He would show them how the Jewish state, created by Holocaust survivors and now led by one of them, comes altruistically to the rescue of a Christian minority also threatened by a holocaust.

The use and abuse of the Holocaust, a salient characteristic of Israel's political discourse, reached new heights with Menachem Begin. Arafat in Beirut was to him Hitler in his Berlin bunker. 'It was', Abba Eban would say, 'as if we were a kind of disarmed Costa Rica and that the PLO was Napoleon Bonaparte, Alexander the Great and Attila the Hun all wrapped into one.' Begin was someone who saw himself as a victim and as such he would not allow his moral motives to be judged by others, nor would he himself set limits on his actions. He was the best proof Israel's critics needed that the Zionist revolution, although it created a state from the ashes of the Holocaust, nevertheless failed to eradicate the collective self-image of the Jew and the Israeli as a victim. The Israelis, through Begin, cast themselves in the role of a nation totally incapable of breaking out of the prison of her past.

But the war in Lebanon, which started in deceit and with grand strategic designs, ended in military disaster, political defeat and human disgrace. It developed into an all-out confrontation between almost all the ethnic and national forces in Lebanon, and its saddest episodes were the massacre of hundreds of Palestinians in the Sabra and Chatila refugee camps and Israel's siege of Beirut. Bashir Gumayel, the head of the Christian militias, a local version of an Italian condottiere, refused to be Israel's puppet president of Lebanon; he would not make peace with her and break, in her favour, the delicate balance of his country between its Christian legacy and its Arab loyalties. He did not hesitate personally to make this clear to Prime Minister Begin. His assassination by Syrian agents was the prelude to the massacre of Sabra and Chatila that was perpetrated by Israel's allies in the Christian militias with the IDF's connivance.

The United States added her own contribution to the series of political setbacks suffered by Israel in Lebanon when, through the Reagan Peace Plan, she signalled to Israel that, although she precluded the creation of a Palestinian state, she did not share Israel's political designs and would not allow the war in Lebanon to be the prelude to the annexation of the West Bank. The plan referred to the settlements as a serious obstacle to peace, rejected the annexation of Jerusalem by Israel and advanced a scheme for a Palestinian autonomy linked to Jordan. The Reagan plan was a timely reminder to Israel that her Lebanese adventure did not bury the Palestinian dilemma as she had hoped; it only focused even more international attention on the Palestinian tragedy through the Sabra and Chatila massacre, and enhanced its international prominence, as well as the urgency of finding a homeland for a displaced people.

Ariel Sharon's brutality and bellicose lack of realism in Lebanon culminated in a political farce in the form of a peace agreement that Bashir's brother and successor, Amin Gumayel, was forced to sign with Israel. Almost twenty years later George Shultz, the hyperactive mediator in that peace deal, would criticise the Barak government for its performance at Camp David II, where the Israeli negotiators, he implied, were not attentive enough to the subtleties of the art of negotiation. Mr Shultz's remark shows once again that the best negotiator is always the one who does not take part in the negotiations. Barak's team certainly could not learn that secret art of negotiation from Shultz's farcical peace mediation in Lebanon. On what grounds did he assume that a weak and fragmented Lebanon led by a hardly legitimate president could resist a peace deal with Israel that emanated from a war of occupation and was practically imposed on Lebanon against the will of the most important ethnic groups in the country, with the active opposition of the Big Brother in Damascus, who still managed to safeguard his position as the major broker of Lebanese politics? How could Secretary Shultz believe that a peace treaty in Lebanon that depended on Syria's acquiescence could last? Of course the Lebanese were interested in Israel's withdrawal as stipulated by the treaty. But to make this conditional on Syria's withdrawal from its most vital strategic asset in Lebanon, the Bekaa Valley, made the peace treaty with Israel inherently invalid.

The war in Lebanon proved to future Israeli peacemakers, if proof were needed, that Lebanon was too weak and fragile to sustain a separate peace deal with Israel and that it would therefore first require peace with Syria. The future structure of peacemaking on the northern front would have to be not 'Lebanon first', but 'the Golan Heights first'. Lebanon was the home court of Syrian diplomacy. In general, Assad's basic premise assumed that separate agreements with Israel legitimised Israel's superiority – which was why he had opposed the Camp David accords – and that in order to defend themselves, the Arabs must either insist on a comprehensive peace on all fronts or give up on the peace process altogether.

By blindly supporting Amin Gumayel, who ran into Israel's arms under the pressure of the Christian militias, and by not curtailing Israel's demands for a peace treaty with a regime created by invasion and occupation, the Reagan administration had tipped the scales in favour of one Lebanese tribe – the Maronites – and against many others, primarily Muslims. How did the Americans not realise that an imposed peace could not last and that ultimately the Christians themselves would rebel against the risk of being tagged by their Arab brethren as the Quislings of Israel, and would therefore desperately look for the earliest opportunity to tear apart that document? Pierre Gumayel, the senior statesman of Christian politics in Lebanon, had warned Sharon even before the invasion – that is, when the Christians were doing their utmost to drag Israel into an open war with Syria by deliberately provoking clashes with the Syrian forces in Lebanon – not to force his country into a peace treaty. 'We are not like Major Saad Hadad [the commander of Israel's Lebanese army in the south]. We are not traitors! We must remain on good terms with the Arab world. We are part of it.' It was only a question of time before Amin Gumayel would return to the Syrian fold and to the safety of the inter-ethnic balance, however precarious, from which the Lebanese state drew its legitimacy.

Lebanon was the proof that a tactical victory on the battlefield can frequently turn into a strategic defeat. Eventually, the foundation of the whole military and political structure that underpinned the war collapsed.

The Maronites of Lebanon brought home to Israel the message that she was an alien element in the region; she could serve as a concubine, not as a legitimate wife. Israel was culturally ill equipped to act as the supreme broker in inter-Arab disputes, in Lebanon or elsewhere. This was a task for Lebanon's Syrian patrons. Syria's was the subtle and frequently brutal art of manipulation and coercion. Israel could never match that art.

Israel succeeded in destroying the military infrastructure of the PLO in Lebanon, but she unleashed an even more formidable threat on its northern border, the Shiite militias of the Hezbollah. In fact, the war brought Iran through its proxies, the Hezbollah militias, to Israel's doorstep. This dynamic was not dissimilar to that created by Israel in the Gaza Strip at about the same time. Her obsession with the PLO there would end up enthroning the Hamas and other fundamentalist groups as the hegemonic power in the Strip.

In the annals of policies that turned out to be marches of folly in modern history, Israel's Lebanese adventure will undoubtedly receive the standing it deserves. One of the absurdities of her presence in that torn land was that she invaded it in the first place to 'solve' the Palestinian question and destroy the PLO's infrastructure, yet long years after the invasion Israel continued to be mired down in the mud and to bleed when no connection existed any longer between her presence in Lebanon and the Palestinian question. In 1993 Israel reached an agreement with the PLO – the Oslo accords – but in Lebanon she remained bogged down in a struggle with the local Shiite militias determined 'to expel the foreign invader'. And if that were not enough, Lebanon held Israel in the clamps of Syrian blackmail: no way out in Lebanon was allowed without payment in Syrian currency, namely, withdrawal from the Golan Heights.

The war in Lebanon would last for eighteen years; it ended in June 2000 when the last Israeli soldier left Lebanese territory under the instructions of a government in which the present author had the privilege of serving. Lebanon taught us that wars that cannot be ended are sometimes worse than those that are lost. It was in Lebanon, not in the Yom Kippur War, that Israeli power lost its credibility for the first time. Given the wide political and national consensus that surrounded that war in Israel – the Labour opposition also supported the invasion – one might perhaps draw the lesson that when the entire establishment is united on a move, it would be advisable to worry whether the whole enterprise might not have been based on entirely wrong assumptions.

To the long list of the victims of the war in Lebanon one prominent name needs to be added, that of Menachem Begin. By leading a country that could go united to war only if this was patently unavoidable, a war of *Ein Brerah*, into what he himself had defined as an 'optional' war, 'a war of choice', he broke the consensual pattern traditionally assumed by the Israelis for the conduct of war and opened a deep divide within society. Eventually, he himself felt manipulated and cheated by his own Minister of Defence, Ariel Sharon. The victims of the war burdened his conscience and he was unable to find comfort in the peace treaty he had achieved with Egypt. A broken man, he would resign from office in the summer of 1983 in a way that was never fully explained. From then until his death, he lived secluded at home, only occasionally leaving it to visit his wife's grave at the Mount of Olives.

There was, nevertheless, a bright side to this sad story. Begin and Sharon certainly did not expect their invasion of Lebanon to result in the PLO drawing the necessary political lessons, moderating its political concepts, being recognised by the Reagan administration as a valid interlocutor, then eventually joining the peace process. Instead of the war becoming the platform for the destruction of the PLO, it became the trigger for its renewal. Once again made homeless, the Palestinians would now opt for diplomacy as a vehicle, always accompanied, however, by armed struggle and terror, for the fulfilment of their national objectives. The PLO's military defeat forced it to shift the focus of its confrontation with Israel to the political arena, precisely where Israel was weakest. In Lebanon the conception collapsed of the PLO in a struggle against the 'Zionist entity' from outside. The willingness of the surrounding Arab countries to sustain Israel's ruthless retaliations for hosting the PLO militias was definitely exhausted. A new strategy aimed at establishing a political and military power base inside the occupied territories, preferably with Israel's consent, was now the priority.

However, the oddities of Israeli politics – the national unity government of 1984–8 based on a rotation of the post of prime minister between Shamir and the Labour leader Shimon Peres was one such oddity – would create the conditions for an Israeli response of sorts to the new political opportunities.

Israel was still anything but ripe for a deal with the PLO. Which is why Peres's premiership of the National Unity government was almost exclusively dedicated to rescuing from oblivion the famous Jordanian option. As a whole, there seemed to be improved conditions for the recuperation of the peace process. Israel's withdrawal to a security zone in southern Lebanon certainly helped to improve the atmosphere. The move of the PLO to a political path was also a vitally important change. Another positive development was that the return of Egypt to a position of leadership in the Arab world helped vindicate in the eyes of other potential Arab interlocutors of Israel the validity of the peace process as a legitimate vehicle for recovering Arab lands.

President Mubarak of Egypt was throughout loyal to the Camp David settlement. He positioned himself between the two legacies of his predecessors, Nasser and Sadat. Unlike Nasser, he would not engage in revolutionary regional politics and would not encourage a Nasserite platform of popular nationalism to captivate the imagination of the masses throughout the Arab world. But neither would he give up on Egypt's active leadership of the Arab world nor disengage, like Sadat, from pan-Arab concerns, mainly on the Palestinian question. Mubarak insisted that an intimate correlation should exist between progress in the peace process and the temperature of Egypt's peace with Israel.

As to King Hussein, he now believed he once again had the right conditions to recover the old strategic course of the Hashemite monarchy, by filling the void of the restless peace seeker left by Sadat's death. He was eager to engage with Peres in advancing the Jordanian option. But the resolution of the Rabat summit in 1974, which gave the PLO the exclusive responsibility to negotiate the future of the territories, and that of the Fez summit of 1982, which stipulated that negotiations with Israel could only take place within the framework of an international conference, limited the King's space for diplomatic manoeuvre. He proposed squaring the circle by convening a conference of the five permanent members of the Security Council and the parties directly involved, with the Palestinians as part of a Jordanian delegation. In February 1985 Hussein even seemed to have reached an understanding with Arafat on the objectives of the process: Palestinian self-determination through a Jordanian–Palestinian confederation. But to join the process and allow the participation of an initially non-PLO Palestinian delegation in the international conference the PLO had to meet three conditions: acceptance of SCR 242, recognition of Israel's right to exist, and renunciation of terrorism and violence.

Not only was the PLO unwilling to accept these conditions, they also represented a problem for Israel even, perhaps especially, if she had accepted them. Hussein could not move without the PLO and Peres could not move with it, regardless of whether or not it agreed to depart from its traditional positions. Nor were the Americans ready to confront Foreign Minister Shamir by admitting into the process a PLO that had not yet met the conditions required by the United States. Moreover, the whole idea of an international conference where the Soviet Union would have a role was not appealing to the Reagan administration. Eager as Hussein was to follow in the footsteps of Egypt and have his own peace breakthrough – he would even meet Prime Minister Peres four days after a raid by the Israeli air force on PLO headquarters in Tunis – he could not but second the Americans' insistence on their conditions for the PLO's participation in the peace process.

Zionism has always relied on Palestinian rejectionism to save it from the need to make hard choices. In a move that was the culmination of a difficult and painful evolution within the Palestinian national movement that had begun in the mid-1970s, the PLO would finally endorse the two-state solution. But not until 1988, when the PLO changed its strategy and assumed the two-state principle, did Israel come really close to its moment of truth. Now, however, typically, the PLO still persisted in its self-defeating attitude and, happily for the Israeli government, it resisted the required changes. Moreover, Arafat's refusal to assume 242 and renounce terrorism precipitated a showdown with the King, who now announced that he would no longer seek the participation of the PLO in the process. In March 1986 he closed the PLO's Amman offices and expelled Arafat's deputy, Abu-Jihad, from Jordan. In July he met Peres and Rabin to renew the efforts for a Jordanian–Palestinian option divorced from any PLO connection. The diplomatic blunders of the PLO paved the way for the Peres–Hussein London Agreement. Israel was also encouraged by a change in the Soviets' attitude. They now agreed to a non-coercive international conference, one that would only serve as a launching platform for free bilateral negotiations between the parties. Hussein was determined not to miss this train.

Essentially, the London agreement of April 1987 was much less of a breakthrough than Mr Peres insisted on claiming. It was about the modalities and the mechanisms of the negotiations, not about their content. Moreover, the agreement meant that both Peres and Hussein still compulsively subscribed to a major fallacy, that of the possibility of 'Jordanising' the solution to the Palestinian problem. They both believed that they could still derail the course of history leading to independent and full Palestinian statehood. The London agreement was the last-ditch attempt of the old peace diplomacy to rescue the Jordanian option from oblivion and give it a fresh lease of life by adapting it to the new diplomatic conditions, but not to the compelling logic of Palestinian nationalism and its legitimate aspirations. Hussein would soon realise that his attempt to turn back the clock of history could not prevail and a year later he announced Jordan's total disengagement from the affairs of the West Bank.

But however weak in substance, the London agreement was nevertheless a major step forward, for it established the structure and mechanisms for the future peace process. Built on concepts agreed at Camp David, it established the modalities that would later serve the Madrid Peace Conference and defined what would eventually be the incremental nature of the Oslo accords. The parties in London agreed that a non-coercive international conference would only serve as an umbrella for bilateral talks between Israel and a joint Jordanian–non-PLO Palestinian delegation. All the parties to the conference, it was stipulated, would publicly endorse SCR 242 and renounce violence and terrorism.

But Yitzhak Shamir, now the Prime Minister of the National Unity government, proved to be an obstacle no less formidable than the PLO. He disavowed his Foreign Minister and rejected the London package altogether. To him, all this was a trap he would not fall into. Shamir was not wrong to assume that once the dynamic of negotiations on the future of the West Bank had been unleashed, however innocent the modalities of such talks might be, this would inevitably lead to territorial concessions in Judaea and Samaria. He was therefore determined to nip in the bud the entire adventure. Shamir then convinced Secretary of State Shultz, who pretended 'to sell' him the agreement as an American idea, not to bother to come to Jerusalem at all.

Strange as this might sound, the Likud–Labour rift over the London agreement was practically the first time since 1967 that the political consensus between these two parties on making war or peace was broken. Until 1987 there existed, for all practical purposes, a national coalition on issues of war and peace. Both parties had encouraged the expansion of settlements in the West Bank, they both ruled out Palestinian self-determination, they went into Lebanon hand in hand, they agreed that the 1967 borders could not be the basis for a future peace agreement, and they displayed passivity in their search for peace. And now, twenty years after a Labour Defence Minister, Moshe Dayan, had said he would wait for a telephone call from King Hussein, Hussein was finally ready to lift the phone, only to find that Israel's line was out of order, blocked by a paralysing breakdown between her two major political parties. Nor was Washington's line especially open for business. The irony was that not Peres but Shamir, who did his utmost to torpedo the international conference, would be the one to preside over an Israeli delegation to precisely such a conference in October 1991. This was admittedly in different historical conditions and with a Soviet Union in the last stages of disintegration.

Shamir was not operating in a political void and he was not entirely out of tune with the *Zeitgeist*. The very political breakdown between Right and Left in the government, with the Left itself not especially radical, reflected an underlying socio-cultural reality that was not unfriendly to Shamir's immobilism. A clear shift to the right could be detected in the mood and opinion of the Israelis throughout the 1980s. Israel's expansionist drive in the territories and her daily oppression of Palestinian sentiments was bound to contaminate the environment on the Israeli side of the Green Line. This was reflected in the emergence of radical movements like Rabbi Kahane's Kach, Rehavam Zeevi's transfer party Moledet, the nationalist Thya movement under Professor Yuval Neeman's leadership and even in underground terrorist cells of settlers. Opinion polls indicated a clear correlation between non-democratic attitudes in Israel proper and those towards the Palestinians in the territories. All this was a vivid reflection of a public mood that supported the uncompromising policies of Shamir.

A popular prejudice in Israel about the Arabs is that 'they only understand the language of force'. But this can just as well be said of the Israelis and some of the other parties to the conflict. Sadly, another war was now needed to recover the momentum for peace and radically change the mood in Israel towards a settlement of land for peace. This came in the form of a genuinely popular Palestinian uprising, the Intifada, which was unleashed in the early days of December 1987. Both in its strategic surprise and in its initial impact, the Intifada was a kind of Palestinian Yom Kippur War. The result of the natural growth of rage and frustration that was soon to develop into a struggle for independence, the Intifada helped the Palestinians recover their pride and national dignity, and forced the main actors – the PLO, Israel and the United States – to readjust their political attitudes in accordance with the new realities.

First came Shimon Peres's idea of a 'Gaza First' deal that was immediately thwarted by Prime Minister Shamir. It is a disheartening reflection on the cumbersome Israeli politics of peace and the intractability of the Israeli–Palestinian tragedy that the same idea is still with us today, albeit in an updated unilateral version of disengagement, to nourish the discourse of peace in Israel.

Much to Yitzhak Shamir's discomfort, the Intifada shifted the attitude of all the parties. America was the first to move. The Intifada could not leave the United States indifferent and it eventually led to a gradual change in America's policy that would culminate in its momentous recognition of the PLO in late 1988. The Shultz initiative of 4 March 1988, clearly triggered by the Intifada, was the most assertive attempt by the US since the abortive Reagan plan to solve the Israeli–Palestinian conflict. Shultz's initiative called for a non-coercive international conference, and created a linkage between the idea of Palestinian autonomy and the future talks on the final status of the territories. What Begin considered to be a major achievement of his Camp David deal was now, to the dismay of his successors, sacrificed by a friendly American administration in its desperate quest for regional stability that depended on calming down the Palestinian Intifada.

But once again a coalition of tough-minded Rejectionists – Shamir and Arafat – derailed the American plan. Shamir, who had voted against the Camp David accords, suddenly discovered the marvels of Camp David and questioned the Shultz plan on the grounds that the linkage it created between the interim and the final agreements contradicted the modalities established at Camp David. American policy in the Middle East, and with it the chances of a credible peace process, had clearly fallen hostage to the PLO's and Israel's intransigence or inability to make decisions.

The parties were nonetheless approaching their moment of truth. King Hussein was about to make a move that would greatly enhance the chances of an Israeli–Palestinian settlement. The political void created by the collapse of the London agreement – and now also by the evaporation of the Shultz initiative and the threat that the Intifada posed to the stability, and perhaps even to the very existence, of the Hashemite kingdom – encouraged King Hussein to take a dramatic step. He cancelled the Act of Annexation of the West Bank to Jordan and cut all administrative links to the West Bank. His attempts so far to reconcile Jordan's historical claims to the West Bank, his commitment to the Arab consensus on the predominant role of the PLO, and his search for a settlement with Israel was an exercise in diplomatic juggling that was no longer sustainable. He left the stage to the PLO and in one stroke eliminated for ever the so-called Jordanian option from the diplomacy of peace. From now on, if the PLO wanted the territories back it had to change its policies and come to terms directly with Israel and the United States. Jordan would no longer serve as a diplomatic buffer or bridge.

If Israel's Jordanian option turned out to be an utter failure, she had only herself to blame. The only thing Israeli would-be peacemakers had ever proposed to King Hussein was to be their collaborator in sterilising Palestinian nationalism, in relieving Israel from the demographic burden entailed in the direct rule of the densely populated Palestinian areas of the West Bank and in legitimising her control of the strategic assets in the area. Now there was no longer a Hussein to pull the parties' chestnuts out of the fire; they had to do it themselves.

It was either Intifada or a direct Israeli–Palestinian deal. The Intifada was not only a revolt against the Israeli occupation. In many ways it was also a popular Palestinian rebellion against the PLO whose sterility, indiscriminate international terror and refusal of all compromise compounded Palestinian suffering. The pressure from the territories on the PLO to modify its policies and join the peace process was now at least as powerful as that forcing Israel, clearly incapable of suppressing the uprising, to devise a political way out of this impasse of blood and despair. Incapable of coping with the demoralising effects of the Intifada on both the army and society, and of dealing with its adverse impact on Israel's international standing, Israel needed a peace platform of her own if she was to reconcile herself with world opinion, calm down the territories and address the internal moral crisis. The military way was clearly inadequate.

The status quo which the politicians, mainly on the right, had long regarded as the best of all possible worlds was shattered for ever. The meaning of the Intifada was that decades of self-delusive and dim-sighted Israeli policies now lay defeated in the streets and alleys of the West Bank and Gaza. The Intifada provided Israel with yet another lesson in the limits of power. Her mythical military might had already displayed its ineptitude when it was sent to serve the cause of a 'megalomaniac strategy in Lebanon. Now the same army that in a matter of days in 1967 took over Gaza and the West Bank, and defeated three Arab armies in such an elegant way, was being humiliated by a children's revolt of stones and was unable to suppress the riots in the slums throughout the territories. In the Intifada, as Amos Elon succinctly put it, the Palestinians discovered the power of their weakness and the Israelis the weakness of their power.

The PLO was also in dire straits. Like Israel, it was taken by surprise by the Palestinian uprising. It suddenly realised that the real showdown with Israel was taking a totally different course from that preached and executed for years by an organisation of professional revolutionaries and terrorists. It was an irony of history that the biggest revolt by the Palestinians since the 1930s had begun without PLO direction. Its supremacy was now being effectively undermined by grass-roots revolutionary committees and a non-PLO United National Leadership of the Uprising (UNLU) that emerged throughout the territories and succeeded in establishing areas of Palestinian self-rule in different parts of the occupied lands. The PLO was also challenged by the dramatic surge of Islamic fundamentalist organisations like Hamas and Jihad, especially in Gaza.

The PLO had two ways of reasserting itself. One was to use its financial leverage and the local leadership's fear of retribution should it fail to accept the PLO's supremacy; another was that of seizing the first opportunity to lead the peace process. From that perspective the future Oslo accords should be seen not only as the major peace breakthrough that they certainly were, but also as a desperate move by the PLO to sideline the local Palestinian leadership, reassert its hegemony and stem the fundamentalist tide in the territories. Eventually, the Intifada helped recover Arafat's and the PLO's relevance. As always, it was not some great personal initiative that would resurrect Arafat, but his role as the embodiment of the collective national will of his people, a symbol of their struggle and yearnings, that brought him back to life.

This is perhaps the moment to reflect on a fundamental difference between Zionism and the Palestinian national movement. Both had their 'Yishuv', as it were, and their 'diasporas'. In the case of Zionism, however, the diaspora was never the centre of decision making as was the case with the Palestinians. The diaspora gave to the Jewish Yishuv the logistic, the moral and the political support it needed, but the decisions about strategy, and the effective leadership in the struggle for statehood and institution-building, were all centred in the Yishuv. In the Palestinian case the diaspora and the institutions it created were the main source of legitimacy for the entire movement, the focus of the struggle for national liberation, and the platform where the major decisions and strategic moves were made. And when, during the Intifada, the Palestinian Yishuv asserted itself and threatened the supremacy of the diaspora, the diaspora reacted swiftly with all the means at its disposal. Ironically, it was even ready to make peace and far-reaching concessions to the Israelis in order to reassert itself.

It was now clear to the PLO that only through a deal with Israel could it be allowed to return to the territories and to exercise effective leadership on the Palestinian people. The move in the wake of the Oslo accords of Arafat and his men from Tunis to Gaza, with their culture of terror and their dictatorial practices, would also eventually mean the end of the grass-roots Palestinian uprising. One of the meanings of Oslo was that the PLO was eventually Israel's collaborator in the task of stifling the Intifada and cutting short what was clearly an authentically democratic struggle for Palestinian independence. That the first Intifada was a popular uprising and the second, the Al-Aqsa Intifada, a display of military rebellion and of the practices of the most abominable brand of mass terrorism, was one more expression of the difference between a spontaneous, popular and democratic uprising without PLO direction, and a revolt under PLO and Arafat inspiration and leadership.

The first Intifada forced both Israel and the PLO, each for its own reasons, to opt for a political solution and assume more realistic policies. The old PLO strategy based on the rejection of the legitimacy of a Jewish state and on the concept of a one-state solution in the whole of Palestine had led the Palestinians up a political blind alley. 'We would rather be frozen ten more years than move towards treason' was how Arafat's deputy, Abu Yiad, had put it in 1984. By 1988 the PLO had realised that such political immobilism would only condemn it and its people to a hopeless journey in the wilderness. Egypt's peace with Israel was a major additional factor in the PLO's change of strategy. It meant that the already remote possibility that Israel would be forced by an all-Arab war to relinquish the territories, and perhaps even disintegrate as a state altogether, became more unrealistic than ever.

The Arab–Israeli conflict was, and in important ways continues to be, essential for the stability of the Arab regimes, a convenient diversion of attention and energies away from governments' incompetence in domestic matters, and from the hopelessness of destitution and the sad reality of corruption as an almost institutionalised system of government. Israel is the ultimate pretext to justify repression and lack of political and civil liberties throughout the Arab world. Egypt's peace with Israel signalled a careful third way between an unsustainable state of permanent war and a full-fledged, positive peace that might end up unleashing the kind of uncontrollable democratic changes that no Arab regime wanted. Egypt's way was conceived to reconcile, through a cold, even tense and armed peace, the need to relieve the regime from the unbearable burden of war with the requirements of domestic stability.

The Palestinians were forced to realise that, although far less outspoken and theatrical than Anwar Sadat, Hosni Mubarak was not abandoning Egypt's peace strategy with Israel and therefore could not be relied upon to lead, or back, a return to the old days of total struggle against her. Mubarak's motives and policies were laid down by him very candidly in a speech in 1989. It could be interpreted as a call by the leader of the Arab world to his brethren throughout the region to change their policies if they wanted to be able to tackle the new realities and respond to the new challenges:

> We fought for many years, but where did we get? We also spent 100 billion on wars, apart from thousands of martyrs until we reached the present situation from which we are now suffering. I am therefore not ready to take more risks.... Wars have generally not solved any problem. Regardless of the difficulties or obstacles surrounding the present peace process, our real effort focuses on removing these obstacles.

The PLO's change of policy in 1988 clearly removed one of these obstacles. In November 1988 a ground-breaking PLO event took place in Algiers. In a declaration of Palestinian independence the Palestinian National Council (PNC) accepted the existence of the State of Israel and endorsed 'all relevant UN Resolutions', paradoxically including two mutually exclusive Resolutions, namely 242 and 181. These ambiguities and the contradictory language that accompanied them would continue to characterise PLO rhetoric in the coming years. The commitment to a step-by-step doctrine of first Gaza and later Acre and Jaffa died hard in the PLO's discourse. But for now the good news was that the claim to all Palestine that was embedded in the PLO's charter was diluted, if not waived altogether, as the Declaration of Independence was to be applied only to the West Bank, Gaza and Jerusalem.

As in the case of Sadat's peace overtures towards Israel, Arafat's change of strategy was mainly meant to shift the Palestinian diplomatic effort from its ineffective reliance on the Soviet bloc to an alliance with the United States. Recognising Israel was for Arafat the introduction to a Palestinian dialogue with the United States more than a demarche aimed at Israel. It was about opening the gates of Washington, not those of Jerusalem. The truth of the matter was, then, that both the Declaration of Independence and Arafat's speech were aimed mainly at the US, not at Israel. Arafat's major objective now was to meet the Americans' demands for a modification of PLO policies in a way that could allow US recognition of the organisation with all the political and strategic benefits this was supposed to entail. But America was not satisfied with the ambiguities and the double language that surrounded the Algiers event. Additional pressure would still have to be brought to bear on Arafat, and a formula whereby he 'totally and absolutely renounced all forms of terrorism' and unequivocally endorsed SCRs 242 and 338 had to be practically dictated to, and imposed on, him by the Americans.

How difficult it was for Arafat to renounce terrorism, even if only verbally, may perhaps be indicated by an anecdote the present author was told years later by Abu-Ala, my counterpart at the time as the Palestinian chief negotiator and today the Prime Minister of the Palestinian Authority. He told me how Arafat failed three consecutive times to pronounce correctly the formula dictated to him. Instead of 'renounce terrorism', he repeated three times 'renounce tourism'.

It is a reflection on the unique character of the Israelis' Palestinian dilemma, as compared with their conflict with the Arab states, that they remained indifferent to, even suspicious of, Arafat's recognition of Israel, while they went out of their way to acclaim Anwar Sadat's gestures. The reason lay not only in the difference in the nature of the two conflicts – Palestinianism is a challenge that threatens the most intimate dreams of the Israelis, touches their innermost complexes and arouses their most acute fears – but also in the fact that it was clear to all that Arafat's declaration was not authentic and natural; it was wrested from, and dictated to, him by the Americans, and it was aimed at them and not at the hearts and minds of the Israelis, as was the case with Sadat. Sadat was always careful to submerge his grand strategic considerations into an emotional appeal to the Israeli conscience. Arafat never mastered that art.

These were the last days of the Reagan administration in Washington and it was another irony of history that this most friendly of American presidents, Ronald Reagan, should have been the one who extended America's recognition to the PLO and gave legitimacy to an organisation that the Israelis perceived to be their arch-enemy, their demon, Satan incarnate. All this was too much for Shamir. He knew that negotiations with the PLO could only lead to a Palestinian state. Himself an underground terrorist leader in the past, Shamir did not see the PLO's terrorism as the main problem. The problem was in the objectives of the movement: independence and statehood. It was not the nature of the partner that troubled Shamir's mind; it was the inevitable agenda of the negotiations that he could not stomach.

But to stand still in revolutionary times and completely overlook the winds of change was too dangerous. It could only mean international isolation, conflict with America and no end to the Intifada. This was how the so-called Shamir Peace Initiative was born. The initiative originated in a series of ideas prepared in January 1989, as an immediate response by Defence Minister Rabin to the PLO move of November 1988 in Algiers, and in a desperate attempt to curtail the ascendancy of Arafat's organisation. Rabin, a major exponent of the Jordanian option, finally understood that it was not through the Jordanians that the Palestinian problem would be solved, but rather it was the solution to the Palestinian problem that would pave the way to peace with Jordan. Rabin's plan now called for a Palestinian move to end the Intifada as a condition and prelude to elections in the territories. The leadership that would emerge from the elections would be Israel's partner for negotiating a Palestinian autonomy first and the final status of the territories later. The deal was simple: autonomy in exchange for an end to the Intifada.

The Rabin–Shamir initiative was clearly aiming at very high stakes with inadequate resources. Both the PLO and the local Palestinian leadership rejected it as a transparent attempt to stifle the Intifada at the cheapest possible political price. This was also the American view. A new American administration had now settled down in Washington and its two most visible members, the new resident of the White House, George Bush, and his Secretary of State, James Baker, had their own strategic vision for the Middle East, at the centre of which there was an Arab–Israeli peace. And, no less important, neither Bush nor Baker was particularly susceptible to Jewish lobbies or to Israel's influence in Washington. Sometimes they even seemed to be blind and deaf to the Jewish factor in America's policy making on the Arab–Israeli front. Secretary of State James Baker made this clear, in a frontal assault on Shamir's right-wing philosophy. 'Israel', he said in a speech to Aipac, Israel's Jewish lobby in

Washington on 22 May 1989, should 'lay aside, once and for all, the unrealistic vision of a Greater Israel'. And in a direct dramatic appeal to Israel, he added, 'Forswear annexation. Stop settlement activity. Allow schools to reopen. Reach out to the Palestinians as neighbours who deserve political rights!'

But Shamir was a hard nut to crack. He remained unimpressed. He would not only not improve his proposal, he even went back on it under pressure from his rivals in the Likud Party. The Prime Minister was now ready to place in jeopardy his National Unity government with the Labour Party by withdrawing from even the semblance of a peace process. He retreated to his narrow political and mental ghetto at a time when the region bubbled with peace initiatives of all kinds, in an attempt to break the dangerous deadlock.

In September 1989 it was Mubarak's turn to try his luck as a peacemaker. Egypt's role as a regional broker needed to be preserved – this was Mubarak's vision – as a way of legitimising Egypt's peace with Israel and vindicating it in the eyes of the Arab world while, at the same time, cementing its links with the United States as an indispensable ally. Mubarak proposed a ten-point plan at the core of which lay concepts such as elections in the territories with the participation of the residents of east Jerusalem as well, 'land for peace' and an end to settlement expansion. A month later James Baker himself came out with a five-point plan essentially focused on the modalities of the elections. In a boost to Mubarak's strategy, he suggested Cairo as the venue for the negotiations.

National unity governments in Israel were normally created to respond either to a threat of imminent war or to the paralysis between the two major political blocs in the country. The reason for their dissolution was, however, almost invariably the same: their incapacity to articulate a common peace policy or to advance a coherent response to a peace initiative. The need to respond to such a barrage of peace initiatives in the late 1980s was too much for the government of National Unity. It could neither digest them nor agree upon a coherent response to them and this was therefore its end. The Labour Party preferred to see the bright side of both Mubarak's and Baker's plans, for neither mentioned the PLO or a Palestinian state. The resignation of the Labour ministers in March 1990 left the most right-wing, hardline government in Israel's history to face the avalanche of peace opportunities that were being produced by a unique combination of local, regional and global changes ranging from the Intifada and the Gulf War, to the collapse of the Soviet Union.

*

Baker succeeded where Shultz had failed because he had on his side an entirely different global context and a Middle East that went through a momentous shock with the Gulf War. A total restructuring of geopolitical realities was about to create the conditions for a new, vigorous stage in Israeli–Arab peacemaking and divert the Intifada to a political path where the emergence of a Palestinian state could be, for the first time, a realistic option.

Yasser Arafat's and the PLO's support for Saddam Hussein's invasion of Kuwait was certainly a major strategic blunder of the Palestinian leadership. Once again, as so often in the past, one could watch with stupor and bewilderment the self-defeating nature of Palestinian nationalism. The PLO's failure to join a coalition based on the same key principle on which the Palestinians had built their case – a principle that was, moreover, embedded in SCR 242, about the 'inadmissibility of acquiring territory by force' – was a sad display of political stupidity which, moreover, morally spoiled the Palestinian case. This was how Arafat misunderstood and misrepresented to his people the coalition's war to undo the Iraqi aggression against another Arab country:

> These are days of glory and pride and steadfastness of our Arab nation. ... The real aim of the treacherous American aggression is not to enforce compliance with UN resolutions but to destroy Palestine and the Arab nation and make way for three million Russian Jews in a greater Israel stretching from the Nile to the Euphrates.

One of the Chairman's advisers, Yasser Abd-Rabbo, followed suit when he declared that the whole Gulf War had nothing to do with Iraq's invasion of Kuwait. Rather, it was America's war for the defence of Israel's hegemony in the region. This was exactly the argument that Arab and non-Arab critics of America would manipulate during the war in Iraq twelve years later. 'The Israelis will be taught a bloody lesson in this war,' boasted Abd-Rabbo. Even a moderate like Professor Sari Nusseibah found time to publish an article in a Jerusalem newspaper under the title 'SADDAM SMASHES THE SIX DAY WAR MYTH'.

If the Palestinians were saved from their own self-destruction, this was because their cause was greater than their leaders. It was also because of President Bush's leadership in pursuing the peace process and in being receptive to the pressure exerted on the United States by her Arab allies without whom the war against Iraq would have lacked a vital legitimacy. A Machiavellian reversal of alliances during the Gulf War had indeed opened possibilities never seen before. Syria was in this respect of special concern to the Americans. The apostle of Arab radicalism, Syria was seen by the United States as the indispensable pillar in the edifice of inter-Arab legitimacy it tried to build for its war in Iraq. And Syria, of all Arab states, would not join the 'American imperialists' in their war against another Arab state unless, as Foreign Minister Farouk al-Shara made clear to the Americans, it was done in the service of a higher cause, namely, the end to what was defined as America's policy of double standards in the Middle East. Not only Iraq should be forced to abide by UN resolutions, Israel should also be coaxed into respecting those resolutions pertaining to the Arab–Israeli conflict.

Eventually, by pursuing the peace process and convening the Madrid Peace Conference, President Bush assumed the linkage that Saddam had cynically pretended to create between his invasion of Iraq and the Palestinian question. In a speech on 6 March 1991, the President laid down his commitment to an Israeli–Arab peace: 'We must do all we can to close the gap between Israel and the Arab states and between Israel and the Palestinians. ... The time has come to put an end to the Arab–Israeli conflict.' Like Kissinger after the Yom Kippur War, the Bush–Baker team understood that wars in the Middle East have always offered opportunities for peace that should not be missed.

The way to Madrid was paved by a unique combination of factors. The collapse of the Soviet Union as a world power and a force to be reckoned with in the Middle East, and hence the loss by the Arabs of their military option, made the peace track through the good offices of the sole superpower the only realistic way left to the Arabs to recover the territories. Notwithstanding the support of King Hussein of Jordan for his brutal neighbour Saddam Hussein – one more example of Jordan's delicate predicament, its difficult quest for security and regional balance while sandwiched between powerful neighbours – the war had made clear to the Israelis the necessity of Jordan as a buffer state between Israel and rogue states in the region such as Iraq and Iran. Even the Likud in Israel had now to come to terms with the reality that Jordan as an independent state was more vital to Israel's security than their ideological drive to convert it into a Palestinian state. The Palestinian problem, Likud was forced to realise, had to be solved on its own merits. Neither the benign Jordanian option of the Labourites nor the Likud's aggressive version of a hostile takeover of Jordan in order to convert it into a Palestinian state, could solve Israel's Palestinian dilemma.

The Gulf War also led to a severe psychological and strategic earthquake in Israel. Her entire strategic doctrine was shattered. Instead of being what she always assumed she was, a strategic ally of the United States and the West, she was relegated to the status of a strategic liability whose main contribution to the war effort was that of absorbing without response

Saddam's missile attacks on her civilian population, lest an Israeli response might disband America's carefully built war alliance with the Arab states in the region. Israel's deterrence power was severely shaken and her claim about the extreme importance of territorial depth for her security was shattered. The occupation of the West Bank did not save Tel Aviv from the weapons of modern warfare – guided missiles. Now the proud self-image of an Israel protected by her own independent mighty military machine, always proficient at transferring the war in no time to enemy territory and keeping her civilians out of it, was shattered by the resuscitation of the older image of the diaspora Jew lobbying the Gentiles for protection. The presence of American troops in Israel to operate the Patriot batteries invoked in the public mind the old times of Jewish proverbial helplessness and dependency on the goodwill of the Gentiles. Even the memory of the Holocaust, as Professor Moshe Zuckermann has shown in a perceptive essay,[1] was revived to express the fears of annihilation that permeated the minds of many. The Gulf War dealt a severe blow to the nation's self-esteem and to established military doctrine.

Nor could the Arab regimes remain indifferent to the meaning of the Gulf War. The war brought them closer to the inevitability of an accommodation with Israel. Iraq's invasion of Kuwait taught the Arab leaders that their conflict with Israel weakened rather than strengthened the stability of their regimes and diverted their attention from other vital conflicts in the region in a way that undermined their capacity to handle them. As a result of the war Arab radicalism had been defeated and an American president conspicuously non-sentimental about Israel or the Jews was now making it clear he would not hesitate to twist the arm of Israel's intransigent Prime Minister. He also made it clear that he would not give Israel the badly needed $10 billion loan guarantees for the absorption of Russian Jews if her government persisted in its settlement policy and did not respond to the President's peace initiatives. Shamir was practically dragged to Madrid by President Bush. The message was forcefully, by way of pressure and intimidation, brought home to him that he could have either America's friendship or the territories, not both. President Bush proved to be the architect of a formidable coalition for war. But he also showed an extraordinary diplomatic proficiency in turning that same coalition into an international alliance for peace in the Middle East. It became the envelope that was necessary in order to give international backing and legitimacy to the launching of the Arab–Israeli peace process in Madrid.

---

[1] *Shoah in the Sealed Room. The 'Holocaust' in the Israeli Press During the Gulf War* (Hebrew), Tel Aviv, 1993.

The present author had the privilege of being a member of Israel's delegation in Madrid at a moment when, for the first time in the history of the Arab–Israeli conflict, the attempt was launched, with unprecedented international backing, for a comprehensive solution of the conflict. I could see the arrival of a jovial and excited Palestinian delegation, again for the first time in so many years, at the Middle Eastern conference table, on an equal footing with the other participants. That the PLO was there only by proxy and new authentic Palestinian leaders of the territories formed the Palestinian delegation boded well for the international image of an embattled nation in search of dignity and freedom from occupation.

The beginnings of an American–Palestinian partnership in the peace process could be detected in Madrid, where the Bush–Baker team seemed to be putting all the pressure almost exclusively on Prime Minister Shamir. The meeting in Madrid, prior to the conference, between the President and the Prime Minister was not exactly a congenial encounter between two allies who had just successfully co-ordinated their strategies against an Arab aggressor. Rather, it was a most unpleasant occasion where the President insisted that he had never promised to acquiesce to Israel's settlement policy as a reward for her restraint during the Gulf War, as the Prime Minister for some reason believed. Shamir's mood throughout the conference oscillated between two extremes: the feeling of being under siege and indifference. The indifferent attitude was made clear to me when, following Gorbachev's speech at the opening session of the conference, I approached the Prime Minister to ask him about his reaction. 'I don't know,' he said to me, 'I fell asleep ...'

But the Americans would not let him sleep for long. Without prior consultation with Israel and to Shamir's dismay, they summoned the parties immediately after the conference to bilateral talks in Washington. The Prime Minister was forced against his will and judgement to send his delegations to the American capital, but this did not mean that he had any intention of budging from his known positions. The talks were a sheer waste of time, and the gap between the parties was simply unbridgeable. Israel's withdrawal from Sinai was *the* implementation of SCR 242 and Israel would not execute any additional withdrawals on the other fronts. Such was the guiding concept behind the instructions given to the Israeli delegations to Washington. Nor would Israel agree to the Palestinians' pretensions that the autonomy should be a stage leading to statehood. And if this were not enough, Shamir made it abundantly clear to the Americans that he would pursue his expansive settlement policy.

Shamir was marching towards his electoral defeat and political demise. The reasons were twofold. Israelis applaud their leaders when they confront the Arabs or snub the Europeans, never when they so irresponsibly defy Israel's major, and at times only, ally the United States. Bush and Baker made it clear to the Israeli public that if they wanted the loan guarantees, they needed to change their Prime Minister. The second reason was internal. Notwithstanding the ideological divide over the future of the territories and the profound social-political cleavages in the country, the Israelis were far more enthusiastic than their Prime Minister about the opportunities offered by the new era that opened with the collapse of the Soviet Union and the Madrid Peace Conference. They saw how the Prime Minister subverted and frustrated their genuine hopes for peace and how, for the sake of a fundamentally unjust and ideologically driven policy of settlements, he mortgaged the chances of Israel joining in the unprecedented opportunities offered by the new international order and the emerging global economy.

Yitzhak Rabin, the leader of the Labour Party in the June 1992 elections, captured the national mood when he proposed a platform based on a radical change in the scale of national priorities. New times and new challenges required a new leadership. Rabin was the right man in the right place at the right moment.

IX   Oslo: The Glory and the Agony

Give me another example in history where one side allowed the other
to dictate who his representatives at a negotiation must be. We agreed
even to this, because we desired peace.

Arafat to a group of Israeli journalists,
May 1993

It is either Arafat or the Hamas. There is no third partner.

Rabin on his decision to negotiate with the PLO,
(interview with Thomas Friedman, no date)

Oh Brethren. ... We are at a war of hundred years. ... When the
Prophet made peace with the tribe of Quuraysh ... Umar ... called
it the despised peace. ... Our history is our best teacher. ... We stand
by our oath to pursue [the battle] ...

Arafat at Gaza's al-Azhar University,
1 January 1995

... [Peace for Israel] is an exchange of land for a Middle East market.

Mohamed Sid Ahmed, an Egyptian intellectual,
January 1995

It is the total and absolute nature of the Israeli–Palestinian conflict that
has made it into such a protracted dispute. For it is not just a collision
over territory, or a banal border dispute; it is a clash of rights and
memory. The longing for the same landscapes, the mutually exclusive
claims of ownership of land and religious sites and symbols, and the
ethos of dispossession and refugeeism for which the two parties claim a
monopoly make their national narratives practically irreconcilable. It is
also a war of images, contrasted and demonised images, a struggle between
two nationalist mythologies, both of them claiming the monopoly of
justice and martyrdom. The history of Jewish disasters and the way
Zionism has instrumentalised them was a lesson the Palestinians were
quick to absorb. 'Expulsion', 'exile', 'diaspora', 'holocaust', 'return', 'genocide' are Jewish catchwords that became an inextricable part of the
Palestinian national ethos.

The Israeli–Palestinian conflict lends itself to additional manipulations. As we have seen, it has been portrayed by the Palestinians and the wider Arab world as a typically anti-colonial struggle, Israel being a kind of high-tech Crusader state, an artificial, Western-orientated 'entity' that would have been doomed if it were not for the unconditional support of the Jews of the world and the United States. In contrast, the Palestinians are an indigenous nation of Oriental peasants that were cruelly and unjustly eradicated from their historical homeland. And if the depth of the conflict were not enough to explain its persistence, its international implications as a vital platform for superpower competition certainly served powerfully to keep it alive. The Palestinian plight was also a political glue for pan-Arab nationalism, a comfortable excuse for the rejection of Israel. It became inseparable from the wider Arab–Israeli conflict.

Political breakthroughs in such protracted conflicts cannot be produced by sterile diplomatic formulae. They require a stage of maturity in both societies that can only come about when all other alternatives have been exhausted and the parties have learned the need for compromise the hard way, through trial and error. The beginning of a solution cannot be envisaged unless the parties have gone through a defining national trauma that exposes both the limits of power of the supposedly superior side and the ultimate impotence of the weaker. In the Israeli–Palestinian case the disintegrating and corrupting effects of occupation on the one hand, and the incapacity of the occupied to bring about the unconditional capitulation of its enemy through a popular rebellion and international pressure on the other, combined to create conditions for a breakthrough. A combination of the deep social transformations that took place in Israel throughout the 1980s and 1990s, the realisation by the Palestinians that, however successful their Intifada might have been in advancing their case, they could not impose their conditions on the Israelis, and a dramatic change in the structure of international relations from the end of the 1980s created a greater readiness for a compromise.

The Oslo breakthrough was preceded by years in which Israeli society went through a process of demobilisation whereby its cohesion as a frontier society was severely loosened. In the late 1980s and early 1990s it looked for a while as though the mainstream Right and the mainstream Left no longer espoused strong, irreconcilable ideological commitments. The heroic Socialist economy of the past had now given way to a more liberal and profit-orientated economy. That the Zionist agrarian vision of a reborn nation had faded away into a technologically driven market economy was epitomised by the decline of the kibbutz and the egalitarian ethos that it represented. The collective enterprises of the Zionist experience – the Histadrut (the trade unions and their industrial corporations), the kibbutz, the moshav, and the political parties as an instrument of national mobilisation – declined into a state of total decomposition. Conspicuously, the June 1992 elections that brought Rabin to power revolved around a rationalistic debate on the need to change the nation's scale of priorities, not on eternal truths and millenarian claims.

The Gulf War had also made the Israelis riper for compromise. It exposed the vulnerability of their home front. Thousands of Israelis left the big cities in a mass exodus to the safer south of the country. A supposedly nuclear power with a mythologically powerful army under its command, Israel had finally to resort to a passive, pathetically defensive strategy – plastic sheets were used to seal doors and windows – against Saddam's Scud missiles. The plastic sheets in the Gulf War were the ultimate argument for peace.

One should not, of course, underestimate the impact of the Palestinian popular uprising, the Intifada. It had shown the Israelis that democratic societies are ill equipped to fight a national struggle for independence. The Intifada weakened the resolve of the Israelis to stay in the territories and shattered the illusion that theirs was a 'humane occupation', or that there was such a thing at all as humane occupation.

The Israeli and South African dilemmas had different origins and each responded to its own dynamic. One was a racial conflict between a black majority and a white minority. The other is a national struggle about land, occupation and symbols of national and religious identity. However, some useful insights may be drawn from the traits they had in common. As in the Soweto uprising of 1976 in South Africa, the Intifada also came as a shock to the complacent ruling classes. In both cases the revolutionary violence did not have to be successful in order to be effective. It had merely to cause significant shock within the dominant society so that the ability of the government to persist in discarding a political compromise by confining its response to the strictly military became unsustainable. This was not the first time in history that the repressive apparatus of the state proved to be useless when dealing with the threat of a national popular uprising like the Intifada. Machine-guns can perhaps quell a popular uprising, but only at the price of compromising the survival of democracy and the stability of the social order. Neither in Soweto nor in the Palestinian territories was the situation out of control, but in both cases the dominant societies were politically and morally defeated.

Again, as in the case of the white minority in South Africa that hoped to retain through negotiations the reins of power for the ruling class, the Israeli politicians and key constituencies throughout society were encouraged to move to a settlement with the PLO by their perception that the peace process would eventually secure them strategic portions of, and key settlement areas in, the West Bank. Paradoxically, more and more people believed now that the best conservative solution was one that passed through a revolutionary shift of policy.

Interestingly, the breakdown of apartheid in South Africa was related to two fundamental reasons – one demographic and the other economic – that were also present in the Israeli case. White manpower shortage, which developed in both the public and private sectors in South Africa and steadily undermined white supremacy, is not, of course, a phenomenon that reproduced itself in Israel in these exact terms. But Israel's growing dependence on cheap Palestinian labour, a phenomenon that stymied the industrialisation of key sectors of the economy and carried with it serious security hazards, not to mention the moral price it entailed, was less and less easy to maintain, especially when the international market had no difficulty replacing Palestinian labour. The message was gradually percolating to the Israelis that the pattern of their relations with the Palestinians needed to change.

A settlement in both cases was made possible from the moment the hard core of the two societies abandoned their ideological convictions. Once the core leaderships lost their faith in coercion, understood that the cost of domination had come to exceed its benefits and began to conceive change, even dramatic change, as the best conservative solution, the way was opened for a peace process. 'We do not want to live permanently in a state of siege in which hatred and bloodshed reign supreme.' This revolutionary affirmation was uttered by a white South African leader, but the Israeli case can offer hundreds of similar utterances.

But ripeness does not have to affect the dominant society only. In the Israeli–Palestinian case it clearly affected both societies and their respective polities. The disarray of the PLO and its financial crisis as a consequence of its strained relations with the dynasties of the Gulf – following the Gulf War – made the PLO more amenable to a settlement based on a compromise that was unthinkable before. That the PLO would accept 60 per cent of the Gaza Strip with all the agricultural land reserve remaining in the hands of 4,000 Israeli settlers, without getting guarantees that a Palestinian state would eventually be established, the settlements dismantled and the 1948 refugees would be promised a politically acceptable solution to their plight, was made possible only because of the circumstantial weakness of the PLO. The collapse of the Soviet Union and the decomposition of the automatic block of support for the Palestinian cause that the Soviet-inspired Third World offered in the past, as well as the erosion of the pan-Arab ideology as a key factor in inter-

Arab politics, also contributed to bringing home to the Palestinian leadership the need for a direct deal with Israel. In addition the dramatic change in the international situation might have influenced the dominant societies in South Africa and Israel to believe that the ground was now ready for the kind of compromise that had eluded them so far. Both could justify the volte face in their stance on the grounds that the enemy or rival was now a containable force, given that the Soviet Union and international Communism – and in the Israeli case, pan-Arab nationalism – were in disarray.

The PLO was surely pushed to assume a realistic approach to the solution of the conflict by its impotence to translate into practical terms the achievements of the Intifada: the moral ground it had gained and its exploits in the field of propaganda. For in spite of the undeniable damage that the Intifada had inflicted on Israeli society, it sometimes also looked as if the Israelis were learning to live with it. In other words the danger for the Palestinians that the Intifada might become a banal fact of life was a factor that might have urged them to come to terms with Israel.

No American president before Bill Clinton had engaged so deeply and intimately with the intricacies of the Arab–Israeli imbroglio. Clinton had almost a sense of mission to make peace between Arabs and Jews. There was, of course, also a strategy behind the presidential drive. The new administration believed in a policy of 'dual containment' of the radical states in the outer circle of the Middle East, namely Iraq and Iran. A close American involvement in the Arab–Israeli peace process, Clinton believed, would help mobilise the moderate Arab states in favour of his dual containment policy and would at the same time prevent the radical states from derailing the peace process.

However, the open negotiations between the Israeli and Palestinian official delegations in Washington, which produced no result in the last phase of George Bush's presidency, were hardly more successful in Clinton's first year in the White House. As in the case of the secret Egyptian–Israeli track that was started in 1977 as an expression of distrust of grandiloquent peace conferences, the Oslo accords emerged as both Israelis and Palestinians realised that only through a strictly bilateral, and preferably secret, channel could the possibilities of reaching a settlement be fully exhausted.

One of the most intriguing traits of the Arab–Israeli conflict is that in spite of the profound and constant involvement of the international community in both the conflict and in the usually abortive attempts to solve it, the major breakthroughs in peacemaking were reached without the support or even the knowledge of external powers. For in spite of the traditional Arab rhetoric about Israel being an instrument of Western imperialism, an American puppet and so forth, in the last analysis the Arabs came to realise the fallacy of their propaganda even before the collapse of the Soviet Union. Sadat's visit to Jerusalem precisely when the superpowers were planning to reconvene the Geneva Conference was a case in point: his initiative was his way of preventing the Geneva Conference from happening. He understood that Israel would not succumb to international pressure, and international conferences would only fuel the paranoiac mentality of the Israelis, hence making a settlement even less possible. In the last analysis Sadat's visit to Jerusalem, Israel's secret peace with Jordan, as well as the surprise agreement with the Palestinians in a secluded nordic castle, had shown that Israel's protracted conflict with the Arabs had not only brought wars, destruction and mistrust; it had, curiously, brought the parties closer to appreciating each other's fears and sensibilities. One of the more 'international' struggles of the twentieth century, the Arab–Israeli conflict paradoxically experienced its major breakthrough only when stripped of its international dimensions, when those who had shed each other's blood for so many years finally sat down to negotiate a possible settlement.

Oslo was the result of a unique combination of local and global changes; it was almost the by-product of an emergent new world. A major transformation in world affairs took place with the collapse of the Soviet Union, with the Gulf War and its regional and international repercussions, and with the emergence of Islamic fundamentalism as a central challenge of the new times.

At that momentous crossroads, Arafat and the PLO misjudged the post-Cold War opportunities and failed to appreciate the far-reaching shift in the structure of international relations at the end of the Cold War. By supporting Saddam Hussein's occupation of Kuwait they isolated themselves from the international and Arab worlds, especially from their wealthy patrons in the Gulf States, and lost their major sources of income without which, rhetoric apart, the PLO simply could not exist. Arafat's miscalculations were of historic proportions, and they brought the Palestinian cause to the verge of financial and political bankruptcy. How could he not realise that by supporting the occupation of Kuwait he was morally spoiling his case, based since 1967 on the principle inherent in Security Council Resolution 242 about 'the inadmissibility of the acquisition of land by force'? Arafat's miscalculation in supporting Saddam Hussein can only be compared with the Mufti's colossal blunder in throwing in his lot with Nazi Germany in World War Two. The crisis of the PLO boosted the chances of their rivals in the territories, especially the Islamic organisations Hamas and Islamic Jihad, which suffered no financial problems. Both Iran and Saudi Arabia continued to lavish budgets and gifts on them.

And if all this were not enough to force a change of policies by the PLO, President Bush's electoral defeat by Bill Clinton in 1992 dealt a serious blow to the Palestinians and the Arabs in general. The Bush–Baker team had no particular love for Jewish lobbies, and was emotionally deaf to Jewish and Israeli sensibilities. Clinton, however, lost no time in positioning himself as a staunch friend of Israel and of the Jewish people.

In such conditions, with the stakes so high, a failure of the PLO to adapt itself to the new realities before the local Palestinian leadership asserted its political supremacy, or the fundamentalist groups completely took over control of the territories, would have been suicidal for the organisation and the cause it represented. Already Arafat's acceptance of the humiliating conditions for the participation of the Palestinians in the Madrid Peace Conference signalled that the old warrior was now entering the most pragmatic stage of his political career. 'Give me another example in history', he would say to a group of Israeli journalists who came to see him in his headquarters in Tunis, 'where one side allowed the other to dictate who his representatives at a negotiation must be. We agreed even to this, because we desire peace.' To further underline his conciliatory approach, Arafat could have added how he had ordered the exclusion of Saab Erakat from the second session of the conference after he had aroused the anger of the Israelis by ostentatiously wearing a Palestinian keffiyeh during the first. More important, when it came to the actual positions in the negotiations with Israel, it soon became clear that Arafat's men in Oslo were far more accommodating than the Palestinians from the territories in the bilateral negotiations with Israel in Washington.

Oslo was for Arafat more a political manoeuvre aimed at recovering the control of Palestinian politics and affairs than a peace initiative. He went to Oslo to save the PLO from declining into oblivion, not necessarily in search of a peace formula. Arafat needed to establish a foothold in the Palestinian territories at all costs, even at the expense of an agreement with Israel that did not secure vital Palestinian aspirations such as the right of self-determination, an end of Israel's policy of settlements, and an acceptable solution to the issues of Jerusalem and refugees. On all these bones of contention, the Oslo accords were either silent or vague and ambiguous.

As to the Israeli side of the equation, it was Rabin's leadership and his sober interpretation of the new realities that made the difference. Reserved, taciturn, impatient, Rabin was a man of action who despised theatrical gestures and hollow rhetoric. He entered his second term as Prime

Minister as a mature statesman who, fully aware of the flaws of his first term, was now determined to rise to the challenges of the changing times. He saw what he called 'a real window of opportunity' to make peace while the Soviet Union was disappearing as a power the Arabs could rely upon, rogue states like Iran and Iraq had not yet developed nuclear capabilities, and Islamic fundamentalism, which produced most of the terrorist capabilities against Israel and threatened the moderate Arab regimes ready to make peace with her, could still be curtailed. Rabin was probably one of the first world leaders fully to grasp the meaning of the strategic threat posed by Islamic fundamentalism. To cope with this combination of risks and opportunities, he believed that peace and, as he always liked to insist, economic development as well, were the answer: 'Let's make peace. Let's have regional development, bring up the standard of living of the people in the Arab countries, and in this way answer the main threat,' he explained in an interview.

Rabin was throughout his term as Prime Minister a keen friend of Israel's business community. Israeli elites yearned for peace as a vehicle for economic growth and as the necessary condition for Israel's dynamic economy to break new ground, to overcome the sense of siege that had stymied her regional and global expansion, open new markets and be able fully to profit from the vertiginous changes that were taking place in the global economy. Yitzhak Rabin was the major political advocate of this economic drive, for he was eager to lead Israel into a new economic era, to see her overcome her sense of isolation and seize the opportunities offered by the new global economy, by the mass immigration of Soviet Jews with their technological capabilities and by the emerging markets. But all this, he knew, could not be done without peace.

Israel's failure to quell the Intifada and the psychological effects of the missile attacks against its cities during the Gulf War had also taught the Prime Minister the limits of the military answer to Israel's problems. To his dismay, Rabin discovered that the legendary stamina of the Israelis was showing signs of erosion and he became doubtful as to their capacity to withstand the threats facing the country. Israeli society, he confided to me during a flight to the Golan Heights in the spring of 1993, was no longer the pioneering society it used to be; it had lost its fighting spirit. Israel was now a far less cohesive society than the one he knew as Chief of Staff in the Six Day War. The dreams of the younger generation were centred on the opportunities offered by the technological revolution and the new economy. Israelis longed for the normal life they had never enjoyed, a life of personal fulfilment and economic well-being. And this required peace. Opinion polls reflected it consistently: the mood of Israel was changing rapidly. A secular majority of Israelis, open-minded and pragmatic, was now ready to accept a historical compromise with the Arab world. The religious and sentimental weight of Judaea and Samaria was to them too heavy a burden, too high an obstacle on the way to the postmodern, perhaps even post-Zionist, normalcy they longed for.

Rabin did not act in a vacuum. He was responding to a notable change in the national mood. The hubris of power so firmly established in the collective mind of the Israelis after the Six Day War was being shattered by a consecutive series of military setbacks. The Yom Kippur War, the Lebanese quagmire, the Intifada and the effects of the Gulf War had all shown that the era of quick and elegant victories was definitely over, and with its passing some of the constituent myths of the Zionist enterprise were dealt a severe blow. Israel's obsession with an exclusive military answer to what were essentially political challenges was no longer sustainable. It was not only Masada that, rather than an inspiration for the nation's struggle for survival, was now widely perceived as a national trauma, a suicidal pattern of national behaviour that needed to be avoided; other legends were also being questioned.

Of course, the process whereby the erosion of old mythologies, which in any case is always resisted by important segments of the social and political elite, can usher in a practical change of policies is never automatic or immediate. Its effect is cumulative and in any case never clearly causal. It does, however, help shape the *Zeitgeist* in a way that might create a more propitious environment for a change of policies. Professor Yehoshafat Harkabi, who served in the past as Chief of Israel's Military Intelligence, triggered a heated national debate in an essay he had published in the early 1980s where he questioned the wisdom of Bar-Kochba's rebellion against the Roman Empire in AD 132–5. More than in a critique of Bar-Kochba and his spiritual mentor Rabbi Akiva, Harkabi was interested in accusing their present-day successors of leading suicidal policies. Bar-Kochba's rebellion and the practical annihilation of the Jewish Yishuv in Palestine that followed the brutal repression by the Roman legions, a chapter in national history that had been idealised in the past as the heroic stand of a nation fighting for freedom, was now denounced by Harkabi as a reminder to contemporary politicians and generals of the catastrophe that might be repeated here and now if the nation continued to be led by the religious Messianism of its rabbis and the military adventurism of its generals. Bar-Kochba's revolt, Harkabi explained, was not a heroic enterprise. It was a blind march to a national disaster that was almost tantamount to a holocaust. His warning was that the lesson of the Bar-Kochba episode in Jewish history could only be that Israel's Messianic obsession with the territories, the refusal of its leaders to assume realistic positions, move away from Messianic hallucinations, and come to terms with the need for compromise and moderation might end in another national holocaust.

Rabin believed that he had made a deal with the PLO out of a sense of healthy realism and only after he had exhausted all other possibilities. The Jordanian option was now dead, Hamas was gaining ground in the territories, especially in Gaza, and the terms for a settlement with the local leadership proved to be too high. 'It was either Arafat or the Hamas. There is no third partner,' he said to an American journalist. 'It was time to end the masquerade with the West Bankers,' he concluded.

But the truth of the matter was that Rabin was manoeuvred to opt for a deal with the PLO in Oslo rather than for one with the local Palestinian leadership in Washington by the Peres team, whose members managed to convince the PLO delegation to lower its price for a deal to a degree that the local leadership could never accept. Arafat's 'cheap price' for a settlement turned out to be, however, a tactical plot aimed at sidelining the local leadership and gaining a foothold in the occupied territories from which he could move to the next stage in his wider strategy. Gaza and Jericho, the base that he was given in the Oslo accords, were to Arafat like the Faqahani quarter in Beirut from which he controlled throughout the 1970s the life and politics of the entire Lebanese state. The eventual collapse of the Oslo process into an all-out Israeli–Palestinian war, for which successive Israeli governments need of course to assume their share of the blame, was therefore not exactly an unexpected accident; rather it was a failure written into the genetic code of Oslo.

Arafat's strategy was based on permanent negotiations, the desired outcome of which was never clear to him, nor was he ever able to spell it out so that the Israelis could weigh the *final* price they would have to pay to reach the end of the conflict. Arafat never managed, nor did he ever try, to convey to the Israelis that he had a sense of the *finality* of the conflict. Terror, including that perpetrated by Hamas, was to him a strategic weapon he used to soften the resistance of the Israelis. The Oslo accords had made available to him the conditions for waging a total war against Israel, and he would use them at the proper moment. At a Palestinian meeting in the West Bank town of Nablus in January 1996, just before an unprecedented wave of suicide terrorism brought about Shimon Peres's electoral defeat to Benjamin Netanyahu, Nabil Shaath, a close associate of Arafat, explained the deeper meaning of Oslo from the PLO's perspective. If the terms of the Palestinians for a settlement with Israel were not accepted, he said,

> We shall return to violence. But this time this will be done with 30,000 Palestinian soldiers at our disposal and while we control a territory of

our own, and enjoy freedom and liberty ... If we reach a dead end, we will resume the war and struggle exactly as we did forty years ago.

Rabin was not a traditional Israeli peacenik. He came to peacemaking not from lofty idealism about the human and national rights of the Palestinians, or grandiose dreams about a celestial integration between Israelis and Palestinians in a 'New Middle East', a Peresian concept he used to ridicule in private. Peace to Rabin was first and foremost a vehicle to security and a springboard to help unleash the economic and technological energies of the Israelis. In fact, he wanted a peace based on separation, even if this required a wall. Rabin was definitely the conceptual and political father of the Israeli Left's own version of the Jabotinskyan wall. For Jabotinsky the wall was a metaphor. He had in mind a conceptual, not a physical, wall. He spoke of deterrence that would lead to peace on Israel's terms. The Left spoke of peace based on physical separation.

With security uppermost in their minds, the Israelis judged their peace partners on the basis of their credibility as providers of security. Conspicuously, as one of the chief Israeli negotiators in Oslo, Uri Savir, acknowledged, Arafat was chosen as a partner by the Israelis with the hope that he would use his new power base in the territories 'to dismantle Hamas and other violent opposition groups'. The Israelis conceived of Arafat as a collaborator of sorts, a sub-contractor in the task of enhancing Israel's security. For Israel this would be the main test of Arafat's performance.

If the Oslo accords fell short of Palestinian expectations, it was because the agreement was the result of the balance of power. The flexibility of the PLO delegation in the secret talks in Oslo, so substantially different from the rigidity displayed by the delegation of West Bankers in the Washington talks, led it to abandon traditional key conditions such as the recognition by Israel of the Palestinians' right of self-determination, and the linkage between the interim and the final settlements. It was the Palestinians' insistence on these very conditions that had derailed the Shultz initiative in the late 1980s. Now they were ignored.

The result of the talks in September 1993 was expressed in two agreements: the Declaration of Principles (DOP) and a mutual recognition between Israel and the PLO, where the latter committed itself to 'a peaceful resolution of the conflict' and reiterated that it 'renounced terrorism and other acts of violence'. It also affirmed that the articles in the Palestinian Covenant that denied Israel's right to exist 'are now inoperative and no longer valid'. The DOP established the mechanism for handing over the control of Gaza and Jericho to the Palestinians, and stipulated a sequence of stages leading from a five-year autonomy regime to the negotiations on the final settlement that would have to solve the problems of borders, Jerusalem, settlements, refugees and the question of Palestinian statehood. But it is crucial to note that no prior pledge or commitment was made by Israel as to the outcome of the negotiations on either of these chapters. Neither according to the letter of the agreement, nor in the perception of the Israelis was this to be like the case of the Syrian–Israeli track where the outcome of the peace negotiations was practically known in advance. No firm premises were established by the parties for the solution of any of the five issues pertaining to the final settlement.

However creative and even epoch-making the Oslo accords might have been, they also contained the seeds of their own destruction. Ambiguous, cumbersome, full of lacunae – an Israeli politician defined them as a Swiss cheese with more holes than cheese – and essentially built on the unequal relations between the occupied and the occupier, Oslo unleashed expectations that were too high, and were consequently bound to crash into the rocks of conflicting national ethoses and dreams. Nor were the inconsistencies and the dysfunctionality of Israel's political system on the one hand, and the Palestinians' incapacity to move away from revolutionary politics and develop the tools of modern governance on the other, especially helpful in allowing Oslo to succeed.

The Oslo process bequeathed additional fallacies to the teams that were later to negotiate the final settlement at Camp David and Taba. The incremental nature of the process left wide open the shape of the final agreement, certainly in the perception of the Israelis, and hence encouraged their governments to persist in their existing policies in the territories. Through what was, and continues to be, the most absurd march of folly that the State of Israel has ever embarked on – the creation of a dense map of settlements throughout the territories that narrowed the living space of the Palestinian people – Israel destroyed beyond repair the faith of its Palestinian partners in the peace process. But again, amazing as it may sound, there is nothing in the letter of the Oslo accords that prevented the creation of settlements. The blame should be put at the door of the Palestinian negotiators who all came from Tunis and had no knowledge of the conditions on the ground. Local leaders who had been brought up under the occupation, and the arrogance and agrarian hunger of the settlers, would not have let this happen. Loyal to the old archaic Zionist philosophy according to which the last kindergarten also defines the political border, the Israelis tried to influence the nature of the final agreement by a hectic policy of settlement expansion. The Palestinians responded with terrorism. It was this fatal symmetry between settlements and terrorism that became the hallmark of the Oslo years.

The expression 'peace of the brave' used ad nauseam by Arafat never convinced anyone, not even Rabin, that the commitments Arafat undertook were indeed irrevocable. Notwithstanding his pledge to renounce violence, he never really relinquished the terror card. It was precisely this that destroyed Rabin politically before he was destroyed physically by a Jewish zealot. It was that same terror card that would also bring about the defeat of Shimon Peres and the ascendancy of Benjamin Netanyahu in the aftermath of the assassination of Yitzhak Rabin. Arafat excelled in destroying his peace partners and in directly enhancing the prospects of the hard Right in Israel. But the incompatibilities between the leaders were not only a question of differences in personalities. They were also fed by the major fallacies and inconsistencies inherent in the Oslo process.

Oslo was designed to function under the sterile conditions of a laboratory, not in real life, for it assumed that trust could be built between the occupied and the occupier. Hemmed in by irresistible domestic constraints, every new Israeli government asked for a revision of the agreements signed by the previous government. The agreement on Hebron was Netanyahu's version of Rabin's Oslo B (the interim agreement signed in September 1995 which stipulated the withdrawal of Israeli forces from Palestinian cities and the transfer of legislative powers to the Palestinian parliament), and Sharm el Sheikh was Barak's version of the Wye River Memorandum of 23 October 1998 (where Netanyahu agreed to give back 13 per cent of the West Bank in exchange for stricter Palestinian measures against Islamic terrorism). All this, of course, was hardly conducive to the cultivation of trust between the parties.

Notwithstanding its flaws, Oslo was a brilliant exercise in back-door diplomacy. Once again an Israeli and an Arab side slipped away from the suffocating patronage of the American broker, reached an understanding behind its back and presented it later with the fait accompli. That all this was achieved in Oslo, of all places, shows that sometimes a small and unpretentious power like Norway can be better placed than a superpower to inspire confidence in the parties to a protracted conflict, and be effective in brokering an agreement between them. But the execution of the agreement could not be carried through without the guarantees of the superpower and its constant assistance and nursing. The American brokerage became a necessity if only because the Oslo process would immediately prove to be riddled with misunderstandings and ambiguities that bred crises and conflict almost from the first day.

Hardly had the ink on the agreements dried when a Palestinian opposition of Islamic and secular Rejectionists, some from within Fatah itself, started to work against them. In his rush to sideline the local leadership and stem the upsurge of Hamas, Arafat, his critics would say, agreed to turn the PLO from a national movement into the sheriff of a small, destitute ghetto in Gaza. Hamas and Jihad lost no time in unleashing a campaign of terror in the hope that this would lead to the radicalisation of Israeli public opinion and, consequently, to a shift to the right, which they expected would undermine and cripple Rabin's peace policies. On the very eve of the signing of the DOP, three Israeli soldiers were slaughtered by a Hamas squad in Gaza. Suicide terrorism was not the invention of the second Intifada. It had already started in the euphoric days of Oslo. The day after the DOP was signed, on 14 September 1993, a Palestinian terrorist blew himself up in an Israeli police station in Gaza.

But the bad omens for the future of Oslo did not come only from the Islamic opposition. On 11 May 1994, a week after he had signed the Cairo agreement establishing the modalities for Palestinian self-rule in Gaza and Jericho and a few days before he himself returned to an ecstatic reception in Gaza, Arafat called, in a speech behind closed doors in Johannesburg, for a Jihad to recover Jerusalem. He went to the extreme of comparing Oslo with the Prophet's tactical Hudaybiyya agreement of AD 625 with the Qurayish tribe, an expedient peace that could be broken when the circumstances would warrant it. Though he liked to position himself as a Palestinian Mandela, or as the leader of a modern secular movement of national liberation, Arafat remained essentially loyal to his youth as a member of the Muslim Brotherhood and, as such, his real hero and model was the Mufti, Haj Amin al-Huseini, as he himself recognised in an interview with the Palestinian daily *Al-Kuds* of 2 August 2002.

As it turned out, the Johannesburg speech was not an isolated incident where Arafat simply got carried away. He uttered similar notions on other occasions. One such was a speech in Gaza's al-Azhar University on the day celebrating the ascension of the Prophet to heaven, where he spoke again of Hudaybiyya as a 'despised peace'. On another occasion, a meeting with an Arab audience in Stockholm as quoted by Yedidia Atlas from the Norwegian newspaper *Dagen*, Arafat presented the right of return and the demographic weapon as his way to subvert the spirit of the Oslo accords: 'We of the PLO will now concentrate all our efforts on splitting Israel psychologically into two camps. ... We will make life unbearable for the Jews by psychological warfare and population explosion.'[1]

This was to be Arafat's mode of behaviour throughout the Oslo years.

---

[1] For Arafat's speeches in Johannesburg and Gaza, see Raphael Israeli, 'From Oslo to Bethlehem: Arafat's Islamic Message', *Journal of Church and State*, vol. 43, summer 2001, pp. 423–45. For the speech in Stockholm, see Yedidia Atlas, 'Arafat's Secret Agenda is to Wear Israelis Out', *Insight on the News*, 1 April 1946.

His was always the language of battle and Jihad. 'We stand by our oath to pursue the battle,' he promised in his speech at al-Azhar, where he also embraced the memory of Izzedin al-Qassam, the icon of Hamas's struggle against the 'Zionist entity'. He would never convey a clear message of peace and reconciliation to the Israeli public. A born master of double talk, he always preferred the language of ambiguities. Throughout his life as a terrorist and guerrilla leader, Arafat avoided an open confrontation with his rivals in the movement. He preferred to co-opt them. Holding the national movement together at all costs, shunning clear-cut divisive decisions, forever looking for leadership through consensus even when this meant not curbing the terrorist activities of those he had pledged to discipline in the Oslo accords – such was his disastrous and eventually self-defeating way of government throughout. An autocrat with no interest whatever in a modicum of good government or in policies of welfare and economic development, he was unable to create the necessary popular, democratic legitimacy for cracking down on Hamas.

Nevertheless, in Jerusalem there was a prime minister committed to the peace process almost against all odds. Rabin insisted – and he would pay a high political, and eventually the ultimate personal, price – that the fight against terrorism should not interfere with, or slow down, the peace process. In a paraphrase of Ben-Gurion's presentation of his strategy with regard to the need to fight the White Paper yet to support Britain in its war against Hitler, Rabin pledged to fight terrorism as if there were no peace process and to pursue the peace process as if there were no terrorism. Such a double-edged strategy proved eventually to be politically self-defeating. The Israeli public could not stomach a policy whereby the victims of terrorist attacks were buried in the morning and negotiations were resumed in the afternoon. Rabin was adamant nevertheless. A few days before he was gunned down, on 28 September 1995, Oslo II, an agreement practically ending Israel's coercive control over the Palestinians, was signed in Washington.

But Arafat was incapable of delivering; he persisted in his refusal to respect his signature and to discipline the terrorists. Nor was his predicament that simple. He rightly understood that clamping down on Hamas and Jihad would portray him in the eyes of his people as a 'collaborator' of the Israelis who, however willing they might have been to pursue the peace process in line with Rabin's double-edged approach, reacted swiftly against Palestinian violence and, in order to curb the upsurge of terrorist groups, launched a pre-emptive policy of mass arrests, curfews and closures.

A tragic and fatal vicious cycle was created that neither the Israelis nor the Palestinians were able to halt. The disenchantment mounted among the Palestinian masses. They were hit by Israeli closures, collective punishment, unemployment, economic decline, a humiliating dependence on Israel and the expansion of existing settlements, whose population increased under the Labour government (1992–6) by 48 per cent in the West Bank and by 62 per cent in the Gaza Strip, that is, more than under any previous Likud government. Rather than behaving as a modern state bound by, and respectful of, international law, Israel in the territories seemed possessed by an irresistible agrarian hunger that trampled underfoot the natural rights of the occupied population. She settled the territories with the same revolutionary zeal of the Yishuv, and followed the same modes of behaviour with regard to the Palestinian population as those of the Yishuv when it fought the British occupier and outsmarted the indigenous population.

Israel's annexationist policies further undermined Arafat's legitimacy for making concessions and reinforced his instinct that he could not be seen as openly collaborating with the Israelis in fighting terrorism. This, in its turn, limited Rabin's capacity to move forward in the process. Caught between the terror of the fundamentalists, Arafat's passivity, and the inevitable ascendancy of the peace sceptics and the Israeli far right, Rabin was marching to his political demise. The frivolous oxymoron coined by Peres that the Israelis killed in terrorist attacks – between 1993 and 1996 about 300 Israelis were assassinated by suicide squads – were the 'victims of peace' was utterly rejected by the public. Terrorism undermined the legitimacy and the moral foundations of the peace process. Neither Arafat nor Rabin was now in a position to give the other the minimum required to keep Oslo alive. When Rabin was assassinated by a Jewish fanatic as a traitor who sold out Eretz-Israel, he was already severely crippled politically by a series of devastating suicide terrorist attacks, notably in Tel Aviv and Beit Lid, and by Arafat's failure to face the enemies of peace in his own camp.

The following eight months of Shimon Peres's premiership were an utter disaster and a political calamity. In his attempt, or rather obsession, to compete with Rabin's memory he tried to make peace and war on all fronts at the same time: to fight terrorism, eliminate the threat of the Hezbollah through a bloody and costly campaign – Grapes of Wrath – in south Lebanon, make peace with the Syrians and the Palestinians, and advance his far-fetched dream of a New Middle East. The result was a resounding failure. Moreover, against the advice of some in the security services, Peres ordered the assassination of Yehya Ayyash, known as 'the engineer', a Hamas terrorist who was also an extremely popular idol of the Palestinian war against Israel. This in turn triggered the bloodiest response yet by Hamas against Israeli civilian targets. The streets of

Israel's major cities ran with the blood of dozens of innocent victims of a Hamas campaign of suicide terrorism of unprecedented proportions. Clearly, Hamas wanted a Likud victory in the forthcoming elections, a victory that it expected would bring about an immediate disruption of the peace process. It got both: Likud and the subversion of the peace process. Arafat did next to nothing to hinder Hamas's strategy and when he finally decided to act it was already too late. The Israelis would simply not buy the Labour Party's mantra that not only war but also peace needs to claim its victims. Peres lost the elections to Benjamin Netanyahu before he was even able to fulfil his commitment to pull the IDF out of Hebron.

Netanyahu's victory was bad news for the peace process which, admittedly, was in very poor health when he inherited it. But conspicuously, two Arab leaders, Mubarak and Hussein, did not exactly mourn the defeat of Peres. Peres' persistent belief in a 'warm' peace and a 'New Middle East' of economic integration – he even launched the bizarre idea of having Israel join the Arab League – was anathema to Mubarak. He preferred a more controlled, slower, perhaps even reasonably tense peace with Israel, better suited to his domestic concerns and his regional aspirations. As to King Hussein, he was so taken aback by Peres's moves towards a quick deal with Syria and so worried that Oslo under his leadership might usher in a Palestinian state that would not respect Jordan's domestic and regional concerns that he even ventured to make public his preference for Netanyahu.

It would not be long, however, before both Mubarak and Hussein realised how dangerous to their interests could be an Israeli prime minister who, instead of simply slowing down the pace of the peace process, did away with it altogether. The total destruction of the peace process with the Palestinians was as dangerous and threatening to the stability of their respective regimes as the supposedly frenetic peace policy of Mr Peres and his team. Netanyahu was not a man of the *juste milieu*. Not only was the new Prime Minister inexperienced and unpredictable – he himself later confessed that he was totally disorientated during his first eighteen months in office – but he also relied on a coalition of extremists of the Right and the far Right. With Netanyahu, the return to the politics of confrontation and war suddenly became a realistic possibility again, and about this neither Mubarak nor Hussein was happy. An agreement on Hebron was to be Netanyahu's sole contribution to peace with the Palestinians, and even that came about only after the bloody clashes in and around the Temple Mount in September 1996, which cost the lives of sixteen Israeli soldiers and eighty Palestinians. Nor did the PLO do much to recover the credibility of the peace process. It failed to devise a new National Covenant, as it was committed to do, and did almost nothing to uproot the terrorism that originated in the cities under its control.

The macabre complicity between Arafat and Netanyahu in bringing about the total collapse of mutual trust and the dissolution of the tools of dialogue and peacemaking was to cause a major change in the pattern of negotiations. The Americans now stepped in for the first time as active mediators. Oslo was unique in being a strictly bilateral channel built on trust and confidence. American mediation would mean that from now on every step and every bit of progress would have to be wrested from the parties through pressure and arm twisting. And it was precisely American arm twisting that produced the Wye River Memorandum, whereby Israel agreed to withdraw from a further 13 per cent of Palestinian land.

In one key matter Netanyahu did not differ from his predecessors. He opted for a Palestinian deal only after he had exhausted the possibility of reaching an agreement through secret negotiations with Hafez al-Assad. He, too, was then committed to the capsule theory, which essentially reflected a reluctance to engage with the Palestinians and a disbelief in the chances of reaching a viable settlement with them. When the Barak government came into office in the summer of 1999, it discovered that Netanyahu had secretly negotiated with Assad the devolution of the Golan Heights down to the 1967 borders, through the good offices of Ron Lauder, a Jewish American businessman who had served in the past as US ambassador to Austria. But as happened with all the attempts to reach a settlement with Assad, one of the parties or both got cold feet at the last moment and the talks came to nothing.

Netanyahu was incapable of delivering on his Palestinian deal. The Wye agreement remained, for all practical purposes, a dead letter. His religious-nationalist government was a totally inadequate vehicle for peacemaking. Netanyahu's designs for a final settlement, a Palestinian state on 40 per cent of the land, and his wild policy of settlement expansion destroyed any chance of a constructive dialogue with the Palestinians. His legacy to the Barak government was a stalled peace process and a tragic loss of trust by both Palestinians and Israelis in their partners.

The Palestinians, however, came out of the Netanyahu years with a major asset in their hands, an almost strategic intimacy with an American administration weary of Netanyahu's stalling tactics. President Clinton's visit to Gaza on 14 December 1998 and his speech to the Palestinian National Council were the expression of an entirely new phase in Palestinian–American relations. Bill Clinton cast himself in Gaza in the role of the Balfour of the Palestinian cause. Five years later, with Arafat under siege among the debris of his headquarters in the Mukhata and the Bush administration ruling him out as a valid interlocutor, the Palestinian leader should have reflected on his share of responsibility for throwing away the asset of intimate relations with the United States, so vital for the future of his people, that was bequeathed to him, by default, by Benjamin Netanyahu.

But Arafat's miscalculations and Israel's blunders and misconceptions should not overshadow the meaning of Oslo as representing a fundamental change in the structure of Israel's peacemaking strategy. The centrality of the Palestinian problem in the quest for the solution of the wider Arab–Israeli conflict, which Israeli governments had consistently refused to acknowledge, was now unequivocally asserted. The capsule theory, whereby peace with the Arab states would help deliver the Palestinians, did not work out. In fact, Rabin himself had tried it before he opted for a deal with Arafat. His first year in office was almost exclusively dedicated to the Syrian track, for he saw in the Ba'ath regime in Damascus the main strategic threat to Israel. He believed, and expected, that peace with Syria would diminish the centrality of the Palestinian problem and would allow him to reach a not-too-expensive deal with local Palestinian leaders.

Paradoxically, Assad was indirectly responsible for the Oslo agreement. It was the failure of his Syrian enterprise that brought Rabin to the White House lawn in Washington for his historic handshake with Arafat. It was precisely when the Oslo agreement was almost ready in early August 1993 that Rabin made his last and most dramatic attempt to stick to the capsule theory and to reach a deal with Assad. He conveyed to him a hypothetical readiness to accept Syria's territorial claims if Syria would in turn accept Israel's demands on security and normalisation. Assad's disheartening response – he utterly rejected Israel's concept of 'normalisation', and insisted on symmetrical and reciprocal security arrangements that would also affect the Israeli side of the new border – prompted Rabin to give the green light to the completion of the Oslo accords later that month. Israel's chief negotiator with Assad's men, Itamar Rabinovich, later recalled how Rabin expounded his rationale to Secretary of State Warren Christopher: 'If Assad were to come forward and an Israeli–Syrian deal were to be made, then this would be supplemented by a small Palestinian deal. If Assad's response is disappointing, there would be no Israeli–Syrian breakthrough, so then there would be a major Israeli–Palestinian agreement.'

Now it was the Palestinians who were supposed to bring the Arab world to a peace with Israel, not the other way round. Oslo definitely vindicated the Arab claim about the centrality of the Palestinian problem in the Arab–Israeli conflict.

Rabin was less of a peace architect than some commentators believed him to be; his peace strategy developed almost *malgré lui*. His intention was to stick to the capsule theory. He never intended to negotiate with the PLO, nor did he think he would go with the Palestinians beyond the autonomy stage.

As a matter of fact, neither Rabin nor, especially, Peres wanted the autonomy to usher in a Palestinian state. As late as 1997 – that is, four years into the Oslo process when, as the chairman of the Labour Party's Foreign Affairs Committee I proposed for the first time that the party endorse the idea of a Palestinian state – it was Shimon Peres who most vehemently opposed the idea. He still believed in a Jordanian–Israeli– Palestinian condominium in the territories. A Palestinian state was clearly not within Rabin's priorities either. But the failure of his Syrian enterprise brought him to Oslo and this, regardless of the letter of the accord, could only lead sooner or later to Palestinian self-determination and statehood.

And Olso, to Rabin's surprise, created such a panic in Jordan that King Hussein finally came out of the closet and rushed to make peace with Israel. The hysteria in Jordan was such that the moment he knew of the Oslo accord, the King ordered the closure of the bridges linking the West and the East Banks for fear of a mass exodus of Palestinians that would end up subverting the Jordanian state. The May 1994 Israeli– PLO economic agreement was an additional threat to Hussein, who now saw his kingdom's economic ties with the West Bank seriously under- mined. To the King a common Israeli–Palestinian economic space meant unemployment and political instability in Jordan.

The driving force behind the traditional relations between Israel and Jordan had been their joint quest for security in a regional environment hostile to both. They also shared an interest in controlling their common enemy, the Palestinian national movement. The 1994 peace agreement between Jordan and Israel was supposed to invigorate these mutual interests through a delicate balance within a new order of things, where a Palestinian political entity would be sandwiched between two states, Israel and Jordan, living at peace with each other. The negotiations for an Israeli–Jordanian peace proceeded along two channels that were established not long after the Madrid Peace Conference. One was an open channel led by Cabinet Secretary Elyakim Rubinstein; the other was a secret track led in Amman by head of Mossad Efraïm Halevi. By the time the Israeli–Palestinian deal was clinched in Oslo, Jordan and Israel had their own draft of a peace agreement practically ready. But it was Oslo that injected life into the understanding and served as a final catalyst for the parties to reach a peace settlement. The so-called Israeli–Jordanian Common Agenda was formalised on 14 September 1993, on the very morrow of the signing of the Israeli–Palestinian Declaration of Principles (DOP).[1]

Arafat's handshake with Rabin was the alibi and legitimisation that Hussein had been looking for ever since he ascended the throne, in order openly to pursue the legacy of his grandfather's peace policy with Israel. Now it was no longer the Jordanian option at the expense of the Palestinians, as both Israel and Jordan wanted it in the past, but a desperate rush to save Jordan's interests and perhaps its very existence as an independent Bedouin kingdom, at a moment when the Palestinian option was picked up by Israel. It became vital for Hussein to make peace with Israel if he wanted to make sure that his nemesis, Arafat, would not have an exclusive say about the future of Jerusalem and the West Bank.

It is an interesting reflection on the nature of the peace process as it developed in the Rabin years that, notwithstanding the high degree of commitment of the Clinton administration to the process, whatever was achieved – Oslo and the peace with Jordan – was done bilaterally with very little, if any, American involvement. The Americans were throughout sceptical that Hussein would dare to depart from his traditional policy of sitting on the fence. They did not realise how imperative the Oslo agreement made Jordan's necessity to reach a settlement with Israel. Clearly, however, a much needed debt relief that the Clinton administration offered as a lure to the King if he made peace with Israel was a crucially important bonus that Hussein could not afford the luxury of ignoring.

Of all Israel's potential partners for peace, Jordan was the most eager to engage in close economic co-operation with her. Unlike Egypt, where economic co-operation with Israel was never to be especially encouraged, 'the economic fruits of peace' were in Jordan a major driving force behind the quest for an accommodation with Israel. The Jordanians did not share the Egyptian fears about Israel's pursuit of regional economic hegemony. Hence the peace agreement between the two countries included particularly robust chapters about co-operation in matters of commerce, transportation, tourism, water, the joint exploitation of the Dead Sea minerals and the building of a new joint international airport in Eilat-Aqaba. But the frustrations were as high as the expectations. After a reasonably promising start during the Rabin years, there came the decline under Netanyahu.

---

[1] See above, pp. 211–12.

The precarious balance established by Rabin's peace policy in the Israel–Jordan–Palestinian triangle meant that any deterioration in Israel's relations with the Palestinians could have a devastating effect on the degree of popular support in Jordan for the peace agreement with Israel. Netanyahu stalled the peace process with the Palestinians, exhibited an indifferent attitude towards Jordan's economic expectations and even irresponsibly humiliated the King by taking the liberty of allowing an attempt – abortive, as it turned out – by the Mossad against the life of a Hamas leader, Khaled Mashal, in Amman in broad daylight.

As a whole (and this was true to a degree in the Rabin years as well) Israel was not sensitive enough to Jordan's economic interests in the West Bank; her attempt to control the Palestinian market did not leave much room for others. By the time the Barak government came into office, and especially after the death of King Hussein who embodied Jordan's commitment to peace, the popular opposition there to the peace with Israel was overwhelming. A poll taken in 1998 by the *Jordan Times* showed that by then 80 per cent of the Jordanians viewed Israel as an enemy, not as a partner in peace.

Syria was an especially hard nut to crack for Israeli policy makers. It had resisted Sadat's peace initiative and, in the aftermath of the Camp David summit of 1978, it embarked on a strategy aimed at preventing the Israeli–Egyptian peace from extending to other states in the region. An Israeli peace with Lebanon or Jordan was viewed by the Ba'ath regime in Damascus as a strategic threat, a sinister move towards the encirclement and isolation of Syria. Her concept of peace was as simple as it was uncompromising: peace talks would be considered only if the final outcome, namely Israel's full withdrawal to the 1967 lines, was secured in advance, and a genuine reconciliation and normalisation of relations with Israel was not required as the price of peace. But the steadfast front which Hafez al-Assad forged with radical, but marginal, countries such as Libya, Algeria and Yemen in the aftermath of the Camp David accord only served further to underline Syria's isolation. And it was precisely that sense of strategic isolation that drove Damascus, in the 1980s, to an alliance with Iran against Iraq. With the collapse of the united Arab front against Israel in the wake of Sadat's peace initiative, Assad became a leader in a desperate attempt to recover the strategic depth he had lost with Sadat's 'betrayal' of the pan-Arab cause.

However, whatever strategic advantages he might have secured for Syria through his alliance with Iran could not match Assad's losses on other fronts. Siding with Iran against Iraq meant being a member of an anti-Arab alliance and this could only increase his isolation in the region. The Gulf States would not easily forgive him his alliance with Iran, then perceived as the major threat facing Iraq, their Arab champion at the time. The anti-Syrian rage of the dynasties of the Gulf and the dramatic drop in oil prices in the 1980s meant that Syria, like the PLO after the Gulf War in 1990–1, could no longer expect much in the way of financial aid from the oil monarchies.

Assad's options were clearly diminishing and he increasingly looked like a leader hectically shifting strategies in a desperate search for a balance of deterrence with Israel that would allow him to dictate his own terms for a settlement. With the exposure of the immanent weaknesses of his Iran connection, Assad moved now to embrace a new and utterly unrealistic policy of 'strategic parity' with Israel. But the new strategy was stillborn. As from the mid 1980s and especially, of course, with the approaching end of the Cold War, the Soviet Union was in no position, or mood, to assist the isolated Ba'ath regime in its quest for 'parity'. Syria became the Cuba of the Middle East, a state whose chief patron went bankrupt, and had therefore either to adapt herself to the new structure of the international system or decline into a position of utter irrelevance.

True, Assad's shrewd tactics of divide and rule had succeeded in defeating Israel's grand designs in Lebanon, and he managed to keep intact his hegemony there throughout the 1990s. But Lebanon was not enough to change the gravity of Assad's predicament. By the time the Berlin Wall had collapsed, Syria was in a state of financial and strategic decline, its Iranian allies had been defeated by Saddam Hussein, who was now free to subvert Syria's interests in the region, and the Soviet Union had practically abandoned him. In the painful transition from the Soviet Union to Russia, Gorbachev was in no mood to be drawn by Syria into the politics of confrontation in the Middle East. His message to Assad was that the reliance on military force in settling the Arab–Israeli conflict 'has lost its credibility'.

Not unlike Arafat when he decided to go to Oslo, Assad was now driven to join the Madrid Peace Conference – that is, the American-sponsored Arab–Israeli peace process – by his isolation, his economic decline and the demise of the Soviet Union. The peace process was an option taken after all the other ways of recovering the Golan Heights and preserving Syria's regional role had either failed or were exhausted. The strategic choice for him now was to play down his relations with Iran without cutting them altogether, for the Iran–Hezbollah connection was vital for Syria's position in Lebanon. To reconcile the contradictions of his regional position he had to maintain the semblance of a military challenge to Israel while improving at the same time his relations with the Gulf States – he had joined the American-led coalition against Iraq in the Gulf War – and participating in the peace process.

This did not mean that Assad would follow exactly in the footsteps of either Egypt or the PLO. Neither model of peacemaking was acceptable to him. True, by engaging in talks with Israel, Hafez al-Assad departed from his basic premise that in order to defend themselves the Arabs must either insist on a comprehensive peace on all fronts or give up on the peace process altogether. But he was nevertheless adamant when it came to both his territorial claims for the 1967 borders as against Israel's insistence on the international border, and his unwillingness to concede much in the way of normalisation of relations with Israel. Assad was determined to teach the Egyptians what a cold peace with Israel really looked like. Not even in return for a deposit Rabin left with the Americans, according to which the Syrians could have gathered that he did not entirely rule out a return to the 1967 borders, was the Sphinx of Damascus ready to concede much in matters of normalisation and security arrangements. Nor was Shimon Peres, Rabin's successor, more successful in his attempt to reach a rapid breakthrough with Syria by shifting the focus of negotiations to the economic components of peace. Syria was not impressed by Peres's fresh approach, whose rationale was that Rabin had exaggerated the strategic importance of the Golan Heights in an era where the real threat was that of ballistic missiles and fundamentalist terrorism.

Domestic concerns in peacemaking are not, of course, the monopoly of democratic leaders. Assad's reluctance to offer Israel the components of normalisation that she so badly needed, if only in order to legitimise in the eyes of public opinion her pull-out from the legendary Heights, responded to a concern that was more vital to him than the future of the Golan, namely, the stability of his regime. The full peace that Israel asked for was an indigestible price to pay for a regime (the Ba'ath) whose central rationale was the ideological conflict with Zionism. The question of whether or not Assad was ready for peace was then closely dependent on a much more fundamental question to him: was he ready to see his dictatorial and ideologically driven regime eroded and perhaps even drawn into a democratic dynamic under the impact of open borders with Israel, and the end of the politics of conflict? More than anything, Assad feared Israel's pursuit of normalisation. Not unlike the Israeli fundamentalist Right, which queried the peace of open borders preached by the Left as a threat to the Jewish identity of Israel, Assad rejected normalisation as a challenge to 'Arabism'. As it turned out, he was not particularly impressed by the willingness of the Israelis to withdraw from the Golan.

The future of his regime, and the cohesion of the Arab Middle East, were much more vital concerns to him.

Hafez al-Assad wanted a settlement with Israel that was an armed peace between two equal partners. Through this deal he expected to gain three major strategic and political assets: the consolidation of his privileged position in Lebanon, the full restitution of the Golan Heights, and close relations with the United States, from which he expected to receive generous economic, and perhaps even military, assistance. As if to underline the meaning of Lebanon in Assad's overall strategy, he persisted in his Vietnam-style negotiating tactics of talking and shooting at the same time – in which, to Rabin's rage, he continued to encourage his clients in Lebanon, the Hezbollah militias, to harass Israel's northern border throughout the course of the negotiations. But the problem was less with what he demanded from Israel and the United States than with what he was ready to give: very little in the way of normalisation and not enough to Israel's taste in matters of security.

A country whose weight in the politics of the Middle East stemmed more from its role as the engine of the Arab–Israeli conflict than from its objective military or economic power, Syria nevertheless expected that peace with Israel would not undermine the regional position she had acquired thanks to the conflict. For this to be the case, peace with Israel needed to be armed and tense, founded on, and institutionalising, a new balance of power between the two countries. Assad's motives in peace were not essentially different from his motives in war. In both cases it was a matter of deterrence, a question of balance of power, a quest for a regional role. Nor should the Syrian regime, he believed, disarm itself so easily and so quickly from the instruments of ideological and political confrontation with the Zionist state. That was why if, in his view, Rabin was too rigid and stubborn in his conditions for withdrawal, Peres's eagerness for a quick deal was no less threatening. Rabin's successor wanted 'to fly high and fast', as he put it. But his storm-peace strategy horrified the enigmatic Assad no less than Rabin's rigidly gradualist approach and he utterly rejected it, for he knew the Ba'ath regime could not digest it and survive.

Oslo had enough problems in its implementation without its chief architect, Shimon Peres, adding to an already fragile process his own misconceptions. His outlandish idea about a New Middle East was one such fallacy. Hardly had Israel finished handing over Gaza and Jericho to the Palestinians, the bulk of the Palestinian people were under military occupation, Israel was still pursuing her wild policy of settlements and

Arafat was giving no signs of a determination to fight Islamic terrorism, than Peres was hallucinating about the coming of the Messiah.

John Maynard Keynes was right in 1919 when, in *The Economic Consequences of the Peace*, he told the statesmen of post-World War I Europe that the most serious problems were not political or territorial, but financial and economic, and that the perils of the future lay not in frontiers or sovereignties but in food, coal and transport. Moralism, demagoguery and vindictive patriotism appeared to him to be irrelevant and counter-productive in the process of building a future of peace based on co-operation and prosperity. Political myths are indeed bad advisers for an era of peace, as Keynes had warned.

But Keynes was only right in the long run, precisely the perspective that did not matter much to him ('in the long run we'll all be dead' was how he dismissed the belief in long-term economic processes). Mr Peres should have known that the Europeans did not listen to Keynes and it took another world war to turn his prophecy into a working plan for the European community. There was a double fallacy in Shimon Peres's pursuit of far-fetched conceptions. One was his assumption that economic development would convince the Palestinians to lower their political expectations. As late as 1997, one needs to reiterate, Peres was still opposed to a Palestinian state. The second was the assumption that the Arabs would welcome this neo-colonialist Israeli version of the White Man's Burden. It was Zeev Jabotinsky of all people who as early as 1924 warned about the dangers of such a fallacious approach:

> ... against the naïve assumption that the aspiration of the Arabs to keep Palestine as their land will be paralysed by such means as subsidies, economic advantages or bribery. The contempt for the Arabs of Palestine inherent in such plans is utterly unjustified. The Arab may be backward in the cultural sense, but his natural patriotism is pure and noble like ours, and it cannot be bought off.

Mr Peres should have known that even in the case of Europe, it was only after the satisfaction of the national aspirations of the suppressed peoples of the continent and the solution of the major political and border conflicts that quasi-federal systems like the European Union could be seriously contemplated. Notwithstanding Oslo and Israel's peace with Egypt and Jordan, the political aspects of the Arab–Israeli conflict were still to be fully resolved.

And, no less important, real economic spaces of co-operation, let alone integration, are possible only through the existence of common values, similar democratic institutions, homogeneous social structures and sometimes even a common religion. This is certainly the case of the EU. Such vital affinities did not yet exist between Israel and the Arab world. In addition, as was certainly the case with the Palestinians, economic co-operation was absolutely secondary to national and religious aspirations. I had the opportunity to visit Mr Arafat many times, but I never saw on his desk a picture of Jean Monnet. What I saw all over the place were huge pictures of the Al-Aqsa mosque ...

The truth of the matter is that the Arab world was not exactly a fertile ground for Israel's restless business community. There was not much of a bonanza there. The region lagged behind in almost every economic indicator. Trade between the Arab countries themselves was not especially significant, nor was the Arab Middle East the recipient of much capital investment from outside. The flow of capital went, in fact, the other way: from the wealthy oil barons in the region to the capitalist world. For the New Middle East concept to have any chance the Arab world needed first to undergo an internal economic and cultural revolution. And it needed, of course, to see that the conflict with Israel had been truly solved. A vague framework such as the Oslo agreement that left wide open all the core issues of the conflict was not perceived by the Arabs as heralding its end and hence as an invitation to economic integration with Israel.

The Arab response to Peres's New Middle East, that is, to Israel assuming a position of leadership in a future Middle Eastern economic space, was so lukewarm and suspicious that it made the whole idea counter-productive. Arab leaders – this was especially the case with Egypt – rejected what they perceived as an Israeli quest for economic hegemony, and an attempt to drive wedges between the Gulf countries that were presumably more open to economic co-operation with Israel and the countries closer to the core of the conflict that resisted Israel's economic drive.

Israel gave the Egyptians plenty of reasons to justify their cold peace with her, such as the war in Lebanon, Israel's settlement drive in the territories and the application of Israeli law on the Golan Heights. The lack of progress in the Israeli–Palestinian track was the most convenient pretext for Egypt to maintain its peace with Israel as a frosty peace. However, the truth of the matter is that Egypt was, throughout, strategically interested in nothing more than discreet relations with Israel. The state of non-belligerency, rather than a full-fledged peace, which is what in reality emerged now, suited Egypt's needs perfectly. Moreover, in the immediate aftermath of the Camp David peace agreement the American administration itself was not that eager to encourage a warm peace between the Israelis and Egyptians. Rather, it supported Egypt's policy of 'cold peace' as a way of preventing its isolation in the Arab world. The US reliance on Egypt as a major strategic ally in the region required that she recover and hold her leadership position in the Arab world. Egypt's cold peace with Israel and her resistance to the potentially destabilising effects of Israel's New Middle East project were in American eyes a reasonable Egyptian answer to the vital need to strike a delicate balance between these two objectives.

The Egyptians denounced Israel's economic drive as 'an exchange of land for a Middle East market', as Mohammed Sid Ahmed (who in 1975 had called in his revolutionary work *When the Guns Fall Silent* for peace with Israel) put it now in *Al-Ahram*. In his book he had urged the Arabs to realise that in the October war they had succeeded in neutralising Israel's technological superiority, and they should therefore lay down, without any complexities, their conditions for an end to the conflict. He even proposed a degree of economic co-operation with the Jewish state. Like many others throughout the Arab world, Sid Ahmed hoped and believed that Israel's integration into the Middle East would end up changing the nature of the Zionist state to a degree that would make it culturally and sociologically unrecognisable. Israel as such would, for all practical purposes, cease to exist. Now, however, Sid Ahmed was far less enthusiastic. He was one among many Egyptian intellectuals who opposed the peace with Israel, both for being brokered by the United States and for ignoring the rights of the Palestinians.

Israel was the measure of the failure of the Arabs and its drive now to assert its technological supremacy was, especially in the eyes of a frustrated Arab elite, inadmissible. 'Tell Mr Peres that we also have computers here in Jordan,' Crown Prince Hassan told me sarcastically when I visited him in 1995 with the Israeli author Amos Oz. Earlier, during the peace negotiations between the two countries, Prince Hassan lashed out against Mr Peres in a private conversation with another Israeli author, Amos Elon, for talking about economic 'projects' instead of negotiating borders. 'We didn't come here to discuss projects without a concept,' he complained. As to Egypt, she would not allow Israel to dictate the agenda of the Arab Middle East and Peres's condescending discourse on Israel as the agent for the modernisation of the Arabs only exacerbated her fears. Conspicuously outspoken, Egyptian intellectuals and opinion makers saw Israel as a high-tech Crusader state, a foreign enclave in the midst of the Arab world. They portrayed her in anti-Semitic metaphors as avaricious and ethnically and mentally insular.

The editor of *October*, Anis Mansour, not exactly an enemy of Sadat's peace initiative, even wrote in his magazine how the Talmud urges Jews to kill any non-Jew. Needless to say, the Egyptians made clear, peace would require that Israel be reduced to her 'natural size' not only in the territorial sense but also qualitatively. She should start by waiving her nuclear option, which created an unbearable imbalance. Interestingly, before their peace with Israel the Egyptians had never been active in fighting Israel's nuclear status at international forums. It was this 'dangerous strategic imbalance', to use Osama El-Baz's expression, not the future of Gaza and Jericho, that most worried the Egyptians. El-baz questioned Israel's eagerness for a full normalisation of her relations with the Arab world as a threat to the existing equilibrium between the parties. Clearly, he expressed the fear that normalisation would allow Israel to unleash her potentialities, dictate the agenda of the region and reach hegemony, not necessarily at this time by way of territorial conquests.

As a whole, the 1990s were not good years for Egypt. Oslo and its consequences did not make the leaders in Cairo especially happy. Israel's ascendancy as a regional economic power, the openness of Arab countries in the Maghreb and in the Gulf to establishing economic and even diplomatic links with Israel – Israeli diplomatic delegations were opened in Rabat, Tunis, Qatar, Bahrain, Oman – and the dramatic improvement in her international position eroded Egypt's weight as a regional power and her relevance as a peace broker.

Notwithstanding her peace with Israel, the very nature of the Egyptian regime and its regional pretensions made it vital for Cairo that Israel not be totally accepted by the Arabs as a natural neighbour, a fully legitimate member of the regional family. Egypt believed that her strategic interests required that a degree of tension be maintained with Israel in a way that would always allow Egypt to uphold her position as a power that defines and controls the nature of the regional balance of power. Even before the Oslo process had started to show signs of terminal illness, the Egyptians were already forging an Egyptian–Syrian–Saudi front against Israel's regional economic pretensions.[1] This in turn reinforced the opinion of the peace sceptics in Israel that it was not peace that the Arabs wanted, but the necessary land to reduce Israel to her natural size and diminish her strategic and economic potentialities.

When the Barak government came into office in the summer of 1999, trust between Israel and the Palestinian Authority was at its lowest ebb. The Palestinians were by then convinced that Oslo was not a process that could lead to the end of the occupation, but at best to the

---

[1] For the Egyptian–Syrian–Saudi front against Israel's regional claims, see Amos Elon, *A Blood-Dimmed Tide: Dispatches from the Middle East*, Penguin Books, London, 2000, p. 203.

redeployment of Israel's forces in a West Bank planted with Jewish settlements.

Oslo II, which was supposed to clarify the vague premises established in Oslo, brought about Israel's withdrawal from the major Palestinian cities, but at the same time it created a crippled Palestinian Authority. This was essentially confined to ruling over a series of disconnected Palestinian enclaves surrounded by Israeli military forces, bypass roads and an ever-expanding network of settlements. Oslo II legitimised the transformation of the West Bank into what has been called a 'cartographic cheeseboard'. By the time Barak came to office there were about 250,000 Jews living in more than 120 settlements throughout the West Bank, and another 150,000 in new modern Jewish neighbourhoods in east Jerusalem. It was true, as the Israelis were always keen to explain, that less than 2 per cent of the West Bank was actually occupied by settlements. But the inhabited space told only part of the story. The municipal boundaries of the settlements, that is, their recognised (by Israel, of course) potential for growth and expansion amounted to about 7 per cent of the West Bank. Moreover, to protect her strategic interests and defend the settlements from their dispossessed Palestinian neighbours, Israel built throughout the West Bank an impressive network of bypass roads, all strictly for Israeli use, that became for the Palestinians one more sad reflection of an increasingly unbearable colonialist system of domination and land grab.

And if all this were not enough, the Palestinians had incompetently agreed in the Oslo II agreement to a principle that practically put Israel's claim for land and assets in the West Bank on an almost equal footing with that of the Palestinians. The Israeli negotiators of the final agreement under the Barak government were advised by the Oslo II accord that neither side, Palestinian or Israeli, had 'renounced or waived any of its existing rights, claims, or positions'. For the Israelis this meant that the precise nature of the final agreement was wide open to negotiations on all the core issues at stake: borders, settlements, Jerusalem and refugees. The Palestinian perception was, of course, entirely different. To them the margin for negotiations and compromise was minimal, if there at all.

The balance sheet of Oslo does not improve in favour of the Palestinians when the economy and the state of Palestinian society are brought into the equation. For Israel, Oslo was the introduction to one of the most breathtaking eras of economic growth and opening up of markets in her history. Coinciding as it did with the collapse of the Berlin Wall and the removal of the barriers of hostility towards the Jewish state in Russia and Eastern Europe, the period following the launching of the peace process at the Madrid Peace Conference of 1991 witnessed the acceleration of the mass immigration of highly qualified Soviet Jews to

Israel. Israel's population increased in the 1990s, that is in less than ten years, by almost 20 per cent. And by the time the Oslo accords came into effect, Israel could also see how her international status had improved dramatically. With diplomatic relations being established with countries such as China and India, the dynamic markets of Asia were added to the widening horizons for the vibrant Israeli economy. During the Rabin years (1992–5) Israel's economy grew at an average of 7 per cent per year.

The main economic benefit that Israel reaped from the Oslo years did not come from the surrounding Arab markets; it came from the normalisation of her international relations and her concomitant integration into the global economy. New markets, improved global conditions, the psychological atmosphere created by the peace process, the highly skilled Israeli labour force and the cheap Palestinian labour force – Palestinians became the hewers of wood and drawers of water of the Israeli economy (by 1993 about a third of the Palestinian labour force was employed in Israel) – were the cocktail of conditions that made the Oslo years into such a vertiginous economic success for Israel.

The Palestinians could certainly not claim a similar success. The Oslo years represented, at best, a mixed record for them. Inevitably, their per capita income increased, on average of course, thanks to the links with Israel's dynamic economy. In 1996 it stood at the level of $650 and by the time the Barak government came to power it was $1,500. But for many these were years of economic decline and paralysing dependency on the superior Israeli economy. By the end of the Rabin years, 20 per cent of the Palestinian population lived below the poverty line, a figure that represented an increase of 33 per cent in the number of poor compared with that of 1993. The Palestinian economy was programmed by the Israeli–Palestinian economic agreement reached after Oslo, the Paris Protocol, to be essentially dependent on, and subservient to, Israel. With a GNP of $120 billion and a per capita income of $19,000, the Israeli economy dominated the Palestinian market and dictated its priorities. The potential for independent Palestinian economic development remained dormant throughout. Only those Palestinians who lived closer to the industrial centres of Israel could really benefit from a better income, which explains why the level of poverty was greater among those who did not have access to the Israeli labour market. Not only was the trade deficit of the Palestinian Authority with Israel as high as 50 per cent when the Barak government came into office, but Israeli governments also enjoyed the prerogative of collecting on behalf of the Palestinians the indirect taxes and custom duties levied on imported goods. This in itself was not a bad thing, of course. But the pattern was established whereby, in response to terrorist attacks or Palestinian violations of the agreements, governments in Israel would unilaterally withhold the huge sums of money they had collected on behalf of the PA, thus practically crippling the latter's capacity to offer the necessary services to their citizens.

Arafat, his ministers and their acolytes were not free of blame for the declining economic conditions in the territories at this time. An army of incompetent and corrupt bureaucrats spread throughout the territories and operated, to their own benefit, all kinds of sinister deals and monopolies such as cement, tobacco and other vital commodities. Embezzlement of funds from the donor countries by ministers and their dependants were common practice under Arafat's government. For Arafat, corrupting his associates was always a tool of rule and control, a central instrument of power. With the highest police per capita ratio in the world and about fifteen security apparatuses under his direct command, all lavishly financed by public money and salaries in cash, and with an army of informants and a bloated bureaucracy (altogether more than 130,000 people were on the PA's payroll), Arafat ruled over one of the most expensive power machines in the world and certainly one that was utterly disproportionate to the ridiculously small slices of territory it was supposed to govern.

Was the demise of Oslo determined by Rabin's assassination? It is the conventional perception that the day Yitzhak Rabin was gunned down by a Jewish fanatic was also the day that peace died. The popular assumption was, and continues to be to this day, that only Rabin could have brought the peace process to fruition.

That Rabin was a formidable leader in the uphill struggle for peace I personally observed on more than one occasion. Six months after he came to power, I accompanied him on a trip to Kibbutz Ortal. A bastion of the settlers in the Golan Heights, Ortal was the place where Rabin had declared during the 1992 electoral campaign that under no conditions, even if he was offered a full peace by the Syrians, would he agree to pull out from the Golan Heights and evacuate its settlements. 'The leader who would give the order to withdraw from the Golan Heights, even in exchange for peace, must be out of his mind,' he said to the cheering crowd. Now, six months later and with the negotiations with the Syrians well under way, Rabin did not hesitate to come back to Ortal, a kibbutz affiliated to Hakibbutz Hameuhad, the movement from which Rabin drew his main political support within the Labour Party, in order to say to the settlers, head-on, that if the talks with the Syrians succeeded they would have to pay the price and be evacuated, uprooted from the houses they had lived in for the last twenty-five years. I cannot recall that any prime minister before him had the courage to be so blunt in the face of the settlers. I watched with awe how Mr Rabin remained solid as a rock when the excited crowd almost assaulted him physically and, resisting the advice of his nervous bodyguards, refused to budge before he had finished speaking his mind.

It is nevertheless extremely doubtful, sheer wishful thinking, that he would have gone with the Palestinians to the unimaginable limits of concessions that might, possibly, have allowed him to reach an agreement. All political leaders spoke of the need to make 'painful concessions' for peace. But no Israeli leader, including Rabin, really imagined how painful and how far-reaching the concessions would have had to be in order to come close to meeting the expectations of Israel's Palestinian interlocutors. Rabin, who in his inaugural speech at the Casablanca economic summit lashed out against Arafat in the most extreme and harshest terms for daring to challenge Israel's monopoly over Jerusalem, would have by no means agreed – as indeed his widow was to ascertain when she later in her turn criticised Ehud Barak's excessive concessions at Camp David – to the kind of compromises that the Barak government was ready to make on Jerusalem and on the other core issues of the conflict.

That the conditions were ripe in 1993 for the initiation of a peace process did not mean that they were also ripe for the sacrifices needed for its conclusion. It is one thing to initiate a process, another to come to terms with the formidable concessions needed for a final settlement. This is not to underestimate Rabin's statesmanship as the leader who broke eternal taboos, recognised the PLO and embarked on a peace process with it. The existence of leaders capable of taking bold decisions and leading the transition to a new era is always vital to turn ripeness into a settlement. It is highly probable, for example, that Yitzhak Shamir would have used the weakness of the PLO as an opportunity to be exploited in his fight for its destruction. Rabin used it as a vehicle to a possible pragmatic settlement. However successful a government might be in building social and political support for its peacemaking policy, at the moment of truth the real test would always be one of statesmanship and leadership. Rabin indeed behaved as a leader of courage and vision, and when he signed the Oslo agreement he knew only too well that the way to a final settlement was still long, arduous and uncertain. But he never imagined the scope of the concessions that were needed for such a settlement. And even if he had been able to bring himself to shoulder the tremendous price of peace, did he possess the capacity to unite a divided society round such a deal? For the question was also to what extent peace could be reached through a reasonable national consensus, for the terms of peace required so many painful compromises and concessions that consensus might simply not have been possible at all.

The case of Israel's peace with Egypt was different. Begin then enjoyed wide popular support for his move; and Sinai was never the sensitive national issue that Judaea, Samaria and the vitally strategic Golan Heights are. Moreover, in the late 1980s Begin's Likud Party was almost the extreme Right in Israel's political panorama; Begin had no Begin to his right. Rabin still had to go a long way in breaking the fragile internal Israeli equilibrium if he wanted to reach a final settlement with the Palestinians. He had yet to challenge the sanctity of political and national legends such as settlements, the taboo of a Palestinian state, the claim that the River Jordan was Israel's military border, the insistence on Israel's undivided ownership of Jerusalem, etc. Probably one of the deficiencies of the Oslo accord – at the same time the reason for its initial success – was that it started as an agreement on the lowest common denominator possible in Israeli society: the idea of getting rid of Gaza did not entail any national trauma. The Right, too, could live with it. From now on every decision was bound to be tougher than the one that preceded it. Both Arafat and the Israeli leadership would still have to break in a more profound and dramatic way the internal consensus in their respective societies. Arafat would have to fight the extremist organisations in a more frontal and resolute way, and he would have to make concessions on refugees and other sensitive issues he was clearly unwilling to contemplate. As to Israel, she would have to conceive solutions on settlements and Jerusalem no relevant Israeli leader, including Rabin, had ever dreamed he would have to envisage.

The day Rabin was assassinated the Palestinian–Israeli conflict was still a long way from solution. The readiness that was so vital for facilitating the initial breakthrough was as yet insufficient to bring about a more permanent solution to the conflict. Were the Israelis really ripe, as it were, for a more bold and pragmatic approach to questions such as the future of Jerusalem, the settlements or the refugees? Was that generation of Palestinians really prepared to depart from the most fundamental and constituent principles of their national cause and move from war to peace at the same pace as the Israelis, so keen to see the immediate fruits of peace, would have liked? Did the Israeli leadership understand that no negotiating skills, perfect as they might be, could bring the Palestinians to accept anything less than a full-fledged Palestinian state, the division of Jerusalem and some degree of repatriation of refugees? The impersonal forces of history may be stronger than the skills that can be exercised by the personal forces; and the former contained a logic that it was not at all clear the Israelis could digest. In other words Israel was ready for the Oslo breakthrough, a painfully, but at the same time an excessively low point of departure; it was prepared for the price required for a permanent solution.

The truth of the matter was, moreover, that by the time Rabin was murdered the peace process was, for all practical purposes, in a state of political coma. Rampant Palestinian terrorism, an uninterrupted expansion of settlements, and Israel's practice of reprisals in the form of closures and collective punishment had already brought the process to a stalemate. Trapped in the vicious circle created by the fatal symmetry between settlements and terrorism, Rabin was almost inexorably marching to his political demise. By the time he was gunned down, he was already severely politically crippled by the alarming loss of legitimacy of the peace process among growing sectors of opinion. A revered general with the record of one who did not hesitate to order the use of brute force in suppressing the Intifada, Rabin failed in his major political task, that of integrating the Israeli Right and the Centre into his peace policy. Eventually he was assassinated as the spokesman of the Israeli Left, a few moments after he had finished singing in a mass rally the 'song of peace', the anthem, as it were, of Peace Now, an organisation whose members were despised and hated by the popular classes as a bunch of 'traitors'.

In his death, Rabin became a martyr for a generation of Israelis, the Messiah of a secular religion of peace and economic growth whose mission was tragically cut short. No one reflected in his life what the Israelis believed was their own collective biography as he did. No one expressed so well their dilemma in the transition from war to peace. His hesitations and ambiguities were theirs, his scepticism and doubts were theirs and, like him, they feared the risks involved in this leap into the future as much as they were excited by the opportunities it opened.

But the real meaning of Rabin's assassination lay more in its significance for Israel's internal life, for the challenge it posed to Israeli democracy and political culture, than in its importance for the already agonising peace process. By the time Rabin was killed, the Israelis' confidence in the political process was severely undermined. With his death, it was the faith that the democratic debate would prevail over violence, more than the peace process, that the Israelis feared had been dealt a mortal blow. The assassination of their Prime Minister was for them principally the occasion for a collective soul searching in questions related to their identity as a nation. More than the death of the peace process, which after all was left in the hands of its engine, the Nobel Peace Laureate Shimon Peres, they mourned the death of the Israel of their dreams that was now being assaulted by an alliance of 'barbarians' ranging from the

Oriental popular classes on Israel's periphery to the fanatic religious settlers, whose spiritual mentors had issued Halachic rulings that author- ised the assassination of the Prime Minister. The sense of loss did not refer only to Rabin the admired leader. The secular Zionist ethos, as it was embodied in the biography of the slain Prime Minister, the most emblematic son of the founding fathers, was under attack, violently challenged and about to be politically defeated by the religious, theocratic ethos of the settlers and by the revolt of the popular masses against 'the peace of the Ashkenazi elites'. Those elites made up of businessmen who profited from the now vilified peace process, and of intellectuals who were indifferent to Jewish values, were seen as the social base of 'Rabinism'.

The challenge to the democratic legitimacy of Rabin's peace policy did not come only from the lunatic fringes of the settlers' community, the dark core of a religious brand of fanaticism, those who had appointed themselves as the interpreters of the nation's 'eternal interest', but also from the very heart of the political establishment. The parliamentary Right was no less active in the task of vicious incitement. The politicians of the Right, with Benjamin Netanyahu and Ariel Sharon at their head, cynically overlooked an elementary lesson of history: the political assassin has always drawn the necessary sanction for his impulse to subvert the political process from the discourse and what he sees as the implicit encouragement of the 'respectable classes'.

Trapped within its built-in fallacies, nullified by Palestinian terrorism and the PA's corrupt incompetence, crippled by Israel's irresponsible settlement policy, and consumed by the political and cultural earthquake that hit Israeli society in the traumatic, abrupt transition from Rabin to Peres's short-lived and bizarre premiership, then to Netanyahu's destruc- tive strategy of confrontation, Oslo gave clear signs of having run its course when the Barak government came to office. Netanyahu was the zealous undertaker of a patient he had received in an advanced state of illness. If there was ever a chance that the Oslo process might survive the upheavals it had been subjected to, Benjamin Netanyahu's premiership removed any doubts and gave it the *coup de grâce*. Israel has no foreign policy, as Henry Kissinger used to say, it only has domestic political constraints. And it was, indeed, the internal divide, Israel's profound social and cultural cleavages as they were so dramatically reflected in Netanyahu's rise to power, that eventually doomed the chances of Oslo.

This rise was the culmination of a most acute internal social and cultural struggle, whose origin lies deep in Israel's old social cleavages. These were now enhanced further by Rabin's divisive peace policies. Netanyahu surfed to the prime minister's office in Jerusalem on the waves of a *Kulturkampf*, a socio-cultural revolution, a mass revolt that was unleashed as a response against the peace policies as they were represented by the secular left-wing elite that Yitzhak Rabin so genuinely embodied.

The Israel on whose shoulders Netanyahu came to power was the reverse image of the Israel that had supported Rabin in his peace policy. Israel in the last generation had developed into more than one nation. The dream of the founding fathers about a secular society, a melting pot with the native, Israeli-born Sabra as the epitome of the new nation, had now taken the form of an essentially Jewish kaleidoscope of multi-ethnic and multicultural identities. The Sabra, Zionism's version of the Soviet New Man and the Aryan Blond Beast, was the proud, autochthonous answer to the rootless, weedy, cosmopolitan and sometimes over-intellectual to the point of being garrulous, Galuthic Jew. Almost a Gentile Jew, half defiantly secular and half a pagan, the Sabra viewed the diaspora as a Jewish sickness and the Jews who survived it after the Holocaust as, in the words of the prophet and the architect of the 'new nation', David Ben-Gurion, 'human dust'. The poet Haim Guri, himself a Sabra of Rabin's generation, wrote how they 'startled the midwives who saw them being born with a monkey wrench and pistol in hand'. Unlike the Jew of the diaspora, the Sabra did not look for beauty spots on his soul; he preferred to proudly display the calluses of a state builder and a soldier on his hands.

But in the 1996 election, fifty years after the establishment of the State of Israel, the pagan, almost Canaanite myth of the Sabra was defeated by the traditional forces of Jewish history. The 'Jew', the hostage of his own fears, self-secluded in a mental and physical ghetto and still at odds with the 'Goyim', had won the day against the 'Israeli'.

Metaphorically, the Israelis were now divided between 'Tel Aviv' and 'Jerusalem', with the latter clearly more genuinely reflective of the national psyche. Tel Aviv was Rabin's and the Left's political and cultural power base. Jerusalem was Netanyahu's domain. Tel Aviv was the modern evolution of 'Israeliness' that, unlike in the days of the hegemony of the mythical Sabra, no longer gripped an Uzi sub-machine gun or followed in the tracks of the combine harvester, but embraced the culture of secularism, hedonism and economic growth. Tel Aviv believed in the State of Israel as a legal entity opposed to the dangerously amorphous, faith-driven Jerusalemite concept of Eretz-Israel. Tel Aviv had replaced the pioneering ethos of the early years and the traits of a mobilised society with the temptations of modernity, liberalism and normalcy. Tel Aviv aspired to be part and parcel of the global village, no longer an isolated, parochial Jewish village, as Jerusalem would have liked. This was an Israel yearning for peace, for which it was ready to pay a hefty price and go to the outer limits of its capacity for compromise. Tel Aviv's

drive for normalcy at any price was seen by the other Israel, that of
Jerusalem, as a shallow affair, one that was almost criminally indifferent
to the depth of Jewish memory and the lessons of Jewish history.

The Israel of Jerusalem was that of the yearning for Jewish roots; it
was the epitome of a deep-rooted fear of the Arabs and an uncompromising distrust of the Goyim, of the international community. The
peace that the Tel Avivian Left strove to achieve was to the Jerusalemites
not only a naïve exercise in political lunacy, but also an unpardonable
attempt to betray Jewish identity. The Tel Aviv peace was a direct attack
on Jewish roots and tradition, a code word for assimilation and a betrayal
of Jewish spirituality, a synonym for licentiousness and the culture of
happenings presided over by the high priest of Hebrew pop music, Aviv
Gefen, a man whose other crime was that he was not even considered
fit to serve in the army. Paradoxically, the assassination of Prime Minister
Rabin, the idol of the 'Tel Aviv' peace, was also an expression of the
yearning for the murder of this high priest of the non-Jewish behavioural
depravity, Aviv Gefen, with whom Rabin, the hero of the Six Day War,
could become a friend only through their common commitment to the
vilified peace process.

Benjamin Netanyahu was brought to power after Rabin's assassination
by the Jerusalem coalition. This was now a magnet for the fears and
complexes of a broad Jewish rainbow alignment of minorities consisting
of Israel's social periphery of the Oriental community, the Russian
nationalist electorate, the Orthodox Jews, the wide sectors of traditionalist
Israelis and the religious settlers. They all viewed the peace process and
its economic fruits with their concomitant international peace festivals as
the exclusive patrimony of the leftist Tel Aviv elite. The economic
dividends of peace did not spill over to the popular classes; they remained
confined to the elites, while the gap between the haves and have-nots
kept widening. Israel under Rabin did indeed know spectacular growth
rates. But at the same time it moved to being second only to the United
States, among Western economies, in its social disparities.

Whether for economic grievances or for an ideological rejection of the
peace process, or out of cultural estrangement, any person alienated –
ethnically, culturally, socially – from the peace elite joined battle in the
1996 elections against those who had usurped Jewish history and had
betrayed Eretz-Israel.

Netanyahu's incompetent three-year premiership, however, ended by
alienating his supporters and dissolving the social and political alliance
that had brought him to power in the first place. The formula for keeping
together such a disparate socio-political alliance required not to endorse
Oslo, not to engage in peace negotiations with the unreliable Palestinians

who had abandoned their role as partners and turned again into enemies. Needless to say, concessions made to such a vilified Palestinian interlocutor were an almost prohibitive political move. By signing the Wye agreement that gave the Palestinians additional land in Judaea and Samaria (13 per cent of it) Netanyahu sealed his political fate and saw his coalition rapidly melting away. In the pendulous power shift between Right and Left that was the hallmark of Israeli politics since 1992, it was now the turn of the new leader of the Centre-Left to exploit the blunders of Netanyahu's deficient leadership. With Oslo in shambles, the philosophy of interim agreements at a dead end, and the trust upon which Israelis and Palestinians were supposed to build the final settlement at its lowest ebb since 1993, Ehud Barak, who positioned himself as the inheritor of Rabin's legacy of peace with security, emerged as the new hope.

X   The Barak Phase: On Freedom and Innocence

Whoever thinks it is possible to resolve issues such as the refugees, Jerusalem, the settlements and the borders through negotiations is under a delusion.

Marwan Barghouty,
4 March 2000

At Camp David we intended to make the Israelis face the tribunal of history, face the victims of their crime and sin.

Akram Hanya, a member of the Palestinian Delegation at Camp David,
July 2000

We need to put an end to our rule over another people. We all remember how it was possible to maintain a small state of Israel [before 1967] but with a much greater internal cohesion.

Ehud Barak, internal consultations at Camp David,
17 July 2000

Maybe the lights are being turned down. No one can predict when will they be turned on again. It is possible that Arafat is interested in a crisis.

Saab Erakat addressing the Israeli team at Camp David,
24 July 2000

We are going from here into a catastrophe. ... Make no mistake: this is the defeat of the peace camp in Israel for many years to come.

The author to Saab Erakat on the last night at Camp David,
25 July 2000

The option is not either armed struggle or negotiations. We can fight and negotiate at the same time, just as the Algerians and the Vietnamese had done.

Nabil Shaath,
7 October 2000

The post-mortem for the peace process as it unfolded under the Barak government and President Clinton's mediation has now become an issue of heated debate and a major controversy as to the reasons, and the responsibility, for the demise of the process. The debate in Israel, of course, is not a mere intellectual exercise; it is essentially a battle for the political identity of both the Left and the Right. The Left must blame Barak and the negotiating team for 'not offering enough to the Palestinians', and for their 'awkward' and 'insensitive' negotiating tactics. The guilt borne by Barak and his team thus becomes the ultimate lifeline for Israel's extreme Left; it is only through the guilt of the peacemakers that it salvages its worldview from the debris of the entire Oslo edifice, now in ruins. The issue is simpler as far as the Right is concerned. After all, they never believed in a settlement and the failure of the peace process is nothing but the ultimate vindication of their worldview. They – as incidentally some on the Centre-Left, the Nobel laureate Shimon Peres for example – accused the Israeli negotiators of making too many concessions, of going too far ...

This is not to say that the Barak government was free of blame for the sad outcome of its peace enterprise. Mistakes and miscalculations abounded. As it turned out, for example, Barak's insistence on a 'Syria First' strategy had extremely adverse consequences for the entire process. The Palestinian track was taken by Barak only after he had exhausted the Syrian channel. He clearly subscribed to the capsule theory, the traditional Israeli structure of peacemaking, that of first dealing with Arab states and relegating the Palestinian problem to a secondary position. Barak, contrary to the advice of most of his ministers, opted for a Syria First strategy that humiliated the Palestinian leader and made him restless, alienated and hostile. The chief cornerstone of the Arab–Israeli conflict, certainly in Arafat's eyes, the Palestinian question was initially relegated by Ehud Barak to the status of a stone rejected by the builders, in a way that was seen as demeaning by the Palestinian leader.

But Barak's priority for Syria was not entirely illogical. A major rationale of his Syrian emphasis was his desire to fulfil his electoral pledge of pulling out of Lebanon within the wider context of a settlement with Syria, which most of us believed was the key to stability along the Lebanese border once Israel had pulled out its forces. Nor was Assad's surprising eagerness to engage in negotiations with Israel unrelated to what he rightly perceived as Israel's threat to withdraw from Lebanon and deny Syria the vital springboard it had used so effectively in order to harass and pressure her through her Hezbollah clients. The logic of Barak's Syria First strategy lay also in his desire to neutralize the Syrian northern front before he moved on to negotiate a final settlement with

Arafat, whose past record led him to reasonably assume that an all-out war could indeed be the outcome should an agreement not be reached. Barak went to make peace, but prepared himself for war should a peace agreement prove to be unattainable. 'Syria First' was then an attempt to eliminate the risk of a war on two fronts.

Like Rabin, Barak was a military man who better understood and therefore preferred to deal with an interlocutor like Assad who was himself, like him, a military man at the helm of an orderly state, rather than with a terrorist and guerrilla fighter at the head of a revolutionary movement, like Arafat. Assad was a tough negotiator, but one whose conditions for a settlement were clear and well known. With Syria it was essentially a territorial dispute, a 'real estate' affair. In the case of Arafat and the Palestinians the conditions for a settlement were never clearly enunciated, nor was the dispute an exclusively territorial one. For it also, perhaps even mainly, touched upon historical and religious certificates of ownership, holy sites, refugees and an emotionally loaded contention about Jerusalem. Barak shared with Rabin the specious argument that Syria, not the Palestinian problem, was the main strategic challenge that needed to be neutralised. They perceived the threats to Israel in terms of armoured brigades, infantry divisions and missile batteries, and could not appreciate that the challenge posed by a national movement and an oppressed and occupied people was not just an issue of public order, or even of terrorism, but could turn, too, into a strategic threat no less formidable than Syria's conventional military capabilities.

Whether or not he was right to opt for a Syria First strategy was no longer relevant once he took that track. What mattered was that he should have known the price of peace and be ready to pay it. For more than the negotiations as such, it was their failure that was bound to have a devastating effect on the chance of reaching a deal with the Palestinians.

But the Prime Minister embarked on his Syrian voyage armed with wrong assumptions. He, and initially President Clinton as well, accepted at face value the version that later proved to be utterly wrong, of Ron Lauder, the Jewish American businessman whom Netanyahu had used as his go-between in secret talks with the Syrians, according to which Assad was ready for a deal on the basis of the 1923 international border and had also accepted an Israeli military presence in a monitoring station on Mount Hermon. The truth of the matter was that Assad had never agreed to such conditions; he would settle for no less than a confirmation of 'Rabin's deposit' of an Israeli pull-out to the 1967 borders that would be linked to agreed security arrangements. Barak tried different formulae to circumvent the need to endorse the deposit, such as 'we cannot erase the historical record'. He also accepted an American bridging proposal that the 1967 lines 'would guide' the delineation of the final border, but to no avail. Assad would not settle for anything that was not an explicit commitment by Israel to respect the 4 June 1967 lines. True, his delegates in the negotiations, including his Foreign Minister Farouk al-Shara, were prepared for flexible arrangements on the ground, such as allowing Israel the right to use a narrow strip along the north-eastern shores of the Sea of Galilee, provided this did not infringe on Syria's sovereignty there. But Assad never endorsed such Syrian concessions.

Barak, however, missed a unique opportunity to reach an agreement with Assad, admittedly on very difficult conditions. For a very narrow window of time there were clear indications that the Syrian leader wanted an agreement, if only in order to allow his son Bashar to succeed him free of the burden of having to struggle himself for the recovery of the Golan. A proof of the surprising determination of the Sphinx of Damascus to strike a deal with Israel was the dramatic gesture, which he had never agreed to make to Rabin, of sending his Foreign Minister to direct negotiations with Barak even before receiving from him an unequivocal commitment to Rabin's deposit. But instead of seizing the opportunity and assuming the inevitable price for peace, Barak risked losing a vital asset, Assad's trust, and avoided making the necessary commitment on the border. He conveyed to the Americans and the Syrians a sense of urgency, but at the moment of truth and decision he got cold feet and engaged in tactical manoeuvres with the hope of wresting a better deal from Assad.

Assad was forthcoming not only because for a short time a deal suited his domestic concerns, but also because he respected Barak as a strong and determined leader who was capable of delivering. But Barak raised the expectations of the Syrians by his initial boldness and sense of urgency, then moved to a wavering attitude and engaged in transparent tactical exercises. In the Shepardstown peace conference with President Clinton and Foreign Minister Sharaa, he responded to the Syrians' uncharacteristic flexibility (they were ready to delineate the final border ten metres to the east of the lake) by still obstinately resisting committing himself to the 1967 lines. He insisted instead on focusing the talks on the security issues, and refused any clear-cut reference to the Rabin deposit. Barak's tactics ended up humiliating the Syrian President and eroded beyond repair his trust in Barak's leadership.

One should not exaggerate Syria's flexibility, however. It needs to be put in its proper perspective. True, there was a sense that Syria's immovable position during the negotiations with Rabin were being reshaped. But the Syrians continued to be as uncompromising as ever on the issue of Lebanon, on the security arrangements and on their claim to have full sovereignty over the strip of land along the north-eastern shores of the lake. They also refused to allow a separate Israeli–Lebanese channel of negotiations, which Barak needed in order to soften the growing resistance in Israel to what everybody knew was going to be an extremely costly deal with Syria.

As was later the case during the negotiations with the Palestinians, Barak's hesitations were mostly the result of his concerns on the home front. Most of the polls that he kept conducting to take the pulse of public opinion clearly showed that the Israeli public did not trust the Syrians and was not especially keen on a settlement with them in exchange for a full withdrawal from the fabled Golan Heights, which would moreover bring the Syrians to the shores of Israel's only, and no less fabled, lake. Barak was not merely isolated in his own Cabinet on Syria, he was also out of tune with the country's mood with regard to what was widely seen as an extortionate price for a grudging, parsimonious peace. Nor did the army and the security establishment share the Prime Minister's Syrian zeal. Both Chief of Staff Mofaz and Head of the General Security Service (*Shabak*) Ami Ayalon questioned in the Cabinet Barak's preference for a Syrian deal and advised him, as did most of his ministers, to focus on the Palestinians.

Barak expected Assad to help him legitimise his peace enterprise within Israel, and make more palatable the inevitable concessions Israel would have to make by changing his traditional indifferent attitude to the sensibilities of Israeli public opinion and agree to make public gestures of goodwill, as well as give his consent to confidence-building measures. He also asked the Syrians to allow their Lebanese clients to get ready for Israel's forthcoming withdrawal from that country and start peace negotiations accordingly. Never too forthcoming on the issue of economic co-operation, Assad was now asked by the Prime Minister to agree, even before a peace agreement was signed, to the creation of a Free Trade Zone on the Golan Heights. This was utterly unacceptable to the Syrian President. Peace to him was about the end of war, not about co-operation. In addition Barak expected the Americans, as well as making available to Israel an astronomic financial package and agreeing to a strategic upgrading of their relations with her, to convince one or more Arab countries to start full diplomatic ties with the Jewish state. Such was the extravagant package of confidence-building measures and down payments on the fruits of peace that Barak felt he needed in order to convince his sceptical countrymen of his Syrian undertaking.

Assad was not entirely negative, albeit not very helpful either. And though President Clinton was very forthcoming, nothing substantial really happened to convince the Israeli public of the immediate advantages of peace. Lebanon was Assad's backyard and he would not easily allow the Israelis to make any headway with the Lebanese until he knew that they had made an irrevocable commitment to the full territorial price of peace on the Golan.

There might have been a chance for a peace deal with Assad in December 1999 and January 2000 on terms that were not at all easy for the Israeli public to accept. But when in early February Barak finally signalled, in a Cabinet meeting, his readiness for a settlement based on the 4 June 1967 lines, it was already too late. A terminally sick man, Assad had by then lost interest. His priority now was managing the succession of his son, not the agonising complexities of a peace deal with Israel.

The Clinton–Assad Geneva summit that put the lid on this last essay in peacemaking between Israel and Syria was one of the most bizarre and humiliating experiences of President Clinton's international diplomacy.[1] Barak practically forced the President to put pressure on a clearly unwilling Syrian President to come to a summit in order to hear Israel's latest proposals. But Assad was clearly no longer interested, whatever the content of Israel's latest proposals might have been. In an embarrassingly short and precipitate meeting Assad rejected out of hand, and without even allowing Mr Clinton to elaborate any further, all and every hint of a new Israeli concession. He even castigated his Foreign Minister in front of the American team for having presumably pledged, without his authorisation, that Israel could have control of the north-eastern strip along the Lake of Galilee. To leave no room for further talks, Assad added that Syria had claims on the lake itself: 'The lake has always been our lake.'

Once again peace eluded Israelis and Arabs. The Syrians, like all the other Arab countries that had never truly prepared their people for peace and reconciliation with Israel, were now as adamant as ever with regard to the substance of peace and the degree of normalisation of their relations with Israel that they were ready to contemplate. Peace for Assad was essentially a transition from a strategy of war and conflict to one of competition and armed peace. And as for the Israeli side, it acted in a political void as a front without a home front, with no popular legitimacy, among other reasons because for years governments and leaders had consistently avoided spelling out to the people the very high price of peace. As would soon happen with the Palestinian track, Barak went further on the Syrian front than any Israeli leader before him. But he was

---

[1] For a first-hand account of the Geneva summit see Dennis Ross, *The Missing Peace: The Inside Story of the Fight for the Middle East Peace*, Farrar, Straus & Giroux, New York, 2004, pp. 583–4.

eventually defeated by his own fears about the fragility of the home front and by the lack of incentives he believed he should have got from the other side in order to legitimise his peace enterprise.

The Syrian track ended with no deal, but with a twofold legacy that Arafat was both forced and happy to embrace. Assad taught him that it was perfectly possible to say 'no' to America, and even publicly humiliate her President, without paying a price, and that, regardless of the ambiguities of the Oslo agreement, the 1967 borders were sacrosanct and therefore needed to be a categorical requirement in any future peace negotiations with Israel. Peace, Assad taught the Palestinians about to start their negotiations with Israel for a final settlement, needs to be based on one unyielding condition: full and unequivocal withdrawal from the occupied territories.

Addressing the Camp David summit, as some commentators do, separately from the entire negotiating process – that is, independently of the negotiations that were conducted for many subsequent months in Tel Aviv, Jerusalem, the Bolling air base on the outskirts of the American capital, where on 23 December 2000 President Clinton presented his final parameters for a settlement, and finally Taba – distorts, of course, the picture as to what exactly were the proposals that Arafat refused to accept. To his last day, the Palestinian leader was still reluctant to acknowledge the real nature of the deal he was offered, and he obstinately kept repeating that he had no option but to reject the ridiculous map of enclaves and 'Bantustans' that was presented to him by an American–Israeli conspiracy.

But this is to anticipate later events. The negotiating process fell victim to the conflicting expectations of the parties, and to their diverging interpretations of the meaning of the process and of what exactly were the actual premises upon which it was built. The Israelis came to the negotiations with the conviction, inherited from, and inherent in, the letter of the Oslo accords, that this was an open-ended process where no preconceived solutions existed. To them, not all 'the territories' were under discussion, but 'territories', for not only did Oslo leave open to free negotiation the nature of the final border, but also just one UN resolution was relevant to the negotiations, Resolution 242, which indeed was the exclusive platform upon which the entire Madrid process was based. For the Palestinians this was a simple, clear-cut process of decolonisation based on 'international legitimacy' and 'UN relevant Resolutions' that compelled Israel to withdraw to the 1967 borders, divide Jerusalem, dismantle the settlements for being illegal and acknowledge the refugees' right of return. Neither Rabin nor Peres thought that Oslo had unleashed a process that should and must culminate in a full withdrawal to the 1967 lines, the clear and unambiguous division of Jerusalem into two capitals, and a substantial implementation of the right of return of Palestinian refugees. Constructive ambiguity facilitated an agreement in Oslo at the price of creating potentially irreconcilable misconceptions with regard to the final settlement. Moreover, the Israeli negotiators came to solve the problems created by the 1967 war and were surprised to discover that the intractable issues of 1948, first and foremost that of the refugees' right of return, were now high on the Palestinian agenda.

In the course of the Oslo years Israel came to assimilate the inevitability of a Palestinian state. Such an assumption was not the exclusive domain of the Left; many on the Right were forced to come to terms with the idea. Netanyahu, for example, used to speak grudgingly of a 'Puerto Rico' or 'Andorra' style Palestinian state. Both Right and Left assumed, however, that the borders and the degrees of sovereignty of the future Palestinian state would be open to discussion, a concept they believed was implicit in the Oslo accords. The endorsement by Labour of Palestinian statehood in its May 1997 party conference was, consequently, qualified by the need to limit the sovereignty of that state, in order to satisfy vital Israeli concerns. The party's resolution stipulated that, though the Palestinian state should have most of the West Bank and the practical totality of the Gaza Strip, it should not encompass the major settlement blocs or any part of Jerusalem, if only because, it was then assumed, no government that would dismantle the settlements and divide Jerusalem had much of a chance of surviving. After all, the Labour Party had just lost the 1996 elections to Likud due in part to Netanyahu's ingenious campaign that 'Peres will divide Jerusalem'.

'Instead of making peace you always look more as if you are getting ready for the next war.' This complaint, made to me by Abu-Ala during our secret negotiations in May 2000 in Harpsund, the summer residence of Sweden's prime minister south of Stockholm, was not entirely baseless. Peace, just like war, has always been a military or militarised affair in Israel. Throughout the Oslo process, although less so during the negotiations for the final settlement under the Barak government, the security establishment was deeply, sometimes overwhelmingly, involved in the negotiations, and it certainly injected a strong military and security rationale into Israel's negotiating positions.

Israel aspired to an agreement that would allow her to respond effectively to the risk of potential Palestinian revisionism and to a subsequent renewed belligerency by the future Palestinian state, either by resorting again to practices of terrorism or by fomenting instability on a regional scale. Israel also contemplated the risk that Palestinian belligerency might be expressed in the future as part of an all-out confrontation by an Arab or Islamic coalition against the Jewish state. The demilitarisation of the future Palestinian state had therefore been, throughout, a standard, primary Israeli requirement. The axiom already established in the Palestinian chapter of the Camp David accords in 1979 was that Palestinian security forces ('a strong police force') should be designed solely for internal security assignments. Hardly anybody in Israel saw the Palestinian state as a conventional military threat. But in the wider context of an all-Arab war against Israel, as a result of either domestic upheavals – a fundamentalist takeover in one or more of the neighbouring countries – or following an attempt by an Arab country to assert its regional ambitions, the use of Palestinian territory by an Arab coalition could pose a serious threat and hinder Israel's capacity to react effectively and deploy her forces in accordance with the nature of the threat. This was the rationale behind Israel's traditional claim to the Jordan Valley as a forward defence line, a claim that did not necessarily require Israeli sovereignty on the valley. Long-term lease arrangements could also be explored.

But Camp David did not fail because of territory. And the issues of security looked throughout the negotiating process, down to the Taba talks, manageable and solvable. Moreover, as the process evolved, Israel was forced to trim down her territorial ambitions to the level where, in late December 2000, she agreed to pull out from 97 per cent of the West Bank and from the entire Gaza Strip. And to make them as palatable as possible to the Palestinians, Israel's security requirements were reduced to their most essential core, a far cry from the initial lavish expectations of her security establishment. As to the attitude of the Palestinian leader to the territorial question, it might be worth recalling how, under the pressure of an Israeli proposal on Jerusalem, which I was personally responsible for at Camp David – both President Clinton and his envoy to the Middle East, Dennis Ross, refer in their respective memoirs to this moment in the talks as potentially heralding a breakthrough[1] – Arafat, notwithstanding his frequent complaints about Israel's humiliating proposals of a state built by fragmented Bantustans, himself put the territorial question in the proper perspective. He deposited with President Clinton his consent to border modifications of between 8 and 10 per cent without even insisting on equal swaps. 'And as to the swaps,' he said to the President, 'I trust you and I accept your judgement. You decide.' Arafat later reversed his position, but this moment in the summit

---

[1] Bill Clinton, *My Life*, Hutchinson, London, 2004, pp. 913–14.

clearly reflected his view of the peace process as not being about a mundane bargaining over real estate. Land mattered to him far less than emotional, legendary and Islamic values such as Jerusalem, the Temple Mount (Haram al-Sharif for the Muslims), and the core of the Palestinian national ethos, namely refugees.

Arafat's 8 per cent 'deposit' can indeed be interpreted as a brilliant manoeuvre by the Palestinian leader aimed at focusing everybody's attention on Jerusalem, the issue that really mattered to him. By pretending to show flexibility on the question of territory he managed to move Jerusalem to the very centre of the negotiations, and put the entire onus for the success or failure of the summit onto the Israelis. He knew only too well that his demands for an unequivocal Palestinian sovereignty on the Temple Mount and a clear-cut division of the city were positions the Israelis could not accept. As it turned out, Arafat's 'deposit' became the deathtrap in which the summit was eventually consumed.

Peace with the Arab states is a strictly political undertaking based on the restitution of territory. In contrast, peacemaking with the Palestinians is an attempt almost to break the genetic code of the Arab–Israeli conflict, and perhaps even of the Jewish–Muslim dispute, by touching religious and historical certificates of ownership. Arafat clearly refused to be the first and only Arab leader to recognise the unique historical and religious roots of the bond of the Jews to their millenarian homeland and to their holy shrines. Refugeeism, Jerusalem and Islamic values more than land and real estate were the insurmountable obstacles that prevented an agreement at Camp David and later at Taba.

Throughout, Arafat perceived himself as a warrior engaged in a mythological campaign of moral decision against a state born in sin, which must be forced to acknowledge Palestinian justice by opening a wide window to the implementation of the refugees' right of return. 'How many refugees do you intend to ask that should return?' Nabil Shaath was asked by the President in the negotiations on refugees at Camp David.

His answer was, 'Between 10 and 20 per cent of the total number.'

'Do you really expect Israel to accept between 400,000 to 800,000 refugees? Is this the agreement you expect them to subscribe to?'

'We insist on the right of every refugee to go back to his home,' was Akram Hania's response. He later published a series of articles in *El-Ayam*, the Palestinian Authority's official newspaper, where he elaborated on the Palestinian rationale on refugees at Camp David, and on the reason why Israel refused to endorse it. Akram Hania, one of Arafat's closest men at Camp David, put it this way: 'At Camp David we intended to make the Israelis face the tribunal of history, face the victims of their crime and sin. Israel wanted to silence for ever the voice of the witnesses to the crime and erase the proof of the Naqbah.'

Arguably, and in the eyes of many, Akram Hania's might be a legitimate and even commendable attitude. But it was not conducive to an agreement that Israel could accept. It only strengthened the Israelis' perception that Arafat was unable or unwilling to endorse the two-state solution and, as Rob Malley, the President's adviser on the Israeli–Palestinian question, and Hussein Agha were fair enough to admit in a joint account of Camp David in the *New York Review of Books* that was not exactly favourable to the Israeli interpretation of the summit, to assume the moral legitimacy for the existence of a Jewish state.

As to Jerusalem, Arafat never ceased nurturing his image as a conqueror, as a modern Saladin or Umar el-Kutab who would liberate Jerusalem from the infidels and redeem the holy places of Islam. In a long meeting I had with him in Nablus through the night of 25 June 2000, that is, a fortnight before Camp David, he was careful to remind me, when our conversation moved to the chapter on Jerusalem, of the Umar Treaty of AD 638, signed between the Khalif Umar, the conqueror of Jerusalem, and the Byzantine Patriarch Sopronius, where, so Arafat instructed me, the conditions of the capitulation of the Christians included a prohibition on the Jews living in Jerusalem. Arafat's ambition to emulate Umar el-Kutab was no mere anecdote. This was so important to him that on one occasion, as related in one of Edward Said's articles, he even ordered the arrest of a Palestinian journalist of *al-Quds*, Maher al-Alami, for daring to relegate to the third page of the newspaper an article comparing him with that legendary seventh-century Muslim conqueror of Jerusalem and liberator of its holy places.

'Instead of repeatedly rejecting the Israelis' proposals, make counter proposals,' Clinton would tell the Palestinians at Camp David. Rob Malley, in the analysis of the summit he co-authored with Hussein Agha, repeated this remark: 'Indeed, the Palestinians' principal failing is that from the beginning of the Camp David summit onward they were unable either to say yes to the American ideas or to present a cogent and specific counterproposal of their own.'

Tactical shortcomings were not, of course, a Palestinian monopoly. Barak and his team were full of them. For example, the Prime Minister was too slow to grasp the centrality of the issue of Jerusalem at this conference and was therefore unprepared for the far-reaching concessions that were required. Nor were Barak's bargaining positions on the territorial issue reasonable enough to be seen by the Palestinians as credible. To start, as he did, with a proposal of a Palestinian state on 66 per cent of the West Bank in order to offer later at Camp David 87 per cent, and not reject out of hand Clinton's proposal at the summit of 91 per cent, was an indication to the Palestinians that he did not really have red lines. Barak's negotiating tactics were a standing invitation to the Palestinians to keep the pressure on the Israelis and never say 'yes' to what Barak liked to call his 'generous proposals'.

This question of Israel's unreasonable point of departure for negotiations with potential Arab interlocutors, whether Palestinians, Syrians or Egyptians, is of far-reaching significance. Israel's unrealistic bargaining positions failed to convince the Arabs of the seriousness of her professed quest for peace and only invited them never to accept an Israeli position as final. The Israeli internal discourse on the price of peace has therefore always been an exercise in wishful thinking and self-deceit, not least, of course, with regard to the Palestinian question. I cannot but recall a revealing comment made to me by Ahmed Aboul Gheit, Egypt's ambassador to the UN and today his country's Foreign Minister, after I finished delivering my speech at the General Assembly in New York on 25 September 2000. To my remark in the speech that Israel had come to the limits of her capacity for compromise with the Palestinians, the ambassador rightly and cunningly responded, 'Why should we believe you when everybody remembers that you started your voyage into the Palestinian question with Golda Meir denying that a Palestinian people existed at all, and at Camp David you agreed to give away the bulk of the West Bank for an independent Palestinian state and divide Jerusalem? These certainly cannot be the outer limits of your concessions.'

Ehud Barak and his team were criticised by both the Right and the Left in Israel for prematurely rushing into a peace summit to tackle extremely intractable issues that were simply not ready for solution. That such a critique should come from the Right for whom there is never an appropriate moment to compromise on Jerusalem or on borders is perfectly understandable. But for the Left, who had devised the entire Oslo framework that stipulated that negotiations for a final settlement should have started in 1996, and had to be concluded in 1998, to say that an attempt to reach a final settlement in 2000 was 'premature' is, to say the least, puzzling. Our decision to go to Camp David in the summer of 2000 was prompted by the need to cut short the process whereby the piecemeal devolution of territories did not produce any progress towards peace; it only became a progressive reinforcement of Arafat's state of terror and corruption, a state which, moreover, encouraged regional instability as a legitimate tool in its struggle. Our intention was to stop the decline of the Oslo process from leading to general war and a regional flare-up. And if indeed our failure to reach an agreement ushered in yet one more round of violent confrontation between Israelis and Palestinians, this would at least take place before Arafat had taken control of the bulk of the territories.

Of course, as critics asserted, the conference at Camp David could have been better prepared, although it is not at all clear what is really meant by that. We made enormous progress at the secret channel in Stockholm between Abu-Ala and Hassan Asfour on the Palestinian side and myself and Gilead Sher on the Israeli side. But the exposure of the channel by the Palestinians themselves – as part of an internal political struggle within the Palestinian camp, Abu-Mazen's people leaked the talks to *Al-Hayat* – destroyed any possibility for further progress. The channel stopped because it was not producing any longer. Exposed by his political rivals back home, who leaked imaginary details about his 'irresponsible' concessions, Abu-Ala quickly retreated to the safety of old, unyielding positions. The dynamic of give and take in a secluded environment was nipped in the bud and was not allowed to prosper. And if this were not enough, by 15 May, the day of the Naqbah, the Palestinians, with Arafat's connivance (he ignored advance warnings by both Israelis and Secretary Madeleine Albright), unleashed throughout the territories days of violent disturbances that ended in the inevitable clashes with Israel's security forces. Now it was Barak's turn to be exposed in Israel as the one who was making concessions to a partner who continued to behave as an enemy.

As the Al-Aqsa Intifada would also show, Arafat could never resist the temptation of the revolutionary way of fighting and talking at the same time, forcing his interlocutor to soften and change his positions under the constant threat of war and terror. By the time we came to negotiate in the pastoral surroundings of the summer residence of Sweden's prime minister, we were advised by the intelligence services that Arafat's security apparatus, not just 'the masses', was already busy resuming its preparations for a war of terror. Arafat's revolutionary way would prove to have devastating effects for the chances of peace with an Israeli side whose public opinion could only lose trust in a peace process that was accompanied throughout by war and terror. The most visible political effect of the peace process was the constant drift to the right of the Israeli electorate. Arafat was the sin, Ariel Sharon is the punishment. The victims are both a Palestinian people whose Intifada and Israel's reprisals would end up devastating their society and dismantling their institutions in what would amount practically to a second Naqbah, and the Israelis who, haunted by the fear of terror, would decide to lock themselves behind the protective walls of a new ghetto for them and for their neighbours. From the moment the Swedish channel was dissolved it became clear that Arafat's insistence that the summit be 'better prepared' was just a euphemism which meant that Israel should come closer to his positions under the threat of war without him having to budge from them.

I must admit, however, that Abu-Ala came to me on the eve of Camp David with an initiative to renew the secret channel, this time in Cairo. He even advanced flexibilities he had been unwilling to show before in order to increase the bait. But I failed to convince Barak, who feared an erosion of his position before the summit. It later became clear, however, that Abu-Ala was not authorised to make these concessions – he agreed, for example, to border modifications of 4 per cent of the West Bank – and his initiative was his way of recovering the political ground he had lost in much of the Palestinian political family. 'We need more time to prepare' for the summit was perhaps a legitimate Palestinian argument, but the truth of the matter was that nothing was being done to facilitate the process of preparation.

It is also true that the lack of trust between Barak and Arafat was not helpful. Barak was never really capable of communicating, or levelling, with Arafat. The Palestinian leader, a curious combination of a megalomaniac possessed at the same time by an inferiority complex, felt humiliated and overmastered by his arrogant interlocutor, always more inclined to dictate his positions than to negotiate them. 'He treats me like a slave,' shouted Arafat at Madeleine Albright on one tense occasion at the Camp David summit.

It is difficult to imagine a greater incompatibility than that which existed between the Israeli Prime Minister, an intellectually arrogant and undoubtedly brilliant general who was totally blind and deaf to cultural nuances and always convinced that he possessed the powerful Cartesian logic that would surely persuade his interlocutor of the invalidity of his own arguments on the one hand, and Arafat, a mythological leader who to his last day continued to embody the general will of his people, but at the same time was full of personal complexes and was incapable, or pretended to be so, of conducting a fluid dialogue on the other. He would only speak in slogans, catchwords, Islamic metaphors; and would always leave his opponent with the frustrating feeling that whatever concessions he might be willing to make, he still owed much more. Elusive, non-committal, the master of double talk, Arafat turned the negotiations with him, to use Lloyd George's description of a similar occasion with De Valera, into a futile exercise of 'trying to pick up Mercury with a fork'. At no point throughout the entire peace process as it unfolded since Oslo, not even in the best days that Arafat later claimed to miss, those he shared with Rabin who he liked to say was his friend, did Arafat convey in private or in public a positive message of hope, or a promise of friendship and co-operation with those with whom he had signed the Oslo accords. Nor did he ever really try to advance a positive ethos for the Palestinian Authority in the areas of development, education and the image of the future Palestinian state.

At a meeting in Lisbon prior to the Camp David summit, Clinton warned Barak that if the summit failed, 'this will kill Oslo'. The President should have known better, for the truth of the matter was that Israelis and Palestinians had already jointly killed Oslo. But his warning to Barak should anyway have been sent to Arafat's address as well. It is true that Arafat had been asking the Americans for more time to prepare for the summit, but he wanted it nonetheless. In fact, he had been constantly pushing the Americans to solve all the issues. 'No more limited deals, no more interim agreements,' he kept saying to the President and, as a close confidant of Arafat, Akram Hania, recalls in his articles in *El-Ayam*, when I personally suggested to Arafat that the negotiations on Jerusalem be postponed for two years and an agreement should first be reached on all the other core issues, his answer was that he would postpone Jerusalem 'not even for two hours'.

Arafat and his men like to insist that he was dragged to the Camp David summit against his will. This is only partly, if at all, true. His tactics were *always* to pretend that he was being dragged against his will to conferences and negotiations in order that the onus of proof should rest with his interlocutors who would have to make the necessary concessions to justify their insistence. I was personally witness to another typical case where Arafat was 'dragged against his will' to the Sharm el Sheikh international summit in mid October 2000, whose purpose was to reach a ceasefire in the Intifada. But Arafat, who had just embarked on a war of attrition against Israel that he believed was bearing fruit for the Palestinian cause, had no interest whatever in a ceasefire. A master of the art of extricating himself from desperate situations, he bowed to international pressure, came to Sharm el Sheikh, subscribed to a ceasefire agreement and immediately turned it into a dead letter by ignoring its provisions. Camp David was perceived by Arafat as a trap and, just as in the case of Sharm el Sheikh, his main preoccupation throughout the summit was how to extricate himself from the ambush prepared for him by Americans and Israelis.

Another criticism frequently made with regard to Camp David is that, given Arafat's well-known unyielding positions on the parameters for a final settlement, the entire premise upon which the Americans and the Israelis built their assumption about the possibility of reaching a settlement was utterly false. It is true, of course, that there was a very substantial gap between the professed positions of the parties on the eve of the summit. But such was also the case at the Camp David summit of 1979.

One always assumes that at the moment of truth, when a historical decision is called for, leaders might change their position, sometimes even radically. This was certainly the case with Menachem Begin in 1979. It was not entirely outlandish to expect that, as Charles de Gaulle once put it, 'a true leader always keeps an element of surprise in his sleeve which others cannot grasp.' It was that element of surprise that is the essence of leadership in times of historic change that everybody expected would appear at the vital moments in the summit.

It is therefore unfair to claim, as Rob Malley and Hussein Agha did in their *New York Review of Books* article, that Barak's all-or-nothing approach was a corridor leading either to an agreement or to confrontation. If this is true, the blame should clearly be shared with Arafat. But the truth of the matter is that at key moments at Camp David, when it was clear that a final settlement was impossible to reach, both the Israelis and the Americans tried fall-back plans for interim or partial settlements that were rejected out of hand by the Palestinians.

Prime Minister Barak insisted, amid criticism from both Left and Right that he was being presumptuous and acting precipitously, on an all-engulfing approach that would solve all and every one of the core issues and bring about an end to the conflict. His rationale was not entirely outlandish. He knew of the assessment of the intelligence services that the Palestinians were like a volcano about to erupt in rage at the never-ending peace process. He used to warn his ministers that Israel was like the *Titanic* about to crash into the iceberg, and she urgently needed to change course by bringing an end to the conflict with the Palestinians before it became too late.

There was a political consideration as well. The fragility and dys-functionality of Israel's political system was such that, as the history of the peace process since Oslo had proved more than once, it simply could not resist the upheavals that followed the redeployments and the withdrawals carried out in the framework of the interim agreements. Governments fell, and a prime minister was even tragically assassinated, amid the hysterical mass mobilisation of the settlers and the parties of the Right, when only minor redeployments were carried out. Today, it is Ariel Sharon's turn to discover the sad truth about the dysfunctionality of Israel's political system when his plan for a unilateral pull-out from Gaza is being constantly torpedoed and derailed by the system, in fact by his own party. Barak rightly assumed that the political price for a final settlement might not be higher than that he would have to pay for yet another crisis-ridden interim agreement. In fact, it was assumed that it might even be lower, for contrary to the interim agreements where Israel gave away portions of the West Bank without any guarantee whatsoever that this would secure Palestinian compliance and stability, the final agreement would leave no issue unsolved. The promise of a full peace, Barak assumed, would induce the Israelis to swallow the 'painful concessions' in a way that might even save the political system from an uncontrolled upheaval.

To turn back to Camp David, one may say that it was his inability to appreciate the unique relationship between the USA and Israel that cost Arafat dearly. America was not there, as some Palestinians might have thought, just to deliver Israel to a passive and rejectionist Arab side that was unwilling to engage in a serious negotiating process, nor would Israel allow herself to be delivered unconditionally. By failing to advance clear proposals and counter-proposals, that is, by refusing to engage in a real negotiating dynamic, the Palestinians deprived the Americans of the vital tools they needed to be able to put pressure on the Israelis. The President and his team could never ascertain whether the Palestinians were at all serious and genuine in their commitment to reach a settlement. As the President repeatedly told Arafat, he was not expecting him to agree to US or Israeli proposals, but he was counting on him to offer something, to produce a new idea that he could take back to Barak in order to convince him to make more concessions. 'I need something to tell him,' he implored. 'So far I have nothing.'

'Do you want to come to my funeral?' was a frequent warning that Arafat manipulated throughout the summit to repel the President's pressure on him. He knew only too well that in the Arab Middle East the leader who makes compromises for the sake of peace – Sadat, King Abdullah – ends up as a prophet without honour and risks being assassinated. The hero to be remembered and revered is the one who stands against the foreign power, even when he is eventually defeated. Arafat preferred to die as a defeated hero who did not give in, like Nasser, than be slain as a man of peace like Sadat.

Barak's major tactical blunder was, however, that by not being able to make up his mind as to his red lines – for these kept changing – he only encouraged Arafat to persist in his refusal to negotiate. The Palestinian leader could always trust Barak to come forward with a new concession in order to break the deadlock. This was true until the moment when Arafat's refusal to budge, mainly on Jerusalem, brought the summit to its unhappy end.

In the final working session of the Camp David summit at the President's residence, Aspen, Mr Clinton made a last-ditch attempt to surmount the formidable hurdle that Jerusalem represented. To no avail. Arafat would not budge from his position and would not agree to a qualified Palestinian sovereignty on the Temple Mount – he was offered in the site a 'sovereign custodianship' that was free of any Israeli interference – or to anything that was not the unequivocal partition of the city. He was offered a capital in Arab Jerusalem (not just Abu-Dis, as all kinds of non-official back channels had suggested in the past) that would include some Palestinian quarters under full Palestinian sovereignty and the others under a more qualified Palestinian sovereignty. Arafat demanded the sovereignty of three-quarters of the Old City and rejected out of hand any bridging ideas such as a special regime, which I had the opportunity to defend throughout the summit, or the President's proposal, accepted by the Israelis, to divide the holy basin into two equal parts, the Christian and Muslim quarters to the Palestinians and the Jewish and Armenian quarters to the Israelis.

Members of the Palestinian delegation at Camp David used to say to their Israeli counterparts that Jerusalem and the Temple Mount, the issues that more than any others wrecked the summit and prevented an agreement, were 'Arafat's personal obsession', which they did not necessarily share.

How genuine was their critique of their leader is difficult to know, for being free of the burden of responsibility for making a historic decision on Jerusalem, they could allow themselves the luxury of sounding more rational and conciliatory. The truth of the matter is, however, that Arafat did not act in a political and cultural vacuum. Jerusalem and the Temple Mount were central components in the shaping of Palestinian nationalism and identity. Jerusalem may not be the most sacred city for Islam and during long periods of Muslim history it had indeed declined into obscurity. But the rise in the modern era of the new Crusaders, the Western imperialists and the Zionist infidels, and their drive to again assert themselves in Jerusalem helped reinvigorate throughout the Muslim world the memory and the spirit of Saladin, the Muslim hero who redeemed Jerusalem from the Crusaders in 1187.

Jerusalem acquired its contemporary weight in the Arab mind precisely as a reaction to the ambition of the Jews to return to it during the Yishuv years and to Israel's hold on the city in the aftermath of the 1967 war. The Mufti's leadership and the way he shaped Palestinian nationalism in the 1930s was essentially religious, for he understood that the Palestinian lower classes could not identify with an exclusively modern brand of secular nationalism. It was in this context that he turned Al-Quds and the Haram al-Sharif into the defining symbols of the Palestinian cause. Protecting the Muslim character of Jerusalem against the Zionists' sinister designs in the city, especially allegedly that of demolishing the Al-Aqsa mosque and building their Temple on its ruins, became a convenient platform for the mobilisation of the Palestinian masses, a device that proved its efficiency in the 1929 riots that were triggered precisely by Arab–Jewish clashes around the Temple Mount. The Prophet's ascension to heaven from Jerusalem (the 'Alissra Day') would from then on become a major celebration in Palestinian nationalism; it was even called the 'Palestine Day'.

As from the 1930s, the centrality of Jerusalem in the Arab reaction to Zionism's aggressive presence in Palestine also became part of pan-Arab, as well as Palestinian, mythology. Jihad and Al-Quds would be used almost as synonymous terms. Indeed, the battalions of the Muslim Brotherhood that fought in Jerusalem in 1948, and in which the young Yasser Arafat served as a militiaman, carried the name of 'Al-Jihad Al Muqades'.

The 1967 war clearly enhanced the role of Jerusalem in the Arab and Palestinian national and religious ethos. So much so that in a book of self-critical reflection following the Six Day War, a young Syrian intellectual, Tsadeq Jilal el-Azzam, questioned the sudden centrality that Jerusalem had acquired in the pan-Arab agenda. He believed that this was a most unwelcome return of the Arabs to a useless and anachronistic religious mythology. 'The struggle for the liberation of Palestine should not be epitomised in the retrieval of churches and mosques that only serve as an attraction for tourists,'[1] he wrote. Unwelcome, as el-Azzam put it, the issue of Jerusalem might have been. But it was nonetheless a central item in the Arab and Palestinian ethos which needed now to be addressed by Israel if an accommodation was to be reached with the Palestinians and through them with the entire Arab and Muslim world.

Nor was Arafat's obsession with Saladin an entirely outlandish preoccupation. It was embedded in the political and religious culture from which the Palestinian leader drew his inspiration. Saladin as the redeemer of Arab lands and the Muslim holy shrines in Palestine had been throughout a vital ingredient in the Palestinian national ethos. When in the 1930s the unstoppable expansion of the Jewish Yishuv triggered violent Arab resistance, it was to the memory of Saladin that their leaders resorted as a mobilising myth. It was then that 'The Day of Hitin' (the battle in 1187 where Saladin defeated the armies of Richard Lionheart and expelled them from Palestine) was established as an important celebration throughout the Palestinian community.

Arafat may not have been especially versed in the history of Islam or in Islamic religious doctrine but, as is frequently the case with Muslim leaders, he was keenly aware of, and always ready to instrumentalise, Arab

---

[1] 'Self-Criticism in the Wake of the Defeat', as analysed by Emmanuel Sivan, *Arab Political Myths* (Hebrew), Tel Aviv, 1988, pp. 85–6.

history and Islam's religious symbols. The rush towards the past is a salient characteristic of the Arab political discourse. As Edward Said had observed, this is an attempt to find refuge in the glories of the past instead of confronting with reason the difficulties of the present and the challenges of the future.

The leader of a supposedly secular national movement shaped along the lines of the Third World movements of national liberation of the 1960s, such as the Algerian FLN for example, Arafat remained nonetheless fully immersed in the religious imagery of his early years as a member of the Muslim Brotherhood in Cairo. His use of Islamic symbols was consistent throughout his speeches from Johannesburg to Gaza. Nor was it accidental that the regiments of his Palestine Liberation Army carried names with a clear religious connotation, such as 'Al-Aqsa', 'Hitin', 'Ein Jalut' (the victory over the Mongol invasion). There was simply no way that Arafat could bring himself to disengage from his self-image as a religious, not just a secular, leader in his quest for Palestinian statehood.

As a committed Muslim, he knew that Islam is fundamentally a political religion that admits no real separation from temporal concerns. It was, after all, none other than Ayatollah Khomeini who acknowledged that 'Islam is politics or it is nothing'. Hence Arafat would not accept a solution to the Palestinian problem that was strictly temporal and exclusively political. It needed to include, for example, the full and unconditional sovereignty over the holy places, first and foremost the Haram al-Sharif, where the Dome of the Rock is the architectural expression of Islam as a religion that supersedes and is superior to all other religions. The Jews' claim to a sovereign right in the Temple Mount on the basis of historical and religious links to the site was, as far as he was concerned, to be utterly excluded.

It was not just Arafat's positions throughout the summit, but his entire attitude to the negotiations, the bunker mentality with which he and his team came, that enraged the President and his staff. At Camp David Arafat destroyed with his own hands the unique, even intimate, relationship that he had developed with the American administration in recent years. I personally had the opportunity to warn Mr Arafat, in the course of a meeting at his residence at Camp David, where I came, together with General Amnon Shahak, to make up for Barak's obstinate refusal to meet the Palestinian leader. 'Your relations with the US', I told him in the presence of his entire team, 'are good, but skin deep. They will not survive the failure of Camp David.' It was indeed at that juncture that the United States' disenchantment with Arafat as a leader capable of making a historic compromise and bringing the conflict to an end started. For the first time since Oslo, the Americans started to have serious doubts as to whether he was a partner for peace. This divorce between the Palestinian leadership and the United States was to have devastating effects for the future of the peace process.

The Camp David proposals as formulated by Clinton in his meetings with the different negotiating teams – a Palestinian state in the entire Gaza Strip and 91 per cent of the West Bank in exchange for 1 per cent land swap in addition to a safe passage that would link Gaza with the West Bank, a division of Jerusalem that was not perhaps clear-cut, but included nevertheless a division of the Old City into two equal parts, a Palestinian 'sovereign custodianship' on the Temple Mount and no right of return for the refugees, but yes, the deployment of a massive global effort that would provide financial compensation to the refugees and facilitate their resettlement in the Palestinian state – might perhaps not have been the best deal the Palestinians could have expected. But nor was this the humiliating deal of 'Bantustans' and 'enclaves' they kept saying it was. How can a Palestinian state that includes the entire Gaza Strip, 92 per cent of the West Bank and a safe passage, under full and unconditional Palestinian control, to link them be defined as a state of Bantustans?

To some among the Palestinians, Arafat's rejectionism was reminiscent of a familiar pattern of behaviour of the Palestinian leadership ever since it confronted the Zionist movement. Nabil Amr, a minister in Arafat's Cabinet, was courageous enough to spell out his criticism in an article in *Al-Hayat-el-Jadida*, a mouthpiece of the Palestinian Authority, two years into the Al-Aqsa Intifada, that is, when it was becoming tragically clear that Arafat's abandonment of the political path had brought about the destruction of the very backbone of Palestinian society:

> Didn't we dance when we heard of the failure of the Camp David talks? Didn't we destroy the pictures of President Clinton who so boldly presented us with proposals for a Palestinian state with border modifications? We are not being honest, for today, after two years of bloodshed we ask exactly that which we then rejected. ... How many times did we agree to compromises, which we later rejected in order to miss them later on? And we were never willing to draw the lessons from our behaviour. ... And then, when the solution was no longer available, we travelled the world in order to plead with the international community for what we had just rejected. But then we learnt the hard way that in the span of time between our rejection and our acceptance the world has changed and left us behind. ... We clearly failed to rise up to the challenge of history.

*

An understanding of the abortive Camp David summit of the summer of 2000 can perhaps benefit from a comparison with the 1979 successful Camp David peace summit. The lack of trust between the leaders should not be given excessive weight. In both cases there was no trust between them. As with Barak and Arafat, throughout the first ten days of the 1979 summit, Sadat and Begin hardly met or spoke to each other. The degree of mutual resentment, sometimes even abhorrence, between the two leaders could hardly be concealed. Interestingly, in Camp David I Begin was manoeuvred into the position of Arafat in Camp David II: he was the one who feared an Egyptian–American trap (in 2000, Arafat was suspicious of an Israeli–American conspiracy and resisted it with a bunker mentality). Indeed, most of the American pressure was put on Begin and, as in Arafat's case, it was upon him that the Americans warned the blame would be put if the summit failed. And it was he who was given to understand that he would pay the price in terms of a deterioration of Israel's relations with America.

The American pressure was definitely a factor in Begin's decisions at Camp David, but it could not move Arafat from his unyielding positions. Both Arafat and Begin behaved as if they were entrenched, confined in a bunker, resisting to the bitter end an enemy onslaught. Drawing his metaphors from his experience during the Holocaust, Begin complained to the members of the Israeli team at the summit, 'It is beginning to feel like a concentration camp.' Neither Arafat nor Begin would initiate ideas or table proposals in search of a breakthrough. But the Israeli leader nevertheless left the summit a different man, one who had the courage to depart from his old archaic beliefs. Arafat, however, would confine himself to rejecting American and Israeli proposals without ever advancing his own counter-proposals. Unlike both Begin and Sadat, Arafat acted throughout the summit more like a politician than a statesman bent on looking for a solution and seeking a historical breakthrough. Sadat in Camp David I and Barak in Camp David II were more restless, far more creative. The two also shared a similar political predicament. They both operated as a front without a solid political rearguard at home. Indeed, the two lost the support of their Foreign Ministers during the summit. In the case of Israel, the present author had the privilege of being there to assume the practical functions of foreign minister. The case of Arafat and Begin was different. They both had their people and their political home front solidly behind them.

True, Begin, like Arafat, might not have been the most creative or flexible of negotiators, but he was surrounded by an excellent team of people who did not cease generating ideas and looking for a breakthrough. Moshe Dayan, Ezer Weizmann and Aharon Barak would always look for new ideas and possible compromises. And when the moment of truth arrived and Begin was required to take an agonising decision on the settlements in northern Sinai, he received a vitally crucial telephone call from the most hawkish of his ministers back home, Ariel Sharon, which encouraged him to dismantle them. The only telephone calls Ehud Barak would receive from Israel during the summit were those with the disheartening news about the disintegration of his coalition and the collapse of his home front.

Admittedly the conditions of the Israeli–Palestinian track and the issues at stake were different from those at Camp David I and clearly the manoeuvring space of the Palestinians was far more limited than that of Sadat when he negotiated the future of the West Bank. But the Palestinians refrained from using even the little space for compromise that they might have possessed. Whereas Begin was surrounded by men of compromise and generators of ideas, the immobile Arafat was flanked by mourners incapable of producing any new idea, launching an initiative that would break the deadlock, or challenging their leader for his adamant immobilism. 'I don't even know what is exactly my mandate in these negotiations,' the Israelis were once told by Saab Erakat, the Palestinian chief negotiator at the summit. The resignation of Foreign Minister Ibrahim Kamel in the middle of the summit in protest at what he believed was Sadat's move towards a separate peace agreement with Israel was one proof of both the tensions in the Egyptian delegation and the courage displayed by President Sadat in exploring new and bold ideas for a breakthrough. Notwithstanding some obvious differences in attitude between the old and the younger generation in the Palestinian team, when it came to the fundamental issues, the Palestinian delegation in Camp David II knew no dissent and posed no challenge to Arafat's impregnable positions, and therefore no reason existed for resignations or protests of any kind.

A fundamental difference between the two summits was the position and performance of the President of the United States. Clinton, his reputation tarnished by personal scandals, came to Camp David to save the record of his presidency when he no longer had much qualitative political time in his hands and consequently not much leverage on the parties. Carter was still in the middle of his presidency and was determined, if that was the price, to sacrifice a second term for the sake of peace. He also had at his disposal all the leverage he wanted to bring pressure to bear on the parties. And there was, too, a difference in performance. At Camp David Bill Clinton let himself be perceived by the parties as what Moshe Dayan would have cynically called 'a nice fellow in the ineffectual sense of the expression'. Notwithstanding the President's explosions of rage, mostly directed at Arafat, at no time during the summit could either the Israelis or the Palestinians see an irresistible American pressure being built up. Clinton had an extraordinary capacity to untie diplomatic knots; he uniquely combined the vision of the statesman with the skills of a negotiator capable of mastering the most minute details. Brilliant, passionate, humane and hard-working, proverbially patient, tolerant and good-humoured, always shunning confrontation and with his days at the White House numbered, Clinton was not a president who was capable of browbeating the parties. Carter had a bulldog-like persistence about him that was absent in Clinton's performance. Clinton did not lack Carter's Messianic zeal; but he lacked his capacity to intimidate, nor were he and his team capable of employing the kind of brutal manipulative tactics that the Nixon–Kissinger team had used in launching the peace process in the aftermath of the 1973 war, or those that would be used by the Bush–Baker tandem in the diplomatic arm twisting leading to the Madrid Conference in 1991. At Camp David, America looked like a diminished and humbled superpower, unable to assert its will.

The issues at Camp David I were indeed difficult and tough to crack, but always clearer and simpler than those at Camp David II. Which might help explain why President Carter could easily detect, at a fairly early stage in the summit, the contours of a possible agreement, the framework for a quid pro quo between the parties, and lead towards it with persistence and determination. At no time during Camp David II could Clinton see the precise outline of a settlement or the ideas that would bridge the gaps and rescue the summit from collapse. Carter could also clearly see the red lines of both Sadat and Begin. Clinton had no firm Israeli red lines to work upon, for these kept changing, to the embarrassment of the President, who could never confront Arafat with a final Israeli position.

None of the delegations at Camp David could claim to be free of blame for the collapse of the summit. But the deficiencies in the performance of the United States obviously had an extraordinarily negative effect. The President's team, from Secretary Albright through National Security Adviser Sandy Berger and Middle East envoy Dennis Ross, down to the most junior assistants, had all accumulated long years of invaluable experience. They failed not because they were ill-equipped for the task. The unique complexity of the problems at stake and the adverse effects of a presidency that was fading by the day, made them insecure and erratic in their tactics. The Clinton team did not hold the reins of the summit with authority. Rather than have it under their command, they kept changing the negotiating patterns to adapt them to the whims and constraints of the parties. As early as the first day of the conclave, and intimidated by the violent reaction of both Barak and Arafat, the American team withdrew its working paper where premises and guidelines for the negotiations were established, and left the summit to run itself without direction, without a compass, without leadership. A recent inside account offers plenty of evidence about the erratic way the American mediator handled the summit.[1]

Although it eventually developed into an attempt to force Israel to propose a better deal than the one that had been put together at Camp David, the Al-Aqsa Intifada did not start merely as a tactical move. It erupted out of the accumulated rage and frustration of the Palestinian masses at the colossal failure of the peace process since the early days of Oslo to offer them a life of dignity and well-being, and at the incompetence and corruption of their own leaders in the Palestinian Authority. The Intifada was also almost the inevitable consequence of a major mis-conception of Oslo, namely the notion that a kind of post-Westphalian phase was opened in September 1993, whereby the parties had already overcome the constraints of their respective mythologies, religious con-flicts and conflicting memories. The fallacy was embraced that from then on this was going to be a banal and mundane process of 'land for peace' that would be settled in a civilised way on the basis of an accepted code of international behaviour and through a 'reasonable compromise' between two political entities, both inherently interested in bilateral and regional stability.

But the creation of the Palestinian Authority did not eliminate or dilute the essence of the Palestinian national movement as a revolutionary enterprise which, if the political track failed to vindicate its aspirations, would again resort to armed struggle and to a strategy of war and regional instability.

From the moment Pope John Paul II left Israel in March 2000, that is, even before I came to Sweden for a discreet channel of negotiations with Abu-Ala, the Palestinians started their preparations once again to unleash the weapon of terror and violence. As early as 4 March 2000 Marwan Barghouti, the head of the Fatah militias ('Tanzim') in Ramallah and a future leader of the Intifada, could not have been more specific when he made it clear to a Palestinian newspaper, *Akhbar-el-Khalil*, that:

Whoever thinks it is possible to resolve issues such as the refugees, Jerusalem, the settlements and the borders through negotiations is under

---

[1] Clayton Swisher, *The Truth About Camp David: The Untold Story about the Collapse of the Middle East Peace Process*, New York, 2004.

a delusion. On these issues, we have to wage a campaign on the ground alongside the negotiations. I mean armed confrontation. We need dozens of campaigns like the Al-Aqsa Tunnel Campaign.

But it was Israel's withdrawal from Lebanon in June 2000 that served as a major incentive for the Palestinian Intifada. It certainly left a profound mark on Arafat's mind. He felt humiliated and embarrassed that he should negotiate border modifications with Israel when 500 Hezbollah guerrillas had forced Israel to withdraw to the international border in Lebanon. 'These are our disciples, we taught them and we financed them.' This was how Arafat referred to the Hezbollah in a conversation with me in Nablus on 25 June 2000, where he harshly criticised me for our precipitate pull-out from Lebanon. I could not fail to notice a sense of admiration and envy in the voice of the old warrior, a man still in uniform, who despised the notion that the national liberation of a people was something to be negotiated with the occupier instead of being achieved by means of military force and through a popular uprising. Armed struggle was his element. The same evening and in the same city, Nablus, driven and inspired by the example of the Hezbollah, Arafat would say to a grand gathering of Fatah youth, 'We are fighting for our land and we are prepared to erase the peace process and restart the armed struggle.' 'I am a general who never lost a battle,' he told me at the same meeting in Nablus, where I tried to convince him of the need to go to a negotiating summit at Camp David. He rejected the possibility that anybody, even the President of the United States, would expect him to engage in negotiations. 'I am a decision maker, not a negotiator,' he told me. In retrospect, I am not sure he was a decision maker either.

Arafat carried with him to Camp David his envy of the Hezbollah model. Israel's pull-out from Lebanon under military and guerrilla pressure obsessed him. In an additional meeting I had with him at Andrews air base in Washington a week later, he once again mentioned the Hezbollah example and told me that our pull-out from Lebanon had exposed him to domestic criticism for not following in the footsteps of his old disciples. At Camp David, or probably before, Arafat came to a decision that if the summit failed to satisfy his aspirations, he would emulate the Hezbollah way. The Lebanonisation of the struggle against Israel, he believed, would break the capacity of resistance of the Israelis. The lesson he drew from Israel's Lebanon defeat was that the Israeli people was worn out and riddled with doubts about its own capacity to sustain casualties in a low-intensity conflict. Seen from the perspective of the last four years of Intifada and of the Palestinians' appalling defeat, it would seem that Arafat was wrong once again.

Arafat never operated as a field marshal who plans military operations in detail and then issues specific orders for their execution. Instead, he offered the inspiration, he helped create the conditions, and he skilfully knew how to divert the popular rage away from him and from his incompetent and corrupt regime towards the occupation and the occupier. And, most important, rather than controlling or stemming the tide of a spontaneous uprising he preferred to ride on it, thus practically turning it into official policy. It was he who had encouraged the outburst of violence on the Naqbah Day of May 2000, thus undermining the Swedish secret channel of negotiations, and he later gave more than one indication that he would welcome a return to armed struggle if Camp David failed.

Mamduh Nufal, an adviser of his, quoted him to this effect in the *Nouvel Observateur* of 1 March 2001. His Minister of Posts and Communications, Imad Faluji, declared in a speech in a refugee camp in south Lebanon that the Intifada against Israel was carefully planned after the failed Camp David talks in July 2000 'by request of President Yasser Arafat, who predicted the outbreak of the Intifada as a complementary stage to the Palestinian steadfastness in the negotiations, and not as a specific protest against Sharon's visit to Al-Haram Al-Quds. ... The Palestinian Authority instructed the political forces and factions to run all materials of the Intifada.'[1] In a telephone conversation with Marwan Barghouti, the head of the Tanzim militia in Ramallah, in early August I was personally advised that if a settlement was not reached by 13 September, the day a unilateral declaration of Palestinian independence was presumably planned, the Palestinians would resume the armed struggle. As Nabil Shaath would put it later in a TV interview in London on 7 October 2000, what the Palestinians had in mind was a Vietnam or Algeria model of revolutionary war and negotiations at the same time:

> The option is not either armed struggle or negotiations. We can fight and negotiate at the same time, just as the Algerians and the Vietnamese had done. This is the reason behind the war of the Palestinian people with weapons, with Jihad, with Intifada and with suicide operations. ... Our people are destined to fight and negotiate at the same time.

Characteristically, Arafat all too willingly seized upon the fortuitous eruption of the Intifada following Ariel Sharon's visit to the Temple Mount on 28 September 2000, a visit that was conceived by the then chief of opposition more as an affront to a government willing to waive

---

[1] Imad Faluji is quoted in different sources, among others: Khaled Abu Toameh, 'How the War Began', *Jerusalem Post*, 20 September 2002.

Jewish sovereignty on the Mount than as an aggression against the Muslims, in order to extricate himself from a predicament he was incapable of solving. He gave an implicit green light to the uprising by doing what he frequently liked to do in such conditions: he left the country in the very first days of the Intifada in order not to have to assume responsibility. Only through the Intifada could he restore his and the Palestinians' international standing that had been so seriously eroded by the worldwide perception after the Camp David summit – a perception strongly enhanced by Clinton's finger-wagging at Arafat as chiefly responsible for the collapse of the summit – of an Israeli government ready for a far-reaching compromise facing obstinate Palestinian rejectionism. Arafat knew that Palestinian casualties played in his favour in world opinion and helped increase the international pressure on Israel. He therefore cynically martialled the harsh arithmetic of death to his advantage. The Intifada and the daily death toll of Palestinians allowed Arafat not only to mobilise the always vociferous support throughout the Arab world, and internationally turn the political tables on Israel, it also helped him stave off what was then an imminent peace package that President Clinton was planning to disclose by the end of September.

Designed by the American peace team in the course of the negotiations that Israelis and Palestinians continued to maintain throughout the months that followed the Camp David summit, the package was prepared along lines that were similar to those of the future Clinton parameters of 23 December 2000. It deterred Arafat precisely because it might have brought him closer to the moment of decision and compromise he was utterly unable to stand up to. Arafat had been portrayed by Clinton after the Camp David summit as a peace rejectionist. Now he pre-empted the possibility that a second peace package would undermine beyond repair his international legitimacy by slipping into the comfort of the role of victim and underdog secured for him by the Intifada.

Israel's disproportionate response to what had started as a popular uprising with young, unarmed men confronting Israeli soldiers armed with lethal weapons fuelled the Intifada beyond control and turned it into an all-out war. This was one more case in Israel's history where the overreaction of the military ended up defining the national agenda in terms that the politicians never planned. Nevertheless, the Intifada's resort to armed struggle and suicide terrorism was to have fatal consequences for the peace process. Incapable of defining attainable objectives for the Intifada and unable to offer the Israelis the temptation of a political horizon they could not resist, Arafat's desperately ambiguous and vague strategy only enhanced the drift to the right and even to the extreme right of Israel's public. The Hezbollah's objectives in Lebanon – Israel's withdrawal to the international border – were attainable if only because they were in line with the wish of the practical totality of Israeli society. But 'the end of occupation', the battle-cry of the Al-Aqsa Intifada, which in the Lebanese context had a clear meaning, was not in the Palestinian context a precise political strategy with a realistic chance of success. As Dr Yezid Sayigh put it in a brilliant critique of the Intifada – 'Arafat and the Anatomy of a Revolt' – the Palestinians failed to lay down concrete and attainable demands that the Israeli public could evaluate, just as it did those of the Hezbollah in Lebanon. The Israelis were left to assume the worst about Palestinian intentions, such as that they had never really intended to reach a settlement and that Oslo was for the Palestinians nothing but a strategic ploy aimed at doing away with the State of Israel altogether. Which is why opinion polls showed that two years into the Intifada only 20 per cent of Israelis believed that not even a signed peace agreement with the Palestinians would bring with it the end of violence and conflict.

But Arafat refused to take notice of the impact that the Intifada had on Israeli public opinion and politics. Through all my conversations with him I was struck, time and again, by the degree to which he did not grasp the depth of the shift in Israeli politics and public opinion. At a meeting in Cairo four weeks before the elections that brought about the downfall of our government and with it the demise of the peace process, he still dismissed my warnings that general elections under fire and suicide terrorism would end up bringing Sharon and the far Right to power, as sheer negotiating tactics. He was also still totally deaf to the sensibilities of Israel, for example when it came to the unconditional rejection by her political system of his demands on refugees. When I told him, at another meeting this time in Gaza, that his insistence on the right of return at such a late stage of the negotiations would not only doom to failure our attempt to reach a settlement but could under no conditions be accepted even by parties on the left of the government, he responded by drawing from his pocket an old excerpt from the English edition of *Haaretz*, where it was said that about 50 per cent of those who immigrated from Russia to Israel were actually not Jewish at all. 'If you can admit them, I am sure you will have no problem admitting our refugees as well. Your people will understand that ...' he told me with an air of certainty and self-conviction.

As it turned out, the Intifada could not usher in a negotiated settlement precisely because, lacking attainable objectives, it raised the expectations of the Palestinians to unrealistic heights. Not an Israeli negotiator, but Hani al-Hassan, an old-time associate of Arafat, was forced to acknowledge that not only was the Intifada devoid of clear strategic objectives, it also raised the expectations of the Palestinian masses to such heights that it became impossible for their own leaders to meet. The Intifada, he wrote, 'obliges our negotiators to raise the level of demands in the negotiations' in a way that made it out of the question for Israel to accept them.

Arafat might not have been a major strategic thinker and his miscalculations led eventually to his failure to go down in history as the founder of an independent Palestinian state, but his behaviour was not necessarily irrational. More a politician than a statesman, Arafat had throughout put the interests of the PLO and that of his own personal rule before the Palestinian cause. Arguably, since he always identified the cause of his people with his own person as the embodiment of their national will, he believed that safeguarding the interests of the PLO and his own personal rule was tantamount to promoting the national cause.

This can best be exemplified by his attitude to the two Intifadas. In the first he was stunned to discover how a grass roots, democratic uprising was unleashed in the territories without any PLO initiative or guidance. The Intifada was therefore seen by him as a threat not only to Israel's rule but also to the political supremacy of the PLO. More than a peace move by Arafat and his men in Tunis, Oslo was a desperate attempt by the Palestinian leader to recover control of the Palestinian cause and agenda and, in the process, sideline the local leadership and cut short what was clearly a democratic struggle for national independence. Reaching those objectives was so urgent and vital to Arafat that his delegates in Oslo were manifestly far more flexible, to the degree of even being negligent, than the local leaders who represented the Palestinians in the official talks in Washington.

The same rationale prevailed in Arafat's attitude to the second Intifada. Although there were plenty of indications that he had been for some time pushing for a shift of strategy from negotiations to violence, he probably did not initiate the uprising with specific orders. But as much of the popular rage was directed at the incompetence of the Palestinian Authority, and indirectly at Arafat himself, he preferred to surf on its waves rather than become its victim. The PLO, or rather its new embodiment, the PA, was now in a state of political bankruptcy with the peace process, the very *raison d'être* of the PA, no longer inspiring any confidence. Riding the crest of a popular uprising against the Israelis was the best way Arafat and his acolytes could think of to save their collapsing rule. Again, as in the first Intifada, leading the uprising was for Arafat a move of political survival, not the insight of a statesman with a clear strategic objective.

Arafat's irresistible penchant for the politics of brinkmanship and his tendency to swim with events rather than lead them, and frequently ride on the back of a tiger, cost his people and its national cause dearly. His misjudgement in the autumn of 2000 and his strategic blunders were of real historic proportions, for they threatened to throw his people back into the tunnel of history, as far away as ever from statehood and from a life of freedom and dignity.

Admittedly, however, Camp David might not have been the deal the Palestinians could have accepted. The real lost opportunities came later on. The negotiations continued after Camp David. More than fifty meetings between the parties and the American mediators, both in Israel and in the United States, took place throughout the summer and autumn of 2000. This was a sequence of round tables that culminated on 23 December in a meeting in the Cabinet room adjacent to the Oval Office, where President Clinton presented to an Israeli delegation presided over by this author and a Palestinian team headed by Yasser Abd-Rabbo his final parameters for a peace treaty between the parties. The parameters were not the arbitrary and sudden whim of a lame-duck president. They represented a brilliantly devised point of equilibrium between the positions of the parties as they stood at that particular moment in the negotiations. The peace package consisted of the following principles:

– A Palestinian sovereign state on 97 per cent of the West Bank and a safe passage, in the running of which Israel should not interfere, that would link the Gaza Strip, all of which, clean of Jewish settlements, would be also part of the Palestinian state, to the West Bank. Additional assets within Israel – such as docks in the ports of Ashdod and Haifa – could be used by the Palestinians so as to wrap up a deal that for all practical purposes could be tantamount to 100 per cent territory. Needless to say, the Jordan Valley, the mythological strategic asset sanctified by generations of Israeli generals, would be gradually handed over to full Palestinian sovereignty.
– Jerusalem would be divided to create two capitals, Jerusalem and Al-Quds, along ethnic lines. What is Jewish would be Israeli and what is Arab would be Palestinian.
– The Palestinians would have full and unconditional sovereignty on the Temple Mount, that is, Haram al-Sharif. Israel would retain her sovereignty on the Western Wall and a symbolic link to the Holy of Holies in the depths of the Mount.
– With regard to refugees, it was stated that the Palestinians would have the right 'to return to historical Palestine' but with 'no explicit right of return to the State of Israel'. They could be admitted to Israel

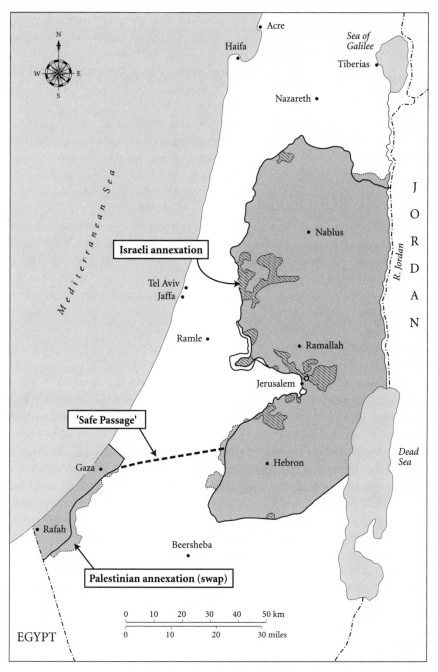

N

W ← → E

S

• Acre

Haifa •

Sea of Galilee

Tiberias •

Nazareth •

J O R D A N

M e d i t e r r a n e a n   S e a

Israeli annexation

• Nablus

Tel Aviv •
Jaffa •

Ramle •

• Ramallah

Jerusalem ○

R. Jordan

'Safe Passage'

Gaza •

• Hebron

Dead Sea

• Rafah

Beersheba •

Palestinian annexation (swap)

0	10	20	30	40	50 km

| 0 | | 10 | | 20 | | 30 miles |

EGYPT

Clinton's peace plan, 2000

in limited numbers and on the basis of humanitarian considerations, but Israel would retain her sovereign right of admission. Refugees could be settled, of course, in unlimited numbers not only in the Palestinian state, but also in those areas within Israel that would be handed over to the Palestinians in the framework of land swaps (the Palestinians were supposed to receive an Israeli territory equivalent to 3 per cent of the surface of the West Bank). In addition, a multi-billion-dollar fund would be put together to finance a comprehensive international effort of compensation and resettlement that would be put in place.

– In matters of security the President endorsed the Palestinians' rejection of the concept of a completely 'demilitarised state' and proposed instead the concept of a 'non-militarised state' whose weaponry would have to be negotiated with Israel. A multinational force would be deployed along the Jordan Valley to replace the IDF. (The President recognised the need of the Israeli air force to co-ordinate with the Palestinians the use of their air space, as well as the IDF's necessity to have three advance warning stations for a period of time.)

Clinton presented his parameters as a 'take it or leave it deal'. It was not the ceiling, explained his envoy to the region, Dennis Ross, it was the roof. It was not supposed to be the basis for further negotiations but a set of principles to be translated by the parties into a peace treaty. The President also presented the delegations with a deadline. He wanted an answer of yes or no by 27 December.

The Israeli government met the deadline. Our decision, at the height of the Palestinian Intifada, in the midst of sweeping opposition on the part of the army – it was almost tantamount to a *coup d'état* that the Chief of Staff, General Mofaz, should have gone public to criticise the government's endorsement of the parameters as an 'existential threat to Israel' – and strong reservations from the opposition and public opinion, was a daring decision of a government (then already a minority government) of peace that stretched itself to the outer limits of its legitimacy in order to endorse positions its opponents labelled as suicidal, and as being an affront to Jewish values and history.

But Arafat lingered. He refused to respond. As usual, he resumed his journeys throughout the world as if he were the travelling Emperor Hadrian, in the hope of evading any decision: another meeting with Mubarak, one more trip to Ben-Ali, another trip to Jordan, a further meeting of the Arab foreign ministers, dozens of calls from world leaders from the President of China to the Grand Duke of Luxembourg urging the Palestinian leader to seize this last opportunity, to grab the historic moment. Time passes. Clinton's presidency is fading away. The Intifada runs wild. The days of the Barak government are numbered. And Arafat lingers. The phone calls continue to pour in from all corners of the world and, ten days after the deadline, he still does not answer. Instead, he asks to come to Washington to see the President. There, at the White House, in a typical Arafat ploy, he said to the President, 'I accept your ideas,' and then he proceeded to tick off a number of reservations, each of which completely vitiated those ideas. He never formally said no, but his yes was a no.

Both the Saudi and the Egyptian ambassadors in Washington, Bandar Bin Sultan and Nabil Fahmi, who came to encourage Arafat, in the name of their respective governments, to accept the President's parameters as a last opportunity for peace that should not be missed, were dismayed at the behaviour of the Palestinian leader. And so was the Saudi Crown Prince Abdullah. He was said to be shocked that Arafat had wasted such an opportunity and that he had lied about the President's offer on Jerusalem. Arafat's rejection of the peace parameters was a 'crime' not only against the Palestinians but against the entire region, concluded the Saudi ambassador in a long interview published in the *New Yorker* on 24 March 2002.

While escorting his guest to the door, Clinton could see from the windows of the Oval Office the swearing-in stage for incoming President George W. Bush on Wisconsin Avenue across from the White House. This was melancholic enough for a president fanatically in love with his job, but he still had to listen to Arafat impudently telling him that he was committed to reaching an agreement under his waning presidency.

A week later I had the chance to make it clear to Arafat at a meeting in Cairo, arranged by President Mubarak, that Israel was ready even at such a late stage to negotiate, but only in order to translate the President's principles into an agreement, not in order to change the parameters. This was what he should have understood when he agreed to send his delegation to Taba.

The Taba talks, where I had the privilege of leading the Israeli delegation, were indeed very practical and detailed. Maps were exchanged and a serious attempt to negotiate was made by the two parties. With the new American administration almost demonstratively uninterested in, and indifferent to, the talks, the parties were denied the bait and the incentives that a robust American involvement could offer, but they were also free from the cumbersome negotiation through a third party. It was the businesslike spirit of the Stockholm talks being resuscitated. There were moments in Taba when we all believed that an agreement might be possible, that the differences could perhaps be bridged.

Political constraints and electoral concerns would later cause Barak to dismiss Taba as a meaningless exercise aimed to placate the Israeli Left. But the truth of the matter was that, in real time, he did his utmost to encourage the Israeli team to reach an agreement. I was personally surprised to receive the blessing of the Prime Minister when, on the eve of my departure for Taba, he called to express his support for the things I said in an interview to *Yedioth Aharonoth*. Among other reflections I advanced in that interview, I said,

> A normal state is not supposed to settle beyond its legitimate borders. We have created a state, we have been admitted to the UN, we strive to have orderly relations with the international community, yet we still continue to behave as if we are a Yishuv. The entire peace enterprise of this government is aimed at leading the nation to opt, once and for all, between being a state or a Yishuv.

Barak's attitude to Taba was genuinely expressed on two occasions. One was when he allowed me to open, in Taba, a secret channel with Abu-Ala in order to explore freely the possibility of bridging the gaps and come to a last-moment breakthrough. The second occasion was when he made a radical shift in his position and virtually agreed to the concept of equal swaps of land. He always thought that Israel could not accommodate the blocs of settlements within the constraints of the Clinton parameters of between 3 and 6 per cent of the West Bank; she needed, he insisted, 8 per cent. But for the first time he was now ready to pay with an 8 per cent swap by leasing to the Palestinians the necessary amount of land within Israel. The Palestinians, however, rejected Barak's ideas when I tabled them, and the secret channel with Abu-Ala did not bear fruit.

The reason the Palestinians dismissed the proposal of an equal 8 per cent swap, admittedly based partly on the principle of lease, lies in their rejection of the very rationale behind the concept of land swaps. A guiding principle of Israel's territorial proposals throughout the negotiations, and of the Clinton final peace parameters, was that border modifications were aimed at accommodating some, certainly not all, of the new demographic realities that were created since 1967. Israel proposed in Taba physically to dismantle, or hand over to the Palestinians for the use of returning refugees, more than one hundred settlements. But those that formed coherent blocs adjacent to the 1967 line were supposed to remain as such under Israel's sovereignty. However, as the maps that the Palestinians produced at Taba showed, our interlocutors totally rejected the very concept of blocs and referred to the settlements more as isolated outposts that would have to be linked separately from each other to Israel. Israel could not accept such an approach for it contradicted her entire peace strategy, and the Palestinians not only knew it but have always accepted it. All the back-track channels, either official or freelance, ever conducted by Israelis and Palestinians before Taba and after, were based on the acceptance by the Palestinians of the principle of settlement blocs.

Another myth about Taba was advanced by Mr Yossi Beilin, the Minister of Justice at the time and a member of the Israeli delegation. Encouraged by his reports about the progress he said he had been making in the working groups on refugees with his counterpart Nabil Shaath, I allowed him, against the advice of the Prime Minister, to continue the negotiations of his team with the Palestinians even when the entire Israeli delegation had to interrupt the talks following a Palestinian terrorist attack that shocked the country. Some progress was presumably made in the working group on refugees mainly on a preamble that would describe an agreed narrative on the origins of the refugee problem, a component of moral compensation that was always deemed to be vital for a settlement. But no agreement was reached about the narrative, nor was any headway made on two other vital questions. 'Only' two questions remained open for further discussion, reported Mr Beilin later. These were the number of refugees that would be admitted to Israel and whether or not Israel would endorse the 'principle' of the right of return. These two 'minor' questions were exactly the same ones that had remained open since the Swedish secret track and they stayed so after Taba.

The Palestinians' lack of interest in a deal in Taba was made patently clear when Yossi Sarid, probably the most emblematic 'dove' of Israeli politics and now a member of the Israeli delegation, proposed a Solomonic solution to the differences still pending between the parties on Jerusalem: the Temple Mount, the Western Wall, the Old City and the holy belt leading from the Old City to the Mount of Olives. Had the Palestinians agreed to stick to the letter and the spirit of the Clinton parameters there should have been no reason for such differences to exist, but Mr Sarid thought nevertheless that an attempt should be made to reach a compromise by going the extra mile towards meeting the reservations of the Palestinians. 'Let us split the burden between us,' he suggested; 'two of the four issues pending will be solved according to your position, and two according to ours, which is, as you know, respectful of the Clinton parameters.' But to no avail. The Palestinians remained unimpressed.

Mythologies apart, Taba did not allow an agreement, not because of the fact that the Israelis' qualitative political time was a desperately diminishing asset, but because the Palestinians treated the parameters as non-committal, and insisted on changing and challenging them on each and every point. For us the parameters represented the outer limits of our capacity for compromise as Israelis and as Jews; for the Palestinians it was a non-binding platform, 'a prison', as Abu-Ala put it to me, they could not operate within. 'The boss does not want an agreement,' was Abu-Ala's comment to my colleague Gilead Sher when the Palestinians refused to make use of the helicopter the Israelis had put at their disposal in order to travel to Gaza to consult Arafat on whether to rubricate an agreement or a Declaration of Principles on the basis of the outline of our talks. This was one more case in a long and unhappy series of Arafat's almost built-in incapacity to make decisions.

It might simply be the case that the Palestinian leader did not want to strike a deal with what looked to him a moribund Israeli government that was indeed about to suffer a major electoral débâcle. He might also have felt the need to know more about the new Bush administration before he made such a historic leap. The conventional wisdom throughout the Arab world at the time was that George W. Bush's was to be a friendlier White House to the Arab cause than Clinton's. Arafat might have thought that a Bush administration would allow him to have an even better deal than the Clinton parameters.

If such was his rationale, he might have had a point with regard to the Israeli government, but he was utterly wrong with regard to the Bush administration. George W. Bush has broken records in American friendship with, and support for, Israel. Never since Jimmy Carter had advocated a 'homeland for the Palestinians', thus inaugurating America's active involvement in peacemaking on the Palestinian front as well, was the Palestinian question so marginal to America's foreign policy, and the Palestinian leadership so sidelined and humiliated, as during the Bush administration.

However, even in the case of the Israeli government Arafat proved to be short-sighted. An agreement rubricated with Barak would have established the legal and political foundations of a peace agreement that neither the American administration nor the international community could have ignored. And assuming that even with such a peace agreement in its hands the Labour Party had still lost the elections, the new Israeli government would have found it hard to overlook such a historic understanding between Israelis and Palestinians on all the core issues of the conflict. One needs to recall in this context that Benjamin Netanyahu came to power in 1996 amid a virulent campaign against the illegitimacy of the suicidal Oslo accords, but was eventually forced to endorse them once in office.

The weakness of the Barak government was of course due in great part to its own political blunders. But Arafat should also have wondered whether he would ever be able to reach an agreement with a 'strong' Israeli government when he so much excelled in weakening and eventually destroying his peace partners. Yitzhak Rabin paid with his life when he went for a dramatic breakthrough while Palestinian terrorism continued unabated, exposing him to Jewish extremists. In 1996 Shimon Peres was defeated amid an unprecedented wave of Palestinian suicide terror. And Ehud Barak suffered the greatest electoral débâcle in Israel's political history because the voters saw the Intifada as Arafat's counter-proposal to his peace initiative. To weaken and undermine Israeli left-wing governments, as he consistently did, and then refuse to make an agreement with them because they were 'weak' is a pattern that might keep the Palestinians in a permanent impasse. Ariel Sharon's policies of scorched earth in the territories have been proof for Arafat that he who sows a wind ends by reaping a whirlwind.

Arafat was a victim of his own illusions. He had a tendency to attribute to himself characteristics of a brilliant strategist and distinguished military man, 'a general who never lost a war', as he liked to introduce himself. But the truth is that as a strategist, of all people he proved his failure again and again. He always pushed his luck to the point where he lost all his achievements and what appeared to be a chance for reasonable victory ultimately became a disgraceful defeat. With Arafat, brinkmanship had no brakes; it was the art of bringing both his people and the Israelis to the edge of the abyss and beyond.

I will never be able to erase from my memory my feelings in Taba. Here, I wrote in my diary, an outline of a reasonable settlement was lying on the table. One would have had to be blind not to understand that these were also the last days of the Israeli Left in power, maybe for many years. An Israeli team consisting of Yossi Sarid, Yossi Beilin, Amnon Shahak and myself as its head cannot be repeated in years to come. In other words if an agreement was not to be reached then, there would be no agreement at all, and both Israelis and Palestinians would be thrown into a wilderness of blood, despair and economic decline. Nevertheless, I discerned no sense of urgency or missed opportunity among my Palestinian friends.

Zionism, at least up to 1948, would never have functioned this way when faced with what is always and inevitably an imperfect settlement. It always acted with its back to the wall, which is why it was blessed with the capacity for pragmatic decision making. There are two essential reasons that can explain the pragmatic wisdom of Zionism at decisive crossroads. One is the fact that, in contrast to the anti-Semitic cliché about 'Jewish power', Zionism was always the national movement of a weak Jewish people lacking support, a persecuted people decimated by holocaust and genocide, a people that in case of failure at the time of taking a decision might be annihilated. The Palestinians, the presumed weak side of the conflict, never acted out of lack of choice as Zionism did. Until 1948 the Zionists certainly excelled in their capacity to mobilise international support and market their case. The Palestinians, however, stumbled on every road block, avoided no mistake and displayed no savoir faire in the field of diplomacy and public relations. They always seemed to take the wrong option.

After the Six Day War, however, the balance of forces in the war on public opinion clearly changed. Rarely – if ever – is history familiar with a similar case of a disparity between the high degree of international support enjoyed by a national movement and the poor results of such a support. In fact, after that war the overwhelming international support for the Palestinian cause almost became a handicap to the degree that it could be said that the Palestinians very nearly 'suffered' from an excess. At every junction of historical decision making, the international community gave them – and this is certainly true with regard to the Arab world – the sense that they were entitled to expect more and could therefore avoid a decision. The international pampering of the national Palestinian movement is unparalleled in modern history and, no less important, was at vital crossroads of the conflict an obstacle to a settlement. For it was frequently interpreted by the Palestinian leadership as an implicit encouragement to persist in its almost built-in incapacity to take decisions and find instead satisfaction in Israel's decline into the position of a state put in the dock of the tribunal of international opinion.

The second difference between Zionism and the Palestinian movement refers to the ethos. Zionism was a social revolution, an attempt to change the patterns of existence of the Jewish people, no less than it was a journey into the soil of the Land of Israel. Though never abandoning wider territorial dreams, it would not have occurred to Ben-Gurion to delay the establishment of the Jewish state because he would not have access to the Western Wall or the Temple Mount. The positive ethos of building a new society was supposed to compensate for the poverty of the territorial solution. The Palestinian leadership failed its people primarily due to the lack of will or capacity to process a positive founding ethos that would enable them to assume a reasonable compromise. The Palestinian leadership under Arafat did not prove that it was prepared to discard, once and for all, the paralysing narrative of the underdog and the victim.

It is a matter of tactics and of ethos. The Zionist leadership prior to 1948 looked for solutions, not for justice, that is for a deal that would respond to its own brand of justice. The Palestinian national movement has been more about vindication and justice than about finding a solution. It therefore never possessed the capacity to make a positive decision. Seen from the perspective of the Palestinian tragedy of refugeeism, the loss of a homeland, long years of dispossession, homelessness and exile, and the deprivation of personal and national rights, the Palestinian ethos of vindication is fully understandable. However, peace is frequently not about justice but about stability. The tragedy of the Israeli–Palestinian conflict stemmed from discrepant historical rhythms. The history of the Jews' modern national movement, again mainly up until the establishment of the State of Israel in 1948, had been characterised by realistic responses to objective historical conditions. The Palestinians have consistently fought for the solutions of yesterday, those they had rejected a generation or two earlier. This persistent attempt to turn back the clock of history lies at the root of many of the misfortunes that have befallen the peoples of the region.

Is it possible that Arafat was someone who was capable of launching a process but was incapable of concluding it? Is it possible that all he tried to do in Taba was hook the new administration – another fatal miscalculation, for they all thought in the Arab world that Bush Jr was a replica of Bush Sr, while it turned out that he is an updated Reagan who champions his own Manichaean view of international relations – and create a sense of continuity with the Clinton ideas? Is it possible that Arafat, who claimed he dreamed of superseding all these interim agreements, was at the same time simply incapable psychologically of ending the conflict? He, whose whole life was characterised by ambiguities, double talk, closing a door yet always leaving it half open, could simply not bring himself to bring down the curtain on this eternal conflict. Is it possible that the old guard of the Palestinian movement that spent a lifetime trading in international forums with the Palestinian tragedy in a way that succeeded in building the case against the wicked Israeli occupier in the law court of international opinion and put Israel in the dock, is incapable of producing the transition to state and institution building, exactly the same kind of accusation made by Nabil Amr in his article in *Al-Hayat-el-Jadida* and implicit in Yezid Sayigh's brilliant essay 'Arafat and the Anatomy of a Revolt'?

One should not underestimate the dilemma of Arafat. Since, for all our difficulties and the practical collapse of our political home front in the course of the negotiations, we, the Israelis, never lost our confidence in our capacity to resolve by democratic means and through the established institutions the internal earthquake that would have inevitably followed a deeply divisive peace agreement. Arafat lacked such tools, nor did he ever try to develop them. A major reason for his incapacity to reach a reasonable compromise with Israel was precisely that the Palestinian Authority under his leadership was unwilling to develop a positive ethos of democracy, civil society, economic development and education. Instead, an old-style autocracy based on a negative ethos of confrontation was created. National cohesion was built around constituent values of radical 'Palestinianism', 'refugeeism' and Islam that left no room for compromise. Arafat's was a regime, as Edward Said has so eloquently described it, based on fear, and on a repressive apparatus of government, a regime devoid of a minimal conception of democratic accountability or free debate. Arafat's responsibility for this appalling state of affairs can be gauged by looking at Abu-Mazen's performance. Occupation was of course a major obstacle to the development of Palestinian life. But for Arafat the occupation was the pretext for, not the cause of, his dictatorial practices. With occupation still in place, road-blocks still obstructing the vital arteries of Palestinian life, and settlements still in expansion, Abu-Mazen has nonetheless engaged in a difficult, yet admirable, process of democratisation. Abu-Mazen seems to be determined to co-opt all the Palestinian factions into the institutions of democracy.

Arafat's rivals were outside the PLO – Hamas, Jihad and a plethora of left-wing splinter groups – not within it. Peace for Arafat, if it were to respond to vital Israeli requirements, could automatically mean a civil war. In fact, Fatah understood that particular dilemma only too well, by explicitly admitting that that was exactly the reason they had rejected the Clinton parameters. To them, as they put it when trying to explain their rejection on the organisation's website, 'the parameters [were] the biggest trick' and one that meant moving the conflict from a Palestinian–Israeli dispute to 'an internal Palestinian–Palestinian conflict that will destroy the Intifada'.

For both Israelis and Palestinians war is a cohesive enterprise, and peace is bound to bisect the nation. The Israelis believed that they could solve the internal divisions by democratic means, which allowed us in the Barak government to opt for decision – inevitably divisive – instead of seeking a (paralysing) wide national consensus. The Palestinians knew only too well that they lacked such tools of democratic decision. Hence Arafat pushed for an impossible settlement, the exact parameters of which were never clear to him either, that would allow him to preserve the widest national consensus possible, the unity of the entire Palestinian family. But a settlement acceptable to Hamas was not a settlement Israel could accept, just as a settlement subscribed to by the Israeli far Right was not the kind of peace that the Palestinians could be expected to endorse.

But the major weakness in our peace enterprise was political and domestic. Ours was the case of a front without a home front. On the way to Camp David, I wrote in my diary:

> Sunday, 9 July, on the night flight from Tel Aviv to New York. I am troubled, and I wish the reason were only the enormity of the task ahead. The government is falling apart, and I wonder during this tense flight who it is exactly that we are representing in this gruelling political undertaking. ... We are approaching our moment of truth like a front line without a home front. ... The latest rumours have been that in addition to Minister Nathan Sharansky of the Russian party 'Israel Ba'alia', and Yitzhak Levy of the National Religious Party, who have already announced their resignation from the government, the 'Shas' party of the Sephardi traditionalists also intends to follow suit. Upon landing in the US, I hear that David Levy, the Foreign Minister, has announced that he will not be attending the summit. ... The rumour about 'Shas', meanwhile, has become fact. They have announced their resignation. The government that started off as a government for 'everyone' has shrunk into its most basic foundations, the traditional Left.

The lesson from Barak's experience – in a way it was also the case of Rabin – is that however grandiose and enlightened the peace vision of a leader might be, he would be doomed if he is not sustained by a careful domestic political organisation. Of course, the Israeli peacemaker is always condemned to break national unity and split the nation if he wants to conclude a difficult agreement. Consensus may sometimes be the negation of leadership. The Israeli case – and indeed, this is also the Palestinian predicament – proves that, tragically, war unites and peace divides. Much will always then depend on the calibre of leadership. A leader should not be a trivial mind, a hostage of the state apparatus and bureaucracy. But he should not ignore them either. Inspiration alone is not sufficient for a bold peace enterprise. A sensible balance is always needed between inspiration and political manoeuvring. A foreign policy needs to have domestic foundations.

Barak was dreadfully awkward in putting together these vital foundations for peace. Inspiration in leadership does not mean ignoring *realpolitik*. An inspired leader does not have to be a political adventurer. Barak clearly failed to legitimise his policy in public opinion and, no less important, within the polity and the government apparatus including the army. Barak's was clearly the case of a leader with a constantly diminishing constituency. By the sad end of our voyage to the boundaries of the peace process he was an authentic example of what Bernard Baruch, the American financier and presidential adviser, described as a leader without a following: 'A political leader must keep looking over his shoulder all the time to see if the boys are still there. If they aren't still there, he is no longer a political leader.' The line of 'boys' following Barak was becoming thinner and thinner by the day.

A legendary military hero, it was especially surprising that he should have been so utterly incapable of co-opting the army bureaucracy to his peace endeavour. This was to have devastating effects in the early phases of the Intifada, when the army freely interpreted the instructions of the government and responded with excessive force to Palestinian attacks, thus fuelling the cycle of violence. The army conducted its own independent war as if it were trying to overcome the frustrations it had accumulated during the first Intifada. The loose control of politicians over the army is a built-in weakness and inconsistency in Israel's political system.

Nor were the Palestinians immune to serious problems on their home front. For years they had been yearning for a Palestinian state, and when the moment of truth arrived they met it in a condition of deep internal divisions and rivalries that made it even harder for them to take a decision. An intra-Palestinian crisis, which stemmed from a battle for the post-Arafat succession, developed between the Gaza group of the younger generation (Muhamed Dahlan, Muhamed Rashid, Hassan Assfour) and the old guard represented by Abu-Mazen and Abu-Ala. The Palestinians were far more impressed by the Israeli proposals than they liked to admit in public or than some of the later commentators were ready to acknowledge. For they all felt that they were nearing the final-status agreement and they believed that whoever brought about the settlement would become Arafat's successor.

This dramatic internal battle within the Palestinian camp erupted during the Stockholm secret talks in May 2000. The Palestinians grasped that the Israelis were making far-reaching proposals and concessions, but they were unable to endorse them precisely because of their internal disputes. Abu-Mazen, who had initiated the Swedish track in the first place, felt that he was now being bypassed in the talks, so his people leaked them to the *Al-Hayat* newspaper in a way that built resistance in the territories to the presumed concessions that the Palestinian delegation was making at Harpsund. We, the Israelis, were aware of this disastrous development and we made efforts to co-opt Abu-Mazen and convince him not to torpedo the process. His answer was that he needed time 'to stabilise things'. But then came the idea of going to a summit in Camp David that enraged Abu-Mazen, who now said that he must continue to oppose the process. And throughout the summit he displayed a mixture of hostile indifference with a fundamentalist ideological attitude that was hardly conducive to a reasonable negotiating atmosphere.

Months later, during the Sharm el Sheikh international summit of early October, where a concerted attempt was made by President Clinton, Secretary General Kofi Annan, President Mubarak and the EU representative Javier Solana to coax Arafat into stopping the Intifada and allowing a resumption of the peace talks, I asked Abu-Mazen directly about his unhelpful approach. His answer was that we, the Israelis, were negotiating 'with the wrong people', as if it was our responsibility to appoint the Palestinian delegation for the talks. At the moment of truth of this desperately long and erratic negotiating process, when an Israeli government was ready for a historic deal, the Palestinians, and in a way the Americans and the Israelis as well, failed to address what was clearly a major obstacle: the internal Palestinian squabbles and the premature but nevertheless fierce struggle for succession.

> We are going from here into a catastrophe. You will forge an alliance with Hamas and we shall go into a paralysing national unity government with the Israeli Right. When we meet again this will be with the West Bank replete with settlements. Make no mistake: this is the defeat of the peace camp in Israel for many years to come.

This was how I addressed my Palestinian counterpart Saab Erakat, on the last night at Camp David, in the presence of Mr Clinton and his entire team gathered in Aspen, the President's residence, when it was clear to all that we were not going to reach an agreement. For Arafat continued to be adamantly opposed to all the President's proposals on Jerusalem as a basis for prolonging the summit and pursuing the negotiations.

Unfortunately, I was not wrong in my prediction. The peace that eluded us became the prelude to the bloodiest and longest confrontation between Israelis and Palestinians since the 1948 war. All the tools of peacemaking were broken, and today, four years after that last-ditch attempt to salvage the Camp David summit, the parties stand once more in front of the debris of the peace process in an unconvincing attempt to inject it with a new lease of life. One more peace plan, an additional initiative, another road map ... Will they succeed now where so many have failed in the past? Or will the Quartet's road map follow in the footsteps of all previous peace plans into this graveyard of peace initiatives that is the Israeli–Palestinian tragedy?

XI   The Politics of Doomsday

[We need] one authority, one law and one democratic and national decision that applies to us all.

Abu-Mazen, upon assuming the office of prime minister,
29 April 2003

We eliminated all the terrorist squads except one. The problem is that this one consists of 3.5 million Palestinians.

A high-ranking Israeli officer,
January 2004

... there was a dangerous erosion in our domestic and international position. Everything was falling apart in Israel.

Dov Weissglass, Sharon's Chief of Cabinet, on the effects of the Intifada,
8 October 2004

You have developed among you a dangerous Messianic spirit. ... I have learnt from my own experience that the sword alone offers no solution. ... Israel will not survive as a democratic state if she continues being a society that occupies another nation.

Ariel Sharon, presenting his Gaza plan to the Knesset,
25 October 2004

The Arafat–Sharon encounter was an exercise in history's irony, a trip back in the time machine to the core of the conflict. In contrast to what could have been anticipated, this was not a meeting between two strong leaders capable of rising to the challenge of extricating their nations from the grip of conflict and producing a historic breakthrough. Sharon and Arafat were the sad embodiment of an archaic political orthodoxy devoid of a vision for the future.

Societies and peoples condemn themselves to ruin if they fail to build a culture of fair compromise when settling conflicts. The loss of the middle ground, the lack of the culture of compromise and the absence of agreed patterns for settling differences have invariably been the prelude to war. With regard to the Israeli–Palestinian conflict, the principle of compromise was now gone, the middle ground had been fatally wounded, and the so-called peace camp in Israel had been severely diminished and morally undermined by Arafat's rejection of its peace platform. Both the discourse and the tools of peacemaking went into the fire of the bloodiest confrontation since 1948 between Israelis and Palestinians. The two nations returned to the fundamentalist roots of the issue, and to the complete demonisation of one another. They went back to a primordial struggle, to believing that the salvation of one could only be founded on the destruction of the other. For the Palestinians, the Intifada has developed into a struggle aimed at ending the occupation through the shaping of a constituent myth of national and Islamic independence.

The Israeli Right's crude blunder lies in its assumption that it can 'solve' the Palestinian issue and domesticate a national movement by means of a military crackdown. In fact, the mistake lies not just in confusing preponderance with omnipotence, and in assuming that over-whelming firepower is enough to win a war against a rebellious national movement, or in the seemingly technical question of whether or not a military solution can be applied to an amorphous body like the Palestinian Authority, but rather in a more fundamental question. The problem is whether, even after a 'victory', Israel would be able to dictate a political settlement as it sees fit. And this is where the tragic error of Ariel Sharon lay, at least during his first government. Zionism's major strategic success to date was that it *forced* its enemies to agree to make peace; but it could not force the *terms of peace* on them. Contrary to Sharon's assumption, a military victory will definitely not spare Israel the high and heavy price of a settlement.

Leaders in Israel's history who succeeded in creating a wide national consensus around them did it mostly by leading the nation through historic accomplishments. Such was the case of the founder of the State of Israel, David Ben-Gurion, of Menachem Begin, the architect of the peace with Egypt, and Yitzhak Rabin, the hero of the Six Day War who later paved the way for the mutual recognition between Israel and the PLO, and made peace with Jordan.

Ariel Sharon's case represents an entirely different phenomenon. The wide national support he managed to elicit at different crossroads in his controversial career as a military man and politician was born out of his ability to manoeuvre through periods of despair that he himself had often been instrumental in generating in the first place. His was a unique talent to produce political blind alleys as a consequence of which his erroneous, frequently destructive moves were seen as an 'inevitable evil', the 'only option left' in an otherwise desperate situation. The support for Sharon was always the result of the hopelessness and despair he himself had generated. Somehow the national consensus around him invariably looked like a collective voyage into the abyss. Sharon's career has frequently defied Napoleon's definition of the leader as 'a dealer in hope'. He dealt with despair, hopelessness and fear.

Such was the case with the invasion of Lebanon in 1982, when an entire nation followed him into an adventure that all were led to believe was inevitable, the last resort. His gamble ended by sinking Israel into a quagmire of blood, bereavement and destruction for more than eighteen years. And such was the situation when he embarked on an initiative to dismantle the settlements in the Gaza Strip that he himself had created in the first place. He was directly responsible for the calamitous network of settlements spread throughout the territories and in the midst of the dispossessed Palestinian population. In the spring of 2001 he was elected on the back of an overwhelming national consensus to the position of Israel's Prime Minister in order to respond to Arafat's macabre flirtation with suicide terrorism and conduct the dirtiest war in Israel's history, albeit a fully justified one in the eyes of the overwhelming majority of the nation. Terrified by what looked like unstoppable Palestinian terrorism, the people supported Sharon's war of targeted killings and practical reoccupation of the territories as a legitimate campaign of self-defence. But Sharon had a strategic objective that went well beyond that of legitimately protecting his fellow Israelis from the Palestinians' own brand of pathological terrorism. He demolished and pulverised the Palestinian Authority, the product of the vilified Oslo accords, with the objective of changing by military means what many continue to see as the unchangeable compelling necessity of creating a Palestinian state along the 1967 borders and dismantling the bulk of the settlements he had himself created. This gap between the people's perception of the objectives of Sharon's wars and his real intentions was already there during the war in Lebanon, where Sharon led the people to perceive the conflict as a legitimate move of self-defence while he had in mind a wider strategic objective: to reshape the entire political map of the region, to change the Lebanese leadership and to do away altogether with the political challenge posed by Palestinian nationalism.

The popularity of Ariel Sharon was often that of the prince of opacity and fog, the master in the tactics of political and military deception. Moreover, in both cases – Lebanon in the 1980s and now in the Palestinian territories – he tended to create such an intractable maze that 'salvation' came through a mounting popular outcry for a unilateral disengagement, a precipitated escape, a pull-out without a settlement – in short, a policy of scorched earth. Sharon is the first prime minister since Oslo who did not aspire to solve Israel's conflict with the Palestinians, something that in his own twisted and tortuous way even Netanyahu had tried to do with the Hebron and the Wye agreements. Sharon's current endorsement of the concept of a unilateral political process, as reflected in both the Gaza disengagement scheme and in his attempt to define Israel's permanent borders with the construction of a security fence ('the wall') leads one to the conclusion that he does not seek written agreements with the Palestinians. He has still to prove that he has a strategy of conflict resolution and that as a statesman he has finally outgrown his attitude as a general when violence was his method of 'resolving' contradictions.

Generally, and in almost every situation, Israelis love national unity governments. They enable them, and primarily their leaders, to avoid the schism and torment involved in confronting the unbearably tough and divisive decisions facing the country.

It was typical behaviour on the part of the Labour Party to succumb to Shimon Peres's lust for power and rush to join Sharon's National Unity government in March 2001. That government had only a military strategy and no political platform whatever. Instead of serving as an opposition fighting for an alternative peace policy, the party defeated the motion I personally presented in the Central Committee: to stick to the peace policy of the Barak government and resist the temptation of the cosmetic power it was offered in Sharon's government. But Labour preferred to go, without any soul searching, from being part of the most daring political voyage since Oslo – the voyage we undertook as a government – to battling over portfolios in the Sharon government, which, in advance, assumed that the Barak team, as Mr Peres himself had claimed, 'went too far in its concessions'. The Labour Party turned its back on its own political audacity while in office and now endorsed the groundless political assumption of Ariel Sharon that the volcanic eruption of rage among the Palestinians could be calmed down by another interim settlement.

From the moment the Palestinians saw the Promised Land placed before them during the last phase of the negotiations under the Barak government, and in the light of the explosive nationalistic atmosphere permeating the Palestinian camp throughout the Al-Aqsa Intifada, it had become utterly inconceivable for the Palestinians to consider returning to the framework of interim agreements. Sharon's assumption, now shared by his new partner Shimon Peres, that the Islamic and nationalist mythological aspirations that were unleashed by this Palestinian War of Independence could be quelled through one more interim agreement was utterly unsustainable. It was totally far-fetched to expect that the Palestinians would accept a deal where Israel would give away a slice of land in exchange for security, a security that Arafat could provide only by cracking down on his allies from Hamas and Jihad, something he had refused to do even when the Clinton parameters for a final settlement were offered to him.

The Sharon-Peres policies were utterly unsustainable also because of Arafat's style of leadership. Alexandre Ledru-Rollin's revealing affirmation during the 1848 Revolution in Paris, 'I've got to follow [the masses], [for] I am their leader,' perfectly expresses Arafat's own style of leadership. He would never risk a civil war, he would always shun confrontation with his rivals; his political intuition would always lead him to be in tune with the national mood, never against it. Violence, Hamas violence included, was for him a legitimate expression of the national will, of which he saw himself as the major interpreter, the exclusive embodiment. And in any case he regarded Hamas's violence as a major strategic tool of the Palestinian cause he would not undermine, so long as it did not directly challenge his personal rule.

Arafat was no Ben-Gurion who transformed the fanatic militants of the Irgun, and even Lehi, into politicians. He was no state builder who draws the line and disciplines a rebellious opposition as Ben-Gurion did when he ordered the shelling of the *Altalena*, the ship importing weapons and fighters from France for the Irgun, with Begin aboard. But of course, in spite of Ben-Gurion's attitude to the extremists as 'Jewish Nazis', the Revisionists – unlike Hamas that dreams of a theocratic Islamic Palestine – were essentially committed to a democratic Jewish state and never really believed they could establish an alternative Jewish society in Palestine.

Abu-Mazen, who was imposed on Arafat by the international community as the Prime Minister of the Palestinian Authority, was quick to understand and to share Ben-Gurion's predicament. But like Arafat, he also avoided the showdown with the extremists that Ben-Gurion did not hesitate to go for. Abu-Mazen acknowledged that for an orderly Palestinian national movement to inspire vital international trust there should be, as he put it in a speech to the Palestinian parliament upon assuming the office of prime minister, 'one authority, one law and one democratic and national decision that applies to us all'. But he was either too weak to challenge Arafat's way, or simply unwilling himself to risk civil strife in order to enforce his national vision.

It was a reflection of the poor state of the peace process and of the fatalistic loss of public confidence in any kind of accommodation with the Palestinians that the second elections of the Sharon era, on 28 January 2003, were about anything but peace plans. In what amounted to an overwhelming vote of confidence in Sharon's hardline military response to Palestinian terrorism, the elections ended in a landslide victory for the

Prime Minister. The peace process was simply irrelevant in the electoral campaign. The Israelis have allowed their leaders to reduce their foreign policy platform to that of punishing and retaliating against those who, to paraphrase Ernest Bevin's definition of his foreign policy in 1951, would not allow them to take a ticket at Tel Aviv Central Bus Station (Bevin spoke of Victoria Station) and go anywhere they 'damn well please' without getting blown up on the way. Very few now believed in a negotiated peace. And Labour, which for the past two years had served as the fifth wheel of Ariel Sharon's chariot, was hardly credible when it postured as the standard-bearer of the peace process.

But it is also clearly the case that Israel's absurdly proportional electoral system is no longer capable of producing workable majorities and efficient governments. It only mirrors the kaleidoscopic constitution of a fragmented society. The always arduous task of coalition building in such conditions almost invariably produces governments that are paralysed by internal political equilibriums. Sharon's second government is a typical case in point. Rather than serving as a vehicle for the resolution of the Palestinian conflict, or any other internal conflict for that matter, the political system is so dysfunctional that it becomes the major obstacle to conflict resolution. The government is incapable of responding to the popular yearnings for peace. For, regardless of party loyalties and according to most studies, the overwhelming majority of Israelis would support a peace settlement that is based on the Clinton parameters – two states, withdrawal from territories, massive dismantling of settlements, two capitals in Jerusalem – but they trust neither their political system nor, of course, the Palestinian leadership to come to an accommodation on that basis. Which may explain the results of a poll conducted in 2002 by the Steinmetz Centre for Peace at Tel Aviv University indicating that, convinced of the incapacity of their political system to produce solutions, 67 per cent of Israeli Jews would support an American effort to recruit an international alliance that would coax the parties into endorsing such a settlement.

But was America under President George W. Bush ready to assume this sort of responsibility? Definitely not.

The Left in Israel has been defeated twice, once in the polls and again through the vindication by President Bush of the Right's strategic vision. The Israeli Left traditionally maintained that only through a settlement with the Palestinians could Israel reach a viable reconciliation with the Arab world and establish a reasonable system of peace and security in the Middle East. The Right conveniently relegated the Palestinian dilemma to the fullness of time. It promised 'painful concessions' to the Palestinians, but only after the strategic threats emanating from the 'rogue' states in the region – Iran, Iraq – had been neutralised. The preference that President Bush has given to the Iraqi situation, clearly relegating the Palestinian issue to a secondary position, was seen by Mr Sharon and his right-wing coalition as a defeat of the Arab thesis and a vindication of their own policies.

ABC – 'Anything But Clinton' – seemed to have been President Bush's attitude to the legacy of the Clinton administration on most domestic and international issues. This was particularly the case with the Israeli–Palestinian track. Probably nothing expresses better this change of attitude than Colin Powell's instruction to the officials in the State Department, as soon as the new administration took over in January 2001, no longer to make use of the term 'peace process'. This now much vilified Clintonian, naïve Middle Eastern jargon was to be superseded by an entirely different language and a distinctive approach.

President George W. Bush embarked on a presumptuous grand strategy, a titanic enterprise aimed at dismantling the Iraqi tyranny, restructuring the Middle East, knocking down Al-Qaeda and helping democracy put down roots throughout the Arab world. It is in the context of this ambitious, all-engulfing and in many senses fallacious undertaking that Mr Bush expected to see the emergence of a solution to the Israeli–Palestinian conflict. Baghdad and Jerusalem were supposed to be connected vessels. An Arab–Israeli peace was meant to emerge almost as an inevitable by-product of an American victory in Iraq.

It is a challenge to common sense to link an Israeli–Palestinian peace to regime change in Iraq, let alone to a solution of the most fundamental problems of the Arab and Muslim world. 'Victory' in cultural wars and in those against terror is always an elusive affair. Mr Bush should have known that an Israeli–Palestinian peace should not be allowed to wait until victory is declared, because there might be no such thing.

America's plan of bringing democracy to the Arab world on the wings of squadrons of F-16s and on the tails of Tomahawk missiles was from the start a dangerous miscalculation. The Middle East has moved in the wake of the Iraq war from stability to uncertainty and the Arab world remains as far away as ever from democratic norms of governance. The regional balance has been upset, but no alternative architecture of peace and regional stability has been put in place. America's credibility as an honest peace broker throughout the region has been mortally wounded. Nor has its fall-back plan for the peaceful democratisation of the Middle East – the broader Middle East strategy – been any more successful or been acclaimed more warmly by the Arab world than the project of democracy through war. Democracy is not a *project* one devises and implements with rigid timetables; democracy is a *process* and the Arab world will have to go through it with hardly any short cuts.

For short cuts may lead to abrupt transitions from the secular dictatorships now prevailing throughout the entire Arab world to Islamic democracies. The Algerian case in the early 1990s may be a relevant reminder. The free elections that were then allowed by the military ushered in a resounding victory for the Islamic Front (FIS) and hence an invitation for the army once again to take over, revert the verdict of the polls and install a military regime. The powerful emergence of Islamic options in Iraq in the wake of the collapse of Saddam Hussein's secular dictatorship is a lesson that would not go unnoticed by regimes throughout the Arab world.

None of the major endemic problems of the Arab and Muslim world has a military solution. Nor, of course, is the Israeli–Palestinian tragedy susceptible to a solution that is not diplomatic and political. The lesson from Iraq and from Israel's war with the Palestinians is that the exercise of political and diplomatic skills, and the forging of international and regional alliances around a legitimate objective, are more vital than sheer military capacity for tackling complex political situations. It would be dangerously naïve to believe that the exercise of power and the capacity to intimidate are unnecessary. But they will always need to be backed by reasonable compromises, to be reached through diplomacy and negotiations.

In many ways Iraq has become the battleground for the future of the entire Middle East. For the major question has now become whether President Bush is only a leader for war or an architect of a new regional system of peace and stability. There can be no escape from the conclusion that such a new order needs to pass through a solution of the Arab–Israeli conflict. One does not have to second the cynical discourse of the Bin-Ladens and the Saddam Husseins, and of many other much more benign figures throughout the region according to whom all the ills of the Arab world stem from Israel's occupation of the West Bank and America's support for Sharon's repressive policies, in order to accept that the Palestinian problem is a major cause of regional instability and a comfortable platform for mass hysteria throughout the region. It certainly serves the Arab rulers as a convenient pretext for the diversion of attention and energies from vital domestic concerns.

Contrary to what the Israeli Right and the neo-conservatives around President Bush would have liked us to believe, the necessity, if not the centrality, for the solution of the Palestinian question for the wider problems of the Middle East remains unchallenged. The real test of

America's leadership, therefore, once the war in Iraq had ended, Syria had presumably been 'disciplined' and a formidable American military machine had been deployed on the Iranian border, lay in whether President Bush was willing or able to bring Mr Sharon and the Israeli Right to their moment of truth with regard to the Palestinian problem. In other words, was President Bush ready to impress upon Mr Sharon the need to move to the implementation of the 'painful concessions' he had been promising to make and, if it was a bluff, to call it?

After all, the immediate effect of the war in Iraq should have created improved conditions for the reactivation of the Israeli–Palestinian peace process. The concern of the Arab regimes for their stability in its wake and their fear of Islamic terrorism combined with American pressure produced better regional conditions for any attempt to create an all-Arab envelope of active support for an Israeli–Palestinian peace than those that existed when Bill Clinton invited the parties to Camp David. Clearly, the Saudi peace initiative, and its eventual endorsement by the Arab League at its Beirut summit in the spring of 2002, were closely linked to the effects of September 11 and the Iraq war on the Arab regimes.

The launching by the United States and the other members of the 'Madrid Quartet' of the road map for an Israeli–Palestinian peace created, for a moment, the illusion that the Middle East might have been witnessing a repetition of the logic of the first Gulf War. Then, the same coalition that made the war came to Madrid, under resolute American leadership, for an international peace conference on the Middle East. However, President Bush did not follow in the footsteps of his father who, precisely because he knew how to build a coalition for war, could also forge in its aftermath a solid international alliance for peace. Neither a coalition builder nor a political architect, George W. Bush proved to be as maladroit in his post-war strategy as he was diplomatically awkward in preparing for the war.

Does this mean that the President abandoned the road map and brushed aside the Palestinian issue altogether? Not necessarily. He had publicly committed himself to advancing his 'vision' of a two-state solution to the conflict and was obliged by his European allies to pursue the process. But he did it the White House way and not the State Department way. This meant working on the road map *with* Sharon, not *against* him. For a while such an attitude kept the road map alive as a broad, albeit not strictly binding, framework for peace within which 'things' happened, some confidence-building steps were taken, summit meetings were even held and a semblance of progress was created. But all this fell short of the level of resolve, commitment and arm twisting that was required to make this road map – whose inconsistencies, vague assumptions and built-in fallacies make it an unrealistic road to peace – a binding platform for peace.

The truth of the matter was that none of the parties was politically ready to give the road map a real chance. Four years into the Intifada and with Arafat as ambiguous as ever in his attitude to terror – or to making peace for that matter – it was becoming evident that no reliable Palestinian political force was left to make peace with. The Palestinian institutions that could secure an orderly return to peace negotiations and stability were in shambles, practically dismantled by war. The escalating violence in the Palestinian territories degenerated, in the wake of the Iraq war and the formation of Sharon's second government, into an all-out dirty war between Israel and Hamas that served the purposes of both. Neither Hamas nor the newly established right-wing government in Jerusalem was keen to see a credible revival of the peace process. Daily Israeli incursions into the Hamas strongholds in Gaza with their appalling toll of civilian casualties, the targeted killing of Hamas leaders from Sheikh Yassin to his successor at the head of the movement, Abd-el-Aziz Rantisi, and Palestinian terrorist suicide attacks against the civilian population in Israel were all the reflection of a macabre alliance between two sides for which a ceasefire would have meant facing political choices they were unwilling or unable to make.

In spite of the appointment of a Palestinian prime minister – first the ill-fated Abu-Mazen and then the astute political survivor Abu-Ala – further reform of the Palestinian Authority was bound to falter in the face of the continuing violence, and Arafat's unyielding resistance to any attempt to curtail his power and transfer portions of it to his ministers. Neither Ariel Sharon nor Yasser Arafat shed tears for the failure of reform. For the Israeli Prime Minister the call for reform of the Palestinian Authority has been a comfortable pretext for avoiding taking tough decisions on a negotiated withdrawal from the territories and the dismantling of settlements. For the Authority's President, 'occupation' had been his ultimate excuse for failing to undertake reforms. When Arafat agreed 'on principle' with an initiative – the need for reforms is a case in point – it invariably meant that he did not have the slightest intention of carrying it out.

Nor was Hamas especially interested in allowing the reforms to succeed, for these were linked to a road map to peace that the organisation despised and rejected. Rather than allowing the shattered Palestinian Authority to regain the trust of the public and recover its international credibility, the ambition of Hamas was to speed up its demise and eventually take its place.

The Palestinian case is one more reminder of an important fallacy to which Mr Bush has subscribed. The real, and certainly the immediate, choice in the Arab world is not between dictatorship and democracy but between secular dictatorship and Islamic democracy. With the collapse of the Palestinian Authority into lawlessness and banditry, and the shattering by Israel of Arafat's secular apparatus of government, it was the Islamic option that was gaining ground and filling the vacuum in the Palestinian territories. The Palestinian Authority and Mr Arafat's personal rule were clearly being displaced in the hearts and minds of the Palestinian masses by the fundamentalist Hamas. Never especially competent, the Palestinian Authority's institutions had virtually collapsed and its security apparatus had been severely shaken, if not practically dismantled; it certainly could not be relied upon effectively to curtail the terrorism of Hamas and Islamic Jihad, both of which have gained in popularity among the Palestinian masses not only for being, unlike the PA, incorruptible, but also for bearing the brunt of Israel's attacks and leading the terrorist war of attrition against its civilian population.

Nor even within Fatah, Mr Arafat's party, had a tolerable chain of hierarchical command been maintained throughout the Intifada. Fatah militias such as the Martyrs of Al-Aqsa and Tanzim conducted their own independent war against Israel as the only way they knew to vie for political supremacy in the Palestinian street against Hamas. In such conditions free elections in the Palestinian territories could either result in a victory for Hamas or in a considerable increase of its political power in a way that could pose a major challenge to Arafat's personal rule.

Too susceptible to procrastination and evasion by the two sides, the road map for a Middle East peace was stillborn. Both Palestinians and Israelis paid it nothing but lip service with only one objective in mind: not to be seen by the United States as the party responsible for its subversion. Having obtained from America the best of all possible worlds – the elimination, even if temporary, of major regional military threats that had haunted Israel for years, the destruction of Saddam Hussein's rogue regime, the disciplining of Syria, the build-up of pressure on Iran, a licence to confine Arafat in his headquarters and discard him as an interlocutor, and a green light to bury unceremoniously whatever remained of the spirit and the letter of Oslo – Sharon had no particular reason to risk alienating one of the friendliest American presidents ever to sit in the White House. As to the Palestinians, they could certainly not claim to have received any special boost to their cause from the Bush administration. But they nevertheless knew that confronting America – the only power capable of delivering Israel or at least putting effective pressure on it – by turning down yet another presidential peace plan would serve no useful purpose.

Neither Israelis nor Palestinians even started to implement the road map's most primary provisions. The Palestinians did not crack down on terrorism and the Israelis dragged their feet when it came to removing the so-called 'illegal' outposts, let alone when addressing the need to stop the expansion of the 'legal' settlements. The fatal symmetry between terrorism and settlements that was born with the Oslo accords and was eventually to wreck them was the same that subverted the road map from the first moment.

The road map shares with the defunct Oslo process some of its major fallacies. They both assume that peace between a dispossessed, desperate nation in a state of revolt and an occupying force driven by the claim of historical rights and a longing for total security can be built on the inevitably diminishing asset of mutual trust. Both peace plans, therefore, contained no binding third-party mechanisms for monitoring and enforcement. It is likewise utterly unrealistic to expect the parties, particularly the Palestinians, genuinely to engage once again in a process that leaves wide open the precise contours of the final settlement. The road map, just like Oslo, thus became a standing invitation for the parties to dictate the nature of the final deal through unilateral acts, such as the expansion of settlements by the Israelis and the wild campaign of suicide terrorism and armed uprising by the Palestinians. Clearly, salvaging the chances of peace required much more robust international assistance, even pressure and coercion, than was envisaged by the road map, or that which President Bush was ready to exercise. The American way – the supervision of the process by remote control and without a task force on the ground – was clearly inadequate.

It has not been uncommon throughout history for national movements to split in order to be able to reach a pragmatic solution to their aspirations. Zionism is certainly a case in point. The Palestinians will sooner or later have to share the same predicament. The question is when and in exchange for what. Clearly, however, the bait of the road map's first stage – the removal of a few scattered outposts and Israel's withdrawal to the positions she held prior to the start of the Intifada – was not enough for the Palestinians to justify a civil war.

Not even the bizarre idea reserved for the second stage of the road map, of a Palestinian state with 'temporary borders', could be seen as especially enticing by the Palestinians. They already had such a 'state' in the form of the Palestinian Authority. It is inconceivable that the Palestinians would agree to repeat the experience if the parameters of the final settlement were not agreed upon in advance. The temporary borders looked to them like a trap, and they rightly suspected that it was Sharon's intention to interrupt the process once the provisional borders were decided and never go beyond that stage. A 'temporary state' could not, in any case, offer the popular legitimacy needed for an uncompromising war on Hamas and Islamic Jihad. Such legitimacy can emerge only if and when the Palestinians are convinced that Islamic terrorism is no longer a response to Israel's strategy of occupation but an obstacle that needs to be removed on the way to a final settlement with dignity.

Political platitudes apart, Sharon and Arafat both had their own particular objectives, and these did not coincide with the road map. Sharon's hidden agenda, which he has been harbouring for years, remains unchanged. The sterilisation of the Palestinian national movement, which he has always seen as a major strategic, even existential, threat to Israel, and the confinement of a Palestinian homeland within scattered enclaves surrounded by Israeli settlements, strategic military areas and a network of bypass roads for the exclusive use of the Israeli occupier, remain, in broad lines, his grand design. He does not seek the annexation of the territories to Israel, for this would inevitably lead to an apartheid state where the nature of Israel as a Jewish state would be lost for ever. He would rather agree to an independent Palestinian state, provided, of course, it is downsized and militarily encircled by Israel, than risk putting in jeopardy the Jewishness of Israel.

Ariel Sharon is wrong, of course, if he believes that he can trivialise the Palestinian problem by turning it from a major national conflict into a unresolved border dispute. For even if such a Palestinian state with temporary borders as is envisaged by the road map is eventually created, it would follow in the footsteps of the Palestinian Authority and revert to a revolutionary strategy the moment it realised that its minimal requirements for a final settlement were not met.

Arafat, just like his nemesis Sharon, did not believe in the road map either. Nor did he share, of course, its provisions about the need to introduce democratic reforms in the Palestinian Authority. He succumbed to international pressure and agreed to appoint a prime minister, but he remained as adamant as ever in refusing to transfer to the minister of the interior any authority over, or control of, the security forces. Even when confined to the debris of his encircled headquarters in the Mukata in Ramallah, Arafat continued to be the centre of power, the superior and practically unchallenged authority, the almost mythological embodiment of Palestine. The road map was a trivial issue to him, who had seen so many peace plans in the past melt away when confronted with the inalienable rights of the Palestinians and the deviating objectives he himself had set for his disinherited people. The real issue, as far as Arafat was concerned, was resisting, displaying determination and resilience, sticking against all odds to his positions, those that formed the hard core of the Palestinian ethos he so fully believed he embodied, and waiting for the moment when the conditions would again work in his favour.

He was not blind to the heavy price that his people was paying for his unwillingness to change his ways, settle for a compromise and assume a positive ethos of reform, democracy and human and economic development. But Arafat's was the soul of a fedayeen, not that of a statesman or a state builder. He saw himself leading a war of attrition, not a political process. Much of the price paid by the Palestinian people during the Intifada was the responsibility of Arafat himself. The *rais* allowed the street and grass-roots organisations to create a state of lawlessness, anarchy and sheer banditry. Even the local leaders of the Intifada, people like Marwan Barghouti and Hussein e-Sheikh, lost control in favour of criminal gangs. The degree of collapse of the Palestinian Authority was such that in Gaza, where for all practical purposes an independent entity emerged, Dahlan and his men boldly challenged Arafat's rule. Amos Harel and Avi Isacharoff wrote in their exhaustive study of the Intifada of a 'Dahlanistan' in Gaza.

But Arafat did not despair. He drew comfort from the terrible ordeal suffered by the Israelis and he did not think for a moment that he was losing the war. Israel's economy was in decline – indeed, a Bank of Israel report published in March 2004 calculated the losses of the Israeli economy during the Intifada at about forty billion shekel, not including defence expenditures – the country's international isolation was growing and Jewish immigration had practically ceased. Not only was the entire world community now convinced of the need for Israel to withdraw to the 1967 borders, but the overwhelming majority of Israelis had finally come to terms with such conditions for a settlement. Arafat knew that this was mainly due to the impact of the Intifada on the Israelis and to Zionism's defeat in the most important battle of all, the demographic race. He also believed that the idea so dear to him of an international solution to the conflict was gaining ground. Time, Arafat was convinced, was definitely on the Palestinians' side.

George W. Bush's departure from Clinton's Middle East strategy and from his personal commitment to the solution of the Arab–Israeli conflict affected the Syrian track as well. It took some time and no small wavering for Syria to adapt herself, albeit as always in her own oblique and ambivalent manner, to the new conditions created by the Iraq war. Israel and the United States, however, failed to respond.

Syria's defiant attitude to the American accusations, once the war ended, that she sheltered fleeing Iraqi leaders after having actively supported them during the war, and the provocative response from

Damascus to the implicit American threats that Syria might be the next in line to bear the brunt of America's rage were either acts of folly or a calculated exercise in brinkmanship, probably the latter.

American accusations were anything but baseless. Before the flare-up in Iraq, Syria was already on America's list of states supporting terrorism. For many years Damascus has been host to a plethora of terrorist organisations from Hamas and Islamic Jihad to Hezbollah. And during the war in Iraq there were indications that not only did the Syrians facilitate the passage of Arab volunteers to Iraq, but they also transferred military equipment from their territory to Saddam's forces. In a deliberate disregard of America's request, Damascus refused to seal her border with Iraq. If this were not enough, 'Tishrin', the Syrian regime's mouthpiece, asked that the International Criminal Court should judge the American leaders 'as war criminals, equal in rank to the Nazi war criminals'. Syria's behaviour has led some in the American administration to adopt the view that Damascus's strategy was that of helping turn Iraq into a new Lebanon, where terrorist attacks and guerrilla tactics would undermine America's occupation.

The Syrian attitude, of course, is not inconsistent with the hardline nature of the Ba'ath regime, probably the last secular ideological system in the Arab world. Syria has always seen herself as the standard-bearer of the Arab cause against 'Western imperialism and the Zionist conspiracy'. Under Hafez al-Assad, she developed into a Middle Eastern version of North Korea, an immobile economy and society ruled by a hermetically closed and disciplined political system resting on two central pillars, the party and the army. But Hafez al-Assad, precisely because his formative experience was the disastrous and humiliating defeat in the Six Day War, tended to be cautious and calculating. He would not lend himself easily to political or strategic adventures. The Israelis and the Americans knew throughout that he actively supported Hezbollah attacks against Israel, but Assad would never admit it publicly.

Bashar al-Assad inherited his father's paranoid attitudes, narrow vision and confrontational strategies, but without the prudence and astuteness that characterised the latter. The young President has proved so far to be a disappointment to those who expected him to engage in a double strategy of internal reforms and a foreign policy of peace and regional stability. Instead, he sometimes looked and sounded like the outspoken ideologue of philosophies of confrontation and vulgar anti-Semitism. Such was his speech in the presence of Pope John Paul II in Damascus. He also made no secret of his active support for Hezbollah as 'a legitimate movement of liberation'. More than being the leader of a new Syria, a member of the club of promising young Arab leaders like King Abdullah

---

of Jordan, King Muhammed VI of Morocco and the ruler of Bahrain, Issa Bin Salman el-Halifa, Bashar has behaved so far as the hostage of the Old Guard inherited from his father.

But the picture may nevertheless be more nuanced and less monolithic. Until very recently, the Syrian regime seemed to be engaged in a double strategy that did not preclude an accommodation with Washington. If Bashar was doing everything to irritate the Americans, he was at the same time showing bursts of co-operation that signalled to them that he could be a valuable ally for the US in the region. In the aftermath of 9/11 the Syrians helped locate and even arrest key figures in Al-Qaeda. It was the Syrians who arrested Mohammed Haydar Zammar, a German citizen of Syrian descent, who had recruited Mohammed Atta, the ringleader of the 9/11 hijackers. The Syrians co-operated in additional ways with the American war against terror, seemingly even helping to foil an Al-Qaeda-planned attack on American forces in the Gulf. And there was, of course, also Syria's vital vote for Security Council Resolution 1441 that allowed the US a much needed diplomatic achievement on the way to its onslaught on the Iraqi regime.

Syria was not, of course, inviting an American invasion, nor did such an invasion seem probable. Rather, the Syrians, whose aspirations have always been to perform as the defiant champions of pan-Arabism, were now trying to occupy the vacuum of leadership in the Arab world, which was going through one of its gloomiest moments in recent history. Many saw the easy defeat of Saddam Hussein combined with the complacent behaviour of Arab leaders as a Naqbah (disaster) comparable only to the Naqbah of 1948, which resulted in the creation of the State of Israel. In those hours of Arab humiliation, Syria aspired to appear as the only one attempting, however ambivalently, to redeem Arab honour.

As in the case of North Korea's defiant nuclear policies, Syria is inviting the Americans to a dialogue, not an invasion. They would expect such a dialogue to lead to the restitution of the Golan Heights to Syrian sovereignty, and to the legitimisation of her special status in Lebanon. The Syrians believed that the risk of not bowing unconditionally to America's diktats was worth taking because even a victorious hyper-power like the US cannot allow herself the luxury of invading Arab countries one after the other. They also know that, the split in the international community notwithstanding, Iraq was a legitimate target. Neither international nor American opinion will now see an attack on Syria as justified, for which the Americans would not have even the semblance of an international coalition.

A Damascene conversion should not be ruled out, then. The Syrians definitely want a dialogue with both America and Israel; to them they are two sides of the same coin. The Iraq war, the Syrians claim, should be followed by a road map for peace not only on the Palestinian track, but also between Syria and Israel. The Syrians were clearly taken aback by the way both Prime Minister Sharon and President Bush brushed aside their call for the resumption of negotiations for a settlement with Israel. There even seem to be indications, as Israel's former military Chief of Staff General Yaalon has hinted recently, of their readiness for a deal based on the international border, rather than on the 1967 lines that Hafez al-Assad so adamantly insisted upon to the extent of making impossible a settlement with Israel.

Both Mr Sharon and Mr Bush may be committing here the typical mistake of leaders lacking the sense of timing and the capacity of decision of the statesman. The weakness of your rival is a reason to reach an agreement with him, not the trigger to humiliate him even further. The stress under which the Syrian regime found itself in the wake of America's global war on terror and the invasion of Iraq propelled it to try to improve relations with America and with the international community at large. It is in this context that, even if out of sheer tactical considerations, the Syrians launched their initiative for a Syrian–Israeli peace. General Yaalon was right to see that as a golden opportunity which, if seized, might contribute immensely to regional peace and stability.

The haughty rejection of the Syrian overture exposed the weakness and, indeed, the fallacy of the philosophy of the Israeli Right and its neo-conservative counterparts in America. They both maintained that the neutralisation of strategic threats in the outer circle of the Middle East would create the ideal conditions for, and would be followed by, peace between Israel and its immediate Arab neighbours. But neither on the Palestinian front nor in the Syrian track was this philosophy being vindicated. Both Israel and America were clearly hesitant to seize the opportunity created by the neutralisation, even if temporary and still precarious, of the strategic threats in the outer Middle East in order to pacify the inner Middle East. On the contrary, they seemed to be overlooking them.

On the Palestinian front, the Israeli argument, seconded by the American administration, was that the chaos and lack of credible leadership made it impossible for Israel to use her improved strategic position in order to strike a peace deal, thus leaving only one alternative out of the impasse: unilateral disengagement. As to Syria, President Bush's policy of too many sticks and hardly any carrots is clearly an impediment on the way to co-opting that country into a regional system of peace and security. Ariel Sharon's rejection of the Syrian overture stems from his knowledge of the inevitable territorial price – a full withdrawal from the Golan

Heights – that he is clearly not ready to pay. Nor is his dilemma an easy one. He knows he cannot tackle and absorb two major political earthquakes at one time, one that would emanate from his disengagement plan from Gaza and another that would inevitably emerge from the pull-out from the Golan. A coalition of the Golan settlers with those of Gaza and the West Bank is a politically lethal alliance that had already contributed to doom Rabin's peace efforts. Ever the tactician, rather than the bold visionary statesman, Ariel Sharon prefers not to tempt fate or to court political disaster.

It was an irony of history that precisely when the gravity of most of the strategic threats that haunted the Jewish state for years was reduced, thanks to America's war in Iraq, Israel found herself trapped in a deadly conundrum of her own making, and with only doomsday scenarios on the horizon. Though Israel could be said to have won tactically the war of the Intifada, she could by no means claim a strategic victory, for she was incapable of turning her military superiority into a strategic breakthrough. Moreover, with no political solution in sight, the spectre of an apartheid, bi-national state of South African characteristics, but with no conceivable South African solution to it, was suddenly no longer a hollow threat. With Israel incapable of halting the cancerous expansion of settlements and removing the bulk of them, while the Palestinians under Arafat's leadership persisted in their impotence to stem the tide of violence and continued to waver about whether to respect the Jewish character of Israel, the two-state solution, which had been the platform of every peace plan so far, started to look like no longer being possible.

By erasing the Green Line, Israel has gained in territory but lost a most central battle of Zionism, that of demography. Among the most fertile peoples on earth, the Palestinians and Israeli Arabs together have already reached demographic parity with the Jews. Only 50 per cent of the ten million people living between the River Jordan and the Mediterranean are Jews. By the year 2020 they will be reduced to 42 per cent with no chance of reversing the trend. From a Zionist perspective this is nothing short of a demographic doomsday. The fear was that if the two-state solution continued to elude the parties, it was also by no means inconceivable that the PLO should cancel its 1988 endorsement of the two-state principle and revert to its old stand about one single Jewish–Arab state.

It was precisely in order to curb such a possibility that Ariel Sharon and the 'civilised' Israeli Right, as opposed to the Messianic settlers and their supporters on the far Right, endorsed the concept of unilateral disengagement. Separation between the two communities in Palestine, a concept that was inherent in the Zionist enterprise from its early days and was later institutionalised through all the mechanisms of governance put in place by the British Mandate, was always staunchly opposed by the Revisionists as a betrayal of Eretz-Israel. Jabotinsky never had in mind a physical iron wall to cut through the heart of Judaea and Samaria. His was a metaphorical wall, a concept of deterrence, a call never to give in to Arab intimidation. But now his disciples did give in. In the 1990s Yitzhak Rabin was the first to initiate plans for a fence that would physically separate Israel from the territories. The same politician who then led a vicious campaign against Rabin for giving in to terror, Ariel Sharon, rushed to endorse the same concept of separation of the Israeli Left, but now it was a pharaonic project of concrete, a Chinese wall hundreds of kilometres long to keep at bay the new barbarians. Important sections of the Israeli Right were compelled, against their dearest ideological belief, to erect a wall in Judaea and Samaria, thus breaking the historical unity of the biblical lands of Eretz-Israel.

Sharon's wall, though it certainly is not a contribution to mutual trust, was conceived as a clear move against the one-state solution. It is an acknowledgement that Zionism has lost the demographic race. Demography and the dream of Greater Eretz-Israel simply could not be reconciled. The wall is a defiant, resolute and bold manifestation that Israel would not allow this fact to usher in a one-state solution. But it is also an acknowledgement by the Israeli Right that it has lost the battle for Eretz-Israel. But unlike the case of Gaza, a small and compact area with not too many 'ideological' settlers, where Sharon plans a total withdrawal, if he ever advances a disengagement plan from the West Bank this will surely be a far more modest affair. There, he might try to remove only a small number of settlements in a way that would leave the Palestinians essentially confined to scattered autonomous enclaves surrounded by settlements and encircled by a dense network of bypass roads.

There is, of course, not the slightest chance that the Palestinians would acquiesce to such a plan. A Palestinian international campaign for a one-state solution backed by a wide popular insurgence cannot be discarded if indeed the Palestinians come to the conclusion that a viable state is not in the offing for them. That the Palestinian insurgence might even expand into the Arab population of Israel as well is not, in such conditions, a far-fetched possibility. Nor is the potential response of the extremists in Israel difficult to imagine. Transfer schemes of all kinds against the Palestinian population and the Arab community in Israel could certainly be violently advanced and a resurgence of Jewish terrorism against Arab targets cannot be dismissed. What started in the 1930s as a civil war between Jews and Arabs in mandatory Palestine and had become since 1988 a struggle for separate statehood, would thus revert to its original condition of a ruthless civil war.

Such a scenario can be averted either through an immediate resumption of negotiations on the basis of a two-state solution along the 1967 borders, or through a unilateral disengagement where Israel would pull out from the bulk of the West Bank and allow a contiguous, viable Palestinian space to exist. Ideally, if the latter option is taken, Israel should leave the door open at the same time for future negotiations for a contractual settlement with the Palestinians. Alas, neither of these options enjoyed a realistic chance in Sharon's right-of-centre coalition, especially as long as Arafat was in control of the Palestinian Authority. There seemed to be no political conditions to produce such bold moves.

Israel's march of folly in the occupied territories represented by her absurdly adventurist policy of settlements has created a reality on the ground that can no longer be solved only through traditional diplomatic means. If and when the conflict becomes so acute and so unbearable, with a civil war between Jews and Arabs claiming its frightening daily toll and the Arab states being drawn into the conflict again, an imposed settlement by an international alliance for peace in the Middle East, led by the United States, might be the last resort. However reluctant the Americans might be to lead such a coalition, they could be compelled to do so when weighing the price in terms of the regional instability and the international indignation that a Jewish–Arab civil war might produce against the difficulties of an imposed solution.

Each and every one of the options, including that of the imposed settlement, that are theoretically open to the parties would inevitably unleash internal earthquakes of unprecedented dimensions within both societies, the Palestinian and the Israeli. If the parties fail to return to the two-state solution, a civil war between Jews and Arabs within the one 'South African' state is inevitable. In either of the remaining options, profound cleavages would also open, and civil strife would certainly be unleashed, this time, however, within each of the separate societies. But this, at least, would be a sacrifice in the service of a moral cause: a life of independence and dignity for each nation in its own state. In the Israeli–Palestinian conflict the possibility of peace without agony was missed years ago. From now on nobody can spare the parties their Calvary. Both Palestinians and Israelis rightly earned it with their political short-sightedness and sometimes sheer human stupidity.

A one-state solution is a nightmare only the extreme Right and the most fanatic settlers would strive for, but even then with the hope that the mass transfer of Palestinians would make it bearable. But the two-state solution is not necessarily the alternative preferred by all the opponents of one state. A withdrawal from the bulk of the territories without allowing the creation of an independent Palestinian state is an option that was being toyed with during the last days of Arafat by members of Israel's security establishment. Moshe Yaalon was certainly one who believed that the two-state paradigm was obsolete and needed to be replaced by agreements with the Arab states bordering with Israel, essentially a return to the armistice agreements of 1949. According to this old-new paradigm, Israel cannot reach peace with security with a revolutionary national movement that is inherently incapable of reforming itself and offering stability in exchange for land and sovereignty.

The impossibility of reaching a negotiated settlement with an invertebrate national movement, and the unresolved war with an anarchic enemy in a state of constant turmoil like the Palestinians, finally brought home to some Israeli generals the lesson that security depends on the political stability of your neighbour, not on the amount of land that you occupy. The idea was then to resuscitate the Jordanian option in the West Bank, encourage Egypt to return to the Gaza Strip and reach a settlement with the Syrians on the Golan Heights. This, the return to the 'capsule doctrine' whereby the Palestinians are encircled and their national movement is sterilised by a ring of peace agreements between Israel and the dictatorial, but stable and orderly, Arab states surrounding it, is what really lay behind General Yaalon's desire for peace talks with Syria.

General Yaalon provided proof of a political resourcefulness of sorts. But by trying to rescue from oblivion such an anachronistic, and indeed obsolete, concept as the capsule doctrine, he displayed his failure to understand the most fundamental lessons of history. National movements that cannot be suppressed by military means cannot be obliterated by simply ignoring them, or by changing the identity of the occupier.

Ariel Sharon's plan to disengage unilaterally from Gaza and dismantle all the settlements throughout the Strip is one concrete proof that the Prime Minister has totally discarded the option of direct negotiations for a two-state solution and has opted for the unilateral approach.

Typically, Mr Sharon did not conceive his plan as part of a grand strategic design or as a component in a wider vision of peace with Israel's Palestinian neighbours. Always the tactical projector and hardly ever the strategic planner, Sharon took the decision to withdraw from Gaza in the autumn of 2003 in a desperate attempt 'to do something' to relieve the international and domestic pressure on him. These were days when the Prime Minister was in dire straits. The dirty war in the territories had unleashed waves of protest among soldiers and reservists; even members of elite commando units and fighter pilots demonstratively questioned the moral legitimacy of the ruthless and indiscriminate war they were ordered to wage. Four prestigious ex-chiefs of Israel's security services (Shabak) warned in a joint interview that Sharon was leading the country 'to the abyss', track II peace plans such as the Geneva accords indicated a potential way out of the impasse of blood, a way Sharon was by no means willing to take, and there was also a real possibility that the Left might be able to repeat the kind of anti-Sharon mass campaign that had brought him down in the wake of the Sabra and Chatila massacre. As Sharon's Chief of Cabinet, Dov Weissglass, put it later in a revealing interview, 'there was a dangerous erosion in our domestic and international position. Everything was falling apart in Israel.'

The Prime Minister now faced a number of choices, none of which was very appealing to him. One was that of totally dismantling the Palestinian Authority and reoccupying all the territories. Another theoretical option was to start direct negotiations for a peace deal that would inevitably entail the almost complete withdrawal from the territories. Sharon's Foreign Minister, Silvan Shalom, had his own brilliant contribution to the pool of ideas put forward by the Prime Minister's advisers. He proposed to simulate a peace process, to pretend negotiations, to meet every now and then 'with some Abu', and do nothing. Mr Sharon ruled out all these options as too risky or impractical and, in a secret meeting he held in Rome on 18 November 2003 with Elliot Abrams, the head of the Middle East desk at the White House, communicated to the Americans his raw plan to withdraw unilaterally from Gaza and dismantle all the settlements in the Strip.

As it turned out, Sharon managed with a whim born out of desperation to kill several birds with one stone. The man of war was suddenly cast in the role of the peacemaker, or at least as somebody who could claim that he also had a plan to keep his domestic and international critics busy, and eventually force them to accept his agenda. Weary of the chances of pushing ahead the ill-fated road map, the Bush administration seized Sharon's idea as if it had suddenly found great spoil. Sharon's reward was that by endorsing the concept of unilateral disengagement, the United States implicitly reiterated her support for a principle that was the cornerstone of Sharon's policy, and indeed the key to his political standing at home, namely, that no negotiations with the Palestinian Authority would start before there was an end to terror. And since the chances that Palestinian terror might end without a political horizon in sight were non-existent, this meant that the option of negotiations was, for all practical purposes, removed from the agenda altogether.

Sharon drew additional benefits from his whimsical plan. He stifled the mounting protest within Israel, he managed to domesticate the Labour Party that asked now to be allowed into his coalition, and he sidelined left-wing track II plans such as Geneva, which hardly anybody speaks of any more; it more or less went into oblivion. And if all this were not enough, he almost managed to nip in the bud an American initiative, communicated to him at his Paris meeting with Elliot Abrams, to start peace negotiations with the Syrians, the outcome of which could only be the devolution of the Golan in exchange for Syria's abandonment of a war option, which Sharon is convinced she does not possess in any case.

But however cynical, and opportunist, and certainly imperfect in its details Sharon's plan may be, it nevertheless offers chances as much as it entails enormous risks. The international community can and should play a vital role in enhancing the opportunities and in curtailing the risks. In other words the disengagement should not be allowed to be wholly unilateral.

Never before has an Israeli leader seriously contemplated dismantling settlements. And, notwithstanding the enormous political difficulties that Mr Sharon has encountered in the embarrassingly dysfunctional institutions of his own party, it is reasonable to say that never has a prime minister in the past enjoyed the political conditions necessary to carry through such a divisive move. Even at the height of his political power, Yitzhak Rabin did not dare to dismantle Netzarim, an isolated settlement in the Gaza Strip that is protected by ten times more soldiers than it has inhabitants. And when, in the wake of the massacre perpetrated in 1994 by a Jewish fundamentalist against Muslim worshippers in Hebron's Tomb of the Patriarchs, a unique opportunity emerged to evacuate the hotbed of politico-religious extremism that is the Jewish Quarter in Hebron, Rabin again wavered and gave in to the settlers.

If Mr Sharon is not bluffing and if he manages to overcome his political constraints (which is still far from certain) he will be setting a precedent with far-reaching consequences. He will again vindicate the mantra that only a hawk is capable of pulling out from Palestinian territory, confronting hardline religious settlers and surviving politically. And whatever his rhetoric may be, he will also signal to some, not all, settlers in Judaea and Samaria that they are not immune from evacuation either.

Ariel Sharon, like his predecessors since 1993, came to his moment of truth with a broken coalition, a divided government and a spineless parliament. Once again it is the dilemma of a leader with a front without a political home front. The fate of any Israeli leader who has tried to withdraw from the territories, either through an agreement like Rabin and Barak, or in a violent way, like Sharon, has been to face political defeat and in Rabin's case even assassination. Israeli politics defy the rule that stability and equilibrium are only maintained by pedalling the bicycle. It is precisely by pedalling, moving and initiating that a leader paves the way for his political demise. Rabin, Peres and Barak were defeated because they tried to break the old, paralysing inertia of war and conflict. And even in the case of Netanyahu, it was only when he ventured, however hesitantly, into an agreement with the Palestinians, the Wye River Memorandum, that he lost his political base and ended up losing power.

Ariel Sharon might still prevail, although this remains to be seen. His political survival, now that his party has abandoned him, requires a miraculous degree of luck and much political astuteness. Not even now that the Knesset has approved the disengagement plan and the Labour Party has joined his coalition, are Sharon's political survival or the implementation of his plan a foregone conclusion. What is refreshing, though, is that Sharon, the unscrupulous and ruthless man of action, has finally realised the limits of force. No one who knew his personal and political history would have imagined him delivering a speech like the one he gave on the day the Knesset approved his plan. Addressing the settlers, those whom he had spoiled and cultivated for years, he said,

> You have developed among you a dangerous Messianic spirit. We have no chance to survive in this part of the world that has no mercy for the weak if we persist in this path. I have learnt from my own experience that the sword alone offers no solution. We do not want to rule over millions of Palestinians who multiply every year. Israel will not survive as a democratic state if she continues being a society that occupies another nation. The withdrawal from Gaza will open the gates of a new reality.

Sharon's disengagement plan is politically courageous, but potentially ominous. The main risk in his move is the 'Lebanonisation' of the Gaza Strip once Israel has withdrawn its settlements and military forces. Pulling out from Gaza without co-ordinating it with a Palestinian or an international body that could help secure stability, while maintaining the control of the crossing points to and from the Strip, and keeping Israeli forces along the Philadelphi Road – the border of Gaza with Egypt – in a way that can by no means be defined as the end of occupation, can only be an introduction to a new phase in the Israeli–Palestinian war of attrition. 'Philadelphi' would certainly become the centre of gravity of all the indigenous, and probably also of regional, terrorist groups committed to the war against the Israeli occupation. Nor is it that outlandish to assume that Hamas would develop, or acquire, missiles with a longer range than that of their home-made Kassams, which could hit targets deep in Israel, a city like Ashkelon for example. Moreover, the assumption is far-fetched that one can undermine the logic of the Palestinian struggle for independence by driving a wedge between the two organic components of the Palestinian nation, Gaza and the West Bank. Gazans would not offer security to Israel so long as their brethren in the West Bank remain under occupation.

However incomplete Israel's pull-out from Gaza might be, the Palestinians will see it as a major victory, as an embarrassing capitulation by the Israeli occupier. A direct line would be drawn in the Palestinian mind between what they perceive as Israel's shameful flight from Lebanon and its even more traumatic disengagement from Gaza in a way that would fire the imagination of young Palestinian fighters and inspire the next phase of Palestine's war of independence. If a credible peace process does not accompany, or immediately follow, the Gaza disengagement, next in line to try to get rid of the Israeli occupier would have to be the West Bank and it is by no means improbable that the withdrawal from Gaza would be followed by an even more ferocious stage in the Intifada throughout the West Bank.

There can be little doubt that Hamas, the dominant power in Gaza, would claim – as Hezbollah did in Lebanon – that Israel's pull-out represents a victory for its campaign and a vindication of suicide terrorism. If Hamas is allowed to become the governing authority in the Gaza Strip, this could usher in the establishment of a mini-Taliban state at permanent war against Israel. That would send a dreadful message throughout the region. It would also deal an additional blow to the Palestinian Authority and to those within it who still hope for a negotiated settlement.

President Bush's support for Mr Sharon's disengagement plan from Gaza was seen as a setback by the Palestinians. They are rightly concerned that Israel would not only control the airspace of the Strip but also the land passages. They should not be surprised either if Israel were to maintain complete freedom of military action should they fail to combat terrorism effectively. Sharon was right to abandon the idea of keeping under Israeli military control the Philadelphi Road, for this could be a source of friction, as was the case of the Shabaa Farms in southern Lebanon. The major Palestinian concern, however, is that of Gaza being both 'first' and 'last', and that no further stages of disengagement are envisaged by Mr Sharon.

But with all its evident shortcomings, the Gaza disengagement project, if it is executed in the framework of an overall peace plan – a reformed Quartet's road map, for example – and a co-ordinated international effort to prevent a chaotic vacuum of authority in the Gaza Strip after Israel has withdrawn its military and civilian presence, can still be a platform worth supporting by both the Palestinians and the international community.

The Americans' sad experience in Iraq has, it must be hoped, taught them that international legitimacy can be no less vital than overwhelming military might. Sooner or later Israel would have to come to the same conclusion if she is to have solid peace arrangements with her Palestinian neighbours. If she persists in discarding the Palestinians as valid interlocutors, Israel's unilateral move needs the support and active assistance of the international community to acquire legitimacy.

Lack of legitimacy is the main problem, too, with the recent exchange of letters between Prime Minister Sharon and President Bush on the contours of a final Israeli–Palestinian peace settlement, an exchange that was offered to Mr Sharon as an American reward for his Gaza plan.

To be sure, the key principles subscribed to by President Bush – blocks of settlements in the West Bank and the stipulation that the right of return should only apply to the Palestinian state, not to Israel – are not altogether new. The Clinton Parameters of December 2000 outlined similar contours for a final status agreement. In fact, Clinton was far more elaborate and specific. His outline embraced every particular item in such a final deal, including precise percentages of land for the blocks of settlements, the ratio of swaps, the ruling out of the right of return to Israel, and the future of Jerusalem and the Temple Mount.

There are, however, major differences between the two presidential documents. Mr Bush did not seem to have assimilated fully the lessons of Iraq, and his pledge to Ariel Sharon was as unilateral and as illegitimate as America's invasion of Iraq. Bush's letter recalls the Balfour Declaration only in one vital point. Both were exchanges of letters between a Western power and the Zionists, while totally ignoring the wishes and positions of the Arabs. Another difference between the two documents is that the Clinton parameters were not the sudden political whim of a president desperately looking for re-election, nor an attempt to throw a lifebelt to a politically drowning Israeli prime minister. The parameters were a brilliantly devised point of equilibrium between the positions of the Israelis and the Palestinians as they stood in that advanced stage of the peace process. The Clinton ideas were born out of negotiations between the parties. They were not an arbitrary imposition.

It is again the question of legitimacy, without which a peace platform cannot endure and would not be viable, that is at stake here. Being the result of negotiations between Israelis and Palestinians for an overall settlement, the Clinton parameters were acclaimed by the international community. Leaders throughout the world from Secretary General Kofi Annan to President Putin of Russia, practically all the European leaders and those of key Arab states, joined the American effort to convince Yassir Arafat to seize the historic opportunity and endorse the parameters. This is not the case with President Bush's pledge to Mr Sharon. It is the unilateralism of the move, perhaps more than its content, that has alienated the Europeans, the Arab states and, of course, the Palestinians.

For all its deficiencies, the Gaza project, being now the only game in town, might still be seen by the Palestinian leadership as an opportunity of recovering their relevance and moving back to the forefront of the peacemaking efforts. Their performance in creating a reliable Palestinian Authority in Gaza that would fight terrorism, create an orderly environment throughout the Gaza Strip and build decent public institutions there, can turn that land of desolation and despair into a model for the wider Palestinian state that would include, in future, the West Bank as well.

Sharon's plan is also a challenge for the international community. The Palestinian institutions are shattered and their economy is in shambles. There are indications that key members of the international community are ready to move from declaratory policies and the familiar inertia of condemnations of the policies of Ariel Sharon to a practical and pragmatic approach. Many now believe that only an active and robust involvement of the international community closely to assist the Palestinians in their task can ensure that Israel's disengagement does not start and end in Gaza, but could be the prelude to a wider and more credible peace process. This might require persuading Sharon to turn his move into an internationally supervised disengagement, leading to an active foreign presence in the Gaza Strip. Since Israel intends to run away, whatever the consequences, only the robust involvement of the international community in assisting the Palestinians in rebuilding their security forces, in institution building, and in laying the foundations for economic growth can turn the politics of despair and devastation into those of hope and peace.

XII   Conclusions

The State of Israel was born in war and it has lived by the sword ever since. This has given the generals and the military way of thinking, at least since the Arab Revolt in the late 1930s, a paramount role in the Jewish state and too central a function in defining both Israel's war aims and her peace policies. Throughout, the army preached 'activism' and frequently overreacted to real and sometimes imaginary threats. The army has also opposed most of the political breakthroughs in Israel's history. Chief of Staff General 'Motta' Gur misread Sadat's peace initiative and was against it; his successor in 2000, General Shaul Mofaz, fiercely opposed Israel's withdrawal from Lebanon as well as the Clinton Peace Parameters, and more recently the army again resisted the Gaza dis-engagement, which had to be practically imposed on it by the Prime Minister.

It is because of the preponderance of the military ethos that the extraordinary achievements of diplomatic Zionism in the early years of the Zionist movement were relegated to a marginal corner in the Israelis' collective memory. In the Ben-Gurion years, 'security' was elevated to the status of a sacred cow, and the concept of pre-emptive war and the nation in arms to that of a vital existential philosophy. For years, peace with a hostile and vindictive Arab world was not viewed as a credible option by the Zionist leadership. To try to break the Arab siege, attempts were made therefore to dilute the centrality of the conflict with the Arabs, and provide manoeuvring space to Israeli diplomacy by diverting its energies to wider regional and even global issues. In the 1950s, the diversion took the form of moves to put together regional alliances, like the Alliance of the Periphery. Attempts, mainly by right-wing governments in Israel, to escape the consequences of the Arab–Israeli conflict by joining global wars persisted until very recently. Such was the case of the war against Communism in the Reagan era and the War on Terror under George W. Bush.

But neither of these attempts could solve Israel's predicament. The centrality of the Arab–Israeli conflict could never be diluted. Frequently lonely and powerless in the world parliamentary arena, but with a disproportionate military strength at her disposal, Israel has always generated apprehension throughout the international community, which the Arabs were wise to cultivate. A major success of the Arabs in their war against Israel has been to prevent her from evading the international consequences of the conflict. It was because of the conflict that Israel was put in the dock of world opinion. It remains a major strategic necessity for the Jewish state to extricate itself from that position.

Two schools did exist in Israel, and indeed in the Zionist movement, with regard to the diplomacy of peace and the conditions that justify going to war. In the 1940s, however, and in the history of the peace overtures in the aftermath of the 1948 war, the two-school theory was just that, a theory. It simply did not exist in real life. The differences, if any, between moderates and activists were then microscopic, more a question of style and tactics than of substance. But both in the 1950s, in the struggle between the diplomatic school led by Moshe Sharett and the 'activists' led and inspired by Ben-Gurion, and in the 1960s when Levi Eshkol tried vainly to stem the tide of war and later enhance the chances of peace, it was the activists and the militants who prevailed.

More important, however, the history of peacemaking between Israel and her Arab neighbours showed that it was the change of mind of the hawks and the shift in their positions, not the preaching of the doves, that allowed Israel to exploit chances of peace at vital crossroads. The major breakthroughs in peacemaking were made and legitimised by the hawks. Such was certainly the case with Menachem Begin and Moshe Dayan in 1978, and Yitzhak Rabin in 1993. This is a pattern that continues to be valid today. The Israeli doves, unelectable in times of conflict and lacking the popular legitimacy for making the inevitable concessions for peace, have come to assume the role of a docile, auxiliary political force in the service of the staunchest military hawk ever to become Israel's prime minister, Ariel Sharon. He is their hope for the future of the peace process.

History has shown that Israel's crushing victories and the humiliation of the Arab armies could never be conducive to peace. That was certainly the case in the aftermath of the 1948 war, where neither side was capable of solving the conflict before it became an intractable dispute. A similar pattern prevailed in the years of nationalistic drunkenness and military triumphalism that followed the 1967 victory. The military stalemate in the 1973 war, the Intifada of the late 1980s and the effects of the Gulf War on the Israeli home front enhanced the chances of peace more than Israel's overwhelming victories. And though defeated and ruthlessly repressed in their second Intifada, the Palestinians can rightly claim to have imposed severe reverses on their Israeli enemies. Israel's unilateral pull-out from Gaza and the construction of the wall in the West Bank are tantamount to an acknowledgement by the Israeli Right of the defeat of its dreams of Greater Eretz-Israel. This is another reflection of the way that Israel is forced to make concessions for peace only under the impact of military pressure and major setbacks. The 'peace of the brave' announced by Yitzhak Rabin and Yasser Arafat in 1993 is now declining into unilateral disengagement. This is not the peace of the brave, but it might be the peace of the exhausted.

Not until the Yom Kippur War were Arabs and Israelis really capable of making the big leap to peace and, surprising as this might sound, not until the first Intifada could a real distinction be made between the policies of the supposedly moderate Labourites and the radical Likud with regard to the West Bank and the Palestinian question. At Camp David, Menachem Begin vindicated Ben-Gurion's concept of the centrality of Egypt to any attempt to reach peace with the Arab world. By taking Egypt out of the war cycle, and thus eliminating the threat of another all-out Arab war against Israel, Begin inaugurated a new era in the region. For all practical purposes, he was the Israeli father, Sadat being the Arab father, of what later became known as 'the peace process'. Sooner or later the Syrians had to follow suit, in their own tortuous, peculiar way. With the demise of the Soviet Union, the provider of an Arab war option, the leaders in Damascus were left with no alternative. Hafez al-Assad, just like Sadat before him, did not of course join the Zionist movement. He was simply forced to respond to changing global conditions. Mr Assad did not change; it was the world around him that changed and from sheer survival instinct, he had to respond.

It was not for the sake of the Palestinians that the Arab armies had invaded Palestine in 1948; the Arab leaders had their own territorial and political ambitions. But, paradoxically, if it was not Palestine that drew them into the war, the war ended by drawing them into the Palestinian question. The boldness of Sadat's peace initiative of 1977 lay in his being the first Arab leader to disengage from the paralysing pan-Arab inertia of 'Palestine first', that is, from a policy that mortgaged the chances of an Arab–Israeli peace to the solution of a problem that looked more and more insoluble. Anwar Sadat reduced the Arab–Israeli conflict to a solvable territorial dispute between sovereign states whose internationally legitimate borders needed to be respected and he thus gave the Israelis space to live in the midst of the Arab Middle East, a space very few among them believed they would ever enjoy.

It was Abba Eban who said that the Palestinian leadership never missed an opportunity to miss an opportunity for peace. In the aftermath of the 1967 war this could just as well be said of Israel's leaders who rejected one after another Sadat's peace overtures. Neither in 1948 nor in 1967 was Israel subjected to irresistible international pressure to relinquish her territorial gains because her victory was perceived as the result of a legitimate war of self-defence. But the international acquiescence created by Israel's victory in 1967 was to be extremely short-lived. Reasonable border modifications are one thing, legitimising a Jewish empire is another. When the war of salvation and survival turned into a war of conquest, occupation and settlement, the international community recoiled and Israel went on the defensive. She has remained there ever since.

The Yom Kippur War could have been avoided, but Israel's politicians and military failed to gauge the real meaning and extent of Sadat's vision and intentions. His was a revolutionary approach that radically changed the politics of the Middle East by paving the way for the ascendancy of the United States to a hegemonic position in the region. Sadat also taught a lesson to his Arab counterparts that, once accepted by them, would change the politics of the Arab–Israeli conflict from war to peacemaking. Fifteen years before the Madrid Peace Conference, which was only possible because of the decline of the Soviet Union as a world superpower, Sadat understood that Moscow was a major obstacle to peace and that only through the good offices of America and its extraordinary leverage on the Jewish state could the Arabs realistically expect to get back their territories. All the Soviet Union could offer the Arabs was a war option that, as the Yom Kippur War had shown, fell short of bringing Israel to her knees, and simply succeeded in draining the resources of the Arab world. Sadat laid down the fundamental truths of any Arab–Israeli peace in the future: Israel cannot expect to have both territories and peace; but nor can the Arabs get away with their territories, as Nasser expected, without offering full peace and recognition to the Jewish state.

Early Zionism was blessed with a sense of pragmatism and diplomatic *savoir-faire*, not exactly the hallmark of the State of Israel in later years. Grand territorial designs were always on the agenda of the Zionist movement, but in the early years they were tempered by a sober acknowledgement of the limits of power. Moderation and humility were not, however, characteristics of Israel's leaders in the 1950s and especially after the 1967 victory. As from the late 1930s, the notion developed among the leaders of the Yishuv that any territorial deal proposed to them, however modest and insufficient, should not be turned down automatically – the mini-Jewish state proposed in 1937 by the Peel Commission, for example, and the UN resolution on partition in 1947 – but, rather, tactically endorsed as a first step. Conditions would arise in the future, they believed, that would allow for further territorial accomplishments. The Zionist leaders had their own 'strategy of phases', to borrow a highly loaded expression later used to define the PLO's strategy of settling first for a small Palestinian state in the West Bank and continuing the struggle for 'all Palestine complete' in a later stage. Israel's territorial gains in the 1948 war did not altogether shelve the dreams of further expansion. In the 1950s, Israel's leaders looked for a pre-emptive war with Egypt and harboured fantasies of additional territorial gains.

It took years of trial and error, and some very dire lessons, for both Israelis and Arabs to appreciate the limits of their capacity to impose their will on one another. Israel's dreams seemed to have been, for all practical purposes, shelved, when she was forced by international pressure to relinquish the Sinai Peninsula in 1957. But her lightning victory in 1967 reopened the debate about Zionism's territorial objectives. Sadat's Clausewitzian war of 1973 and his subsequent peace initiative forced Israel to face the dilemma of peace versus territories. Today, thirty-two years later, the Israeli debate continues, but very few are really convinced that Israel can have both peace with the Palestinians and territories. And, as Sadat anticipated, neither the Assad family in Damascus, nor Arafat's successors in Ramallah, continue to expect that they can get back their land without offering Israel a full-fledged peace agreement. 'The traces of Israeli aggression', as Nasser was the first to establish, do not refer any longer to Israel's territorial exploits in the 1948 war, but only to the lands taken in 1967. The Six Day War, it is now clear to the entire Arab world, has legitimised the 1948 borders.

Israel has never accepted the Arab claim that the Palestinian problem is the core issue of the Arab–Israeli conflict, and for many years she preferred to overlook its centrality. But when it became a challenge no responsible Israeli leader could ignore, a 'capsule theory' was developed, namely a strategy of reaching agreements with the surrounding Arab states in a way that would capsulate, or limit, the Palestinian problem and prevent it from triggering another Arab–Israeli war or creating dangerous regional turmoil. Menachem Begin believed that at Camp David he had secured for Israel the control of Judaea and Samaria. But the Palestinian problem that practically disappeared from the scene as a meaningful political challenge after the débâcle of 1948, and re-emerged after 1967 as a powerful political movement that did not hesitate to resort to the tactics of mass terrorism, could not simply be brushed aside. The capsule doctrine was thwarted by Arafat and his renovated PLO. Arafat's success lay in keeping alive the centrality of the Palestinian problem in the politics of the region despite Egypt's separate peace with Israel. That the formal peace agreement signed at Camp David remained throughout a cold peace had much to do with the persistence of the Israeli–Palestinian conflict.

Menachem Begin's attempt to capsulate and sterilise the Palestinian challenge, and later to eliminate it through his war in Lebanon, was doomed to failure. In fact, Begin's failure was written in the very text of the Camp David accords. It was he, after all, who subscribed to such revolutionary clauses as those referring to the 'recognition of the legitimate rights of the Palestinian people and their just requirements', and to 'the resolution of the Palestinian problem in all its aspects'. However much he later tried to undermine the chances of a meaningful, as opposed to a token, Palestinian autonomy and fill the West Bank with settlements, Begin would go down in history as the one who laid down at Camp David the political foundations of the Oslo process, and consequently established the premises upon which a future Palestinian state would have to emerge. Begin's mysterious retirement from political life and his seclusion in his humble Jerusalem apartment until his last day was his way of admitting that he had failed to secure Israel's hold on the biblical lands of Judaea and Samaria, and that he had in fact paved the way for the emergence of an independent Palestinian state.

The tragedy of the Arab–Israeli conflict stemmed from discrepant historical rhythms. Driven by the dire lessons of Jewish history, the modern Jewish national movement, certainly until 1948, was characterised by its pragmatic and realistic responses to objective historical conditions, a spirit of cautious realism that was later abandoned by the State of Israel. The Arabs, and especially the Palestinians, have consistently fought for the solutions of yesterday, those they had rejected a generation or two earlier. This persistent attempt to turn back the clock of history lies at the root of many of the misfortunes that have befallen the peoples of the region. But, eventually, it was the Arab side that led the strategic shift from war to political accommodation.

Peace breakthroughs in the Arab–Israeli conflict began almost invariably thanks to Arab, not Israeli, moves. Such was the case of the Yom Kippur War that was started by President Sadat with the aim of breaking the political deadlock and unleashing a peace process with Israel; such was likewise the case of his 1977 peace initiative, and so also the first Palestinian Intifada that forced Israel to abandon the convenient politics of inertia with regard to the Palestinian problem.

Resistance to seizing the opportunities for a settlement was never an Arab monopoly. True, in the aftermath of the 1948 war, peace was not yet a realistic possibility. Encircled, embattled, boycotted, but also enamoured with its newfound military prowess, the Israel of the late 1940s and the 1950s was in no mood for a peace that entailed giving up the territorial gains of her War of Independence. But when after 1967, and especially after 1971, Egypt started to signal her readiness for a settlement based on the international borders, and the Arab discourse about 'the traces of Israeli aggression' clearly referred to the territories acquired in the Six Day War, not to those gained in 1948, Israel failed to rise to the challenge and missed clear opportunities for peace. It was then the Arab side, specifically Egypt, that was active in devising initiatives aimed at breaking the deadlock and unleashing a political process that could have led to peace. The Yom Kippur Egyptian onslaught on the Bar-Lev Line in 1973 and the Palestinian Intifada in 1987 were both essentially Arab political moves aimed at forcing Israel to come to the negotiating table. Without the Yom Kippur War, Israel's peace with Egypt would not have been possible. Nor could the Oslo accords, which are Israel's recognition that the Palestinian problem needed to be addressed on its own merits rather than be 'solved' through Jordan or ignored altogether, have emerged without the Intifada.

But for the Palestinians to begin seeing a tangible solution to their plight, their leaders needed to change their strategy and display, for a change, a sense of statesmanship. Arafat will go down in history as the father of a major strategic change in the history of the Palestinian movement. He was the initiator of the Israeli–Palestinian peace process through the PLO's 1988 Algiers declaration. In Algiers, the PLO abandoned the utterly unrealistic concept of a solution based on one Arab–Jewish state in Palestine and endorsed instead the concept of a two-state solution, thus extending an implicit recognition of an independent Jewish state in Palestine. However unwilling Israeli governments might have been to negotiate with the PLO, and notwithstanding the fact that the Algiers declaration was mainly aimed at responding to the requirements of the Reagan administration for it to recognise the PLO, Arafat's courageous move would leave Israel no option but to open, sooner or later, negotiations with the PLO. Arafat's endorsement of the two-state solution would also turn out to be the trigger for a momentous change in the Israeli political set-up. It forced for the first time since 1967 a real political debate in Israel on the future of the territories, and helped expose the real political differences between Right and Left, Likud and Labour, with regard to the Palestinian question.

Nothing could be the same after 1988, a year when another momentous decision was made by an Arab leader, King Hussein of Jordan. He unceremoniously buried the so-called 'Jordanian option', another futile Israeli strategy aimed at 'capsulating' the Palestinian problem within an Israeli–Jordanian peace, with his announcement that he disengaged Jordan from the affairs of the West Bank and handed over to the PLO the responsibility for the future of the Palestinian territories. Nowhere is the reality of connected vessels between the Arab states and the Palestinian question more patently clear than in the case of Jordan. 'The best of enemies' since at least 1946, Israel and Jordan would nevertheless only come to a peace agreement in 1994, and even then only because Israel had reached an accommodation with the Palestinians through the Oslo accords. There is a strong Palestinian dimension to the profile of the Jordanian state, and its peace with Israel was conceived as a move vital for the existence of the kingdom in the context of the delicate triangle of Israel–Jordan–Palestine relations.

Sadat's 1977 peace initiative and Hussein's and Arafat's momentous moves in 1988 were also crucial for the politics of peacemaking because they relieved Israel of some of the false assumptions upon which it had based its peace strategy. Israel always saw Lebanon and Jordan as the weakest links in the Arab front, and the misconception prevailed among her leaders that these countries would be the first to come to a peace settlement with the Jewish state. But fragile states sandwiched between strong regional powers and suffering from a serious gap of legitimacy – Jordan a Hashemite monarchy perceived as a product and client of the West and a covert ally of the Zionists, and Lebanon torn between its Christian identity and its Arab destiny – they could never be free to lead the big leap. Nor did Israel ever propose to them a deal they could not resist. The 'Jordanian option' existed only in the imaginations of the Israelis, and their drive to establish an alliance of minorities with the Maronites of Lebanon was never going to be a meeting between equals. Sharon and Begin inherited from Ben-Gurion and Dayan the notion that Israel would reshape the political as well as the physical map of Lebanon. The resounding failure of Israel's adventure in 1982, and the rapid collapse of her peace agreement in 1983 with a Christian president in Beirut, were the inevitable outcome of an ill-conceived strategy. Not even today when, isolated and subjected to the uncompromising pressure of the Bush administration, the Ba'ath regime in Damascus has sunk into the deepest crisis in its history, is it possible to disentangle the Lebanese–Syrian connection and reach a separate deal between Israel and Lebanon. Peace with Beirut would have to be either simultaneous with, or sequential to, peace with Damascus.

Yitzhak Rabin will go down in history as the man who overrode many of the inconsistencies in Israel's peace policy. With the change in 1992 from the paralysing experience of Shamir's government to Rabin's extraordinary resolve to exploit what he called 'the window of opportunities' for an Arab–Israeli peace, Israel embarked on an entirely different course of action. Rabin was the first Israeli leader to address the Palestinian problem on its own merits and not as a collateral, secondary effort. Rabin's determination to break taboos that were deeply embedded in the Israeli mind unleashed hopes for peace that would tragically clash with the hard realities of a Syrian regime incapable of assuming normal relations with the Jewish state even in exchange for all the land.

That the hopes for an Israeli–Palestinian peace were frustrated was the responsibility of both sides. The inbred incapacity of the Israelis to abandon the politics of fait accompli, and their obsession with settlements in the occupied territories, were a major reason for the despair of the Palestinians. The hopes of peace were also wrecked on the rocks of a dysfunctional Palestinian system led by a leader, Arafat, incapable of renouncing the drug of Palestinian martyrdom, and fearful of the task of leading the big leap to the end of the conflict. This was made patently clear when Ehud Barak's bold, even if awkward and sometimes erratic, pursuit for peace, and President Clinton's readiness to compromise the legacy of his entire presidency by advancing the most far-reaching parameters for an Israeli–Palestinian peace, were turned down by the Palestinian leader. Arafat's rejection of the Clinton peace parameters was, as a close witness to the process, the Saudi ambassador in Washington, Bandar Bin Sultan, defined it, 'a crime against the Palestinian people' and the peoples of the region. Arafat should be given credit for being the initiator of the political process with his 1988 Algiers Declaration. But in Algiers he also established the conditions for a settlement with Israel from which he never deviated. To him, the peace process was not meant to be an open-ended give and take. He had already given, now he had only to take: a Palestinian state in the 1967 borders, the right of return for the refugees, Jerusalem and the Temple Mount. The Israelis, including Rabin who signed the Oslo accords with him, did not concur with Arafat's interpretation of the peace process. Arafat believed that in 1988 he had made his major historic compromise, and that it was now up to the Israelis to make the necessary concessions. He believed that the onus was now on them, not on him.

Does the Middle East enjoy now, in the wake of the Iraq War and President Bush's War On Terror, a new 'window of opportunity' for an Arab–Israeli peace? As the Arab–Israeli peace process in the 1991 Madrid International Peace Conference has shown, the prospects of peace in the Middle East always depended on a synchrony between global changes and regional conditions. With the election of George W. Bush to a second term in the White House, the prospects for a resolution of the 125-year-old conflict look somewhat brighter. Notwithstanding America's difficulties in Iraq, the brutal determination of the President in pursuing his policies in the region, the threats to the stability of the Arab regimes from Islamic fundamentalism, and their fear that the persistence of the

Palestinian problem might end up dissolving their home front and undermining their regimes, have all helped create more favourable conditions for an all-Arab accommodation with Israel. The endorsement in the spring of 2002 by the Arab League of the Saudi initiative for peace with Israel was the Arab response to America's War on Terror.

More recently, Syria's international isolation and the pressure exerted on the Ba'ath regime by the United States and its European allies brought President Assad to plead publicly for peace with Israel. Free of the chaotic style of governance of Yasser Arafat and of his macabre flirtation with terrorism, the Palestinian Authority, defeated and pulverized by Ariel Sharon's ruthless methods of repression, is more ready now to move back to a pragmatic course of action. Even the serial producers of suicide squads, Hamas and Islamic Jihad, exhausted and decapitated of their historical leaders by Israel's merciless campaign of targeted assassinations, are now pleading for a truce (*hudna*), and are even ready to contemplate an accommodation, albeit limited in time, with Israel on the basis of the 1967 borders. And as for Abu-Mazen, he knows only too well that the Palestinians could only have the upper hand if they shift the struggle from Israel's marketplaces and kindergartens to the negotiating table. It is there that Mr Sharon lacks answers, not in the military field, and it is there that the Palestinians run a chance of calling his bluff.

Another key to the reactivation of the peace process is Egypt. Ariel Sharon, who, unlike most of his predecessors, especially those of Labour, never courted the friendship of President Mubarak and never thought of making the traditional pilgrimage of Israeli leaders to Cairo to plead for Egypt's mediation with the Palestinians, nevertheless succeeded in warming up Israel's relations with the *rais*. The latter even recently advised the Palestinians that 'only with Sharon do you run a chance of having peace'. Israel's planned pull-out from Gaza, and the alarming prospects that this might create for Egypt an unstable common border with an anarchic Palestinian entity in Gaza, are a major reason for Mubarak's sudden infatuation with Sharon. Sharon's determination to use force mercilessly and unscrupulously, and his success in maintaining his intimate alliance with an American president who has just been re-elected for a second term, conveyed an unequivocal message to President Mubarak: improving relations with Israel, contributing to making possible its Gaza plan and exerting pressure on the Palestinians in favour of more pragmatic policies are all vital Egyptian interests. Not peace but the continuity of his regime is President Mubarak's priority, and this requires that he adapt his policies to the changing conditions.

A note of caution would not be misplaced, however, in assessing the chances that these improved conditions will usher in a permanent

Arab–Israeli settlement. The Arab–Israeli peace process has known more than one moment of euphoria in the past; nor is this the first time that regional and global conditions seemed so favourable for the chances of peace and, indeed, the parties were more than once on the brink of peace. The Middle East is a cemetery of missed opportunities. Today, the forces that might still derail the possibility of peace have anything but laid down their arms. Iran's nuclear ambitions and her hostility to the Arab–Israeli peace process are major destabilising factors. Iran's Hezbollah clients have already started to strike roots among radical Palestinian organisations in the territories in order to undermine the chances for a ceasefire or a smooth execution of Sharon's Gaza plan.

Three times in their history the Palestinians were offered statehood – in 1937, in 1947 and through the Clinton parameters in 2000 – and three times they have rejected it. Arafat was known for always being more conscious of what he was denied than of what he had obtained. Will Abu-Mazen be able to supersede this obsession with the unobtainable and build a positive ethos of democratic governance and human development around a pragmatic peace with Israel? Abu-Mazen is leading the post-Arafat transition with admirable wisdom and a commendable display of diplomatic skills. It is an irony of history that the only Arabs in the world that were allowed the sovereign right of electing their leader in fully democratic elections are those living under Israeli occupation. It is no less true, of course, that the Palestinians have shown the world a commendable sense of democratic maturity. But it nevertheless remains to be seen how the non-charismatic Mahmoud Abbas fills the void of revolutionary legitimacy created by Arafat's departure, and consolidates his leadership by controlling the plethora of anarchic grass-roots militias which, if not disarmed, will only serve as a pretext for the hardliners in Israel to stick to a military course of action.

Despite some promising signals from Hamas both with regard to their eagerness for a ceasefire and to their readiness to move to a more constructive political phase, I doubt if they can really reconcile their desire to maintain their distinct identity with such a radical shift of strategy. Their predicament is tough. For them to go to elections and be defeated could be a serious embarrassment. But nor would a victory be so welcome either, for this would force them to make the choice of recognising Israel and joining the peace process, a decision they seem at present utterly incapable of making. In one way or another, Hamas would have to keep alive its military option, its terrorist capabilities, and its political purity if it wants to survive. Moreover, a PA under Abu-Mazen would probably follow Arafat's legacy and avoid a frontal clash, let alone an all-out civil war, against Hamas so long as the Israelis and the Americans do not offer the ultimate bait, that is, the contours of a final settlement that could be acceptable to the Palestinians.

It is of course possible that everybody will now look for a diplomatic solution by resuscitating the Road Map. It would have to be a reformed road map, however. I do not believe that the bizarre idea, reserved for the second stage of the road map, of a Palestinian state with 'temporary borders' can be seen as enticing by the Palestinians. They already had such a 'state' in the form of the Palestinian Authority. It is inconceivable that the Palestinians will agree to repeat the experience if the parameters of the final settlement are not agreed upon in advance. They will probably see it as a trap, or as the introduction to a long interim agreement whose end would depend on whether or not they finally 'turn into Finns', as Sharon's aide Dov Weissglass remarked sarcastically in a recent interview. Any attempt by Israel to trivialize the Palestinian problem by turning it into a banal border dispute will fail with Abu-Mazen just as it would have failed with Arafat. For, even if such a temporary state is eventually created, it will follow in the footsteps of the Palestinian Authority and revert to a revolutionary strategy the moment it realises that its minimal requirements for a final settlement are not met.

Arafat was a difficult partner. But at the same time he was the ultimate defender of the two-state solution. Without him, stemming the threat of a one-state paradigm is a much more formidable task. Many in the Palestinian leadership are troubled by the difficulty of pursuing the two-state course without the backing of Arafat's authority and the legitimacy that only he could provide. The Palestinian factions that are openly opposed to, or simply sceptical of, the principle of a second partition of Palestine have gained considerable power and moral authority during the Intifada. They now include not only Hamas, which is especially dominant in the Gaza Strip, but also grass-roots militias within Fatah itself, such as the Al-Aqsa Martyrs' Brigades. In other words, Arafat's death does not necessarily eliminate the threat of the demise of the idea of two states for two peoples, and of the mutual recognition of the PLO and Israel. In fact, it removes from the scene the ultimate legitimiser of these two historic shifts in the Palestinian strategy. His successors might be far less capable of defending the Oslo legacy in conditions of conflict and persistent war with Israel. Oslo is the most vilified term in Palestinian political discourse. Abu-Mazen was chosen as the heir not because he was the architect of Oslo, but in spite of it.

And even if an entirely new and promising chapter in the Egypt–Israel–Palestinian Authority triangle does unfold, and the Gaza withdrawal turns out to be the most successful and peaceful undertaking, when the moment of truth arrives and the parties sit down to explore the parameters for a final settlement – for after all *this* is the objective of it all – the Israelis may find that the Palestinians changed their tactics and leadership, but not the price of peace. The Israeli government would then once again realise that it is a prohibitive price it cannot afford or is politically incapable of paying.

The Israeli Left is bound to admit that its policy of fighting terrorism and negotiating peace at the same time was a resounding failure, and that it was Ariel Sharon's ruthless crackdown on Palestinian terrorism that brought the Palestinians to their knees and forced even Hamas to plead for a truce. But the Right was, and continues to be, equally wrong in its far-fetched assumptions about the price of peace and its capacity to impose it on the Palestinians.

Abu-Mazen's conditions for a peace deal with Israel are no different from those that prevented an agreement with Arafat. In fact, he had already spelled them out: a Palestinian state within the 1967 borders with its capital in Jerusalem, and a just solution of the refugee problem in accordance with UN Resolution 194. Arafat's positions were not the child of his whims and what Abu-Mazen did was merely to reiterate what have been the undeviating, official Palestinian positions since 1988. The Palestinians do not believe that these are overly radical positions. On the contrary, to them they represent the most moderate deal they can offer to Israel. Before he was being dubbed 'engineer of the Intifada', Marwan Barghouti used to proclaim that these positions were exactly what made Fatah the equivalent of a Palestinian 'Peace Now' movement.

A change of leadership among the Palestinians does not alter, then, the conditions for peace or its price. Peace will not be cheaper because of Arafat's disappearance. The tragedy of this conflict is that the only man whose signature on an agreement of compromise and reconciliation, which would include giving up unattainable dreams, could have been legitimate in the eyes of his people was incapable of bringing himself to sign. He took this legitimacy with him to the grave, and left his heirs with the same positions and the same beliefs on which compromise will be beyond their reach and their capacity. That is his terrible legacy. And, as if this were not enough, it is also possible that in his heirs' eagerness to fill the vacuum of revolutionary legitimacy the founding father left behind him, they will be compelled not only to stick to his well-known positions, but perhaps even to be more radical, if they wish to survive.

The fact that Sharon's intentions with regard to the post-Gaza process are not exactly those of 'Peace Now', to use Barghouti's metaphor, does not make the chances of a negotiated Israeli–Palestinian settlement any easier. Mr Sharon has recently given sufficient indications of his intention to turn the struggle for a greater Jewish Jerusalem into the main effort of his policy after the completion of the Gaza disengagement. He has already started to put into practice the scheme to link Jerusalem with Maale Adumim in a way that will not allow for a contiguous Palestinian state. Was, for example, Mr Sharon's readiness to allow the Palestinians in Jerusalem to participate in the elections for Arafat's successor really an indication that he has finally assumed that there would be no solution unless the Palestinians have their capital in Arab Jerusalem? It is not entirely implausible that what he has in mind is to establish a precedent whereby a functional, rather than a territorial, division of at least part of the West Bank would be the essence of the future peace deal. 'Palestinians living in Israel's capital can vote in the Palestinian elections just as American citizens living in Israel are entitled to vote for the president of the United States', is how Mr Sharon's entourage explained his surprisingly forthcoming attitude to the voting rights of the Palestinian Jerusalemites. The Arabs of Jerusalem, and maybe even those of the State of Israel proper, might be asked in a future final settlement to vote in the Palestinian state without the territories they live in being part of the State of Palestine, just as the settlers throughout the West Bank could remain in their settlements, be citizens of the State of Israel and vote in the elections for the Israeli parliament. Sharon, who is so surprisingly sanguine in allowing the Palestinians of Jerusalem to vote, may believe that this is the best way to reconcile his demographic worries with his territorial ambitions.

The political culture prevailing throughout the region is also a formidable hurdle on the way to a final settlement. The Middle East remains a region in flux, the legitimacy and stability of its political regimes as questionable as ever. It was always easier for an Arab leader to achieve popularity with the masses when he confronted the enemy on the battlefield, even if he was defeated and humiliated, rather than gain legitimacy for a peace with Israel that is based on compromise and concessions. Left to their own devices, the countries of the region do not possess the necessary culture of conflict resolution to solve their differences.

The dysfunctionality of Israel's political system is no less an impediment to an agreement with the Palestinians than Abu-Mazen's difficulties in consolidating an orderly polity and a hierarchical system of decision making in the Palestinian territories. Moreover, if the Palestinians have understandably lost their trust in the Israelis as partners for peace, the devastating effect of the Intifada on the Israeli public has been anything but conducive to enhancing trust in the Palestinian partner. Oslo was made possible when an almost post-Zionist clamour for 'normalcy' and peace took possession of Israeli society. The Israelis' 'Tel Avivian' secular and hedonistic existence has always vied for supremacy in a constant *Kulturkampf* with the other Israel, a 'Jerusalemite' traditionalist and xeno-phobic Israel, sceptical of modernity and suspicious of peace with the Arabs. This internal struggle was never conducted in a vacuum. Its outcome depended on the perception that the Israelis had of their Arab neighbours, particularly the Palestinians. Arafat's rejection of the peace deal offered to him in December 2000, and his endorsement of the Intifada, not only set fire to all the mechanisms of peacemaking, but also dealt an almost mortal blow to the peace camp in Israel, and allowed Jerusalemite Israel the upper hand once more in her politico-cultural civil war.

In a number of articles I wrote after the collapse of the Israeli–Palestinian peace talks under President Clinton's mediation (for example, 'The Only Way Out', *Newsweek*, 27 August 2001; 'A New Paradigm for the Middle East', *Financial Times*, 31 October 2001), I argued that our failure to reach a peace agreement needed to be seen as a defining moment, not just a technical failure, and therefore the conclusion needed to be drawn that the old peace paradigm of Oslo had run its course and was no longer valid as a framework for peacemaking. I then advanced the idea that an Israeli–Palestinian peace would require a tight international envelope to make it possible. I argued that an international alliance for peace under American leadership was needed in order to articulate a new peace paradigm. The Madrid Quartet and the 'road map' it has produced are steps in that direction, although this new international endeavour still suffers from many weaknesses. It is my view that neither the unilateral approach now prevailing in Ariel Sharon's government, nor bilateral peace talks can lead to a final Israeli–Palestinian peace settlement. The legitimacy for Israel's permanent borders and for a viable Palestinian state would have to come through an international peace scheme.

The State of Israel was born out of an international proclamation – the UN's General Assembly Resolution of 29 November 1947 – and its borders were decided in the spring and summer of 1949 in Armistice Agreements brokered by the international community, represented by the UN's deputy secretary general, Ralph Bunche. What had started out as an international endeavour will now, sixty years later, have to be completed as such. If the all-powerful Arafat attributed such importance to having an international umbrella escort him to the altar of an agreement, is it likely that lesser figures, saddled with such difficult terms of inheritance, will be able on their own to overcome the belief in the right of return and the Temple Mount without a tight-fitting envelope of support from the international community, especially from the Arab states and the Palestinians' allies in Europe? Palestinians and Israelis would simply not be capable of accommodating themselves to each other's minimal requirements for peace.

We stand, then, at the end of the peace process as we have known it to date. From now on, our options will be between a violent and unilateral separation or disengagement, such as the one being led by Ariel Sharon, and a comprehensive peace plan that will be annexed to the road map and will lead to its practical imposition on the parties by an international peace coalition headed and led by the United States. I believe that this peace plan should follow the letter and spirit of the Clinton plan, and I have proposed that this be anchored in a special Security Council resolution that will view the plan as the authoritative international interpretation of Resolution 242 on the Palestinian issue. The Clinton Peace Parameters, a sensible and judicious point of equilibrium between the positions of the parties as they stood at the last stage of the negotiations in December 2000, provide the most advanced and precise set of principles upon which a reasonable compromise with overwhelming international legitimacy can be articulated. The 'parameters' do not contradict any of the principles laid down by the Saudi peace initiative that was later endorsed by the entire Arab League. The two platforms are not mutually exclusive; they are complementary. Only when such a precise peace platform is established will the parties be able to develop a vested interest in securing an orderly transition to the final settlement. Clinton's failure did not lie in the nature of his peace platform, but in the deficiencies of his international diplomacy. He was unable to rally the Arab governments to his peace enterprise, and he did not build a solid and effective international foundation to sustain and internationally legitimise his peace deal.

A major fallacy of the Oslo accords is precisely that they contained no binding mechanisms that would lead the Palestinian people from a state of revolutionary struggle to orderly and democratic statehood. An orderly Palestinian polity is crucial if it is to meet Israel's elementary security requirements. Before Arafat's death, I was of the view that the Palestinian system could not be reformed from within, certainly not as long as there was no *binding* road map for peace and an end to occupation. The only way out of the impasse, I believed, was the establishment of an international mandate in the Palestinian territories that should accompany the Palestinian Authority in its transition to democratic independence, real free elections, economic order and a resolute security system.

The Palestinian elections and Abu-Mazen's admirable achievement in changing the nature of the Palestinian discourse will hopefully make the trusteeship concept redundant. A nation that goes into fully democratic elections with such a display of civic spirit is a nation whose march to independence is unstoppable. But given the strength of the Islamic challenge to the new Palestinian Authority, it still remains to be seen whether Abu-Mazen's leadership changes the need for such a close international nursing of the Palestinians' transition to democratic governance. Abu-Mazen himself has not rejected the concept of such international assistance to the struggle for Palestinian democracy when he agreed to participate in the London International Conference for Palestinian internal reforms. If the political horizons of a final peace deal remain unclear, and Abu-Mazen's new strategy fails to deliver a settlement that is acceptable to his people, especially to the more radical groups, his internal legitimacy would certainly be questioned and the militant organisations would again challenge both his reforms and his negotiating strategy.

The idea of a protectorate in the Palestinian territories is not entirely alien to Israeli and Palestinian peacemakers. It was discussed and even established as the main feature of the Israeli–Palestinian Declaration of Principles (DOP) during the first round of talks in the secret channel in Oslo, but was later ruled out in favour of a direct handover of the Gaza Strip to an elected Palestinian Authority. In view of the resounding failure of the road that was taken, and given the total collapse of trust between the parties and the state of decomposition into which the Palestinian Authority has degenerated in the Arafat years, recovering the concept of an international protectorate was not an unreasonable way to extricate the parties from the impasse. It remains to be seen whether Abu-Mazen's rule will make such a concept redundant.

The paradigm of an international envelope that would coax the parties to the Israeli–Palestinian conflict into endorsing an agreed peace plan would not work unless the gulf that has opened in the transatlantic alliance, especially in the wake of America's invasion of Iraq, is bridged. The differences in their approach to the Israeli–Palestinian conflict being a major reason for the chasm between Europe and the United States, a common platform and a joint effort for its solution are deemed vital, certainly by the Europeans, as the bond without which the transatlantic alliance could not be fully restored. Sooner or later, it is in Jerusalem that the future of the alliance that was wrecked in Baghdad will be decided.

It is vital that the Israelis realise that no change in the international system, however radical, will spare them hard and painful choices. They must also learn the lesson from their agonizing attempt to quell the Intifada, as others in history have learned, that states, however strong, have little deterrent power against national uprisings. Internationally legitimised borders will offer Israel more deterrence power than F-16 raids on terrorist targets that end up killing innocent civilians without deterring the terrorists. It is by no means the case that force and the capacity to intimidate one's enemies has become unnecessary, especially in a region whose value system does not allow for such a luxury. But, as the United States has learned the hard way in Iraq, this is an era where power without legitimacy only breeds chaos, and military supremacy without legitimate international consent for the use of force does not offer security.

Israel's respect for her international border with Lebanon has given more security to her northern villages than twenty years of military occupation of that country. Only when a free and independent Palestinian state assumes a vested interest in respecting the regional order and a civilized system of governance can peace prevail. This will have sooner or later to be complemented by a peace agreement between Israel and Syria, whose parameters are known only too well. Only then might the conditions be created for an accommodation between Israel and the Arab and Muslim world, and a regional system of security can perhaps be made possible. Any attempt to develop such a regional system before the Arab–Israeli conflict has been resolved is doomed to failure.

Arabs and Israelis tend to pay great reverence to the past; they are both saturated with history. But the past is frequently the enemy of the future, and nothing in the Arab past has prepared them for the idea of a Jewish sovereign state in their midst. Hostages of their traditional way of dealing with the Jews as nothing more than a tolerated minority, the Arabs only fuelled the paranoiac instincts of the Israelis. Nor were Israel's past and the Jewish historical experience conducive to easy conciliation. Israel's history as a state has been characterised throughout by a traumatic reaction to any initiative that has a bearing on its physical security. The crisis of the Jewish conscience in the transition from Holocaust to statehood may also help explain the rigidity of Israel's approach to peacemaking in its early years of sovereign existence. It always opted for a pessimistic, if not fatalistic, interpretation of regional challenges. The territorial answer to the Jewish atavistic fear, Israel was for too long unable to break the walls of its Jewish heritage.

Israel's agonizing challenge today is to conduct a radical change of strategy by overcoming the traditional tendency of her leaders and policy makers to take, or to avoid, decisions only on the basis of worst-case scenarios. Israel's pre-emptive strategy throughout the 1950s, her embrace of a nuclear option, and the temptation to use it in 1973, the desire of her generals to launch an early strike in May 1967, the invasion of Lebanon in a 'war of choice' in 1982, the vociferous, almost hysterical, rejection of the Clinton parameters by Chief of Staff General Mofaz as 'a threat to the very existence of the State of Israel', and even the building of the wall on the West Bank are all consequences of an Israeli outlook that, as mentioned before, Levi Eshkol defined with typical Jewish humour as a kind of 'Shimshon der Nebechdeiker' (Samson the nebbish). Israel could never really decide whether she was an intimidating regional superpower or just an isolated and frightened Jewish ghetto waiting for the pogrom to happen.

From the perspective of a conflict more than a century old and from that of the politics of war and the all-or-nothing diplomacy that prevailed for so many years in the Arab–Israeli dispute, Zionism can claim that it has prevailed against all odds. The major victory of Zionism that began, in Arab eyes, as a foreign colonial intrusion, is that it succeeded in forcing its enemies to come to terms with it, accept its existence and even contemplate peace with it. Israel even managed to force the entire Arab world, and the international community as well, to accept the legitimacy of the 1948 borders even though these went far beyond the borders that were approved for the Jewish state in 1947. If Israel accepts trimming her post-1967 territorial ambitions – and as both the negotiations conducted during the Barak government and all the recent studies of Israeli public opinion have shown, Israel is ready for a pragmatic, non-ideological approach to peace – and accepts that the territorial phase of Zionism has come to its end, Zionism's victory can still be finally sealed.

This would require the Palestinians to trim their dreams as well. The destruction of Jewish statehood and sovereignty twice in the history of the Jewish people was the result of her failure as a nation to take the right political course, to opt for accommodation with reality instead of engaging in messianic hallucinations. The punishment was very severe: centuries of exile and persecution. This should serve as a lesson to the Palestinians and their leaders who throughout their history have preferred the dangerous inertia of national myths and unrealistic dreams, rather than choosing a wise and prudent political course.

Peace cannot wait for Arab democracy to emerge; it will have to precede it. The end of conflict, and the beginning of a process of ideological disarmament, are vital for the democratisation of the region. Peace should serve as the major agent and trigger for Arab democracy. As long as there is no peace, Arab dictatorships have the ultimate argument for staying in power. Democracy is the key for Arab leaders to be able to end the historically destructive pattern of government whereby they were constantly forced to placate and control an 'Arab street' which they had themselves incited with bellicose rhetoric against the Jewish state and its American 'imperialist' patrons. It was when trapped in that insoluble conundrum of their own making that the Arab leaders man-oeuvred themselves against their own will into the 1956 Sinai Campaign and the 1967 Six Day War.

As from 1948 the Arabs expected Israel 'to behave' in order to be accepted as a state, however small and modest, in their midst. They were proved wrong. It was Israel's behaviour as an unyielding and intimidating regional superpower that threatened the territorial integrity and the political stability of her Arab neighbours, and whose policies even condemned her to international isolation, which eventually forced the Arabs to wish to come to terms with the Jewish state. At the end of the day, it was Israel's 'bad behaviour', Jabotinsky's iron-wall philosophy, and Ben-Gurion's doctrine of offensive defence, backed by the ultimate nuclear deterrence, which changed the Arabs' attitude to the Jewish state.

But forcing Israel's Arab enemies to accept her existence and make peace with her is one thing; imposing on them the territorial terms of a settlement is quite another. Demography and territory, the two pillars of the Zionist enterprise, cannot be reconciled unless Israel abandons her territorial ambitions and departs from the unrealistic, and morally corrupting, dream of possessing the biblical lands of Eretz-Israel. A Palestinian people yearning for freedom and dignity lives under occu-pation. Israel's moral standing as well as vital political imperatives require that the Palestinians recover their rights and dignity as a nation. Democracy and Jewish statehood cannot be reconciled with territorial aggrandizement. 'Transfer' and 'separation' were, one should recall, important concepts that were advocated from the early days of the Zionist enterprise. In the inevitable second partition of Palestine borders might have to be reshaped to accommodate new demographic realities, but the transfer of populations cannot be allowed. The resettlement of refugees in 'historical Palestine', to borrow the expression used in the Clinton parameters to define the Palestinian state in the West Bank and Gaza, is a different matter.

Israel's existence as a nation and as a state derives from the critical lessons of Jewish millenarian history. Her task today is to confront the world around her not only with the traditional defensive tools she has developed and acquired over the years, but also with the audacity of thought and the same creative imagination that have been the hallmark of Jewish elites throughout the centuries. Israel's leaders and her civil society bear a heavy responsibility to conceive bold and generous solutions precisely because of the high ideals upon which the Jewish state was built, and because of the noble values of Jewish civilisation that cannot be reconciled with the denial of the natural right of an occupied people to a life of freedom and dignity. It was with a unique combination of democratic and utopian reason that the Zionist movement enabled the Jews to recover their birthright and endowed them with a key to the future. The same tools need to be put at the service of this most vital task of the Jewish state, bringing an end to the conflict with the Arab world, in particular with the Palestinians. For the Jews have not survived all the horrors of extermination only to entrench themselves behind the walls of their own convictions and remain righteous and immobile. They have survived in order to devise a solution to what for too long looked like an insoluble conundrum: that of making Jewish statehood a legitimate reality in the eyes of those who consider themselves its victims.

No one in this conflict has a monopoly on suffering and martyrdom; nor is the responsibility for war atrocities exclusive to one party. In this tragic tribal dispute, both Jews and Arabs have committed acts of unpardonable violence, and both have succumbed at times to their most bestial instincts. What is no less grave is that they have both too frequently chosen the wrong course, refusing to see the changing realities and adapt their policies accordingly. The time has finally arrived to assume that the complete satisfaction of the parties' respective dreams or presumed rights will only lead them both to perdition. Hence it is incumbent upon each to devise realistic ways that would heal without opening new wounds, that would dignify their existence as free peoples without putting into jeopardy the selective security and the particular identity of the other. The moment has come for the creative energies of the parties to this most protracted of conflicts to be put, at long last, to work in the service of a durable peace, for as the wisest of kings wrote thousands of years ago, there is 'a time for slaying and a time for healing ... a time for war and a time for peace'.

Bibliography

Abbas, Mahmoud (Abu-Mazen), *Through Secret Channels*, Garnet Publishing, Reading, 1995

Aburish, Saïd, *Arafat: From Defender to Dictator*, Bloomsbury Publishing, London, 1998

Ajami, Fouad, *The Arab Predicament: Arab Political Thought and Practice Since 1967*, Cambridge University Press, 1981

al-Gridly, Hassan, 'The Outbreak of the 1973 War Was Unavoidable' (Hebrew), *Maarachot*, 332, Tel Aviv, 1993

Albright, Madeleine, *Madam Secretary*, Miramax Books, New York, 2003

Ali, Kamal Hassan, *Warriors and Peacemakers* (Hebrew), Israel Defence Ministry Press, Tel Aviv, 1993

Alpher, Joseph, *And the Wolf Shall Dwell with the Wolf: The Settlers and the Palestinians* (Hebrew), Hakibbutz Hameuhad Publishing House, Tel Aviv, 2001

Antonius, George, *The Arab Awakening: The Story of the Arab National Movement*, Hamish Hamilton, London, 1938

Aronson, Geoffrey, *Israel, Palestinians and the Intifada: Creating Facts on the West Bank*, Kegan Paul, New York, 1990

Ashrawi, Hanan, *This Side of Peace: A Personal Account*, Simon and Schuster, New York, 1995

Atlas, Yedidia, 'Arafat's Secret Agenda is to Wear Israelis Out', *Insight on the News*, 1 April 1946

Avigur, Shaul, *The Book of the Haganah* (Hebrew), Maarachot, Tel Aviv, 1956

Avineri, Shlomo, *Varieties of Zionist Thought* (Hebrew), Am-Oved Publishers, Tel Aviv, 1991

Avneri, Arieh, *The Claim of Dipossession: Jewish Land Settlement and the Arabs, 1878–1948*, Yad Tabenkin, Efal, Herzl Press, New York, 1982

Baker, James A. III, with DeFrank, Thomas M., *The Politics of Diplomacy: Revolution, War and Peace, 1989–1992*, Putnam, New York, 1995

Bar, Shmuel, *The Yom Kippur War in Arab Eyes* (Hebrew), Maarachot, Tel Aviv, 1986

Bar-Joseph, Uri, *The Best of Enemies: Israel and Transjordan in the War of 1948*, Frank Cass, London, 1987

Bar-Joseph, Uri, *The Watchman Fell Asleep: The Surprise of Yom Kippur and its Sources* (Hebrew), Zmora-Bitan Publishers, Lod, 2001

Bar-On, Mordechai, *Challenge and Quarrel: The Road to the Sinai Campaign – 1956* (Hebrew), Ben-Gurion University of the Negev Press, Beer Sheva, 1991

Bar-Siman Tov, Yaacov, *The Israeli–Egyptian War of Attrition*, Columbia University Press, New York, 1980

Bar-Siman Tov, Yaacov, *Israel and the Peace Process, 1972–1982: In Search of Legitimacy and Peace*, SUNY Press, New York, 1994

Bar-Zohar, Michael, *Ben-Gurion: A Political Biography* (Hebrew), Am-Oved Publishers, Tel Aviv, 1975–7

Begin, Menachem, *The Revolt*, Dell Pub. Co., New York, 1978

Beilin, Yossi, *Touching Peace* (Hebrew), Yedioth Aharonoth, Tel Aviv, 1997

Beilin, Yossi, *Manual for a Wounded Dove* (Hebrew), Miskal-Yedioth Aharonoth Books and Chemed Books, Tel Aviv, 2001

Ben-Ami, Shlomo, *Quel avenir pour Israel?* (*Entretien avec Yves Charles Zarka, Jeffrey Andrew Barash et Elhanan Yakira*), Presses Universitaires de France, Paris, 2001

Ben-Ami, Shlomo, *A Front Without a Home Front: A Voyage to the Boundaries of the Peace Process* (Hebrew), Miskal-Yedioth Aharonoth Books and Chemed Books, Tel Aviv, 2004

Ben-Eliezer, Uri, *The Emergence of Israeli Militarism 1936–1956* (Hebrew), Dvir Publishing House, Tel Aviv, 1995

Ben-Elissar, Eliahu, *No More War* (Hebrew), Maariv, Jerusalem, 1995

Ben-Gurion, David, *Why Did We Fight? Why Did We Withdraw? What Did We Achieve?* Mapai's Central Committee edition, 1957

Ben-Zvi, Abraham, *Decade of Transition: Eisenhower, Kennedy and the Origins of the American–Israeli Alliance*, Columbia University Press, New York, 1998

Benvenisti, Meron, *Conflicts and Contradictions*, Villard Books, New York, 1986

Bergman, Ronen, *Authority Given: Where Did We Go Wrong? This is how the Palestinian Authority Became a Serial Producer of Corruption and Terror* (Hebrew), Miskal-Yedioth Aharonoth Books and Chemed Books, Tel Aviv, 2002

Bethell, Nicholas, *The Palestine Triangle: The Struggle Between the British, the Jews and the Arabs 1935–48*, Andre Deutsch, London, 1979

Bialer, Uri, *Between East and West: Israel's Foreign Policy Orientation 1948–1956*, Cambridge University Press, 1990

Boutros-Ghali, Boutros, *Egypt's Road to Jerusalem: A Diplomat's Story of the Struggle for Peace in the Middle East*, Random House, New York, 1997

Braun, Arieh, *Moshe Dayan in the Yom Kippur War* (Hebrew), Idanim, Tel Aviv, 1993

Braun, Arieh, *Moshe Dayan and the Six Day War* (Hebrew), Yedioth Aharonoth, Tel Aviv, 1997

Bregman, Ahron and El-Tahri, Jihan, *The Fifty Years' War. Israel and the Arabs*, TV Books, New York, 1999

Brzezinski, Zbigniew, *Power and Principle: Memoirs of the National Security Adviser 1977–1981*, Weidenfeld & Nicolson, London, 1983

Bulloch, John, *The Making of a War. The Middle East from 1967 to 1973*, Longman, London, 1974

Carter, Jimmy, *Keeping Faith: Memoirs of a President*, Bantam Books, Toronto and New York, 1982

Christopher, Warren, *Chances of a Lifetime*, Scribner, New York, 2001

Clinton, Bill, *My Life*, Hutchinson (Random House Group), London, 2004

Cohen, Avner, *Israel and the Bomb*, Columbia University Press, New York, 1998

Cohen, Hillel, *An Army of Shadows: Palestinian Collaborators in the Service of Zionism* (Hebrew), Ivrit Publishing House, Jerusalem, 2004

Cohen, Michael, *Palestine to Israel, from Mandate to Independence*, Frank Cass, London, 1988

Crosbie, Sylvia, *A Tacit Alliance: France and Israel from Suez to the Six Day War*, Princeton University Press, Princeton, NJ, 1974

Dallar, Roland, *King Hussein: A Life on the Edge*, Profile, London, 1999

Dayan, Moshe, *Diary of the Sinai Campaign*, Schoken Books, New York, 1967

Dayan, Moshe, *A New Map, Other Relationships* (Hebrew), Maariv, Tel Aviv, 1969

Dayan, Moshe, *Milestones: An Autobiography* (Hebrew), Yedioth Aharonoth, Jerusalem, 1976

Dayan, Moshe, *Breakthrough: A Personal Account of the Egypt–Israel Peace Negotiations*, Weidenfeld & Nicolson, London, 1981

Dayan, Moshe, *Living with the Bible* (Hebrew), Edanim, Jerusalem, 1981

Eban, Abba, *An Autobiography*, Weidenfeld & Nicolson, London, 1977

Edelist, Ran, *Ehud Barak Fighting the Demons* (Hebrew), Zmora-Bitan Publishers and Miskal-Yedioth Aharonoth and Chemed Books, Tel Aviv, 2003

Eisenberg, Laura, 'Desperate Diplomacy: The Zionist–Maronite Treaty of 1946', *Studies in Zionism*, 13, No. 2, 1992

el-Gamasy, Mohamed Abdel Ghani, *The October War: Memoirs of Field Marshal el-Gamasy of Egypt*, American University Press, Cairo, 1993

Elon, Amos, *A Blood-Dimmed Tide: Dispatches from the Middle East*, Penguin Books, London, 2000

Enderlin, Charles, *Le rêve brisé: Histoire de l'échec du processus de paix au Proche-Orient 1995–2004*, Fayard, Paris, 2002

Eshed, Haggai, *Who Gave the Order? The Lavon Affair* (Hebrew), Edanim, Jerusalem, 1979

Eyal, Yigal, *The First Intifada* (Hebrew), Israel Defence Ministry Press, Tel Aviv, 1998

Fahmy, Ismail, *Negotiating for Peace in the Middle East*, Johns Hopkins University Press, Baltimore, 1983

Finkelstein, Norman, *Image and Reality of the Israel–Palestine Conflict*, Verso, London and New York, 2003

Fisk, Robert, *Pity the Nation: The Abduction of Lebanon*, Atheneum, New York, 1990

Flapan, Simha, *The Birth of Israel: Myths and Realities*, Pantheon, New York, 1987

Forsythe, David, *UN Peacemaking: The Conciliation Commission for Palestine*, Johns Hopkins University Press, Baltimore, 1972

Freedman, Robert (ed.), *The Middle East Enters the Twenty-first Century*, University Press of Florida, Gainesville, 2002

Friedman, Thomas, *From Beirut to Jerusalem*, second edition, HarperCollins, London, 1995

Gabbay, Rony, *A Political Study of the Arab–Jewish Conflict: The Arab Refugee Problem – A Case Study*, Librarie E. Droz and Librarie Minard, Geneva and Paris, 1959

Gelber, Yoav, *Independence Versus Nakba* (Hebrew), Kinnereth, Zmora-Bitan, Dvir Publishing House, Or Yehudah, 2004

Gilboa, Moshe, *Six Years – Six Days: Origins and History of the Six Day War* (Hebrew), Am-Oved Publishers, Tel Aviv, 1969

Gluska, Ami, *Eshkol, Give the Order! Israel's Army Command and Political Leadership on the Road to the Six Day War, 1963–1967* (Hebrew), Maarachot, Tel Aviv, 2004

Gorny, Yosef, *Zionism and the Arabs 1882–1948: A Study of Ideology*, Oxford University Press, 1987

Haber, Eitan, *'Today War will Break Out.' The Reminiscences of Brig. Gen. Israel Lior, Aide-de-Camp to Prime Ministers Levi Eshkol and Golda Meir* (Hebrew), Edanim Publishers, Yedioth Aharonoth, Tel Aviv, 1987

Harel, Amos and Isacharoff, Avi, *The Seventh War: How Did We Win and Why Did We Lose in our War against the Palestinians?* (Hebrew), Miskal-Yedioth Aharonoth Books and Chemed Books, Tel Aviv, 2004

Harkabi, Yehoshafat, *Arab Attitudes to Israel*, Transaction Publishers, New Jersey, 1974

Harkabi, Yehoshafat, *The Bar Kokhba Syndrome: Risk and Realism in International Politics*, Rossel Books, New York, 1983

Heikal, Mohamed, *The Road to Ramadan*, Collins, London, 1975

Heikal, Mohamed, *Cutting the Lion's Tail: Suez Through Egyptian Eyes*, Andre Deutsch, London, 1986

Helmick, S. J. Raymond, *Negotiating Outside the Law: Why Camp David Failed*, Pluto Press, London and Ann Arbor, MI, 2004

Herzog, Chaim, *The War of Atonement*, Weidenfeld & Nicolson, London, 1975

Hirschfeld, Yair, *Oslo: The Formula for Peace* (Hebrew), Am-Oved Publishers, Tel Aviv, 2000

Horovitz, David (ed.), *Yitzhak Rabin: A Soldier for Peace*, Peter Halban, London, 1996

Hourani, Albert, *A History of the Arab Peoples*, Warner Books, New York, 1991

Israeli, Raphael, 'From Oslo to Bethlehem: Arafat's Islamic Message', *Journal of Church and State*, Vol. 43, Summer 2001, pp. 423–45

Kafkafi, Eyal, *A War of Choice – The Road to Sinai and Back, 1956–1957* (Hebrew), Yad Tabenkin, Tel Aviv, 1994

Kamel, Mohamed Ibrahim, *The Camp David Accords: A Testimony*, KPI, London, 1986

Karsh, Efraim, *The Falsification of Israeli History* (Hebrew), Hakibbutz Hameuhad, Tel Aviv, 1999

Kerr, Malcolm, *The Middle East Conflict*, Foreign Policy Association, New York, 1968

Keynes, John Maynard, *The Economic Consequences of the Peace*, Macmillan, London, 1920

Khalaf, Issa, *Politics in Palestine: Arab Factionalism and Social Disintegration 1939–1948*, SUNY, New York, 1991

Khalidi, Rashid, *Palestinian Identity: The Construction of Modern National Consciousness*, Columbia University Press, New York, 1997

Kimche, Shaul, Eban, Shmuel and Fost, Gerald, *Yasser Arafat: A Psychological Profile and a Strategic Analysis* (Hebrew), International Institute for Counter-Terrorism, Interdisciplinary Centre, Herzlia, September 2001

Kimmerling, Baruch and Migdal, Joel, *Palestinians: The Making of a People*, Free Press, New York, 1992

Kissinger, Henry, *The White House Years*, Little Brown, Boston, 1979

Kissinger, Henry, *Years of Upheaval*, Weidenfeld & Nicolson, London, 1982

Kissinger, Henry, *Crisis: The Anatomy of Two Major Foreign Policy Crises: Based on the Record of Henry Kissinger's Hitherto Secret Telephone Conversations*, Simon & Schuster, New York, 2003

Korn, David, *Stalemate: The War of Attrition and Great Power Diplomacy in the Middle East, 1967–1970*, Westview Press, Boulder, 1992

Laqueur, Walter, *The Road to War: The Origin and Aftermath of the Arab–Israeli Conflict, 1967–1968*, Penguin Books, London, 1969

Laqueur, Walter, *A History of Zionism*, Schoken Books, New York, 1976

Laqueur, Walter and Rubin, Barry, (eds), *The Israel–Arab Reader: A Documentary History of the Middle East Conflict*, Penguin Books, London, 2001

Lavon, Pinhas, *In the Paths of Reflection and Struggle* (Hebrew), Am-Oved Publishers, Tel Aviv, 1968

Lewis, Bernard, *What Went Wrong? Western Impact and Middle Eastern Response*, Weidenfeld & Nicolson, London, 2002

Lewis, Bernard, *The Crisis of Islam: Holy War and Unholy Terror*, Weidenfeld & Nicolson, London, 2003

Lorch, Netanel, *The Edge of the Sword: Israel's War of Independence, 1947–1949*, Putnam, New York, 1961

Louis, Roger and Owen, Roger (eds), *Suez 1956, the Crisis and its Consequences*, Clarendon Press, Oxford, 1989

Makovsky, David, *Making Peace with the PLO*, Westview Press, Boulder, 1996

Malley, Robert and Agha, Hussein, 'Camp David: the Tragedy of Errors', *New York Review of Books*, 9 August 2001

Mandel, Neville, *The Arabs and Zionism Before World War I*, University of California Press, Berkeley, 1976

Mansfield, Peter (ed.), *The Middle East: A Political and Economic Survey*, fourth edition, Oxford University Press, London, New York and Toronto, 1973

Marcus, Yoel, *Camp David: The Gate to Peace* (Hebrew), Schoken Publishing House, Tel Aviv, 1979

Masalha, Nur, *Expulsion of the Palestinians: The Concept of 'Transfer' in Zionist Political Thought, 1882–1948*, Institute for Palestine Studies, Washington DC, 1992

Masalha, Nur, *The Politics of Denial: Israel and the Palestinian Refugee Problem*, Pluto Press, London, 2003

Mattar, Philip, *The Mufti of Jerusalem: Al-Hajj Amin al-Husayni and the Palestinian National Movement*, Columbia University Press, New York, 1988

Meir, Golda, *My Life*, Futura, London, 1976

Meital, Yoram, 'The Khartoum Conference and Egyptian Policy after the 1967 War: A Re-examination', *Middle East Journal*, Vol. 54, No. 1, Winter 2000, pp. 64–82

Ménargues, Alain, *Les secrets de la guerre du Liban. Du coup d'état de Bashir Gémayel aux massacres des camps palestiniens*, Albin Michel, Paris, 2004

Merari, Ariel and Elad, Shlomi, *The International Dimension of Palestinian Terrorism* (Hebrew), Hakibbutz Hameuhad, Tel Aviv, 1986

Mishal, Shaul, *The PLO under Arafat: Between Gun and Olive Branch*, Yale University Press, New Haven, 1986

Mishal, Shaul and Morag, Nadav, 'Political Expectations and Cultural Perceptions in the Arab–Israeli Peace Negotiations', *Political Psychology*, Vol. 23, No. 2, 2002

Mishal, Shaul and Sela, Avraham, *The Hamas Wind – Violence and Coexistence* (Hebrew), Miskal-Yedioth Aharonoth Books and Chemed Books, Tel Aviv, 1999

Moore, John Norton (ed.), *The Arab–Israeli Conflict: Readings and Documents*, Princeton University Press, 1977

Morris, Benny, *The Birth of the Palestinian Refugee Problem 1947–1949*, Cambridge University Press, 1988

Morris, Benny, *Israel's Border Wars, 1949–1956*, Clarendon Press, Oxford, 1993

Morris, Benny, *Righteous Victims: A History of the Zionist–Arab Conflict 1881–1999*, John Murray, London, 2000

Morris, Benny, *The Road to Jerusalem: Glubb Pasha, Palestine and the Jews*, I. B. Tauris, London, 2003

Nasser, Gamal Abdel, *The Philosophy of the Revolution* (Hebrew), Maarachot, Tel Aviv, 1961

Newman, David, *The Impact of Gush Emunim: Politics and Settlement in the West Bank*, Croom Helm, London, 1985

Oren, Michael, *Six Days of War: June 1967 and the Making of the Modern Middle East*, Oxford University Press, New York, 2002

Ovendale, Ritchie, *The Origins of the Arab–Israeli Wars*, Longman, London and New York, 1999

Pappe, Ilan, *Britain and the Arab–Israeli Conflict, 1948–1951*, St Antony's/ Macmillan, London, 1988

Pappe, Ilan, *The Making of the Arab–Israeli Conflict 1947–1951*, I. B. Tauris, London, 1992

Peleg, Ilan, *Begin's Foreign Policy, 1977–1983: Israel's Move to the Right*, Greenwood Press, New York, 1987

Peres, Shimon, *Now, Tomorrow* (Hebrew), Keter, Jerusalem, 1978

Peres, Shimon, *The New Middle East*, Element, Shaftesbury, 1993

Peres, Shimon, *Battling for Peace*, Random House, New York, 1995

Peters, Joan, *From Time Immemorial: The Origins of the Arab–Jewish Conflict Over Palestine*, Harper & Row, New York, 1984

Porath, Yehoshua, *The Palestine–Arab National Movement, 1929–1939: From Riots to Rebellion*, Frank Cass, London, 1977

Quandt, William, *Camp David, Peacemaking and Politics*, Brookings Institution, Washington DC, 1986

Rabin, Yitzhak, *The Rabin Memoirs*, Weidenfeld & Nicolson, London, 1979

Rabinovich, Itamar, *The War for Lebanon 1970–1983*, Cornell University Press, Ithaca and London, 1984

Rabinovich, Itamar, *The Road Not Taken: Early Arab–Israeli Negotiations* (Hebrew), Maxwell-Macmillan-Keter Publishing, Jerusalem, 1991

Rabinovich, Itamar, *The Brink of Peace: Israel and Syria 1992–1996* (Hebrew), Yedioth Aharonoth, Tel Aviv, 1998

Rabinovich, Itamar, *Waging Peace: Israel and the Arabs 1948–2003* (Hebrew), Kinnereth, Zmora-Bitan, Dvir, Or Yehudah, 2004

Rafael, Gideon, *Destination Peace*, Stein and Day, New York, 1981

Reinharz, Jehuda, *Chaim Weizmann: The Making of a Statesman*, Oxford University Press, New York, 1993

Rivlin, Gershon and Oren, Elhanan (eds), *From Ben-Gurion's Diary: The War of Independence*, Ministry of Defence, Tel Aviv, 1987

Rogan, Eugene and Shlaim, Avi (eds), *The War for Palestine: Rewriting the History of 1948*, Cambridge University Press, 2001

Rosenthal, Yemimah (ed.), *Yitzhak Rabin, Prime Minister of Israel: A Selection of Documents from His Life* (Hebrew), Jerusalem, 2005

Ross, Dennis, *The Missing Peace: The Inside Story of the Fight for Middle East Peace*, Farrar, Straus & Giroux, New York, 2004

Rubinstein, Amnon, *From Herzl to Rabin: 100 Years of Zionism* (Hebrew), Schoken Publishing House, Tel Aviv, 1997

Rubinstein, Danny, *The Mystery of Arafat*, Steerforth Press, South Royalton, 1995

Rubinstein, Danny, Malley, Robert, Agha, Hussein, Barak, Ehud and Morris, Benny, *Rashomon Camp David* (Hebrew), Miskal-Yedioth Aharonoth Books and Chemed Books, Tel Aviv, 2003

Rubinstein, Elyakim, *The Peace Between Israel and Jordan: An Anatomy of a Negotiation*, Jaffe Center for Strategic Studies, Tel Aviv, 1996

Rusk, Dean, *As I Saw It*, W. W. Norton, New York, 1990

Sadat, Anwar, *In Search of Identity: An Autobiography*, Harper & Row, New York, 1978

Safran, Nadav, *Israel – The Embattled Ally*, Harvard University Press, Cambridge, Mass., 1978

Said, Edward, *Peace and Its Discontents: Gaza–Jericho, 1993–1995*, Vintage, London, 1995

Said, Edward W., *The End of the Peace Process: Oslo and After*, Granta Books, London, 2002

Savir, Uri, *The Process* (Hebrew), Yedioth Aharonoth, Tel Aviv, 1998

Sayigh, Yezid, *Armed Struggle and the Search for State: The Palestinian National Movement 1949–1993*, Oxford University Press, 1997

Sayigh, Yezid, 'Arafat and the Anatomy of a Revolt', *Survival*, Vol. 43, 2001, pp. 47–60

Sayyid-Ahmad, Muhammad, *After the Guns Fall Silent*, Croom Helm, London, 1976

Schiff, Zeev and Yaari, Ehud, *Israel's Lebanon War*, Unwin, London, 1986

Schiff, Zeev and Yaari, Ehud, *Intifada*, Simon & Schuster, New York, 1990

Schiff, Zeev, *October Earthquake: Yom Kippur 1973*, Transaction Publishers, New York, 1974

Schoenbaum, David, *The United States and the State of Israel*, Oxford University Press, New York, 1993

Seale, Patrick, *Assad: The Struggle for the Middle East*, University of California Press, Berkeley, 1990

Segev, Tom, *One Palestine, Complete: Jews and Arabs Under the British Mandate*, Abacus, London, 2002

Shapira, Anita, *Land and Power: The Zionist Resort to Force 1881–1948*, Oxford University Press, New York, 1992

Shapira, Anita, *Igal Alon: Spring of His Life. A Biography* (Hebrew), Hakibbutz Hameuhad, Tel Aviv, 2004

Shavit, Yaacov, *The Mythologies of the Zionist Right Wing* (Hebrew), Emda Library – Academia Series, published by Beit Berl and the Moshe Sharett Institute, Beit Berl, n.d.

Sheffer, Gabriel, *Moshe Sharett: Biography of a Political Moderate*, Clarendon Press, Oxford, 1996

Shepherd, Naomi, *Ploughing Sand: British Rule in Palestine 1917–1948*, John Murray, London, 1999

Sher, Gilead, *Just Beyond Reach: The Israeli–Palestinian Peace Negotiations 1999–2001* (Hebrew), Miskal-Yedioth Aharonoth and Chemed Books, Tel Aviv, 2001

Shipler, David, *Arab and Jew: Wounded Spirits in a Promised Land*, Times Books, New York and Toronto, 1986

Shlaim, Avi, 'Conflicting Approaches to Israel's Relations with the Arabs: Ben-Gurion and Sharett, 1953–1956', *Middle East Journal*, Spring 1983, pp. 180–202

Shlaim, Avi, *Collusion Across the Jordan: King Abdullah, the Zionist Movement and the Partition of Palestine*, Columbia University Press, New York, 1988

Shlaim, Avi, 'His Royal Shyness: King Hussein and Israel', *New York Review of Books*, 15 July 1990

Shlaim, Avi, 'The Debate about 1948', *International Journal of Middle East Studies*, 27 (1995), pp. 287–304

Shlaim, Avi, 'The Protocol of Sèvres, 1956: Anatomy of a War Plot', *International Affairs*, 73, No. 3, July 1997

Shlaim, Avi, *The Iron Wall: Israel and the Arab World*, Penguin Books, London, 2000

Shlaim, Avi, 'Interview with Abba Eban, 11 March 1976', *Israel Studies*, Vol. 8, No. 1, Spring 2003, pp. 153–77

Shlaim, Avi, 'The Rise and Fall of the Oslo Peace Process', in Louise Fawcett (ed.), *The International Relations of the Middle East*, Oxford University Press, 2003

Shohamy, Elana and Donitsa-Schmidt, Smadar, *Jews vs. Arabs: Language Attitudes and Stereotypes*, Steinmetz Centre, Tel Aviv University, 1998

Shultz, George, *Turmoil and Triumph: My Years as Secretary of State*, Simon & Schuster, New York, 1993

Sivan, Emmanuel, *Arab Political Myths* (Hebrew), Am-Oved Publishers, Tel Aviv, 1988

Snetsinger, John, *Truman, the Jewish Vote and the Creation of Israel*, Hoover Institution Press, Stanford, 1974

Sprinzak, Ehud, *The Ascendance of Israel's Radical Right*, Oxford University Press, New York, 1991

Stein, Kenneth, *The Land Question in Palestine, 1917–1939*, University of North Carolina Press, Chapel Hill, 1984

Stein, Kenneth, *Heroic Diplomacy: Sadat, Kissinger, Carter, Begin and the Quest for the Arab–Israeli Peace* (Hebrew edition), Maarachot, Ministry of Defence, Tel Aviv, 2003 (English original edition Routledge, 1999)

Stephens, Robert, *Nasser: A Political Biography*, Penguin Books, London, 1971

Swisher, Clayton, *The Truth about Camp David: the Untold Story about the Collapse of the Middle East Peace Process*, Nation Books, New York, 2004

Tal, Uriel, 'The Foundations of a Political Messianic Trend in Israel', in *Myth and Reason in Contemporary Jewry* (Hebrew), Sifriat Poalim, Tel Aviv, 1987, pp. 115–25

Tal, Uriel, 'Messianism vs. Political Restraint in Religious Zionism', in *Myth and Reason in Contemporary Jewry* (Hebrew), Tel Aviv, 1987, pp. 98–114

Tamir, Abraham, *A Soldier in Search of Peace: An Inside Look at Israel's Strategy*, Weidenfeld & Nicolson, London, 1988

Teveth, Shabtai, *Ben-Gurion and the Palestinian Arabs: From Peace to War*, Oxford University Press, New York, 1985

Teveth, Shabtai, *Ben-Gurion: The Burning Ground, 1886–1948*, Houghton Mifflin, New York, 1987

Teveth, Shabtai, *The Evolution of 'Transfer' in Zionist Thinking*, Occasional Papers, Moshe Dayan Center for Middle Eastern and African Studies, Tel Aviv University, 1981

Twain, Mark, *The Innocents Abroad: Or the New Pilgrims' Progress*, New American Library, New York, 1980

Vance, Cyrus, *Hard Choices: Critical Years in America's Foreign Policy*, Simon & Schuster, New York, 1983

Wallach, Janet and Wallach, John, *Arafat: In the Eyes of the Beholder*, A Birch Lane Press Book, Carol Publishing Group, Secaucus, NJ, 1997

Wasserstein, Bernard, *The British in Palestine: The Mandatory Government and the Arab–Jewish Conflict 1917–1929*, Basil Blackwell, Oxford, 1991

Wasserstein, Bernard, *Divided Jerusalem: The Struggle for the Holy City*, Yale University Press, New Haven and London, 2002

Wasserstein, Bernard, *Israel and Palestine: Why They Fight and Can They Stop?*, Profile Books, London, 2003

Weizmann, Ezer, *The Battle for Peace* (Hebrew), Edanim Publishers, Jerusalem, 1981

Wistrich, Robert and Ohana, David (eds), *The Shaping of Israeli Identity: Myth, Memory and Trauma*, Frank Cass, London, 1995

Yakobson, Alexander and Rubinstein, Amnon, *Israel and the Family of Nations: Jewish Nation-State and Human Rights* (Hebrew), Shocken Publishing House, Tel Aviv, 2003

Zak, Moshe, *Hussein Makes Peace* (Hebrew), BESA, Ramat Gan, 1996

Zasloff, Joseph Jeremiah, *Great Britain and Palestine: A Study of the Problem before the United Nations*, Libraries E. Droz, Geneva, 1952

Zertal, Idith, *Israel's Holocaust and the Politics of Nationhood*, Cambridge University Press, 2005

Zertal, Idith and Eldar, Akiva, *The Lords of the Land: The Settlers and the State of Israel, 1967–2004*, Dvir, Or Yehudah, 2004

Zuckerman, Moshe, *Shoah in the Sealed Room: The 'Holocaust' in the Israeli Press During the Gulf War* (Hebrew), author's publication, Tel Aviv, 1993

Index